Zambia's Foreign Policy: Studies in Diplomacy and Dependence

Other Titles in This Series

Apartheid and International Organizations, Richard E. Bissell

Ethnicity in Modern Africa, edited by Brian M. du Toit

Botswana: An African Growth Economy, Penelope Hartland-Thunberg

South Africa into the 1980's, edited by Richard E. Bissell and Chester A. Crocker

Crisis in Zimbabwe, edited by Boniface Obichere

The Arab-African Connection: Political and Economic Realities, Victor T. Le Vine and Timothy W. Luke

Westview Special Studies on Africa

Zambia's Foreign Policy: Studies in Diplomacy and Dependence
Douglas G. Anglin and Timothy M. Shaw

This volume examines Zambia's role in the search for African independence, unity, and development, particularly in the context of southern Africa. It also analyzes the problems of dependence and underdevelopment and their impact on foreign policymaking. By concentrating on the key issues and major crises that confronted Zambia's decision makers during the nations's first years, the authors explain the country's current preocoupations and future prospects. Although their primary focus is on Zambia, they also treat a range of substantive and theoretical issues.

Douglas G. Anglin, professor of political science at Carleton University, was previously research associate at the Center for International Studies, Princeton University, and vice-chancellor at the University of Zambia.

Timothy M. Shaw is associate professor of political science and director, Centre for African Studies, Dalhousie University; he has taught at Makerere University in Uganda and at the University of Zambia.

Zambia's Foreign Policy: Studies in Diplomacy and Dependence

Douglas G. Anglin and
Timothy M. Shaw

Westview Press / Boulder, Colorado

Westview Special Studies on Africa

Copyright © 1979 by Westview Press, Inc.

Published in 1979 in the United States of America by
    Westview Press, Inc.
    5500 Central Avenue
    Boulder, Colorado 80301
    Frederick A. Praeger, Publisher

Library of Congress Catalog Card Number: 79-4849
ISBN: 0-89158-191-X

Composition for this book was provided by the authors
Printed and bound in the United States of America

To

Margaret and Deirdre

Benjamin and Amanda

for whom Zambia is also unforgettable

Contents

Tables and Figures

Figures

Preface

Zambia's status as a leading African actor, her strategic situation on the frontier of freedom in Southern Africa, her considerable mineral wealth, and the international stature of her President amply justify the wide interest in her foreign policy among scholars and statesmen, diplomats and development officials. The analysis of the roots and forms of Zambia's external behavior also contributes to an understanding of the foreign policies of other new states, the future of Southern Africa, and global resource politics. This volume of essays examines Zambia's role in the search for African freedom, development and unity, particularly her place in the regional affairs of Southern Africa. It also analyzes the problems of dependence and underdevelopment and their impact on foreign policy making. The inherited political economy of Zambia imposed constraints on her first decade of diplomacy which made her particularly concerned to promote change in the region and to prevent external intervention in her own internal problems. However, the elusiveness of both independence and development has not prevented Zambia's continuing support for the final liberation of the continent nor her quest for a distinctive domestic political economy reflecting her national ideology of Humanism.

While our studies make no claim to being comprehensive, they do focus on several of the core issues of Zambia's external relations. A variety of methods has been employed in an attempt to capture the history and reality of Zambia's foreign policy, as it is expressed and practised in several issue areas—transaction analysis, events data, decision making, external exchange and analysis of ideology. We have sought to explain as well as describe foreign policy through a diversity of techniques, issues and relations. Given the wide range of incidents, crises and questions covered, not all of the analysis presented here is strictly consistent. However, rather than impose an unnatural compatibil-

ity on our work over the last few years, we have let
the debate amongst ourselves and others on methods,
findings and implications continue between the covers of this book. We trust that, overall, the result
is a balanced and logical, sympathetic yet critical
enquiry.

The essays in this volume deal with some of the
major challenges and constraints, triumphs and dis-
appointments that have preoccupied the Zambian nation in its first decade and a half of political
independence. Issues examined include the military
balance and the guerrilla struggle, crisis behavior
and routine interactions, dependence and political
economy, diplomatic initiatives and the search for
external support, confrontation and cooperation, and
the role of institutions and ideology. We explore
a variety of particular problems—from Rhodesia's
UDI to Angola's independence, from détente to liberation, from landlockedness to regional integration,
from nonalignment in global affairs to deep commitment in regional affairs, and from the role of State
House to that of state capitalism. Although the
specific focus is on Zambia, the range of substantive and theoretical concerns dealt with are central
to African and Third World politics, development
studies and international relations generally. In
highlighting some of the key issues and major crises
that have confronted Zambian decision makers during
their nation's formative years, we have attempted to
describe and explain Zambia's past performance, current preoccupations and future aspirations.

This volume is the result of our mutual interest in, analysis of, and writing on Zambian foreign
policy. It is based on a selection of our recent
essays on this theme; several have previously been
published elsewhere, but all have been substantially
revised for this book. The production of such a
joint manuscript always poses problems, for inevitably different authors approach their subjects from
slightly varying perspectives. In preparing our
earlier articles for republication, the original
author first revised, recast or updated them as considered appropriate. They were then subjected to
further careful and critical review and rewriting by
the second author. In this interactive process, a
considerable convergence of views has resulted and
much common ground has emerged, so much so that we
feel able to accept co-authorship of the volume as a
whole. Nevertheless, some variations in emphasis or
interpretation inevitably remain. No attempt has
been made either to obscure these or to reconcile

them completely in order to achieve an acceptable but artificial consensus. On the contrary, we consider our residual differences in perspectives and approaches a strength rather than a weakness. These essays, then, are presented not as definitive studies but as modest contributions to a continuing debate on and understanding of the foreign policy roots and behavior of one of the most significant and fascinating actors in the unfolding drama in Africa generally and Southern Africa in particular.

In the preparation of this volume, our individual and joint debts are numerous and great. We are especially appreciative of our respective opportunities to work at the University of Zambia and to interact with its staff and students; Anglin was first Vice-Chancellor of the University, 1965 to 1969, and Shaw was a Lecturer in Political Science in 1973 and 1974, returning for research visits in 1977 and 1978. We are also grateful for the time and interest given to our research by government, party, diplomatic, and corporate officials, particularly Zambian leaders and officials, in Lusaka and elsewhere. Needless to say, we alone accept responsibility for the conclusions reached, cautious and tentative as they necessarily must be.

Our communication and collaboration could not have occurred without the intellectual and financial support of our respective Departments of Political Science and research affiliations, Anglin with The Norman Paterson School of International Affairs at Carleton and Shaw with the Centre for Foreign Policy Studies at Dalhousie. The authors have received modest research and typing assistance from the Research and Publications Fund of the Faculty of Social Sciences at Carleton and the Research Development Fund for the Humanities and Social Sciences in the Faculty of Graduate Studies at Dalhousie. The preparation of this and earlier manuscripts would have been impossible without the able assistance of Doris Boyle at Dalhousie and Kim Mitchell, Lynne Plummer, Bertha Zimba and Cyril Daddieh at Carleton.

We are grateful to our publishers not only for printing our earlier articles, but also for allowing them to reappear in revised form here. We gladly acknowledge the permission received from the following publishers and journals: Journal of Modern African Studies (chapter 2), African Studies Review (chapter 3), Norman Paterson School of International Affairs (chapter 4), University Press of America (chapter 5), Longmans (chapter 6), International Journal (chapter 7), Sage Publications Inc. (chapter

9), and Canadian Journal of African Studies (chapter 10).

We have decided to bring some of our essays together in this form to make them more readily available to academics, administrators and others interested in the place of Zambia in world affairs. We believe this task to be worthwhile and hope that Zambia's crucial role in the liberation—political, social and economic—of Africa will be better understood because of it.

Douglas G. Anglin
Timothy M. Shaw

Abbreviations

AAC	Anglo-American Corporation
ACR	*Africa Contemporary Record*
ANC	African National Congress (Zambia)
ANC	African National Council (Zimbabwe)
ANCSA	African National Congress of South Africa
ARB	*Africa Research Bulletin*
BSAC	British South Africa Company
CAPC	Central African Power Corporation
CIPEC	Inter-Governmental Council of Copper Exporting Countries
EAC	East African Community
ECA	UN Economic Commission for Africa
EEC	European Economic Community
FINDECO	State Finance and Development Corporation
FLS	Front Line States
FNLA	National Liberation Front of Angola
FRELIMO	Mozambique Liberation Front
FROLIZI	Front for the Liberation of Zimbabwe
IMF	International Monetary Fund
INDECO	Industrial Development Corporation
MEMACO	Metal Marketing Corporation
MINDECO	Mining Development Corporation
MPLA	Popular Movement for the Liberation of Angola
NCCM	Nchanga Consolidated Copper Mines (formerly AAC)
NPP	National Progress Party
OAU	Organization of African Unity
PAC	Pan-Africanist Congress of South Africa
RCM	Roan Consolidated Mines (formerly RST)
RST	Roan Selection Trust
SWAPO	South West African People's Organization
TAZARA	Tanzania Zambia Railway Authority
UDI	Unilateral Declaration of Independence
UN	United Nations
UNIP	United National Independence Party
UNITA	National Union for the Total Liberation of Angola
UPP	United Progressive Party
ZANU	Zimbabwe African National Union
ZAPU	Zimbabwe African People's Union
ZED	Zambia Events Data
ZIMCO	Zambia Industrial and Mining Corporation
ZIS	Zambia Information Services

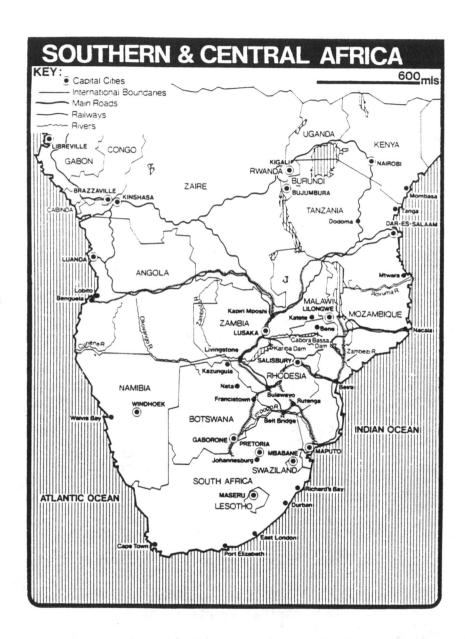

SOUTHERN & CENTRAL AFRICA

KEY:
- ● Capital Cities
- —— International Boundaries
- ═══ Main Roads
- ≡≡≡ Railways
- ∼∼∼ Rivers

600mls

LIBREVILLE
CONGO
GABON
KIGALI
RWANDA ●
BRAZZAVILLE
KINSHASA
CABINDA
ZAIRE
UGANDA
KENYA
● NAIROBI
BURUNDI
BUJUMBURA
TANZANIA
Dodoma
Mombasa
Tanga
DAR-ES-SALAAM
LUANDA
ANGOLA
Lobito
Benguela
Cunene R
Okavango R
Zambezi R
Mtwara
Rovuma R.
Kapiri Mposhi
MALAWI
LILONGWE
MOZAMBIQUE
ZAMBIA
Katete
Bena
LUSAKA
Cabora Bassa
Livingstone
Kariba Dam
Dam
Zambezi R
Nacala
SALISBURY
Kazungula
RHODESIA
Nata ●
Bulawayo
Bera
Francistown
Rutenga
Limpopo R.
NAMIBIA
WINDHOEK
Walvis Bay
BOTSWANA
Beit Bridge
INDIAN OCEAN
GABORONE
PRETORIA
MBABANE
MAPUTO
Johannesburg
SWAZILAND
SOUTH AFRICA
MASERU
Richard's Bay
ATLANTIC OCEAN
LESOTHO
Durban
East London
Cape Town
Port Elizabeth

xxii

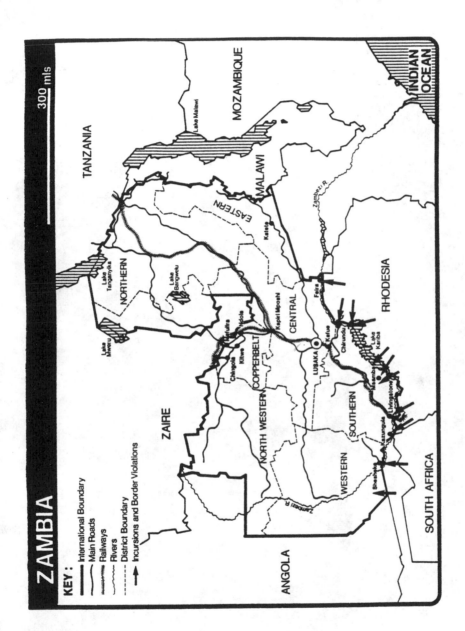

ZAMBIA

KEY:
— International Boundary
— Main Roads
— Railways
— Rivers
--- District Boundary
↑ Incursions and Border Violations

300 mls

xxiii

Part I
The Foreign Policy of Zambia:
Ideology and Institutions

1
Introduction:
Zambia and World Politics

> Central and Southern Africa are passing
> through the worst crises in our history. The
> wars of liberation raging in the region have
> reached a decisive phase in Zimbabwe and
> Namibia. South Africa sits on a deadly time
> bomb. There is a new conflict in the Shaba
> Province of our sister Republic of Zaire.
> These events have produced a new situation . . .
> more critical and dangerous than at any time
> before. . . . For the first time, Africa is
> becoming visibly a battlefield for international
> forces. . . . All these developments are taking
> place at a time when our unity is on trial.
> . . . In the last few years, our economy has
> been going through very difficult times.
>
> President Kenneth D. Kaunda, 12 June 1978

Few African states embarked on independence with
such promising prospects as Zambia in 1964. Her
achievement of statehood had been comparatively nonviolent, her economy was apparently prosperous and
solidly grounded on copper riches, her political
leadership was popular and progressive, her hopes of
building a nonracial society were being realized,
and her reception into the international community
was exceptionally cordial. Yet, even at the moment
of Independence, the seeds of the forces that were to
intensify and, by 1978, all but overwhelm the nation,
were already evident.

Beneath the veneer of unity expressed in the
brave words of the national motto—One Zambia, One
Nation—lay increasing regional, ethnic and incipient
class divisions. Zambia was also a classic case of
a dual economy, with the depressed rural areas contrasting sharply with impressive growth along the
line of rail. In terms of communications, she was
hostage to neighbors who controlled her access to

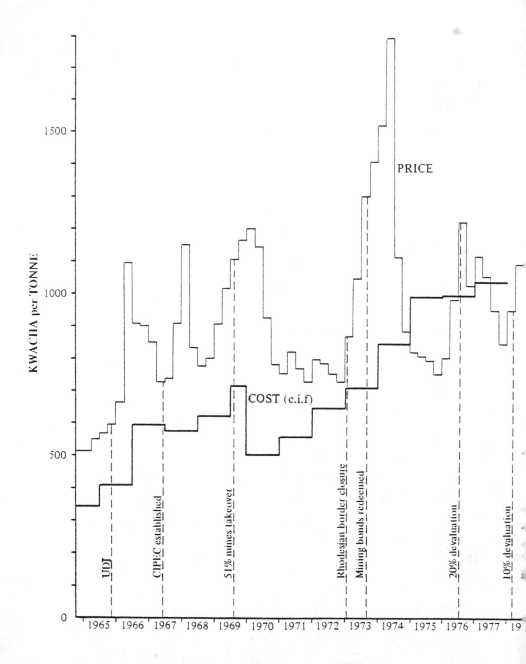

Figure 1.1 Zambian Copper Prices and Costs: 1964—78

4

the sea and, in terms of trade, she was dangerously dependent for foreign exchange on a single export industry whose profitability was at the mercy of global forces beyond Zambian control (figure 1.1). A more immediate menace came from the ominous rumblings across the Zambezi in Rhodesia, where a racial holocaust threatened to erupt and engulf Zambia along with the rest of the subcontinent. Each of these issues—domestic social inequities, regional political conflict, and global economic dependence—has, at different times during the first difficult decade of independence, posed a formidable challenge to the stability of the nation. By 1978, however, they had begun to combine in a new and more menacing way to confront Zambians with one of the severest tests of national will in the history of modern Black Africa.

Three critical events in close conjunction symbolize the intertwined strands—global recession, regional liberation, and the national political economy—that constituted the compound crisis of late 1978. These are the partial reopening of the Rhodesian border in October, the savage Rhodesian assaults on ZAPU camps in Zambia later in October, November and December, and the second general election under the country's one-party participatory democracy in December (see table 1.1).

In this introductory chapter, we attempt to sketch a framework within which to situate the more detailed but less than comprehensive case studies which follow. In particular, we provide a broad overview of the roots and goals of Zambian policy, the emerging patterns of external behavior, the constraints under which national decision makers operate, and the ongoing debate these questions have generated. We also draw attention to three analytically distinct but operationally interrelated levels of analysis—the global, regional and national—to the major issues and factions involved, and to their evolution over time, culminating in the current multiple crises across the domestic and external spheres.

HISTORICAL LEGACY

Zambia did not embark on statehood totally uninitiated into the harsh realities of international relations. Bitter experiences, stemming from the imposition of colonial overrule by the British and economic penetration from the South, had left a lasting legacy of deep distrust of foreign cupidity

5

TABLE 1.1
Principal Zambian Crises and Events, 1964-1978

1964
January 22   Kaunda appointed Prime Minister
February 5   UK offered military bases against
                      Rhodesia
May 18   Barotseland Agreement
June 25-Oct. 15   Lumpa "disturbances"; 710 killed
October 23   BSAC mineral royalties settlement
October 24   Independence

1965
May 23   1st trade agreement (with Japan)
November 11   Rhodesian UDI
December 2   Offer of RAF jet fighter squadron
                      accepted
December 23   Gasoline rationing (for 33 months)

1966
January 1   First National Development Plan,
                      1966-70
May 20-July 22   Rhodesia Railways payments crisis
July 12   Threat to leave Commonwealth

1967
April 26   Humanism in Zambia Part I becomes
                      national ideology
June 1-7   Lusaka conference creates CIPEC
June 21-26   Kaunda visits China
June 30   De facto Rhodesia Railways break-up
August-Sept.   ZAPU-ANCSA incursions into Rhodesia;
                      South African "police" sent to
                      Zambezi border
September 5   Tanzam railway survey agreement
                      with China
October 27-30   Kaunda mediates Kenya-Somalia
                      border dispute
November 28   Decision to apply to join EAC

1968
April 1-Aug. 29   Kaunda-Vorster correspondence
April 19   Mulungushi economic reforms; 51%
                      ownership of 25 major companies
May 20   Recognition of "Biafra"
September 3   Tazama oil pipeline from Dar es
                      Salaam in operation
December 19   Presidential and parliamentary
                      elections

6

1969
April 16   Lusaka Manifesto on Southern Africa
June 19   National referendum on constitution
July 16   Government-judiciary dispute
July 28   UN Security Council condemns
                Portuguese armed attacks since
                May 1966
August 11   51% government ownership of copper
                mining companies (AAC and RST)

1970
July 12   Tanzam railway loan agreement with
                China
September 1   Kaunda elected OAU Chairman
September 8-10 3rd summit Conference of Non-
                Aligned States, Lusaka
November 9   Leadership Code announced
December 5   First Zambian army commander

1971
January 22   Singapore Declaration of Common-
                wealth Principles
February-June   "Unofficial" Portuguese port boy-
                cott of Zambian goods
April 21   Vorster reveals secret 1968
                correspondence with Kaunda
July 10   1.5m bags of Rhodesian maize
                imported following Zambian drought
July 15-Aug. 30 University of Zambia closed follow-
                ing student assault on French
                embassy in protest against arms
                sales to South Africa
August 22   Former Vice-President Kapwepwe
                forms United Progressive Party
October 12   UN Security Council resolution in
                response to Vorster threaten (5
                October) to invade Zambia in
                "hot pursuit" of freedom fighters
December 10   IMF approves first loan (of $19m)
       .   to Zambia (and a second for
                $20.5m on 3 August 1972)

1972
January 12   Second National Development Plan,
                1972-76, launched
February 4   UPP banned and Kapwepwe detained
                (until 31 December)
February 24   Commission on a one-party state
                established
December 13   One-Party Participatory Democracy
                instituted

7

1973
January 9   Closure of Rhodesian border
May 25   Chinese transmitters for Radio
                     Zambia's External Service
                     commissioned
August 25   One-party constitution in force
                     (Second Republic)
August 31   Redemption of ZIMCO mining bonds
December 5   One-party presidential and
                     parliamentary elections

1974
April 25   Coup in Portugal
Apr.-Jan. 1975   Copper price falls from $3000 to
                     $1200 per tonne
June 5-6   FRELIMO-Portuguese negotiations on
September 5-7   Mozambique Independence, Lusaka
October 24   10th anniversary of Independence;
                     Humanism in Zambia Part II issued
November 7-10   1st meeting of Front Line States,
                     Lusaka
November 20-29   Kaunda state visits to Soviet Union
                     and Yugoslavia
December 7   Zimbabwe Declaration of Unity,
                     Lusaka

1975
March 18   Assassination of Herbert Chitepo
                     (ZANU) in Lusaka (Report of
                     Special International Commission,
                     March 1976)
April 11   OAU Dar es Salaam Declaration on
                     Southern Africa
June-March 1976   Angolan civil war
June 30   Kaunda's "watershed speech" on
                     economy
August 21   Closure of Benguela Railway (until
                     4 November 1978)
August 25   Kaunda-Vorster meeting on Victoria
                     Falls Bridge
Dec. 15-Mar. 19   Nkomo-Smith negotiations supported

1976
January 28   Emergency powers extended
Feb. 9-May 10   University of Zambia closed follow-
                     ing student support for MPLA
July 9   Kwacha devalued 20%
July 14   Inauguration of TAZARA
July 30   UN Security Council condemns
                     South African border attacks

8

1977

January 20	Botswana-Zambia (Botzam) road from Nata to Kazungula opened
February 3	Tanzania closes border with Kenya
March 26-29	Soviet President visits Zambia
April 19	Angola agrees to release 24,000 tons of Zambia-bound cargo held in Lobito since August 1975
May 16	Kaunda declares a "state of war" with Rhodesia following Smith threat of pre-emptive strikes against ZAPU bases
July 2	Zambia to sue 17 international oil companies accused of sanction-busting
August 31	Rhodesian air force bombs Feira
September 3-20	Blackout and curfew in Lusaka, Kafue and Livingstone
September 9	Kapwepwe rejoins UNIP
September 25	Kaunda-Smith meeting in Lusaka

1978

January 27	Austerity budget, drastic cuts in government food subsidies
March 17	UN Security council condemns Rhodesian "armed invasion"
March 17	$390m IMF facility; kwacha devalued 10%
May 1	Mining companies declare force majeure; 15% production cutback
June 27-29	World Bank consultative group on aid to Zambia meets in Paris
August 1	Kapwepwe announces candidacy for presidency; later disqualified
August 14	Nkomo-Smith meeting, Lusaka
August 23	South African attack from Namibia on Katima Mulilo
September 9-11	8th UNIP General Conference, Mulungushi Rock
October 6	Partial reopening of Rhodesian border
October 19-21	Massive Rhodesian raids on ZAPU camps in Zambia; also 2 November and 22 December
December 12	Presidential and parliamentary elections; Kaunda re-elected for fourth term

and duplicity. The scandalous behavior of Cecil Rhodes' British South Africa Company in deceiving the Litunga of Barotseland into signing away, under the Lochner concession of 1890, immensely valuable mining rights over a vast and vaguely defined area north of the Zambezi was still vivid in the minds of nationalists three-quarters of a century later. Indeed, so concerned was the UNIP government to rectify this historic injustice that it precipitated a major confrontation with London over the mineral royalties issue on the eve of Independence. Only hours before their withdrawal, the British finally relented and abandoned their untenable position completely rather than destroy the genuine goodwill that otherwise characterized their transfer of power. It was a notable triumph for the fledgling state.[1]

Nevertheless, it was the Zambians' fierce but futile fight in the early 1950s against incorporation into the Federation of Rhodesia and Nyasaland that constituted their real baptism into the tough world of power politics. Having lost the opening battle, their initial reaction appeared to be a resigned acceptance of the fait accompli. However, once they realized that the much-heralded "racial partnership" was a hollow promise and that massive sums of Copperbelt wealth were being drained off to Salisbury, opposition quickly mounted with renewed intensity. Thereafter, Federation came to be detested with even more passion than colonialism, and neighboring Rhodesia became an even greater focus of Zambian hostility than the subimperial center in South Africa.

The searing experience of a decade of Federal domination convinced Zambians that, when it came to the crunch, Britain would always sacrifice their interests to those of her "kith and kin" in Southern Africa. This conviction was powerfully reinforced by the feeble British response to UDI, beginning with the refusal to employ force (see chapter 4), and culminating in the recent devastating revelations of thirteen years of massive oil sanction busting. The cynicism this calculated deception has generated is difficult to exaggerate.

In the course of her own nationalist struggle for freedom from Britain, Zambia developed certain distinctive modes of political agitation which have continued to find reflection in her diplomatic style since Independence. Among the techniques employed were, in ascending order of coercive potential, appeals over the heads of the British government to the consciences of the British people, hurling

bruising personal epithets at the British,[2] indulging in confrontation tactics, threatening violence
and, on occasion, injecting mild doses of it into
the bargaining process. However, the success of
these pressure tactics in eliciting British concessions misled the Zambian government into assuming
that they would prove equally efficacious against
the Southern African settler regimes themselves.
Only after years of frustration did the crucial distinction between the two situations—colonial power
and settler societies—come to be fully appreciated.

    Although their formative contacts with the out-
side world had given Zambians ample grounds for dis-
trusting the intentions and dependability of friend
as well as foe, this suspicious instinct was to some
extent tempered by President Kaunda's generous
spirit. Despite successive, shattering disappoint-
ments, he persisted in his faith that man's inherent
decency would eventually shine through. As the
country's central decision maker, his dominating
personality and humanistic world view powerfully
conditioned the substance and style of Zambia's external behavior (see chapter 3). Morality he saw as
the foundation of foreign policy, nonracialism as a
prerequisite for peace within and between states,
and justice as the key to international cooperation.
It was a remarkably enlightened outlook for the
strong-willed father of a nation caught in the eye
of the gathering Southern African storm. How he
sought to reconcile his moral commitment to the process of liberating the subcontinent with the constraints imposed by his Christian humanist values is
a recurring theme of this book.

NATIONAL UNITY

    The absence of national unity can be seriously
prejudicial to the effective prosecution of a coherent
foreign policy. Internal dissension not only drains
energies off into domestic preoccupations and saps
the sense of national purpose, it also offers scope
for intrusive external influence. This is a threat
to which Zambia is singularly susceptible, having
been thrust by geography, history and conviction
into the forefront of the fight for freedom in
Southern Africa. At the same time, she is even more
an artificial colonial creation than most African
states; this is readily apparent from the curious
figure-of-eight contours of her geographical boundaries. Five mutually reinforcing cleavages have

inhibited the emergence of a strong sense of national identity. These are regional loyalties, ethnic and linguistic particularism, political competition, uneven economic development, and class conflicts. Each of these divisive tendencies has had an external dimension which reinforces their implications for Zambian foreign policy.

The Zambian government has been understandably concerned that the major pockets of political discontent in the country have been in those provinces bordering Southern African regimes. This has been the case notably in the Western Province (formerly Barotseland) and the Southern Province—the political base of the opposition African National Congress (ANC) in the past—but also, to a lesser extent, in the North Western and Eastern provinces. Inevitably, the suspicion has persisted in Lusaka that this geographical concentration is no mere coincidence. Certainly, there is some evidence to suggest that, in the early years after Independence, both the Portuguese and the South Africans periodically sought to exploit existing disaffection among the Lozi[3] as well as the Lunda. A further factor intensifying the secessionist sentiments of the Barotse was Lusaka's decision on principle to end WENELA recruitment of labor in the province for work in South African goldmines (see chapter 5). On at least two occasions, the Pretoria government has been implicated in conspiracies to finance, arm and train Zambian dissidents who were then infiltrated back into the country on destabilization missions. The first was in December 1972, when a hundred Zambians were recruited for military training in Namibia. Subsequently, four of the ringleaders, including the former mayor of Livingstone, were convicted of treason for allegedly plotting to overthrow the government. A more serious incursion occurred in December 1975 when an armed gang, led by a disaffected UNIP official, returned from Namibia via Angola. Since then, the "Mushala gang" has roamed the North Western Province, pillaging and murdering, in what the President has characterized as "a small civil war."[4]

The sense of alienation which certain segments of the population in the North Western Province have felt is basically a reflection of its continued relative underdevelopment. Nevertheless, an additional aggravation is the arbitrary colonial boundary which cuts across traditional tribal polities. In particular, the partitioning of the Lunda empire among Angola, Zaire and Zambia has inevitably created

12

divided loyalties, especially as the tribal capital lies across the border in southern Zaire. The continued strength of these traditional transnational ties helps account for the moral and material support which Moise Tshombe—a member of the Lunda royal family—extended to opponents of UNIP in the North Western Province and elsewhere in Northern Rhodesia in the early 1960s,[5] for the trek which Senior Chief Kanongesha of Mwinilunga and, subsequently, some two thousand of his followers undertook (apparently at the invitation of the Portuguese) into neighboring Angola in February 1965,[6] and for the ease with which the so-called Popular Armed Forces of the Congo—based on the remnants of Tshombe's gendarmerie which fled to Angola a decade earlier—succeeded in transiting the Mwinilunga salient undetected by the Lusaka authorities in the course of their second violent return to Shaba in May 1978.

Recognition of the explosive potential of tribal separatist tendencies for subverting national loyalties also explains President Kaunda's unusually sharp reaction to President Banda's assertion in September 1968 that the boundaries of the ancient empire of Malawi extended to the Luangwa River, thus appearing to lay claim to Zambia's Eastern Province as well as Isoka District in Northern Province. "Malawi imperialism," Kaunda charged angrily, amounted to a "declaration of war."[7]

A recurring complaint of Kaunda's critics has been his alleged preoccupation with external affairs, and especially with Southern African liberation, to the detriment of the country's domestic interests. This was a consistent theme of the settler-based National Progress Party (NPP), of the Tonga-based African National Congress (ANC), of the Lozi-based United Party, and of the Bemba-based United Progressive Party (UPP). Following the establishment of a one-party state in 1972, this criticism not only continued but intensified, as the costs of foreign policy militancy mounted in terms of delayed development, rampant inflation, shortages in the shops, border incursions and, latterly, armed invasion. Thus, in announcing his decision on 1 August 1978 to challenge Kaunda for the presidency, former Vice-President Simon Kapwepwe promised to concentrate on economic reconstruction rather than external relations, and to make Zambian self-interest the sole criterion of policy. Specifically, he advocated reopening the Rhodesian border and openly trading with South Africa in order to eliminate unnecessary costs.[8]

13

However, the emphasis which the disparate opposition elements have placed on a "Zambia first" policy has not spared them in turn from accusations of having sought or accepted external support.[9] The NPP, as the successor to Sir Roy Welensky's United Federal Party (UFP), never managed to rid itself of its public image as the spokesman for Salisbury interests; accordingly, in August 1966, it prudently decided to disband. The ANC, too, was suspect because of its pre-independence affiliations with settler interests, notably its electoral pact with the UFP in 1962, and its alliance with and dependence upon Tshombe in neighboring Katanga.[10] After Independence, it was implicated in at least two series of raids into the Mwinilunga area, in December 1968 and May 1971, by political dissidents armed and trained by the Portuguese in Angola.[11] Kapwepwe's UPP was also accused of collaborating with Southern African patrons. "I am satisfied," the President declared in 1971, "that of late a group of disgruntled politicians has resorted to gun running and sending out our people for military training to countries hostile to Zambia with a view to subverting the tranquility of the Republic." These insinuations against Kapwepwe were never substantiated.[12]

Political protest in the peripheral provinces, arising in part out of persistent inequities in the level of development on and off the line of rail, remains a recurring phenomenon on the Zambian political scene. The situation has been further complicated by the differential impact of the dramatic reorientation in the country's external transport routes since the Rhodesian UDI. The closure of the southern border in 1973 and the inauguration of the railway to Dar es Salaam three and a half years later had beneficial spinoffs for the Northern Province, but left Livingstone at the end of a line to nowhere. Moreover, the prospect of opening direct road and rail connection through the North Western Province to Angola, and through the Eastern Province to Malawi and Mozambique, could generate further centrifugal pressures as the provinces become increasingly oriented to their neighbors and compete among themselves for traffic for their own outlet to the sea. Contemporary communication patterns reinforce traditional transnational tendencies towards fragmentation.

Although the national philosophy of Humanism aspires to a society of equals (see chapter 2), President Kaunda has repeatedly warned of the insidious growth of social classes and economic

14

inequalities. This poses two questions: what is
the character of the class system in Zambia, and
what is the influence of class interests on foreign
policy? In much of the growing body of literature
on the political economy of Zambia,[13] the assumption
that the economic interests of the middle classes
have prevailed politically represents the new orthodoxy. We are impressed by the explanatory potential
of this approach. Nevertheless, we recognize that
no systematic analysis of classes in Zambia has yet
been undertaken, partly no doubt because the task
appears so daunting.[14] As Mafeje has concluded, in
developing countries "classes are still inchoate."
Moreover, what class contradictions exist in independent Africa are, according to Arrighi and Saul,
"blurred by racial, ethnic and nationalist dimensions."[15] We make no attempt to fill this obvious
void here. However, we do recognize as inadequate,
theoretically and empirically, the lumping together
into one undifferentiated ruling elite, commonly
designated a "bureaucratic bourgeoisie" or comprador
class, such disparate interests as the political
leadership, the technocrats, the indigenous business
and professional community, progressive farmers,
military and police officers, and even the labor
aristocracy. As Jack Simons has observed, the
bureaucratic bourgeoisie is less homogeneous than is
often contended: "It too is the center of an ideological struggle. To omit that inner struggle, which
is not always a silent one, is to distort the record
and falsify the analysis."[16]

Recognition of this diversity of interests within the "ruling class" has clear implications for the
formulation of foreign policy. Even within the
business sector, which is often assumed to exercise
decisive influence, conflicting economic interests
may exist, with the commercial elite anxious to ensure cheap and convenient sources of imports, and
local manufacturers fearful of their ability to survive in the face of such foreign competition. What,
then, can we say concerning the impact of class on
external policy? If we acknowledge the existence of
a bourgeois ruling class, many of whose members reject the President's "radical" predilections in the
field of foreign policy, to what extent does the
empirical evidence sustain the claim of the political economy mode of analysis that the economic interests of the dominant class generally prevail in
foreign policy decision making? To seek an answer,
we turn to a consideration of regional liberation
and global interdependence.

Five factors account for Zambia's obsessive
preoccupation with the liberation of Southern Africa
and govern her approaches to the problem: an ideological commitment to the eradication of colonialism
everywhere on the continent of Africa, moral indignation at the gross injustices perpetrated in the
name of civilization south of the Zambezi, fear of
the infectious spread of racialism northward, concern at Zambia's residual dependence on trade with
and transit traffic through Southern Africa, and
suspicions concerning the subversive intentions—
economic as well as military—of the minority
regimes. As with other African states which, at
Independence, found themselves geographically and
economically integral parts of the Southern African
subsystem, Zambia had a choice among three broad
strategic responses. These alternatives were:
first, confrontation, or deliberately forcing an
escalation of the conflict through resort to puni-
tive measures, with a view to precipitating fundamental system transformation in opposition to the
white rulers; secondly, negotiation, or the use of
essentially noncoercive persuasion to convince the
Southern African regimes to accept essential changes
in their own interests; and thirdly, accommodation,
or adaptation to the inherited environment. Zambia's
characteristic behavior has been confrontation,
though she has also experimented with negotiations
as a means of achieving the same end. Accommodation
has been the typical reaction of neighboring
Malawi.[17]

Confrontation

The prime prerequisite for a concerted campaign
of confrontation is a clear set of priorities. While
the ideological unity of the White South was recognized, Zambia also realized that her limited resources could be deployed most effectively if concentrated on a single target. Initially, Rhodesia
headed the list. She was the country with which
Zambia had had the closest associations in the past;
also she had the most developed nationalist movement
and appeared to be the most promising candidate for
early independence. However, with the failure to
crush UDI and fission within Zimbabwean ranks, the
focus in the liberation struggle shifted to Angola
and Mozambique. Following the Portuguese coup in

1974, Rhodesia was restored to center stage along with Namibia. At the same time, preparations were made for the final assault on the South African citadel.

A second requirement was a greater measure of political and economic maneuverability than was possible while the Zambian economy remained hostage to the South. Despite this, Lusaka pressed its liberation support to the point where it provoked serious economic and military punishment in retaliation (see figure 6.1). On two occasions, it overreached itself and was compelled to execute humiliating tactical retreats. Both involved threats to the country's staple food supply. In July 1971, faced with drought and a Portuguese blockade, the government was forced to turn to Rhodesia for 1.5 million bags of maize.[18] Again, in October 1978, when existing routes proved incapable of coping speedily enough with a massive backlog of fertilizer imports, the Rhodesian border, closed since January 1973, was partially reopened.

In spite of these temporary setbacks, the clear trend has been towards much more open and effective assistance to the liberation movements. This has been possible because of the startling success of efforts to disengage economically from dependence on the South generally and Rhodesia in particular (see chapter 5). A further factor has been the rapid strengthening of the country's defense capabilities though, as the recent devastating Rhodesian raids demonstrated, the Zambian armed forces cannot yet offer an adequate deterrent to a major incursion.

The costs to Zambia over the past fifteen years of confrontation have been staggering. Moreover, they continue to multiply and, with the collapse of the world copper price, now amount to more than the economy can bear. Although no precise calculation of Zambia's share of the total costs, or even of that proportion attributable to UN sanctions against Rhodesia is possible, it is clear that no other member of the international community has borne anything like the same burden. The latest annual estimate of the Coordinator of UN Assistance to Zambia of the direct financial outlay is "well in excess of $800 million." If exceptional transport costs are included, Zambian figures run as high as $1,250 million.[19] Yet, even these huge sums fail to take adequate account of the real costs resulting from aggravated inflation, distorted development, the resort to alternative sources of supply, and other contingency planning expenses. The true toll may be

17

closer to Lusaka's claim of $6 billion—the equivalent of two years GNP.[20] The international community has formally recognized its responsibility to share the common burden. Yet, to date, it has been more willing to respond with resounding resolutions than with material assistance. Even more discouraging has been the monumental hypocrisy of British and other governments and corporations which now stand convicted of systematic sabotage of UN sanctions. The irresistible conclusion is that the enormous sacrifices Zambians have endured over many years have largely been in vain.

Negotiation

     Confrontation was never conceived of as an end in itself; rather, it was a means of precipitating meaningful political change. The assumption was that at some stage, well before the minority regimes had been compelled to surrender unconditionally, they would wake up to the need to negotiate a transfer of power to the majority. Negotiations, therefore, were perceived, not as an alternative to confrontation, let alone as evidence of weakness, but as a complementary strategy. The essential precondition for agreeing to "negotiate rather than destroy" was, however, unambiguous acceptance by the white communities of the "principles of human equality and national self-determination."[21] This implied, as a minimum, the eradication of racialism and acquiescence in majority rule. Other issues, particularly the choice of leaders and the ideological orientation of the new governments, were decisions to be left to the people of each country to resolve, though it was hoped that these could be settled peacefully and democratically, if necessary by the formation of governments of national unity. The responsibilities of African states, as Lusaka saw them, were limited to promoting political independence; they had no right to insist upon—or oppose—a "second revolution" or socialist transformation.
     What has distinguished Zambia's liberation support from that of other Front Line States has been, not the strength of her commitment, but her tactical flexibility in response to changes in the external environment. Prior to the Portuguese coup, President Kaunda sought on several occasions to break the Southern African logjam by offering, with the consent of the nationalist parties concerned, to "mediate" between them and the minority regimes on the basis

18

of the Lusaka Manifesto. Since 1974, the emphasis
has been on facilitating direct negotiations amongst
the parties when it appeared that these might serve
the cause of liberation. In the case of Rhodesia,
Kaunda also attempted unsuccessfully, in 1968 and
again in 1974-75, to enlist the support of the regional power, Pretoria, in pressuring Salisbury into
offering significant concessions. There has been no
dialogue on apartheid; that was ruled out from the
start as a subject for negotiation. Nevertheless,
the distinction between bilateral "contacts" with
South Africa over Rhodesia and broader schemes of
regional "détente" was not widely appreciated, especially as Pretoria was doing its best to link the
two. Consequently, Zambia's pursuit of dual tactics
generated considerable misunderstanding, particularly among those critics who were already disposed
to suspect Zambia's motives on ideological grounds
because of her mixed economy and nondialectical
definition of socialism.

Accommodation

Paradoxically, then, the African state that has
sacrificed the most for the liberation of Southern
Africa has also been the subject of some of the
severest strictures for its failure to do more. The
flood of criticism heaped on Zambia has emanated
from three principal sources: from certain factions
within the liberation movements which have, understandably, chafed under any host country constraints,
however reasonable; from a number of progressive
African states, several of whom are far from the
front line and whose militancy has generally found
expression more in revolutionary oratory than in
honoring their financial commitments to the OAU
Liberation Committee; and from a growing number of
radical intellectuals, African and non-African,
whose objections have been essentially ideological.
Each of these interests has, from its own perspective, accused Zambia of accommodating her "external
behavior and internal institutions to the demands
emanating" from her Southern African environment.[22]
Of the three, the radical critique has been the most
reasoned and sustained.
    There can be no disputing that Zambia has ex-
perienced severe economic dislocation and hardship
in recent years. Just as the country appeared on
thè point of coping with the economic consequences
of the determined decision in 1973 to keep the

19

Rhodesian border closed, but before the Tazara railway was opened to traffic in August 1976, it was
confronted with a calamitous fall in the world copper price, a five-fold increase in the cost of imported oil, a mammoth balance of payments deficit,
and the sudden closure, in August 1975, of its one
remaining rail outlet to the sea—a casualty of the
Angolan civil war. Later, Tanzania instituted road
restrictions on transit traffic from Mombasa and
then, in February 1977, closed her border with Kenya
altogether, thus further aggravating the chronic
congestion in the port of Dar es Salaam. So serious
did the situation become that, in March 1978, the
Zambian Minister of Finance was constrained to con-
fess that his country's economy was on the brink of
collapse and that only an international rescue operation could "bail us out."[23]

To what extent have these compound misfortunes
compelled Lusaka to temper its "self-denying revolutionary idealism" in favor of the "competing norms
of realpolitik,"[24] as economic determinists of differing ideological persuasions have so confidently
predicted? On the right, South African Whites have
long shared a conviction with their opponents on the
left that economic realities must ultimately triumph
over political preferences. Accordingly, they have
been keen to exploit Zambia's plight for their own
economic and political advantage.

The radical exponents of the political economy
approach have identified the material interests of
the dominant class, rather than a consensual and ambiguous national interest, as the crucial clue to
foreign policy behavior. The central thrust of
their argument rests on three related propositions
concerning the role of the bourgeois "ruling class"
in the Zambian decision-making process. The first
is that the Zambian middle class has a direct economic stake in an accommodation with the South.
This is undeniable in the case of some groups within
both the public and private sectors; while all
Zambians have suffered from confrontation, certain
businessmen and bureaucrats have been especially
hard hit. Accordingly, and consistent with a class
interest approach, the Zambian bourgeoisie will pursue a policy of accommodation. Again, there is
abundant evidence of some members advocating this,
at least with respect to trade with South Africa as
opposed to Rhodesia. On the other hand, it is
equally evident that many within the elite continue
to uphold a confrontation stance either out of conviction, or a sense of patriotism or, in the case of

some businessmen, fear of foreign competition——a not insignificant alliance against regional collaboration. Finally, it is asserted that, since the national bourgeoisie has become the ruling class, it will by definition attempt to impose its own class interests on the country's affairs. This scenario is seductively simple and superficially plausible; certainly, it compels close scrutiny. Nevertheless, it fails to account adequately for some awkward facts, notably Zambia's unique record of liberation support. It also exhibits a tendency to put the theory cart before the factual horse, to deduce evidence from analytic, even "ideological" assumptions.

The empirical case for an accommodationist interpretation of Zambian relations with Southern Africa relies heavily on four controversial contentions: that the "détente" exercise in 1974-75 represented a shift from militant confrontation with South Africa to cautious coexistence; that Zambia sought to promote neocolonial outcomes in Angola and Zimbabwe in collusion with Pretoria; that she was successfully seduced by South African economic assistance; and that the reopening of the Rhodesian border reflected the economic interests of the Zambian ruling class. As the first two claims are explored in chapters 7 and 8, only the latter two will be examined here.

Few accusations have angered President Kaunda as much as the allegation in 1975 that Zambia had accepted a huge, secret South African loan.[25] The report appears to have originated in South Africa; certainly the media and propaganda organs there eagerly trumpeted it about. However, it only acquired some credibility when a highly sensational account, based on "foreign sources" in Dar es Salaam, appeared in the London Guardian. This sketched a detailed scenario involving a "massive" interest-free loan tied to acceptance of a "moderate" Smith-Nkomo internal settlement designed to usher in a stable and pliant buffer state on South Africa's northern border.[26] Other "rumors" linked the loan to the financing of Zambia's $77 million annual oil import bill.[27] Kaunda was so distressed at the suggestion that he might be a party to such an arrangement "simply to get an advantage for Zambia" that he took the Guardian to court and successfully extracted an abject apology and substantial damages.[28]

Despite this and the absence of any hard evidence, the loan story continues to circulate. One reason for this may be the interest that those disseminating the reports have in crediting them;

certainly, within South Africa, there has been a good deal of wishful thinking about the extent of her regional economic leverage. So anxious, in fact, has Pretoria been to elicit a request from Lusaka for economic assistance that it has repeatedly approached Zambia, directly and indirectly through official and private channels, with a variety of tempting offers, only to be rebuffed. The stock response to every feeler has been that while, economically, Zambia would welcome development assistance, it would be "morally wrong and politically unwise to establish ties with a regime which is committed to things that we find repulsive and repugnant."[29]

Pretoria's overtures have included offers of investment capital, soft loans, and longterm export credits. The export credit option received considerable prominence as a result of the visit of the South African Minister of Economic Affairs to Lusaka in October 1975, reportedly armed with credits totalling as much as $175 million as inducements to expanded Zambian imports from South Africa.[30] Although these enticements were also spurned,[31] so exhilarated were some South African observers at the prospect that they, and others who professed to see a Lusaka-Pretoria axis, were optimistically predicting that South Africa would emerge as Zambia's leading source of supply in 1975 because of her relative geographical proximity and pricing advantage. In fact, imports in 1975 from South Africa declined to a mere 6.8% of total imports—less than a third of the proportion of the market South Africa commanded at Independence (table 1.2).[32]

TABLE 1.2
Zambian Imports from South Africa, 1964-1977

Year	Kwacha millions	% Total Imports
1964	K32.4	20.7%
1966	58.5	23.8%
1973	41.4	11.9%
1974	38.7	7.6%
1975	40.4	6.8%
1976	36.0	7.7%
1977	38.1	7.3%

Sources: Monthly Digest of Statistics, Bank of Zambia Annual Report, 1977

The partial reopening of the Rhodesian border
in October 1978, after nearly six years, offers more
persuasive support for the claims of economic deter-
minism. Clearly, only extreme economic necessity
forced Lusaka into this humiliating climbdown; previously, Kaunda had promised that this would happen
only when "Zimbabwe is free." What is less certain
is whether the interests of the "ruling class" were
the decisive consideration. The timing of the
announcement suggests they were not. Prominent
businessmen, technocrats and parliamentarians had
been openly clamoring for a restoration of the
southern route for at least three years.[33] Yet this
elite pressure was firmly and successfully resisted.
It was only when the supply of fertilizer and, therefore, the staple diet of the urban poor was threatened that the government acted.[34] The alternative
explanation of the timing—that the reopening was an
election ploy designed to dampen growing public disenchantment with the costs of confrontation—also
suggests that the President and the Party were defer-
ring to mass as well as middle class opinion. Moreover, during the run-up to the December 1978 general
elections, the UNIP leadership deliberately clipped
the political wings of the accommodationist lobby by
vetoing the candidatures of two of the most outspoken advocates of a reopened border, former Vice-
President Simon Kapwepwe and former Finance Minister
Arthur Wina.[35]

To date, the results of the search for empirical support for the assertion that Zambian decision
makers have pursued an ambivalent policy of confrontation and accommodation with the White South are
less than conclusive. Economic injury does serve as
an ultimate constraint on Zambian opposition to
minority regimes, though the government has shown it
is prepared to absorb severe damage before that limit
becomes operative. Finally, class interest, while
an essential tool of analysis, is not by itself an
adequate explanation of Zambian behavior with respect
to Southern Africa. On the other hand, it may have
greater potency for an understanding of the political
economy of Zambia's global dependence, which in turn
impacts upon her regional position and policy.[36]

GLOBAL INTERDEPENDENCE

At Independence, Zambia's asymmetrical dependence on racist Southern Africa was politically her
most odious and economically her most onerous

colonial inheritance. At the same time, as the second ranking copper producing country in the world
and the leading copper exporter, her economy was inevitably closely integrated into that of the wider
world.[37] This gave her a strategic significance and
a potential bargaining advantage that few other
African states possessed; yet, it also tied her to
the fluctuating political and economic fortunes of
her customers and competitors around the globe.
Moreover, in the process of disengaging from the
South, she deepened her dependence in some respects
on the North. As a result, by the mid-1970s, her
international linkages had come to rival regional
conflicts as arbiters of her national fate.

     In the immediate aftermath of UDI, Zambia had
little opportunity to plan the pattern of her external relations; under the inexorable pressure of
events, she had no alternative but to turn for emergency assistance wherever she could find it. The
available options were strictly limited—principally
the Commonwealth, African neighbors and the United
States. Gradually, however, as the country recovered
from the initial trauma of economic disruption,
Zambia consciously sought to strike a somewhat different balance among her international partners.
The countries with which, in Zambian perceptions,
she shared the most concerns and, therefore, wished
to collaborate most closely were: first and foremost, fellow OAU members especially the more progressive ones; then, other Third World and nonaligned
states; followed by a broad spectrum of middle powers
ranging from Commonwealth and Scandinavian countries
to Yugoslavia, Rumania and (after some initial suspicion) China (see chapter 9). Friendly relations
were also pursued with the superpowers though Lusaka
never felt fully comfortable with either of them.[38]
Admittedly, traditional interaction patterns have
persisted and remain strong. Nevertheless, over
time, Zambia has made very considerable progress in
reshaping her international relations to reflect her
independence, interests and ideals, notably pan-
Africanism, nonalignment and development.

Pan-Africanism

     In her search for likeminded associates, Zambia
was drawn first to East Africa, and especially to
Tanzania (see chapter 5). By 1964, Kenneth Kaunda
and Julius Nyerere had already established a remarkable personal rapport which, despite recent strains
over Rhodesia, has stood the test of two troubled

decades. Their partnership has been nourished and cemented by a lengthy series of shared endeavors: responding to the challenge of UDI, hosting liberation movements, recognizing Biafra, collaborating with China in the construction of the Tanzam railway, fashioning one-party democracies and seeking to build nonracial societies at home. The two leaders also constituted the common denominator in a number of regional groups of varying degrees of formality, vitality and longevity, which have emerged in East and Central Africa over the years (table 1.3). On the other hand, Zambia never succeeded in joining the East African Community before its collapse in 1977, partly because of second thoughts in Lusaka but also, reportedly, as a result of a Kenyan veto.

On the wider continental stage, Zambia strove to fashion the Organization of African Unity (OAU) into an effective instrument of African unity, with which to confront principally Southern Africa but also imperialist forces elsewhere in the world. Among heads of state, Kaunda was one of the most faithful in his attendance at annual OAU summits; during 1970-71, he served as Chairman. Zambia was also one of a few member states to pay her annual assessment for the OAU's administrative expenses and liberation activities promptly, fully and regularly. Yet, she did not hesitate, on occasion, to challenge the central principle of the Organization—"non-interference in the internal affairs of states"— notably by recognizing secessionist Biafra[39] and by refusing to recognize certain military regimes. Kaunda hoped thereby to discourage coups. He also had an instinctive aversion to militarism. Moreover, he greatly admired many of the victims, especially Ben Bella in Algeria, Nkrumah in Ghana, and Obote in Uganda. Nevertheless, as the rash of coups spread across half the continent, Kaunda was reluctantly compelled to adopt a more pragmatic approach, as he had earlier done in the case of Mobutu's Zaire which lay astride Zambia's vital rail outlet through Angola to the sea. Besides, several of the military leaders proved more progressive than many of the more conservative civilian heads. The close working relationship forged with Nigeria, especially under General Obasanjo, is evidence of the extent to which the original purist position has been abandoned.

Nonalignment

The same intense concern for the moral content of policy has characterized Zambia's distinctive

TABLE 1.3
East and Central African Regional Organizations

Member States	PAFMECSA 1958-63*	Eastern Africa Heads of State 1964-69	ECA Economic Community of Eastern Africa 1965-67†	Conference of East & Central African States 1966-74††	"Mulungushi Club" 1967-73⁺	Tanzania-Zaire-Zambia 1973-74	Front Line States 1974-
Zambia	x	x	x	x	x	x	x
Tanzania	x	x	x	x	x	x	x
Kenya	x	x	x	x	x		
Uganda	x	x		x	x		
Ethiopia	x		x	x			
Somalia	x		x	x			
Burundi	x		x	x	x		
Rwanda	x		x	x			
Zaire	x			x	x	x	
Malawi	x		x	x	x		
Botswana	x				x		x
Mozambique	x						x
Angola							x

*PAFMECSA: Pan-African Freedom Movement of Eastern, Central and Southern Africa. Dependent territories, including Rhodesia, South Africa, Namibia, Lesotho and Swaziland, were represented by one or more nationalist movements.
†Also Madagascar and Mauritius
††Also Central African Empire, Chad, Congo (B), Equatorial Guinea, Gabon and Sudan
⁺Informal meetings of leaders at party conferences. Only representation at UNIP conferences is shown. Swaziland also attended occasionally.

approach to nonalignment. While African states routinely deny that nonalignment represents either a reluctance to get involved in East-West conflicts or a search for a carefully calculated balance between ideological camps in terms of such indicators as UN votes, trade patterns, aid donors, or diplomatic missions,[40] Zambia has taken the "positive" aspect of nonalignment more seriously than most. "We will not lend the virgin name of Zambia," Kaunda declared on the eve of Independence, "to any professional shouting of nonaligned slogans." Moreover, the standard by which the policies of Zambia and other states were to be judged was their contribution to the moral and material uplift of the common man, especially but not exclusively in Africa:

> Zambia's policy of positive nonalignment, centered around our philosophy of the inherent worth and dignity of man as man, . . . is an affirmation that Africa's way must be neither for East nor West, but initially directed towards the emancipation of the continent and her people. In this task of fostering the African revolution, the morality of an action counts more than its form or conditions.

Thus, Zambian nonalignment represents the external dimension of Kaunda's philosophy of Humanism.[41]

Operationally, nonalignment has been implemented at three levels: in Zambia's own behavior, in judgments on the policies of other actors, and in collective action. With respect to the first, there was a conscious campaign, particularly during the early years before Zambians had fully regained their confidence, to minimize foreign and, above all, superpower influences in order to preserve Zambian freedom of action. Accordingly, diplomatic missions in Lusaka were limited in size and their activities, especially their contacts with Zambians, were severely regulated; in 1971, the East German trade commission in Lusaka was expelled for inadmissable behavior. Similarly, foreign assistance was viewed with deep suspicion, and not infrequently rejected, as in the case of the American Peace Corps. Complete self-reliance was the ideal; indeed, the First National Development Plan called for the virtual phasing out of external assistance by 1970.[42] This proved increasingly impractical. Nevertheless, aid proposals—especially the many competing scholarship offers—continued to be carefully coordinated and their political implications closely scrutinized, at

27

least until the late 1970s when massive injections
of external funds became a condition of national
survival. Foreign films and dress styles have also
been targets for occasional outbursts of xenophobia
among zealous UNIP officials.

Secondly, Zambia undertook to judge the international conduct of the superpowers on their merits
without fear or favor. Accordingly, she vigorously
condemned US military involvement in Vietnam and,
less understandably, in Korea, and denounced Soviet
military intervention in Czechoslovakia and Angola.
Despite this apparent symmetry, Zambia has, on balance, been considerably more critical of Western
than of Soviet policies in Africa, in the main because of Western associations with the White regimes
of the region; at the same time, she has clearly
been more sympathetic to Western democratic values
than Soviet ideology. Among the countries notably
successful in striking a responsive chord in Lusaka
have been the independently-minded European states—
Sweden and, curiously,France in the West, and Yugoslavia, Rumania and even, in minor respects, maverick
Albania in the East. China too has served as an inspiration. The frequency with which Zambia has sided
with China on issues in dispute between Peking and
Moscow helps explain the Soviet Union's cautious and
unresponsive attitude—for example, at the time of
UDI and following the 1973 Rhodesian border closure—
though equally important have been Moscow's initial
perceptions of Zambia as a neocolonial outpost of
international capital and its inability to comprehend
or categorize Humanism.

Finally, Zambia saw the nonaligned movement and
related Third World forums as offering scope for
coalition building over issues of importance to her,
such as racial and economic equity. As in the case
of the OAU, her specific concern at first was the
mobilization of world opinion in support of Southern
African liberation. However, she increasingly came
to view Third World unity as crucial to the restructuring of relations with the advanced industrial
states. Significantly, it was the Third Conference
of Nonaligned Nations in Lusaka in September 1970
which marked the reorientation of the movement away
from its previous preoccupation with East-West conflict towards a new awareness of North-South inequalities. By that time, détente between Washington and
Moscow had begun to render classical "strategic"
nonalignment less relevant.

Development

Zambia's awareness of a need for a New International Economic Order has increased greatly since the mid-1970s when the copper bottom fell out of her economy. Nevertheless, as early as May 1967, she hosted the founding conference of the Intergovernmental Council of Copper Exporting Countries (CIPEC) in an attempt to strengthen and stabilize the price of her pre-eminent export. More recently, she joined with other African-Caribbean-Pacific countries in negotiating the 1975 Lome Convention with the European Economic Community (EEC),[43] and has participated actively in the Commonwealth Group of Experts (1975-76), the North-South dialogue in Paris (1975-77), UNCTAD's Group of 77 and other UN organs and agencies. The results of all this unprecedented international activity over global economic restructuring have, to date, been meagre and, for Zambia, particularly unrewarding. CIPEC has signally failed to provide price stability in the copper market, and neither the EEC's export revenue stabilization scheme (STABEX) nor UNCTAD's proposed Common Fund includes copper in its select list of commodities, though Lusaka is pressing for its inclusion. Consequently, Zambia has so far reaped few immediate benefits from Third World collaboration; the diversity of interests within the developing world has been too great, the agenda too long, and the changes too distant. Domestic measures to foster economic independence have been somewhat more successful.

The principal instrument of Zambian economic nationalism has been the 51% nationalization of foreign firms, designed to bring the "commanding heights" of the economy under direct state control. Whether the mere transfer of ownership is adequate for this purpose remains a subject of considerable dispute. The sceptics contend that minority foreign shareholders are still able to manipulate decisions to their own advantage, especially when they also hold management contracts, as the mining companies did from 1969 to 1974; that the Zambian directors have been effectively coopted into a transnational bourgeoisie with extranational loyalties and values and, therefore, cannot be expected to act in the interests of the Zambian people; and that, at least in the case of the copper mines, Zambian "ownership" remains something of a myth as they were "bought" mainly with loans floated overseas.[44] This controversy constitutes part of a wider debate on the role of the multinational corporations in Zambia and on

neocolonial mechanisms generally. To date, there
have been few empirical tests of the various claims
advanced, though what limited evidence is available,
mainly case studies on the mining industry, tends to
call in question, or at least qualify, some of the
conventional wisdom. Moreover, Zambia's parastatal
system has been in an almost continual state of flux
for the last decade.

The two mining conglomerates—the Anglo-American
Corporation (AAC) and the Roan Selection Trust (RST)
—have undoubtedly found the Zambian policy of disengagement from and confrontation with the South an
anathema. Nevertheless, they appear, for broad
policy reasons, to have participated actively and
effectively, and at considerable expense to themselves, in Zambian contingency planning exercises
prior to and since UDI, notably through the development of alternative routes and sources of supply.
They also responded positively, if unenthusiasti-
cally, to the fresh challenges of the 1973 border
closure. Lusaka's decision to exploit domestic
Zambian coal rather than rely on traditional
Rhodesian sources was particularly unpalatable; not
only did it deal a severe financial blow to AAC's
Wankie Colliery, it also committed the companies to
costly and technically difficult conversion operations because of the lower quality of the Zambian
product. Nevertheless, they again "cooperated fully
and loyally" with the government. More significant,
perhaps, are the instances where the government succeeded in overcoming open company hostility to its
policies. Three battles, in particular, have been
documented: the establishment of a copper fabri-
cating plant (ZAMEFA) and the metal marketing corporation (MEMACO), and the installation of the Waelz
Kiln plant at Broken Hill.[45] On the other hand, the
Zambian surrender which ended the railway payments
crisis in July 1966 and the collapse of the Japanese-
American consortium which threatened to challenge
the longstanding duopoly of the AAC and RST,[46] suggest that the victories have not all gone one way.
However, before firm conclusions are possible on the
extent to which the multinational tail is able to
wag the Zambian government dog, further detailed
research will be necessary.

The same is true of transnational class formation within the Zambian context. Pending additional
evidence, all that can be hazarded is that the
search for a significant Zambian comprador class has
been largely unproductive. As Markovitz points out:

The experience of the international copper-
mining companies in Zambia clearly reveals the
difference between a national bourgeoisie and
a comprador class. A comprador class sits in
power at the pleasure of foreign corporations
and governments. Tool and puppet, its loyalties and policies are determined by these
outside forces. Without an independent domestic base, its autonomy is severely circum-
scribed, as are its national loyalties. The
multinational corporation cannot doubt the
patriotic intensity of the national bourgeoisie. . . . As a matter of self-interest,
the national bourgeoisie needs the state to
protect and further its personal and economic
interest.[47]

On the basis of our present knowledge, the Zambian
bourgeoisie appears quite capable of recognizing its
own interests, and of bargaining effectively to promote them. Cooperation with international capitalism is no longer dictated by external forces alone
but involves an almost continual process of renegotiation to reflect both Zambian terms and global
change.

CONCLUSION

Zambia's experience of independence has been an
almost unrelieved succession of escalating and mutually reinforcing crises, some of her own making or
choosing but most beyond her control. Moreover,
none of the major national, regional or global problems confronting the nation is amenable to easy or
early resolution. The outcome of the December 1978
general elections can afford considerable satisfac-
tion to the President personally, but the evidence
they reveal of provincial pockets of discontent must
occasion some concern. In addition, the inability
of the government to meet the material expectations
of the population—whether middle class, urban
workers, unemployed labor, peasant or expatriate—
or even to maintain previous standards in the face
of the declining gross domestic product, let alone
to deal effectively with the structural inequalities
in society, introduces an element of uncertainty and
potential instability into the political system.
Regionally, the partial reopening of the southern border is a painful reminder that, despite the
enormous progress made in disengaging the economy

31

from dependence on the White South, the country has not yet developed completely dependable alternative routes. Moreover, the increasing frequency and destructiveness of Rhodesian armed assaults by land and air underscore Zambia's continuing military vulnerability. Nevertheless, encouraged by his recent electoral mandate, the President appears more determined than ever to press ahead with the liberation of Southern Africa as the only real or acceptable solution to the country's long term security and communication dilemmas. The announcement of increased defense expenditures—despite opposing demands within UNIP for cutbacks—and the renewed assurances that Zambia will continue to offer liberation movements a "reliable rear base," are convincing evidence that the government has not succumbed to the obvious attractions of a strategy of accommodation with the Southern African regimes but, instead, is sticking to its principles despite the ever-mounting costs.

It is in the sphere of Zambia's global relationships that the greatest changes and reverses have been registered in recent years. Economic misfortune, in the form of zero copper revenues, spiralling costs of imports especially oil, shortages of all kinds, and rampant domestic inflation, has forced the country to accept less rather than more self-reliance internationally. In the absence of alternatives, Lusaka has turned to Western governments and financial institutions, not only for its development needs but also for its current cash requirements. The sharp rise in the external debt service ratio and the staggering arrears in the payments "pipeline" resulting from the drastic decline in foreign exchange earnings and reserves, are measures of this new dependence. The long term implications of these emergency developments for Zambia's political economy may well be profound. Their impact as further constraints on foreign policy behavior and choices is only beginning to emerge.

NOTES

1. Northern Rhodesia, The British South Africa Company's Claims to Mineral Royalties in Northern Rhodesia (Lusaka: Government Printer, 1964); Richard Hall, The High Price of Principles: Kaunda and the White South (Harmondsworth: Penguin, 1973), pp. 73-87. Finance Minister Arthur Wina, who conducted the negotiations, was the son of a Barotse Ngambela

32

(traditional prime minister) and acting Litunga.

2. The outstanding postindependence instance of
this was the highly publicized remark of Zambia's
high commissioner-designate to London in April 1967
(and subsequently repeated) characterizing Britain,
somewhat undiplomatically, as a "humbled toothless
bulldog." The truth hurt.

3. David C. Mulford, Zambia: The Politics of Inde-
pendence, 1957-1964 (London: Oxford University
Press, 1967), p. 280; Gerald L. Caplan, "Barotseland:
The Secessionist Challenge to Zambia," Journal of
Modern African Studies 6, no. 3 (October 1968):345-
55.

4. Africa Research Bulletin (ARB), 1976, pp. 4064-
65; UN Security Council, Verbatim Records (S/PV.
1944), 27 July 1976; New African, no. 135 (November
1978):16.

5. In 1965, the Zambian Consul in Lubumbashi offi-
cially represented Zambia at the funeral in Kapanga,
Zaire of Paramount Chief Mwantiyanvwa of the Lunda,
Tshombe's father-in-law. Tshombe's younger brother
David succeeded to the throne.

6. Kanongesha died in a road accident in Angola
shortly afterwards, apparently without learning that
Lusaka had deposed him for antigovernment activities.
As late as 1968, a Zambian minister (and grandson of
Chief Kanongesha) was still alleging that remnants
of the earlier exodus were "undergoing military
training in Angolan jungles, possibly to cause subversion in Zambia" (Zambia Mail, 2 August 1968,
p. 1).

7. Africa Confidential, 1968, no. 20 (11 October
1968):5. A careful reading of Banda's remarks suggests that he was not claiming any territory, merely
establishing an historical point. However, Zambia
was not sure the border tribes would fully appreciate the subtle distinction.

8. Economist, 12 August 1978, pp. 45-46; Times
(London), 8 August 1978, p. 4. Kapwepwe and two
other presidential hopefuls were subsequently dis-
qualified on technical grounds following amendments
to UNIP's constitution. In the election of
12 December 1978, Kaunda received a convincing 80.5%
"yes" vote in a 66.9% poll.

9. As early as April 1966, the Organisations (Control of Assistance) Act prohibited organizations "having, in the opinion of the President, objects of a political nature" from accepting "assistance from any foreign government" except with the "prior approval of the President in writing." A similar provision applied to trade unions.

10. Africa Digest 10, no. 2 (October 1962):44-45; Mulford, Zambia, pp. 241, 277, 290-91, 294, 316-17; Jan Pettman, Zambia: Security and Conflict (New York: St. Martins, 1974), pp. 194-96.

11. Times of Zambia, 6 December 1968, p. 1; Zambia Daily Mail, 20 May 1971, p. 1. The first intrusion may have been intended to disrupt the general elections and the second, UNIP's critical Mulungushi conference. The Nakuru Agreement of 21 June 1975, signed by the three Angolan parties, provided for the disarming of Zambian bands still in Angola (Africa Contemporary Record, 1975-76, p. C82).

12. Times of Zambia, 21 September 1971, p. 1; Times, 28 August 1971, p. 4. Kapwepwe successfully sued the Zambia Broadcasting Service and Zambia's two daily newspapers for $84,000 for publicizing unsubstantiated charges (Times, 20 March 1974, p. 6).

13. See chapter 10 and Karen Eriksen, "Zambia: Class Formation and Detente," Review of African Political Economy 9 (May-August 1978):4-26; Robert Molteno and William Tordoff, "Independent Zambia: Achievements and Prospects," in Politics in Zambia, ed. William Tordoff (Manchester: Manchester University Press, 1974), pp. 388-401; Ian Scott, "Middle Class Politics in Zambia," African Affairs 77, no. 308 (July 1978): 2-14; Ann and Neva Seidman, South Africa and US Multinational Corporations (Westport, Conn.: Lawrence and Hill, 1978), pp. 216-242; Timothy M. Shaw, Dependence and Underdevelopment: The Development and Foreign Policies of Zambia (Athens: Ohio University Center for International Studies, 1976). Cf. William Tordoff, "Zambia: The Politics of Disengagement," African Affairs 76, no. 302 (January 1977):60-69.

14. Richard Sklar, in his Corporate Power in an African State: The Political Impact of Multinational Mining Companies in Zambia (Berkeley: University of California Press, 1975), pp. 205-206, makes the best effort to date. He estimates the size of the

"managerial bourgeoisie" in 1970 at "25,000 persons in addition to their immediate families—a total of some 100,000 to 125,000 . . . or between 2 and 3 percent" of the population. If the ruling class were defined to include all the "leaders" as specified in the Leadership Code, i.e., all public, parastatal and private employees etc., and their families, with an income of $3200 (Statutory Instrument no. 88, 28 May 1976), the number would be much larger.

15. Archie Mafeje, Science, Ideology and Development (Uppsala: Scandinavian Institute of African Studies, 1978), p. 10; Giovanni Arrighi and John S. Saul, Essays on the Political Economy of Africa (New York: Monthly Review Press, 1973), p. 84.

16. African Social Research, no. 23 (June 1977):256.

17. See Douglas G. Anglin, "Zambian versus Malawian Approaches to Political Change in Southern Africa," in David Chanaiwa, ed., Profiles in Self-Determination: African Responses to European Colonialism in Southern Africa, 1652-Present (Northridge: California State University Foundation, 1976), pp. 371-414.

18. Letter: Permanent Representative of Zambia to the United Nations addressed to the Secretary-General (S/10225), 15 June 1971. The near-riots in Lusaka in late 1970, resulting from a local shortage of "mealie-meal," had alerted the government to the explosive potential of this issue (Times of Zambia, 4 December 1970, p. 1).

19. UN Economic and Social Council, Assistance to Zambia: Report of the Secretary-General (E/1978/114), 5 July 1978, Annex, p. 3; Times, 22 September 1978, p. 6.

20. This is the amount that Kaunda claimed in April 1978 from the major oil companies as damages for prolonging the Rhodesian rebellion through their sanction busting. In the opinion of the Times (22 September 1978, p. 15), this sum "perhaps may be taken as his estimate of what twelve years of UDI have cost Zambia."

21. Manifesto on Southern Africa (Lusaka: Government Printer, 1969), pp. 2, 3.

22. James N. Rosenau, The Adaptation of National

Societies: A Theory of Political System Behavior and Transformation (New York: McCaleb-Seiler, 1970), p. 5. Rosenau's term acquiescent adaptation is similar to the concept of accommodation employed here. An alternative formulation is the attempt of a society "to keep its essential structures within acceptable limits by making them consistent with the changes and demands emanating from its present environment" (p. 4).

23. N. A. Deb., 9 March 1978.

24. Sklar, Corporate Power in an African State, p. 177 n.99.

25. Zambia Daily Mail, 21 November 1975, p. 1; 30 March 1976, p. 1; also 26 April 1975, p. 1.

26. Tony Avirgan, "'Secret loan' in Rhodesia package deal," Guardian, 19 November 1975, p. 3. Also, BBC Africa Service "Morning Show," 26 November 1975. Avirgan also alleged that the agreement called for Zambia to detain all "ANC militants" loyal to Muzorewa and Sithole. At that time, these two leaders were denouncing negotiations with Smith and promising to win majority rule through an intensified armed struggle.

27. Tony Hodges in Economist, 20 December 1975, p. 52 and African Development, February 1976, p. 137; Times of Zambia, 23 March 1976, p. 4.

28. Guardian, 25 November 1976, p. 4.

29. Vernon Mwaanga, "US-Africa Relations: The View from Zambia," Africa Report 20, no. 5 (September-October, 1974):38-39.

30. Financial Mail (Johannesburg), 28 November 1975; Economist, 20 December 1975, p. 50; African Development, February 1976, p. 137; Standard Bank Review (Johannesburg), March 1976, p. 6. Jan Marais, a leading South African banker, also visited Lusaka in October 1975.

31. Normal short term suppliers' credit continued, at least until 1978 when, because of the arrears in payments, the Credit Guarantee Insurance Corporation of Africa Limited in Johannesburg refused to underwrite any further credit by South African exporters (CGICA Press Statement, 15 March 1978).

32. In December 1978, South African consumer goods totalling $8 million were specially imported to overcome shortages at Christmas. In addition, some South African products have been purchased in Malawi (N. A. Deb., no. 41, 21 January 1976, c. 159).

33. Times, 18 November 1975, p. 9; N. A. Deb., no. 41, 21 January 1976, cc. 157-59, 195; Economist, 20 December 1975, p. 50. Former Finance Minister Arthur Wina was the most outspoken; his Livingstone constituency had been hardest hit by the closure.

34. Contingency Planning Secretariat, Why Zambia Reopened the Southern Railway Route (Lusaka: Government Printer, 1978); Note Verbale dated 6 October 1978 from the Permanent Representative of Zambia to the United Nations addressed to the Secretary-General (S/12884), 6 October 1978.

35. Times of Zambia, 4 November 1978, p. 1; 17 November 1978, p. 1. In August 1977, the passports of 4 prominent Zambian businessmen with multinational corporation connections were seized.

36. Eriksen concedes that "the rise of an indigenous bourgeoisie" has not been, "by itself, a sufficient factor in promoting" the foreign policy changes she detects ("Zambia: Class Formation and Detente," p. 26).

37. In 1964, Zambia produced 13.3% of the world's copper. By 1970, she had slipped into 4th place, behind the United States, the Soviet Union and Chile, with 10.8% of world production (and, in 1976, 9.0%).

38. This ranking of international actors corresponds more closely to Chinese categories emphasizing size and development than to the more traditional Western-Soviet trichotomy rooted in ideological conflict.

39. See Douglas G. Anglin, "Zambia and the Recognition of Biafra," African Review 1, no. 2 (September 1971):102-36.

40. By this erroneous (but common) definition, Zambia has been more "nonaligned" politically than economically. There were 84 diplomats from NATO countries and 81 from Warsaw Pact countries resident in Zambia in 1978, with China having the largest mission; Zambia had 58 agreements with Western countries and 48 with Eastern countries (N. A. Deb.,

no. 36, 31 July 1974, c. 325); and in the UN General
Assembly, Zambia votes more regularly with the USSR
and against the USA than vice versa. Even the aid
balance (because of the huge Chinese loans) has,
until recently, been relatively even. Trade and investment links, on the other hand, have been mainly
with the West; in 1976, only 2.5% of Zambian trade
was with China and the Soviet bloc.

41. Zambia Information Services, Press Release,
no. 1710/64, 23 October 1964, p. 33; no. 1201/65,
29 July 1965, p. 11; see also, Fola Soremekun,
"Kenneth Kaunda's Cosmic Neo-Humanism," Genève-
Afrique 9, no. 2 (1970):29.

42. First National Development Plan, 1966-1970
(Lusaka: Government Printer, 1966), p. 15.

43. In July 1966, the Zambian cabinet rejected any
association with the EEC—such as the Arusha Convention which the East African states signed in 1968—
as inconsistent with nonalignment. The fact that
Welensky, as Federal Prime Minister, had favored
association with Europe did not count in its favor.

44. $150 million of the $226 million required in
1973 to redeem the bonds issued in 1969 at the time
of the 51% takeover came from international banking
loans.

45. Times of Zambia, 1 November 1965, p. 6;
Economist, 22 April 1967, p. 379; Sklar, Corporate
Power in an African State, pp. 93-95, 144-48, 176-
78, 183; George K. Simwinga, "The Copper Mining
Industry of Zambia: A Case Study of Nationalization
and Control," in What Government Does, eds. Matthew
Holden and Dennis L. Dresang, Sage Yearbooks in
Politics and Public Policy 1 (1975):89, 91-93. The
decision to establish a metal marketing company was
first announced in 1968 as a joint undertaking with
the AAC and RST (N. A. Deb., no. 16, 30 October 1968,
cc. 557-60), but not implemented until 1973 when
MEMACO was incorporated as a wholly-owned parastatal.

46. Sklar, Corporate Power in an African State,
pp. 72-73.

47. Irving L. Markovitz, Power and Class in Africa
(Englewood Cliffs: Prentice-Hall, 1977), p. 94;
Sklar, Corporate Power in an African State, pp. 198-
200, 207-210.

2
The Ideology of
Zambian Foreign Policy

The foreign policy of Zambia is complex; it
encompasses a variety of values and goals, and advances several interests and concerns. This chapter
attempts to examine the continuities and discontinuities, compatibilities and contradictions in her
foreign policy. In particular, it focuses on the
emerging debate in the country over the direction
of the Zambian society and state and over the definition of the national ideology of Humanism. This
analysis is based on the assumption that internal
and international policies and actions are related,
especially for states such as Zambia which are characterized by a high level of dependence. It is also
concerned with the constraints which domestic values,
interests and structures impose on her foreign policy
"choices"

The debate over the content of Humanism and the
orientation of foreign policy in Zambia reflects the
growth in inequalities and divergent interests in
the country during its first decade. The attempt by
the Zambian state to reform both its economy and its
international status are crucial parts of its desire
to enhance its authority and control. Given the
inherited dependence of Zambia on foreign investment,
technology, skills and trade, her foreign policy
values may be seen as an expression of the intent of
the elite to exert control over Zambia's society and
resources. The leadership of Zambia perceives internal and international challenges to its dominance
to be related; if it is to confront these linkages,
it has to develop and articulate a foreign policy
which attacks both. Humanism is designed to serve
these interrelated purposes.

The major advocate of Humanism and the primary
foreign policy spokesman for Zambia is, of course,
President Kaunda. Yet, while his response to crises

and opportunities in international politics is in
some respects representative of the Zambian elite,
he tends to stand outside and above ethnic, regional
and class politics in Zambia. He is more objective
and intolerant of Zambia's international inheritance
and, as the conscience of the nation, often draws
attention to policy problems and contradictions.
Yet, although he is increasingly critical of Zambia's
continuing dependence and of the embourgeoisement
of its elite, he has been more permissive towards
both than he would wish because of the imperatives
of his office. As a philosopher-king, the President
expresses general national concerns and intentions,
but he rules in a pragmatic style to perpetuate his
control and pᵢ ᵣnage. Dr. Kaunda regularly expresses
his preference for a more radical society and policy,
but he cannot compel compliance single-handedly. His
presidential style is one of attrition and encouragement combined with political sensitivity and dexter-
ity. Consequently, the external behavior and social
reality of Zambia tend to lag behind the expression
of presidential priorities and proposals.

This chapter deals both with the preferences of
President Kaunda and with the debate over Humanism
as a response to Zambia's problems of dependence and
underdevelopment. The first section examines the
major foreign policy values of Humanism, pan-Africanism and nonalignment. The second part analyzes continuities and discontinuities in the foreign policy
ideology of Zambia. In the final part, alternative
values advanced by a segment of the Zambian elite are
considered.

THE "NATIONAL INTEREST" OF ZAMBIA: HUMANISM,
NONALIGNMENT AND PAN-AFRICANISM

The "national interest" of Zambia, articulated
by the President and his advisers, is concerned with
the politics of Southern Africa and Zambia's role in
the world. Zambia's inheritance of dependence on
the white regimes and of domestic racial tension led
to advocacy of a rival philosophy — Humanism. Humanism is concerned with people and with dignity; it
is a reaction to Zambia's colonial history and to
the continuing problem of minority rule in Southern
Africa. It is designed not only to overcome internal
racial conflict, but also to advance an alternative
international order in Southern Africa based on racial equality and respect. Humanism has been developed largely by President Kaunda himself and reflects
his Christian beliefs and pacifist preferences.[1] It

represents both Zambia's contribution to new state ideologies and a standard by which state behavior can be justified and judged.

Although Humanism is the core of Zambia's values, to attract support in the confrontation in Southern Africa, she has also advanced the related ideas of pan-Africanism and nonalignment. Lusaka is concerned to maintain African unity in opposition to the white regimes; it is an advocate of functional as well as of political cooperation and remains interested in the prospects of certain forms of integration in Central Africa. Zambia might have protected her security by entering into an alliance with a major power. Instead, she has preferred to appeal for political and material support from nonaligned states in her regional confrontation. After the experience of the Central African Federation, Zambia is cautious about becoming part of a comprehensive regional community, at least until liberation is achieved. Rather, she seeks support among relatively disinterested, smaller powers to enhance both her sovereignty and her security (see chapter 9)

These three core values of Humanism, pan-Africanism and nonalignment are not only responses to the politics of Southern Africa; they also advance Zambia's claims to development. Although Zambia is landlocked, she is clearly not a "least developed" state. However, she remains poor despite the extraction and export of copper. She is concerned, therefore, to participate in the collective Third World demand for significant changes in the structure of the international economy as a means of enhancing her own prospects for development. In summary, Humanism is concerned with the improvement of the welfare of Zambia; pan-africanism advocates continental cooperation as one way to accelerate development; and nonalignment demands changes in the terms of trade and investment. These values, therefore, serve to advance Zambia's position with respect to her twin preoccupations, namely, Southern Africa and development.[2]

Humanism as a response to racism: Zambia and the liberation of Southern Africa

In response to ideologies of racial separation and superiority, Humanism seeks to re-establish the rights of black people to be, to belong and to have. Of all the forms of inequality, President Kaunda has been most consistent and bitter in his denunciation of racial inequality. In particular, he sees "apartheid as practiced to the South of us. . .in direct

contradiction to Humanism."[3]   Hence, his intense
preoccupation with replacing the existing racial regimes in Southern Africa with majority governments.
     The practical interpretation of Humanism and
nonalignment in Zambia's foreign relations has been
strongly influenced by the politics of the subcontinent.   In early 1974, Foreign Minister Vernon Mwaanga
asserted that Zambia would "continue to pursue a
progressive, positive and active foreign policy based
on peaceful coexistence among all nations of the
world."[4]   However, advocacy of dialogue and détente
has excluded Southern Africa, except where this
serves the cause of liberation.   Lusaka considers
itself a "thorn in the flesh" of the white regimes
because it "poses a major threat to their status quo
and indeed to their unholy alliance."[5]
     Moreover, Zambia's crucial support for change in
Southern Africa affects her perceptions of the intentions and behavior of other states.   In particular,
her commitments in Southern Africa have had a profound impact on her ties, especially at the political
and military levels, with Western nations:

>   The main aim of our foreign policy in
>   Southern Africa has been designed to
>   defuse tension by creating the necessary
>   conditions for the transfer of power from
>   irresponsible white hands to responsible
>   black hands. We have supported those
>   who stand for peaceful change and majority
>   rule, but our efforts have constantly
>   been hampered and frustrated by members
>   of NATO who continue to strengthen the
>   forces of white oppression by pouring
>   in investments and sophisticated military
>   hardware.[6]

Zambia has opposed the white regimes and their supporters in a wide variety of international organizations and conferences.   To enhance the visibility
of Southern African problems as well as herself in
world politics, she has been particularly active
over a cluster of issues such as human rights and
opposition to colonialism, imperialism and racism.
Lusaka has faithfully supported international organizations as indispensable for world order, and welcomed access to their platforms in order to advance
its own foreign policy interests.
     Zambia's advocacy of change in Southern Africa
is inseparable from the promotion of her own national
interests and security.   Her three major achievements
in attracting support for her policies towards white
regimes and the issue of race have been the 1969

Lusaka Manifesto,[7] the 1971 Declaration of Commonwealth Principles, and the 1975 Dar es Salaam Declaration. Although these statements were subject to
collective revision, each was powerfully influenced
by the ideals and approaches of President Kaunda when
not actually authored by him and his advisers. The
Manifesto seeks to legitimize the escalation of conflict in Southern Africa while providing terms for
détente and change; the Principles focus on the impact
of racial prejudice and the need for human dignity
and equality; and the Declaration revised Africa's
Southern Africa strategy after political change in
Portugal, Mozambique and Angola.
     Zambia has also supported the reorientation of
nonalignment away from a preoccupation with political
freedom and towards a greater concern for the redistribution of global resources. The 1970 Lusaka Declaration on Peace, Independence, Development, Cooperation and Democratization of International Relations,
agreed at the third nonaligned conference in Lusaka,
stands in contrast to the 1969 Lusaka Manifesto on
Southern Africa. The latter was concerned with the
pace and direction of political change in the region;
the former dealt with the place of the Third World in
the global system and the imperative needed to change
the structures of world politics. The subsequent
1971 Commonwealth Declaration brought these concerns
together, and the 1975 Dar es Salaam Declaration
stressed the importance of solidarity and organizational cooperation in maintaining a sophisticated
strategy of multiple advocacy in Southern Africa.
     The Lusaka Manifesto originated in the State
Houses in Lusaka and Dar es Salaam, was issued as a
collective statement by the heads of East and Central
African states, and was subsequently adopted by both
the Organization of African Unity (OAU) and the United Nations (UN). It was designed to present a comprehensive position on the problems and prospects
of Southern Africa. Accordingly, it dealt with
freedom in the region and an end to racism; but it
also advocated peaceful change if the minority regimes would cooperate in the transition to majority
rule:
     The Liberation of Africa —— for which we
     are struggling —— does not mean a reverse
     racialism nor is it an aspect of African
     Imperialism. . . . We would prefer to nego-
     tiate rather than destroy, to talk rather
     than kill. We do not advocate violence;
     we advocate an end to the violence against
     human dignity which is now being perpetuated

by the oppressors of Africa. If peaceful progress to emancipation were possible, . . . we would urge our brothers
in the resistance movements to use peaceful methods of struggle even at the cost
of some compromise on the timing of change.
But while peaceful progress is blocked by
the actions of those at present in power
in the States of Southern Africa, we have
no choice but to give to the peoples of
those territories all the support of which
we are capable in their struggle against
their oppressors.[8]

    South Africa's "outward-looking" policy of dia-
logue may be regarded as a belated and devious response. When, however, this generated factionalism
within the OAU, the Heads of States of East and Central Africa at their next meeting adopted the Mogadishu Declaration which abandoned the diplomatic reservations of the Lusaka Manifesto and advocated the
necessity of violence in rather Fanonesque terms.[9]
Nevertheless, President Kaunda maintained his own
commitment to the earlier Manifesto and, in March
1974, revived it when offering Lusaka as a site for
negotiations between Frelimo and the Portuguese.[10]
This followed publication of General Spinola's book
on the impossibility of winning anti-nationalist wars,
but preceded the overthrow of the Lisbon government.
After the Portuguese coup, Kaunda was instrumental
in arranging the June and September 1974 negotiations
in Lusaka which led to a transitional government for
Mozambique and to independence in June 1975.[11]
    The new politico-economic vulnerability of Rho-
desia after Mozambique's liberation produced an "understanding" between President Kaunda (on behalf of
himself and President Nyerere) and Prime Minister
Vorster of South Africa. This tentative "détente"
over Rhodesia between the two leading antagonists in
Southern Africa led to negotiations with white and
black politicians from Rhodesia, and to the inclusion
of Presidents Khama of Botswana and Machel of Mozambique in a "Rhodesian détente faction", which subsequently evolved into an informal alliance of Front
Line States. Then, in April 1975, a special meeting
of OAU Foreign Ministers adopted the Dar es Salaam
Declaration on Southern Africa. This document is essentially compatible with and an updated version of
the earlier Lusaka Manifesto, although it focuses on
the liberation of Zimbabwe, Namibia and South Africa
because of the intervening changes in Mozambique and

44

Angola:

> As long as the objective of Majority Rule
> before Independence is not compromised,
> the OAU would support all efforts made
> by the Zimbabwe nationalists to win inde-
> pendence by peaceful means. .... While the
> OAU accepts the task of helping in genuine
> negotiations in order to facilitate the
> transfer of power to the African majority,
> it must remain absolutely vigilant and
> undertake the necessary preparations for
> the intensification of the armed struggle
> should peaceful solution to the Zimbabwean
> conflict be blocked.[12]

Zambia's sophisticated and cautious diplomacy over
decolonization at this time served to enhance further her international image, and led to the creation
of a cooperative regime in Mozambique which has provided crucial transit facilities and other potential
economic opportunities. It may yet lead to significant political change in both Zimbabwe and Namibia
which will further improve Zambia's economic position, diplomatic status and role as a regional power.

By contrast with the Manifesto and Declaration
on Southern Africa, the 1970 Lusaka Declaration of
nonaligned states on development and underdevelopment
is a response to global détente and multipolarity.
It asserts that one cause of such structural change
in the international system is the growth of the nonalignment movement. It demands an end to international inequality, especially of the monopoly of the
technological revolution by the rich and of new forms
of domination:

> International relations are entering a phase
> characterized by increasing interdependence
> and also by the desire of states to pursue
> independent policies. The democratization
> of international relations is therefore an
> imperative necessity of our times. But
> there is an unfortunate tendency on the part
> of some of the big powers to monopolize de-
> cision making on world issues which are of
> vital concern to all countries.[13]

The subsequent 1971 Commonwealth Declaration
was concerned particularly with the impact of inequality and conflict on the issue of race; it brought
together Zambia's concerns with underdevelopment and
Southern Africa around the problem of color. The
Declaration of Commonwealth Principles was introduced by President Kaunda as a direct consequence of

the controversy surrounding the intention of the
British Conservative government to relax its arms
embargo against South Africa:

We recognize racial prejudice as a dangerous sickness threatening the healthy
development of the human race and racial
discrimination as an unmitigated evil of
society. Each of us will vigorously combat this evil within our own nation.

No country will afford to regimes
which practice racial discrimination
assistance which in its own judgment
directly contributes to the pursuit or
consolidation of this evil policy. We
oppose all forms of colonial domination
and racial oppression and are committed
to the principles of human dignity and
equality.[14]

Nonalignment and the demand for a new world order

Zambia seeks support for its policies on Southern Africa and on race in many organizations, especially in the nonaligned movement. She is part of
the new majority in world politics that demands a
redistribution of resources. Lusaka is concerned
with the impact of international inequalities on the
sovereignty of new states. As President Kaunda has
suggested "the poor and weak nations are naked and
defenseless before the greed and self-interest of
powerful and wealthy countries whose affluence is
largely achieved at our expense."[15] At Independence,
he warned foreign diplomats to respect Zambia's integrity and not to attempt to exploit her poverty and
dependence.[16]

The concerns of the nonalignment movement, with
which Zambia is associated, have included nuclear
testing in Africa and the proliferation of nuclear
capability to China and India, superpower interference
in their regions of dominance, Vietnam and the Middle
East, global coexistence and détente. Shortly after
Independence, Dr. Kaunda defined his conception of
nonalignment in an address to the UN General Assembly:

Zambia's policy in external affairs is a
simple one. We believe in nonalignment;
we maintain our right, having won our independence, to make a free choice in the
interests of our people on all the great
issues which today divide the world. We
feel that it is also our duty to make such
sacrifices as are necessary to win freedom

for those men everywhere who are not free
men today . . . our nonalignment is not a
withdrawal from world problems. Indeed it
cannot be, for our geographical position
as a landlocked country brings us into direct contact with eight neighboring states
whose policies and actions are of immense
concern to us.[17]

When President Kaunda opened the third summit
conference of the nonaligned states in Lusaka in
September 1970, he emphasized Zambia's commitment
to the movement and appealed for support in Southern
Africa.[18] He also pointed to the salience of nonalignment in a world of unequal states as a defense
against subordination; nonalignment is the external
dimension of Third World nationalism. Just as the
new demand in the Third World is now for economic
change, so the nonalignment movement has moved away
from disinterested mediation towards more self-in-
terested advocacy of a New International Economic
Order.

Pan-Africanism: from continental conflict to regional integration

Although Zambia's first decade in the world community has been characterized by confrontation in
Southern Africa, she has also been active in continental politics over other issues. As we note in subsequent chapters, Zambia has successfully withstood
Rhodesia's UDI and the border closure in 1973, supported the liberation movements, and encouraged negotiation towards black government in Mozambique and
Angola; she has also promoted Africa's role in world
politics, critized military coups in the continent
and advocated regional integration in Central Africa.
President Kaunda has always been a "continental
thinker".[19] In the quest for security, honor and
support, Zambia has orientated her foreign policy
around the issue of Southern Africa. Yet she has
also at times been outspoken in her criticism of
undemocratic regimes and violations of human rights
elsewhere, including Black Africa. Idi Amin of Uganda
was the "Hitler of Africa", and his expulsion of the
Asians "terrible, horrible, abominable and shameful".[20]

As a Front Line State and a pillar of the OAU
Liberation Committee which has a branch office in
Lusaka, Zambia has helped shape the OAU's consensual
policy on Southern Africa. She has also actively
promoted African issues in other international organizations, from conferences of the nonaligned and the

47

Commonwealth to the UN and its agencies. For two
years 1969 and 1970, she served on the UN Security
Council,[21] and President Kaunda acted as Africa's
spokesman while OAU Chairman in 1970. In addition,
Zambia has participated in formulating general OAU
policies, such as in the complex negotiations between
the European Economic Community (EEC) and Third World,
mainly African states.

     Although Zambia is supportive of OAU efforts
at mediation and development, she is intolerant of
military coups and regimes. She has instituted her
own one-party state to encourage internal order,
participation and development, and is critical of
undemocratic political change elsewhere on the continent. Zambia was particularly outspoken in condemning the Ghanaian and Ugandan coups which toppled
Nkrumah and Obote with whom Kaunda had had close
political and personal associations. On the other
hand, she has been more tolerant of coups in which
the leaders have revived certain democratic forms
as in Nasser's Egypt, Obasanjo's Nigeria and Mobutu's
Zaire. President Kaunda's opposition to coups is
both principled and pragmatic:

          Military coups can never provide solutions
          to problems. . . . Wherever there has been
          a military coup there has been great insta-
          bility. . . . there must be morality in poli-
          tics. The methods you use to organize
          against other people will be used against
          you.[22]

     In the case of the Amin coup, President Kaunda
also denounced the British government's precipitate
recognition as providing extracontinental support
for an undemocratic and bloody change of regime:

          President Obote. . . committed the country
          to free elections under a democratic Con-
          stitution within the next few months. We,
          therefore, strongly condemn the coup as
          clearly the work of reactionary elements
          whose only motive is to further their own
          interests, thereby acting as agents for
          the enemies of African independence, pro-
          gress and unity. It is our hope, as it is
          the hope of all Africa, that leaders of this
          Continent will continue to be united against
          outside forces of destruction.[23]
Since then, Lusaka has continued to withhold formal
recognition and has remained highly critical of the
rule of terror of Idi Amin. Accordingly, Zambia
along with Tanzania boycotted the OAU summit in

Kampala in July 1975 in order not to lend respectability to the Uganda military regime. This opposition to coups has also affected Zambia's relations
with certain other states. Diplomatic relations
were severed with Chile in 1973 following the "brutal assassination" of President Allende.[24] Although
sharing a common interest with Chile in the price of
copper, Zambia was critical of the role of foreign
states and corporations in the coup.

Despite her long struggle to disengage from the
white south (see chapter 5) and bitter memories of
the Central African Federation, Zambia may yet become a center of regional integration in Africa. Although Zambia's landlocked location makes her dependent on transit through other countries to the sea,
her relative affluence and central geographical position may lead to her designation as the core for
regional communications and manufacturing. Even
before Independence, President Kaunda foresaw Zambia
as a good location for industrialization and technological training; he predicted that Zambia would be
able to extend assistance to her neighbors out of her
wealth.[25] Zambia's economic potential and history
explains his preference for functional integration.
He sees five factors as contributing to a trend towards gradual cooperation: the "realities of international and continental politics", the common enemy
of the white regimes, the OAU system, the variety of
proposals for African unity and finally, the youth-
fulness of the African population.[26] Zambia has
advanced regional cooperation because it undermines
the influence of Pretoria and enhances her security,
leadership and development. But she prefers informal
associations such as amongst the Front Line States,
to formal agreements; experience in an integrative
system which advanced settler interests has made her
cautious. Within the subsystem of Central Africa,
the presidents of Zambia, Tanzania, Botswana, Angola
and Mozambique now meet regularly both bilaterally
and multilaterally; and Dr. Kaunda occasionally meets
with Presidents Mobutu or Banda bilaterally. Zambia
sees her growing relationship with both Botswana and
Malawi as a challenge to South Africa; she has also
been active in widening relations with independent
Mozambique and Angola; and she foresees Zimbabwe as
a partner in Central Africa. The policy of "good
neighborliness" has encouraged "harmonious, if not
integrated development in this great belt." While
Zambia has not become a member of the East African
Community (EAC):

these [Central African] consultations have
enabled this area to develop into a belt of
countries engaged in political, economic
industrial, technical, scientific and
cultural cooperation designed to further
the wider interests of Africa, including
the elimination of foreign rule and the
consolidation of African independence.[27]

CONTINUITIES AND DISCONTINUITIES IN THE FOREIGN POLICY IDEOLOGY OF ZAMBIA

In one sense, ideology is a response to reality;
as international politics have evolved, so too has
the foreign policy of Zambia. While she has consistently advocated majority rule, she has also begun
to confront the problems of dependence and underdevelopment. The President has moved towards an
acceptance of violence and has become critical of
the intrusion of neocolonialism. The articulation
of the ideology of Humanism has advanced these new
positions and policies.

From nonviolence to support of the liberation movement in Southern Africa

President Kaunda hoped to influence white politics and perceptions by establishing Zambia as a
peaceful, developing democracy. In early 1964,
Kaunda advocated the opening of a large Zambian mission in Pretoria to encourage a peaceful transition
to majority rule; his only condition was that Zambian diplomats and their families should be treated
equally with other diplomats in South Africa. He
also advocated influencing racial practices in
Southern Rhodesia by making recruitment from Zambia
into the common services institutions nonracial and
by establishing Zambia as a nonracial example.[28] He
offered to mediate between Black and White groups in
Southern Rhodesia in 1960 and advocated pacifism and
example as two means to generate change.[29] "I reject
absolutely violence in any of its forms as a solution
to our problems."[30]

However, with the escalation of violence in
Southern Africa and attacks on her borders, Zambia
increased both her security preparations and her commitment to the liberation movements as examined in
chapters 6 and 8. The President has abandoned his
total belief in pacifism under the impact of the
offensives of the white regimes: "We want peace as
the Lusaka Manifesto bears testimony. . . .The peace

we want is based on justice."[31] Because of her vulnerability and the elusiveness of political change
in the region before 1974, Zambia escalated her commitments:

> Zambia has not hidden the fact that she has
> given all possible assistance to the libera-
> tion movements. She has fearlessly called
> upon the oppressed people in Southern Africa
> to rise against their oppressors. Zambia
> has no moral right to prevent the oppressed
> people from taking up arms against their
> oppressors if these oppressors use arms
> against defenceless and innocent masses.[32]

In 1964, Kaunda advocated personal contact with whites
from the South and continued functional cooperation
with the white regimes; in 1974, Zambia supported
the exclusion and expulsion of South Africa from the
UN and had eliminated all links with Rhodesia. At
Independence, President Kaunda advocated nonviolence
as a strategy whilst recognizing that violence might
be inevitable should the white regimes be intransigent:

> If we use violence before exhausting all
> other means we should be responsible for
> the deaths of many of these very people
> for whom we sought freedom. We must,
> therefore, choose the harder path of non-
> violence and of positive action which great
> Ghandhi first taught us, for we must never
> forget that our battle is to ensure that
> our oppressed brothers shall not die but
> live.[33]

From non-socialism to Zambian Socialism and Humanism

Just as Zambia has moved from nonviolence to
violence if necessary in Southern Africa, so she
has shifted from non-socialism to Zambian socialism
and the ideology of Humanism. Before Independence,
the UNIP leadership was critical of socialism; now
it advocates a moderate and indigenous variety of
socialism. In 1963, President Kaunda foresaw Zambia
as the Switzerland of Africa:[34] "We have no intention
of nationalizing any industries at all."[35] In December 1972 he declared that

> Zambia must move in the direction of egali-
> tarianism and attain the highest possible
> degree of economic and social democracy in
> order to maximize social justice. Humanism
> is a revolutionary philosophy and requires
> revolutionary and self-sacrificing leaders.

51

Our society rejects individualism.[36]
In June 1973, President Kaunda asserted that Zambia
had replaced a foreign style of democracy and government with an indigenous system and had abandoned "a
foreign economic and social system based on capitalism and chosen one based on Humanism."[37] The philosophy of Humanism has become concerned with justice
and equality both within Zambia and in the international system as their interrelatedness has become
clear; it confronts both domestic capitalism and
racial supremacy in Southern Africa. Its declaration
in April 1967 was designed to challenge exploitation
by a political elite, racial group or economic class
and to prevent these collectively from dominating
Zambia as they had done in the colonial and federal
periods.[38] Humanism was intended to revive the traditions of a "man-centric" society, of communality
and of participation. According to Kandeke, until
the Mulungushi reforms, Zambia was following an orthodox strategy of growth. "However, since then
Zambian Humanism has been vigorously promoted to
reverse the situation from property-centeredness to
man-centeredness. Property is to serve man and not
Man to be controlled by property. . . ."[39]
   The growth of inequalities in Zambia and the
associated dependence of Zambia on the global economy
examined in chapter 10 has led the President to adopt
a more critical position towards capitalism and neocolonialism. A serious balance of payments problem
in Zambia consequent upon a decline in the price of
copper and a rise in the cost and quantity of imports,
combined with a mediocre performance of the large
parastatal sector and an increase in crime, prompted
the President in mid-1975 to present further socio-
economic changes. After the successive Mulungushi,
Matero and Lusaka reforms (1968 to 1970),[40] there
were few institutions left to incorporate into the
parastatal sector. On 30 June 1975, however, President Kaunda, responding to four critical reports on
the economy, crime and mismanagement and to his own
concern over the media, leadership code and social
problems, directed in his famous "watershed" speech
that massive state subsidies on maize, fertilizer,
meat and petrol be removed and that the United National Independence Party (UNIP) take control of the
remaining nongovernment newspaper, the Times of Zambia. His major concern, however, was with the continued economic and cultural dependence of Zambia and
the associated increase of inequalities, discontent
and crime. He appealed for discipline, self-reliance
and frugality:

The cause of the revolutionary masses,
workers and peasants is the cause of the
Party. . . . Luxuriousness, lavishness and
all forms of behavior are found in today's
Zambia. . . . Society is sick and the Zambian economy cannot be more sick than the
people who run it. We cannot turn Zambia
into a socialist state we want it to be,
let alone a Humanist one, in a short time. . ..
We are not against foreign capital per se.
Therefore, to those who may wish to invest
in Zambia again they are welcome. . . . We
are building socialism here as an instrument of establishing a Humanist state.[41]

This latest Mulungushi pronouncement, however,
reveals a continued ambivalence over the direction
of the Zambian economy. According to Kandeke:
Zambian Humanism does not accept Capitalism
as a system of socio-economic organization.
But within this system, Zambian Humanism
recognizes certain techniques of industrial
organization and management that can be ad-
vantageously utilized for the purpose of
producing more material wealth in the process of constructing a Humanist society.
This is in accordance with the principle
of ECLECTICISM, the Zambian Humanist MODUS
OPERANDI.[42]
Thus, Humanism remains essentially a liberal ideology
reflecting the tension between idealism and pragmatism. In practice, more emphasis has been placed
on equality of opportunity than an equitable distribution of resources. The President has frequently
commended individual performance and excellence as
essential components and commitments in a Humanist
society as well as crucial to development. Excellence
is "a condition of freedom"[43] and effort an ingredient
of democracy.
The Zambian state has now taken partial control
over most of the means of production, except for the
foreign banks, but it has resisted moving towards a
more egalitarian socialist economy. Despite the rhetoric about UNIP supremacy, the leadership code,
participatory democracy and rural development, Zambia
remains a stratified society in which access to affluence remains the dominant goal. The President
may appeal for popular support in his attempt to make
an opening to the left, but thus far the new Zambian
"bureaucratic bourgeoisie" remains entrenched in new
positions and opulence. Although he has correctly

diagnosed the political, economic and social problems
of Zambia, it is doubtful if he can single-handedly
confront the new Zambian elite in the ministries,
parastatals and barracks of Lusaka. Therefore, the
following complimentary analysis of the "Second Revolution" of the "Second Republic"[44] may be somewhat
premature:

> President Kaunda, it appears, has identified
> his country's problems with considerable
> precision. He has put the danger of
> class warfare high on the list. . . . It is
> expected that this appreciable swing to-
> wards sterner socialism will change the face
> of Zambia and usher in an egalitarian so-
> ciety in the decade ahead.[45]

The President and other Zambians have clearly
begun to appreciate the emergent problems confronting
the national political economy. Nevertheless, many
of the difficulties are inherent and structural rather than superficial and short term. As a recent
ILO report suggests, "Zambia has gone a long way in
recognizing the importance of many of these issues.
What is needed is a firm, determined and consistent
approach to implementation."[46] Kandeke, however,
claims in his analysis of Humanism that:

> Until recently, although Zambia achieved
> political independence, she continued to
> remain in the system of the world capi-
> talist economy. . . . However, after the
> declaration of economic reforms at Mulun-
> gushi on 19 April 1968, Zambia has refused
> to constitute the rear and reserve of
> capitalism. She has since become an ally
> in the struggle for the abolition of ex-
> ploitation of man by man. Capitalism is
> incompatible with Zambian Humanism. Zam-
> bian Humanism strongly condemns and opposes
> Imperialism.[47]

Kandeke goes on to argue that, through Humanism, Zambia is creating a classless society which will go beyond socialism to become a man-centred political economy. He predicts the:

> elimination of exploitation of Man by Man
> through the liquidation of socio-economic
> classes. In Zambia this is being achieved
> by preventing the growth of a national
> bourgeoisie on the one hand and, on the
> other, by encouraging every Zambian to
> cultivate initiative towards personal de-
> velopment and progress through the principle

of self-reliance. . . . socialist principles
in Zambia are only an instrument for
building a Man-centred society which is
the backbone of Zambian Humanism.[48]
He asserts that Humanism is a distinctively Zambian
and uniquely relevant form of social justice and
order, bringing an indigenous solution to problems
within the national political economy:
In Zambia, socio-economic, geo-political
and historical experience is such that
socialist reconstruction is being achieved
without recourse to violence and bloody
revolution. . . . To bring about social
revolution without resorting to force,
without destruction or disorganization is
the objective of Zambian Humanist social
reconstruction.[49]
We return to the debate over the definition, practice
and promise of Humanism in Zambia in the next section.

Dependence: neocolonialism and underdevelopment

One characteristic response of African leaders
to the elusiveness of development has been to shift
the blame to neocolonialism. President Kaunda has
resisted such general explanations of underdevelopment, recognizing that the accusation can be mis-
used by leaders. He has defined neocolonialism as
the attempt made by great powers to undermine the sovereignty of an African state
by the use of subtle economic and political
tools to replace the physical domination of
the old colonialists. It is all too possible
for an African country to emerge from the
colonial prison to find itself enmeshed in
a net of financial, diplomatic and ideological obligations which effectively destroy
its freedom of action.[50]
Although the President recognizes that the exchange
of raw materials for manufactured goods was part of
Zambia's inheritance, he has yet to establish an
autonomous economy in Zambia. Nevertheless, one
inspiration for the policy of "self-management" of
the mines and industries of Zambia has been a more
critical view of the many aspects and activities of
foreign capital. When President Kaunda opened the
Saba Saba celebrations in Tanzania in July 1974, he
warned of the dangers of neocolonialism and dependence on foreign interests: "There is no such thing
as benevolent colonialism. We must therefore, change
these structures in order to consolidate our independence." He identified the multinational corporations

as centers of exploitation which threaten the positive impact of African parties. He charged that they were "invisible opposition parties" and instruments of neocolonialism: "The problem with these interests is that either you control them or they control you. They will exploit the slightest difference in approach to problems for their own selfish ends to the detriment of our interests".51 He has also criticized the impact of external assistance.

Although until recently Zambia has needed and received relatively small injections of foreign aid, the President is critical of its paucity, unpredictability and impact; in place of international in - equalities, he advocates economic interdependence. Shortly after Independence, Kaunda asserted that, although Zambia needed foreign technology, organizations and skills, she would not accept them if her independence were thereby threatened.

We will not purchase economic development at the cost of a new type of colonialism. . . . technical assistance and aid have contained tendencies towards a new type of dependence just as difficult to throw off as the old. It is our view that bargains have no part to play in technical assistance. Therefore, we ask that countries which offer us their aid should not exploit our need in order to infringe our sovereignty, for this is something which we shall guard jealously.52

Kaunda is also aware of ideological neocolonialism and is particularly cautious about international communism. He regards nationalism as a stronger force, but recognized years before the liberation struggles in Angola, Mozambique and Zimbabwe that communism may be more attractive to the majority in Southern Africa than elsewhere in Africa because of their history of oppression. He is critical of the colonial and settler regimes for being so anticommunist, arguing that their authoritarian rule has served to encourage rather than challenge communism. Nevertheless, even in independent Africa, Dr. Kaunda sees ideological infiltration as a threat to nonalignment and to pan-Africanism:

Any success which the communist bloc may achieve in aligning African states with it is destructive of Africa's unity and causes a shift of loyalty from Pan-Africa to Pan-Communism. Ideological subservience must be seen for what it is — a subtle and debilitating form of colonial domination which

can carve up Africa as effectively as anything achieved by the Great Powers in the
late nineteenth century.[53]
Humanism is designed to overcome such ideological
dependence.

Yet, despite the sensitivities of the President
to foreign investment, ideology and culture, a "plan"
by UNIP for the present, second decade of Zambia's
independence reveals more continuity that disconti-
nuity in interpretations of the philosophy of Humanism. According to this plan, foreign policy will
continue to reflect the eclecticism of Humanism
that Kandeke identified. The nine-point plan includes
five concerned with Africa (liberation, good neighborliness, regional cooperation, continental cooperation and support for the OAU) and four based on nonalignment and development (nonalignment, support for
international organizations, trade and exchange, and
international cooperation).[54] The Party also pro-
poses continued state participation, decentralization and an integrated defense system. The somewhat
synthetic and duplicative nature of the UNIP proposal
is a contrast to occasional presidential initiatives
and to the emerging debate within the Zambian elite
over the response to continued dependence and underdevelopment.

ALTERNATIVE VALUES IN THE ZAMBIAN ELITE: THE DEBATE OVER HUMANISM

As Zambian society has become more complex and
unequal, a number of new actors have come to assert
themselves in its foreign policy system as we note
in the next chapter. Although the President dominates
the formulation and presentation of policy, other
institutions and interests are also involved, especially the Ministry of Foreign Afrairs, other ministries, the parastatals and the Party. While these
organizations are all headed by members of the new
"bureaucratic bourgeoisie", they have their distinctive institutional interests. The debate over values
in Zambia also involves the remaining foreign and national private companies, other interest groups and
diplomatic missions in Lusaka. Thus, State House
and the Ministry of Foreign Affairs do not command a
monopoly of Zambia's foreign relations; UNIP and the
parastatals, for instance, have their own "transnational" relations with other ruling parties or with
multinational corporations. Not all these linkages
are equally compatible. For example, Indeco may have
different priorities than, say, the Ministry of Defence:

the interests of Foreign Affairs may diverge from those of Finance, Commerce, Transport or UNIP.

Humanism remains an underdeveloped ideology; it is less than fully comprehensive and is capable of being used as a synthetic rationalization for virtually any action taken by the state. The debate over its content is reminiscent of a continuing argument in Tanzania over the role of parastatals and the growth of social differentiation because of foreign investment and tastes.[55] In Zambia, as we note in chapter 10, dependence on copper and the rise of an indigenous elite and labor aristocracy, plus the constraints of a continued reliance on a few foreign markets and on expatriate skills, all contribute to a more permissive attitude towards international capitalism:

> Because Zambians consider their country to
> be more dependent upon and intertwined with
> the world economy than its more rural and
> agriculturally-based neighbor, Tanzania,
> they are cautious in redefining their rela-
> tionship to the multinational corporations
> in their midst. Such caution carries with
> it an implicit acceptance of an element
> of privilege for the modern sector during
> the transition towards extensive equaliza-
> tion. Thus Zambian reorganization, geared
> to local needs and conditions, is less dra-
> stic in its objectives, costs and regulations
> than that in Tanzania.[56]

This analysis by two expatriates stands in stark contrast to the more positive assertion by a leading Zambian socialist intellectual that the Humanist vanguard in Zambia is overcoming its inheritance of integration within the world capitalist economy through a "continuous struggle":

> Zambia's humanist economy negates the to-
> tality of the capitalist mode of produc-
> tion for the newly created socialist rela-
> tions of production. Local emerging capi-
> talists, for example, are joining hands
> with their foreign counterparts and to-
> gether are vehemently fighting against the
> establishment of an egalitarian humanist
> society in Zambia. However, the revolu-
> tionary power of the masses, through the
> Party, is steadily and decisively winning
> the battle. The contradiction between these
> two is the driving force, the main source
> of effort in the establishment of a truly
> humanist economy.[57]

58

Kandeke also does not perceive the caution and pragmatism suggested by the former analysis either, but
rather considers that struggle for socialism involves
a long-term "confrontation with tremendous resistance
from long-entrenched capitalist forces":

> most people in Zambia although they cannot
> be classified as "capitalists" in the stric-
> test sense of the term, have nevertheless
> become associated both materially and psy-
> chologically with a situation we would
> refer to as a "National Bourgeoisie".
> Their attitude and philosophy of life, as
> a result, is one of "conspicuous consump-
> tion". These people would obviously resist
> any efforts to restructure the economy on
> a socialist basis. "The haves" never take
> dispossession lying down.[53]

The parastatal strategy: towards state capitalism or socialism?

Differential interests in Zambia are, in part,
reflective of such emerging "class" interests. The
two major and interrelated issues in the debate over
the content and direction of Zambian Humanism are
the question of the parastatals and the growth of social inequalities in the country. As we note in
chapter 10, not all actors in Zambia accept the dominant, official interpretation of Zambia's foreign
policy presented by the President and his advisers.
Some oppose the policy of unrelenting confrontation
in Southern Africa because it involves excessive
costs in the form of higher prices of some commodities, an end to labor migration, shortages of certain goods and a redirection of the economy. Some
were critical of the application to join the East
African Community or the development of close relations with China. However, the major debate, around
which other related issues cluster, is over the attractions of state capitalism versus socialism and
over the growth of inequalities. Both of these problems are related to the future development of the
official ideology of Humanism.

Although Humanism has become a rationale for
regular presidential initiatives and does assert a
belief "in economic equality and social harmony,"[59]
it is not completely incompatible with the growth of
state capitalism and inequalities. To be sure, the
President criticizes conspicuous consumption, corrup-
tion, inefficiencies and decadence. Yet, in practice,
moves to control economic and social dependence

have been quite moderate and cautious. Humanism
seeks to reform, not to replace, Zambia's inheritance
of dependence on foreign trade, capital, technology
and skills. The reformation of the copper industry
and expansion of the parastatal sector are accommoda-
tive arrangements, in line with the establishment
interpretation of Humanism. Although the parastatal
sector is still subject to further organizational
change and is moving towards "self-management" in
industries such as copper and transport, nevertheless
the essential structures of collaboration between
foreign capital and the Zambian elite are likely to
be perpetuated. Indeed, the termination of management and marketing contracts in the crucial copper
industry in August 1973 was largely forced on the
government by the uncooperative attitude of the two
multinational corporations involved.60 Further,
Zambia achieved self-management only by becoming in-
debted to international banking consortia for $25 m
in three Eurodollar loans floated between June 1973
and June 1975. Moreover, the relationship between
the parastatals and external interests, though modified, has not been terminated. Anglo-American, for
instance, has "undertaken to supply, on a best endeavors basis, various services which currently relate
to overseas purchasing, recruiting and engineering
services."61

However, most criticism of the management practices and social impact of Zambia's parastatals has
been directed at Indeco; the regime's response has
been rhetorical, with repeated reorganizations and
senior staff shuffles. A critical editorial "Opinion"
in the Times of Zambia on 30 May 1974 for instance,
complained that state industries were essentially
capitalist in their relations between owners and
employers and between workers and employers and in
their quest for profitability. It suggested that any
move towards a more populist economic system must
occur shortly, before state capitalist executives
become too entrenched. In a reply, Indeco's Chairman
rejected any suggestion that parastatals operate only
for profit and not for welfare. He claimed to accept
the need for humanistic operating procedures, and
pointed to the range of normal corporate charitable
and humanitarian activities; he also drew attention
to Indeco's policies of regional development and disengagement from the South. In his 1974 statement,
Mr. Andrew Kashita asserted that:

Indeco cares for the national interest and
the workers. It is a people's organization.
Those who want to see even more radical changes
should remember that it requires a profit (or

60

Santa Claus) to go hell-for-leather in pursuit of these desirable objectives but not
without either. Indeco, like any other institution in Zambia has to operate within the
social, political, economic and cultural environment. Until the people of Zambia through
their representatives order otherwise, depar-
tures from the existing order must be undertaken with thought and careful planning. The
profit motive has been established in this
country and those who decry it have a duty to
set an example, if necessary.[62]

While this response is compatible with Zambia's preoccupation with the issue of Southern Africa, the
philosophy of Humanism is less critical of relations
with capitalist states and corporations outside the
region.

The Bank of Zambia has also expressed reservations about the parastatals, not so much because
they are neocapitalist, but rather because their
growth has tended to squeeze out private initiatives.
It is particularly concerned with the growth of unemployment and debt servicing; it calls for export
diversification, import substitution, employment
creation and an end to inefficiency:

There is a need for redefinition of the role
of state enterprise. In addition to operational
problems, many parastatals suffer from over-
ambitious and inconsistent aims and objectives.
All too often, parastatal organizations are
expected to perform social services as well as
to make a profit, and to keep prices low while
financing expansion from internal sources.
Such a redefinition should be accompanied by
an examination of the role of the private
sector, especially in employment creation.[63]

The Bank suggests that "a careful selective approach
to the encouragement of private investment, both local and foreign" could restore dynamism to the economy; it is quite uncritical of the continued dependence of parastatals on external links: "Now that
the economic reforms have brought the 'commanding
heights' of the economy under national control, the
dangers of foreign investment exercising excessive
leverage have receded."[64] Interests such as those of
Indeco and the Bank resist any major retreat from
capitalism or progress towards a more socialist
definition of Humanism. The entrenched linkages between multinational corporations and the Zimco group
now dominate the economy and cannot readily be restructured by radical or presidential rhetoric. The
ideology of humanism, as now practiced, is largely

compatible with elite interests and the mixed economy.
It may be a relatively enlighted response to Zambia's
inheritance of a racially stratified society in a racially divided region, but it "remains fundamentally
ambivalent in its attitude to the private sector".[65]

Although Kandeke echoes the President's assertion that "as humanists we cannot allow Zambians to
develop into capitalists,"[66] in reality the transition
from state capitalism towards state socialism is very
problematic because of growing resistance from the
new bourgeoisie:

> The adamant proponents of state capitalism
> as opposed to state participation assert that
> the running of all socio-economic affairs
> should be based on a system of MANAGEMENT BY
> EXPERTS. This stand endorses the entrench-
> ment of bureaucratic-technocratic state pro-
> prietorship as a form of production relations.[67]

Kandeke foresees a continuing and intensifying struggle between the advocates of state socialism and those
of state capitalism, between the participatory democracy advocated by State House and the technological
rationality proposed by many members of the bureaucracy. He recognizes that:

> Zambia is at a cross-roads. On the one
> hand lies the establishment of workers'
> committees and councils as a new venture;
> on the other, due to her historical exper-
> ience and current structure of social and
> economic forces, the sources and opportuni-
> ties for the emergence and survival of
> state capitalism and technocratic-bureau-
> cratic monopoly management appear to be
> quite strong. As long as the economy is
> not brought under state control, this
> polarization will continue to bedevil the
> country.[68]

Humanism in Zambia: nationalism and/or socialism?

Humanism has permitted a distinctive Zambian
contribution to the diverse definitions of African
socialism and nonalignment. It tends to be permissive of elite control provided it is exerted with a
Zambian ethos. Henry Meebelo, like Kandeke, emphasizes its indigenous origin and its contribution to
national unity, but is less critical of the political
economy of Zambia's parastatal institutions and of
her embryonic national capitalist class:

> Zambian humanism is drawing on the social
> norms and values of the traditional society

in constructing a system of cooperative
enterprise. There is, necessarily, a
certain degree of pragmatism to be exercised
in the process. . . A measure of private
enterprise is useful and, indeed, indispensable in Zambian humanism, and, accordingly, the Government has taken steps to
encourage the participation of Zambian entrepreneurs in the economic life of the nation.
Only in this way can Zambia advance towards
the elimination of foreign capitalist
influence.[69]

Although Meebelo advocates state control, he remains
somewhat ambivalent about the advantages of national
versus foreign capitalism and over state or workers'
control. Nevertheless, he argues that:

participation in industry, state landowner-
ship, cooperatives and price control are. . .
important for preventing incipient capitalism
and exploitation in Zambian humanism. But
as measures for positively creating an egalitarian society, they fall short of the rai-
son d'être of the philosophy. . . . a humanist
Zambia must be a welfare state as well.
Zambian humanism therefore, aims at both
eradicating capitalist tendencies and
achieving an equitable distribution of
wealth.[70]

Some expatriate intellectuals have been critical
of traditionalist and social democratic interpretations of Humanism; instead they advocate the development of a Zambian socialism. For example, Robert
Molteno laments that the major interpretation of
Humanism has been closer to "reformed capitalism"
than to "scientific socialism". He suggests that
one reason for its moderate tone is the strength of
opposition to any socialist definition. He identifies
several groups in Zambia, centered on the new bureaucratic bourgeoisie in the government and parastatals
as well as resident foreign entrepreneurs, which,
as we have already suggested, are likely to oppose
any moves toward a radical redistribution of wealth,
ownership or control:

The danger is that these multinational corporations will use their links with western
monetary markets, their relations with shipping firms, and their vital role in the
supply of skilled foreign manpower to compel
the Government to go slow on the further
translation of Humanism into practice. In

particular, effective workers' participation, humanist management practices and
significant income redistribution may all
be delayed. This in turn may mean that
solid working class support for Zambian
Humanism may not be forthcoming sufficiently fast in order to provide the
necessary bulwark against reactionary
class elements bent on sabotaging Humanist
objectives.[71]

Finally, Molteno points to the interrelated opposition from the white South and certain Western
states. Humanism, in both its nationalist and socialist varieties, is a challenge to racist regimes and
values. Humanism may yet confront capitalism in
both Zambia and Southern Africa and erode capitalist
investments and markets in the region. To challenge
this formidable coalition of opponents to a socialist
interpretation of Humanism, Molteno argues that
support must come from the rural peasantry and the
urban workers. But these groups are heterogenous.
Moreover, the rise of affluent African farmers and a
labor aristocracy affects the influence of the peasants and workers. It is these groups, along with
senior bureaucrats and managers and black entrepreneurs, that have achieved dominance within the party
structure and in parliament. Their profitable alliance with the nationalist old guard and modern
technocrats now in the cabinet means that a socialist
Humanism is unlikely to be seriously debated or considered. Indeed, given the profitable association
between the Zambian state and multinational corporations, internal and international opposition to a
socialist definition of Humanism is to be expected.[72]
Sefelino Mulenga, then a Cabinet Minister, also
advocated a socialist Humanism and identified groups
similar to those of Molteno and Kandeke which oppose
such a definition. However, now that "materialism
is more firmly entrenched than ever before as the
supreme ethic",[73] Mulenga's appeal for modest consumption and an end to "the elitism of party functionaries, civil servants and the managers of state enterprises" is likely to go unheeded:
Zambian economic reforms so far have brought
not hardship but prosperity and increased
scope to Zambians. There is still the
Zambianization of production which is quite
different from the Zambianization of management. Socialism cannot be attained without
hardship.[74]

64

Given the likely impact of a socialist Humanism on
dominant interests in Zambia, it is difficult to envisage its implementation, as opposed to its declaration, without presidential involvement and/or coercion: "Humanism involves a revolution in the values
of Zambian society and, therefore, a frontal attack
on the interests of the middle class."[75]

Humanism may have constituted an appropriate and
powerful response to the racial problems of Zambia in
Southern Africa at Independence. But its subsequent
development, as a guide to Zambia's development and
foreign policies for the nation's first and second
decades, has been more problematic because of the
inherent difficulties of designing and implementing
any transition to the declared goal of socialism and
because of resistance to any such definition of the
ideology of increasingly entrenched interests in Zambia's political economy. So, whilst the national
philosophy has informed policy statements on Southern
Africa and presidential pronouncements about deficiencies in Zambian society, it has yet to be used
by either the party or the poor to effect fundamental
change in the state capitalist system. Therefore,
the achievement of a truly Humanist society remains
remote. As Kandeke and others envisage it, socialism
is in any case merely a transitional stage on the
long road towards a more fully humanist political
economy: "Socialist principles in Zambia are only
an instrument for building a Man-centred society
which is the backbone of Zambian Humanism."[76]

NOTES

1. On the president's origins and values, see Kenneth
D. Kaunda, Zambia Shall be Free (London: Heinemann
1962) and Fergus Macpherson, Kenneth Kaunda of Zambia:
The Times and the Man (Lusaka: Oxford University
Press 1974). See also John Hatch, Two African States-
men: Kaunda of Zambia and Nyerere of Tanzania (London
Secker & Warburg, 1976).

2. On the relationship of Humanism to pan-Africanism
see Timothy K. Kandeke, Fundamentals of Zambian Humanism (Lusaka: Neczam, 1977), pp. 143-165.

3. Kenneth D. Kaunda, Letter to My Children (London:
Longman, 1973), p. 53.

4. Zambia N.A. Deb., no. 35, 23 January 1974, c. 395.

5. Ibid., c. 396.

6. Ibid., c. 398

7. This manifesto on the future of Southern Africa should not be confused wish subsequent "Lusaka" documents, notably:
    Lusaka Declaration on Peace, Independence, Development, Cooperation and Democratization of International Relations, Third Nonaligned Conference, 10 September 1970.
    Lusaka Programme (on Trends in Portuguese African Territories) 12 September 1973.
    Lusaka Agreement (between FRELIMO and Portugal), 7 September 1974.
    Lusaka Declaration of (Zimbabwean) Unity, 7 December 1974.
    Lusaka Agreement (on Rhodesia), 11 December 1974.
    Lusaka Declaration on Namibia (UN Council for Namibia), March 1978.

8. Manifesto on Southern Africa (Lusaka: Government Printer, April 1969), sections 11 and 12.

9. See Benedict V. Mtshali, "The Mogadishu Conference and Declaration, October 1971", Internationale Spectator, 24, no. 10 (May 1972): 966-977.

10. Zambia Daily Mail, 30 March 1974, p. 1

11. See Zambia 1964-1974: A decade of achievement (Lusaka: Zambia Information Services [ZIS], 1974), pp. 12, 13.

12. "OAU Declaration of Dar es Salaam on Southern Africa", in Colin Legum, ed., Africa Contemporary Record (New York: Africana Publishing, 1976), 8 (1975-1976): C73.

13. Lusaka Declaration on Peace, Independence, Development, Cooperation and Democratization of International Relations (Lusaka: Government Printer, September 1970), p. 5.

14. Declaration of Commonwealth Principles (London: Commonwealth Secretariat, 1971).

15. Kaunda, Letter to My Children, p. 100

16. Cólin Legum, ed., Zambia: independence and beyond, The Speeches of Kenneth Kaunda (London: Thomas Nelson, 1966), p. 162.

17. UN General Assembly Official Records (A/PV.1291), 4 December 1964, p. 2.

18. See Address by President Kaunda on the Occasion of the Opening of the Third Summit Conference of Non-Aligned Countries, Lusaka, 8 September 1970.

19. Macpherson, Kenneth Kaunda of Zambia, p. 99.

20. Times (London, 7 September 1972, p. 1; 10 June 1977, p. 8.

21. See Zambia in the Security Council, 1969 and 1970 (Lusaka: ZIS, 1971).

22. Kenneth D. Kaunda, Africa in the Sixties: the decade of decision and definition (Lusaka: ZIS, 1970), p. 22.

23. ZIS, Background, no. 13/71, 8 February 1971, p. 2.

24. ZIS, Press Release, no. 51/73, 26 October 1973.

25. Legum, Zambia: independence and beyond, pp. 45 and 184-185.

26. Kenneth D. Kaunda, A Humanist in Africa: Letters to Colin M. Morris (London: Longman, 1966), pp. 127-32.

27. Zambia 1964-1974, p. 10.

28. Legum, Zambia: independence and beyond, pp. 46 and 66-67.

29. Macpherson, Kenneth Kaunda of Zambia, p. 418.

30. Black Government? A Discussion between Colin Morris and Kenneth Kaunda (Lusaka: United Society for Christian Literature, 1960), p. 99.

31. The Challenge of the Future (Lusaka: Government Printer, 1973), p. 12.

32. Zambia 1964-1974, p. 12.

33. Legum, Zambia: independence and beyond, p. 192.

34. Ibid., p. 46.

35.   Ibid., p. 10.

36.   'A Nation of Equals' - the Kabwe Declaration
(Lusaka: ZIS, 1972), p. 6

37.   The Challenge of the Future, p. 4

38.   See 'Take up the Challenge' ... Speeches made
by President Kaunda to the UNIP National Council,
Mulungushi Hall, November 1970 (Lusaka: ZIS, 1970),
p. 35.   For a comprehensive statement of Humanism as
an ideology of development, see K. S. Kaunda, Humanism
in Zambia and a guide to its implementation (Lusaka:
ZIS, 1968).

39.   Kandeke, Fundamentals of Zambian Humanism, p. 45.

40.   See Zambia's guideline for the next decade (Lusaka: Government Printer, 1968); Towards complete
independence (Lusaka: Government Printer, 1969);
This completes economic reforms: 'Now Zambia is
ours' (Lusaka: Government Printer, 1970).   For analyses of these reforms, see Bastiaan de Gaay Fortman,
ed., After Mulungushi: the economics of Zambian
Humanism (Nairobi: East African Publishing House,
1969); M.L.O. Faber and J.G. Potter, Towards economic
independence: papers on the nationalisation of the
copper industry in Zambia (Cambridge: Cambridge
University Press, 1971); Mark Bostock and Charles
Harvey, Economic independence and Zambian copper: a
case study of foreign investment (New York: Praeger,
1972); and Anthony Martin, Minding their own business:
Zambia's struggle against Western control (London:
Penguin, 1973).

41.   Zambia Daily Mail, 1 July 1975, pp. 8-11.

42.   Kandeke, Fundamentals of Zambian Humanism,
p. 23.   Emphasis in original.

43.   Kaunda, Letter to My Children, p. 53.

44.   See Jan Pettman "Zambia's Second Republic: the
creation of a one-party state," Journal of Modern
African Studies 12, no. 2 (June 1974):   231-244.

45.   "Zambia: exploiters and exploited", Africa,
no. 48 (August 1975):   29.

46.   International Labour Office, Narrowing the Gaps:
Planning for basic needs and productive employment

in Zambia (Addis Ababa: ILO Jobs and Skills Programme for Africa, January 1977), p. 37.

47. Kandeke, Fundamentals of Zambian Humanism, p.21.

48. Ibid., pp. 25-26 and 26-27.

49. Ibid., p. 26.

50. Kaunda, A Humanist in Africa, p. 115.

51. Zambia Daily Mail, 4 July 1974, p. 1.

52. Legum, Zambia: Independence and Beyond, p. 191.

53. Kaunda, A Humanist in Africa, p. 121.

54. UNIP National Policies for the Next Decade 1974
-1984 (Lusaka: ZIS, 1974), pp. 68-70.

55. See, inter alia, Issa G. Shivji, "Capitalism Un-
limited: Public Corporations in Partnership with
Multinational Corporations," The African Review 3,
no. 3 (1973): 358-381; John Loxley and John S. Saul
"Multinationals, Workers and Parastatals in Tanzania,"
Review of African Political Economy, no. 2 (January-
April 1975): 54-88; and William Tordoff and Ali A.
Mazrui, "The Left and the Super-Left in Tanzania,"
Journal of Modern African Studies 10, no. 3, (October
1972): 427-445.

56. Donald Rothchild, "Rural-urban inequities and
resource allocation in Zambia," Journal of Commonwealth Political Studies 10, no. 3 (November 1972):
232.

57. L. S. Chivuno, "Preface" in Kandeke, Funda-
mentals of Zambian Humanism, p. xxi. Dr. Leonard
Chivuno is Deputy Director of UNIP's Research Bureau.
He obtained his doctorate in the Soviet Union.

58. Kandeke, Fundamentals of Zambian Humanism, pp.
98, 99. Timothy Kandeke is currently a District
Governor in UNIP's Research Bureau. He obtained a
master's degree in sociology from the University of
Warsaw.

59. Robert Molteno and William Tordoff, "Conclusion-
Independent Zambia: Achievements and Prospects," in
Politics in Zambia, ed. William Tordoff (Berkeley:
University of California Press, 1974), p. 389.

60.   See Ministry of Planning and Finance, Economic Report, 1973 (Lusaka: Government Printer, 1974), pp. 181-182.

61.   Anglo-American Corporation of South Africa Limited Annual Report 1974 (Johannesburg, April 1974), p. 15.

62.   "Chairman's Statement", Indeco Annual Report 1973/74 (Lusaka: Indeco, June 1974), p. 9.

63.   Bank of Zambia, Report for 1973 (Lusaka: Bank of Zambia, 1974), p. 7.

64.   Ibid., p. 7.

65.   Molteno and Tordoff, "Conclusion", p. 391.

66.   Kandeke, Fundamentals of Zambian Humanism, p. 123.

67.   Ibid., p. 134.   Capitalization in original.

68.   Ibid., p. 135.

69.   Henry S. Meebelo, Main Currents of Zambian Humanist Thought (Lusaka: Oxford University Press, 1973), pp. 92 and 77.   Meebelo is Director of the Research Bureau and Special Assistant to the Secretary-General of UNIP.   He obtained his doctorate in history from the University of London.

70.   Ibid., p. 95.   See also his analysis of Humanism as an ideology based on the "individual" rather than the "people", a further illustration of the "individualistic" rather than "socialist" content of Humanism ("The concept of man-centredness in Zambian Humanism", African Review 3, no. 4 [1973]:   559-575).

71.   Robert Molteno, "Zambian Humanism: the way ahead", African Review 3, no. 4 (1973):   552.   Molteno, a member of a prominent South African liberal family, taught political science at the University of Zambia from 1968 to 1976, and is now in the publishing business in London.

72.   Ibid., p. 553.   Molteno's article is reprinted as the final chapter in Kandeke, Fundamentals of Zambian Humanism, pp. 212-239.   Cf. J. B. Zulu, Zambian Humanism: some major spiritual and economic challenges (Lusaka: Neczam, 1970) and Fola Soremekun, "The challenge of nation-building: neo-Humanism and

politics in Zambia, 1967-1969", Génève-Afrique 9,
no. 1 (1970):   3-41.

73.   Molteno and Tordoff, "Conclusion", p. 395.

74.   N. S. Mulenga,"Humanism and the logic of self-
sufficiency", mimeographed (Lusaka, 10 September
1973), pp. 10, 8; emphasis in original.   Reprinted
in Zambia Daily Mail, 30 and 31 January 1974.   Dr.
Mulenga is a graduate of the University of Leipzig.
A political activist since the age of eight, he was
first elected to Parliament in 1964, and appointed
successively a Parliamentary Secretary (1967), Minister of State (1969) and Minister (1973).   In 1977,
he was dismissed for alleged "abuse of office", and
is now employed by Intersomer, an Italian firm.

75.   Molteno and Tordoff, "Conclusion", p. 398.

76.   Kandeke, Fundamentals of Zambian Humanism, pp.
26-27.

3
The Foreign Policy System of Zambia

The foreign policy, indeed the political process, in most African states has tended to be personalized both by politicians, publicists and scholars. In the case of Zambia, there continues to be a common assumption that the president "makes" foreign policy, that he conceives, articulates and symbolizes Zambia's external ideology and relationships. In our attempt to go beyond such simplistic and misleading assertions, this chapter identifies and analyzes a variety of actors in the foreign policy system of Zambia.[1] It represents an effort to present a reasonably exhaustive typology of actors in the system as well as a preliminary analysis of the Ministry of Foreign Affairs; it is not concerned either with the ideology of Zambia's foreign policy (see chapter 2) or with the constraints within which decision makers operate in Zambia (see chapter 11). Rather, the limited intent of this essay is to provide a tentative list of actors in the Zambian "foreign policy system" and to begin to analyze the bureaucratic politics which affect the policy of the "system". The focus is on the relevant part of the operational environment which affects foreign policy making in Zambia, especially on the structures of government and industry, domestic and foreign interests, and on communication between these actors. Because of problems of research access, information on institutions is more readily available than information on the processes of decision making.

ACTORS IN THE ZAMBIAN FOREIGN POLICY SYSTEM

This chapter suggests, then, that the foreign policy system of any African state such as Zambia includes a wide range of actors. If we define the foreign policy system as consisting of those relations among

72

all actors within the state who have external relations, then the system includes a range of ministries,
parastatal organizations, foreign missions and local
offices of multinational corporations and international organizations in addition to State House and
the Ministry of Foreign Affairs. Despite the international attention directed at crises and wars in
Africa, most external behavior on the continent is
concerned with routine "low" politics. More international transactions occur in issue areas such as economic exchange than over security; these regular relations are supervised by a variety of actors. "High"
politics are restricted to senior decision makers in
a few institutions such as the President's Office.

This diversity of actors in the sphere of foreign policy leads to problems of coordination and
multiple advocacy, especially in new states which
lack a tradition of organizational effectiveness.
The absence of real national control also advances
penetration of the national polity by foreign interests and institutions. Because new states are characteristically underdeveloped and dependent, some foreign diplomats and corporations at times serve as
authoritative actors in the making of foreign policy
choices. As noted below, the national institutions
that make foreign policy in a state like Zambia often
have insufficient funds, staff or experience and so
tend to adopt some policies by proxy. It is unrealistic to exclude the foreign origin of such policies
from the "national" foreign policy system. However,
the openness of a polity varies according to issue
area and level of interaction.

Moreover, the range of actors involved varies
with the issue and intensity of the external relationship. The primary actors in Zambia's international politics are State House — including the long-
serving Special Assistant to the President on Foreign
Affairs, Mark Chona — the Ministry of Foreign Affairs,
the ruling United National Independence Party (UNIP)
and particularly the Committee of its Central Committee, and other ministries and parastatals. Parliament has a minimal role to play in foreign affairs,
though international issues are sometimes raised
in caucus. Crisis management is largely a function
of the Office of the President. The State House foreign affairs team, augmented as occasion demands by
Central Committee members, ministers and officials,
is most involved in high politics, international initiatives and presidential activities. Zambia's policy
in Southern Africa is executed by State House and the
Ministries of Defence and Foreign Affairs, all represented in the Foreign Affairs Committee of the Cabinet.

Zambia's policy is also coordinated with other Front
Line States, the Lusaka regional office of the OAU
Liberation Committee and the Liberation Centre. The
latter is the organizational center for recognized
movements in the region (see chapter 6), and is controlled by the President's special representative
who is seconded from, and in close touch with Defence.[2] Other African affairs are coordinated by
Foreign Affairs and by UNIP. In global politics,
the national interest is articulated by the parastatals and Foreign Affairs, and other functional ministries. Table 3.1 suggests a framework for the analysis of Zambia's foreign policy system.

     This distribution of responsibilities also coin-
cides with activities and emphases within different
international organizations. Zambia's policy toward
Southern Africa is compatible with the OAU-Front Line
State strategy, and influences her behavior toward
the rest of the international system. The defense of
her national interests involves good neighborliness
with other independent states and support of political changes in minority regimes which continue to
threaten her sovereignty and ideology. This need
for support from the OAU and provision of assistance
to the liberation movements involves the Office of
the President and the Ministries of Defense and Home
Affairs; the army and air force, home guard, national
service, police and para-military police all act in
a variety of ways to defend Zambia's territorial and
political integrity. The State House foreign policy
group is involved in attempting to resolve factional
disputes in the liberation movements, in suggesting
presidential initiatives in the region, and in over-
seeing diplomacy amongst the movements and minority
regimes along the lines of the Lusaka Manifesto.
Continental relations are concentrated in the OAU
and in Eastern Africa, and are concerned with political cooperation and economic integration. Zambia
has been an active member of the OAU and has contributed to the development of its policies; she regularly supplies personnel to its secretariat. She
advances her national interests and change in Southern Africa by her entente with Angola, Botswana, Mozambique and Tanzania; this grouping of Front Line
States advocates change in the minority regimes,
support for the liberation movements and cooperation
among independent African states. Integration is
most advanced in the bilateral Tanzania-Zambia relationship, which involves presidential, party, ministerial and infrastructural ties as noted below.
Cooperation is also growing with Botswana and

TABLE 3.1
Framework of Foreign Policy Making in Zambia

Level of Interaction	Central Actors	Major Issue Area	Primary International Organizations
Regional	State House Defence	Military & political	Front Line States
Continental	Foreign Affairs UNIP Central Committee	Political & economic	Organization of African Unity
Global	Parastatals Foreign Affairs	Economic & political	United Nations Commonwealth

Mozambique. At the international level, Zambia is
dependent on the Western economic system and has developed her parastatal structure to advance her national interests in cooperating with multinational
corporations, especially in the mining, manufacturing and communications sectors. Her global relations are coordinated by Foreign Affairs, but also
by parastatals, other ministries (especially Finance,
Economic and Technical Cooperation, Planning and
Development, Mines and Industry), the Bank of Zambia
and foreign and international organization missions
in Lusaka. Continental and global relations are
generally routine but, whenever they reach a crisis,
the State House group becomes involved.
    These three levels of interaction are interde-
pendent: Southern African policy involves representation at the OAU and the UN and attraction of political and material support; the role of multinational
corporations in Southern Africa affects—positively
and negatively—Zambia's perceptions and treatment
of them in Zambia; her attitude toward military regimes in Africa affects her policy toward similar
governments in countries of particular interest, such
as Chile. However, we may begin to distinguish between the primacy of actors in each issue area and
each level of interaction. The President, or chief
executive, is dominant in regional politics, especially those concerned with security and liberation. Ministries and the party dominate continental
affairs, which are thus characterized by a primacy

FIGURE 3.1
Actors in Zambian Foreign Policy System

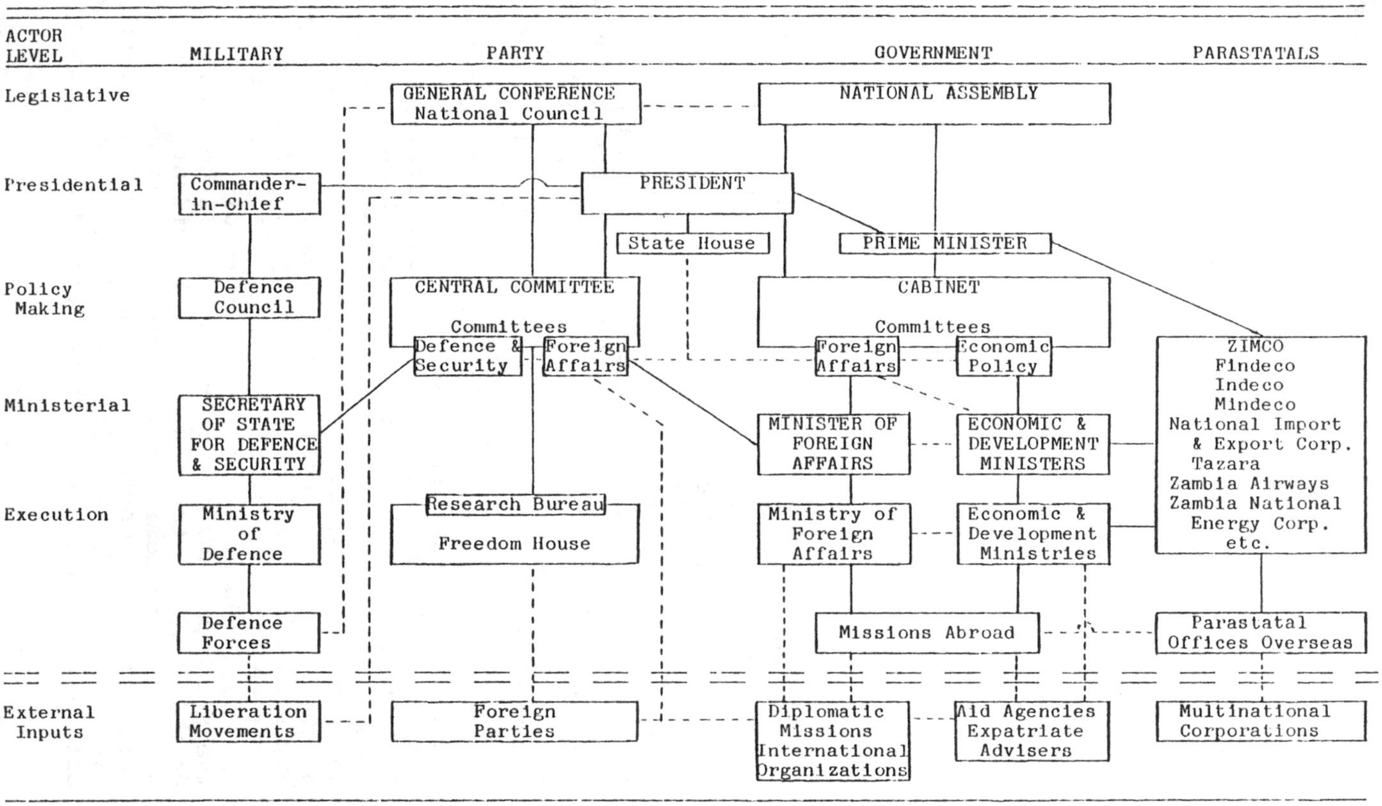

ACTOR LEVEL	MILITARY	PARTY	GOVERNMENT	PARASTATALS

Legislative: GENERAL CONFERENCE National Council — NATIONAL ASSEMBLY

Presidential: Commander-in-Chief — PRESIDENT — State House — PRIME MINISTER

Policy Making: Defence Council — CENTRAL COMMITTEE Committees: Defence & Security, Foreign Affairs — CABINET Committees: Foreign Affairs, Economic Policy — ZIMCO, Findeco, Indeco, Mindeco, National Import & Export Corp., Tazara, Zambia Airways, Zambia National Energy Corp. etc.

Ministerial: SECRETARY OF STATE FOR DEFENCE & SECURITY — Research Bureau, Freedom House — MINISTER OF FOREIGN AFFAIRS, ECONOMIC & DEVELOPMENT MINISTERS

Execution: Ministry of Defence — Defence Forces — Ministry of Foreign Affairs, Economic & Development Ministries — Missions Abroad — Parastatal Offices Overseas

External Inputs: Liberation Movements — Foreign Parties — Diplomatic Missions International Organizations, Aid Agencies Expatriate Advisers — Multinational Corporations

76

of bureaucratic politics, that is, competition and
bargaining within the government. Finally, in world
politics, Zambia's foreign policy system is characterized by organizational politics, conflict both
within and especially between actors, ranging from
ministries and parastatals to missions and multinationals. In this way, bureaucratic and organizational politics are related to low politics, whereas
presidential dominance is associated with high
politics.

The variety of actors and interests in the foreign policy system of Zambia are indicated in figure
3.1. These actors can be categorized into four
types: government ministries, the ruling party, the
parastatal sector and private or foreign interests in
Zambia. This typology draws attention to the range
of actors in the system within different issue areas.
Although the President's Office and the Ministry of
Foreign Affairs attempt to coordinate the nation's
foreign relations, many ministries and parastatals
conduct their own external affairs (table 3.2) with
minimal reference to official or party directives—
to the continual dismay of the foreign minister and
the Central Committee. This approach also suggests
that private or external actors may at times be
treated as authoritative within Zambia, at least for
policy making in particular issue areas. The parastatal sector itself is partially owned and controlled by foreign investors; foreign interests include national and international diplomatic missions
and entrepreneurs. Each of these actors makes an
input into the development of Zambia's foreign
policy, either in specific issue areas or to the
general direction of her external relations. They
may act as a constraint on new policies or advocate
change in particular relationships.

THE MAKING OF FOREIGN POLICY IN ZAMBIA

The general direction and ideology of Zambia's
foreign policy have been set by President Kaunda and
his State House advisers in consultation with appropriate senior ministerial colleagues and Members of
the Central Committee (MCCs), depending on the subject. As noted in the previous chapter, Dr. Kaunda
is the intellectual author and principal exponent of
Humanism, and his stature in the international system
gives him frequent and prestigious occasions on which
to act the role of Zambia's own "philosopher king."
From the first, he has sought to relate Humanism to

77

TABLE 3.2
Foreign Relations of Zambia: Allocation of Subjects
    to Government Ministries, 1977

Ministries	Subjects	Parastatals etc.

Office of the President
  Defense Forces, Home Guards,
    Zambia National Service
  Foreign nationalist organizations
  Security and intelligence

Office of the Prime Minister
  Coordination & supervision
    of government & parastatal
    business & administration
  Cabinet & cabinet committee
    matters
  Contingency planning
  Development planning

Commerce and Foreign Trade	Export Promotion
Commercial policy	Council
Import and export policy	National Import and
Foreign trade	Export Corporation
Trade fairs	Tariff Advisory Board

Economic & Technical Cooperation
  Aid agreements
  Multilateral & bilateral econ-
    omic & technical cooperation
  National estimates of all
    foreign aid
  Negotiation & coordination of
    foreign technical assist-
    ance & economic aid
  Research in foreign aid
  Foreign scholarship coordination

Education
  Zambia National Commission
    for UNESCO

Foreign Affairs
  Diplomatic Corps in Zambia
  Foreign relations
  International organizations
  Official foreign visitors
  Protocol
  Repatriation of destitutes
    from foreign countries
  Treaties and agreements
  Zambia Foreign Service

TABLE 3.2 (continued)

Finance
  Customs and excise   Bank of Zambia
  Financial & fiscal matters FINDECO (State Finance
  Loans and investment   & Development Corp.)

Home Affairs
  Arms and ammunition
  Immigration, citizenship
    passports and deportation
  Law and order
  Refugees
  State security
  Zambia Police

Industry
  Industrial policy and   INDECO (Industrial
    administration   Development Corp.)

Information, Broadcasting & Tourism
  Broadcasting & television Zambia Publishing Co.
    services   Zambia National
  Information services   Tourist Bureau
  Tourism   National Hotels Corp.

Labour & Social Development
  Sports & sports development National Sports
                      Council

Legal Affairs
  Extradition Act

Mines
  Mines and mining policy   MINDECO, MEMACO
                      NCCM AND RCM

Power, Transport & Communications
  Power policy   Central African Power
  Transport policy   Corporation
  Airways policy   National Transport
  Civil aviation   Corporation
  Posts & telecommunications Zambia Airways Corp.
  Shipping   Aeronautical Authority
  Railways policy   Posts and Telecommuni-
                      cations Corporation
                      Zambia Railway
                      Tanzam Railway
                      Zambia Tanzania Road
                        Services
                      National Energy Corp.

Source: Government Gazette, 18 October 1976 and
27 April 1977

79

his preoccupations in foreign affairs, principally crisis management, Southern Africa, and pan-Africanism and the nonalignment movement. Coordination of policy takes place at three levels: in State House, in the Central Committee and its foreign affairs subcommittee, and in the Cabinet and its Foreign Affairs Committee. There is no parliamentary committee on foreign affairs.

Although in practice State House exercises a superior role in defining and articulating the nation's policies, constitutionally Zambia is a one-party state in which the party is formally supreme. The ultimate policy making organ is the quinquennial General Conference and, in intervening years, the National Council which normally meets twice a year. All MPs, heads of diplomatic missions and senior military officers are full members of both bodies. The 25-member Central Committee assumes more immediate supervision of the government's foreign policy, issuing interpretations of Humanism as guidelines for its implementation by the bureaucracies. The Committee is also directly concerned with UNIP's own international relations. Under the party constitution, it is assigned specific responsibility for "the selection of Party members undertaking visits to other African States and overseas."[3] These transnational interparty relations have assumed considerable importance with parties in neighboring states, initially members of the "Mulungushi Club" in East Africa, and currently the ruling parties in other Front Line States. Party leaders in the region meet regularly to discuss party and government structures and strategies and to foster relations among sections of their parties, such as youth and women's groups. In addition, UNIP maintains fraternal relations with certain socialist parties overseas as well as with Southern African liberation movements. Party officials are regularly included on Zambian delegations to foreign states and to international organizations where they are socialized into international diplomacy and issues.

The Central Committee's Political, Constitutional, Legal and Foreign Affairs Committee is able to give closer and more continuous attention to international concerns than its parent body. Nevertheless, as its terms of reference embrace "political, foreign affairs, human rights and constitutional matters,"[4] external affairs takes up only a fraction of the time of its monthly meetings. Moreover, except for purely party affairs, it has no operational or administrative responsibilities. It

80

is concerned with the general direction and orientation of policy, with values and ideology; it is not
concerned with the structure or procedures of the
Ministry. Nevertheless, to ensure relevance, the
ministers of Foreign Affairs and Legal Affairs are
included in its membership along with (usually) five
MCCs, two MPs and representatives of educational institutions, trade unions and the party bureaucracy.
The subcommittee's first chairman was Elijah Mudenda,
who had twice served as Minister of Foreign Affairs
and was subsequently appointed Prime Minister. His
vice-chairman, Daniel Lisulo, was, in June 1978,
promoted Prime Minister.[5] The current subcommittee
chairman, Reuben Kamanga, had been the country's
first Vice-President and second foreign minister.
In a recent development, the President handed over
the chairmanship of the important Defence and Security Committee to the party's former Secretary-
General.
    Under UNIP's 1973 constitution, in the event of
a conflict between the Central Committee and the
Cabinet, decisions of the former are to prevail.[7]
This formula is no assurance of the absence of friction. Nevertheless, the legal supremacy of the party
is freely acknowledged. As a former foreign minister
explained,

    our foreign policy is indeed determined by the
    Party to which we all belong. Foreign policy
    is discussed in the National Council meetings
    of the Party; it is discussed at various Party
    committees. In fact we have a Sub-Committee
    of the Central Committee dealing with foreign
    policy. This Committee decides on the policy
    and my Ministry implements this policy.[8]

    Under the First Republic (1964-1973), the for-
eign ministers were prominent political leaders but,
with the inauguration of a one-party state, the
cabinet has increasingly been composed of technocrats
(table 3.3). All three foreign ministers since 1973
have been career diplomats, having served previously
in at least two senior ambassadorial posts. This
development, and the continued association of established political figures such as Reuben Kamanga and
Elijah Mudenda with the management of Zambia's external affairs, have provided a greater measure of
continuity in personnel and policies than the frequent major reshuffles of senior ministerial, party
and parastatal appointments might suggest. In addition, there has been no change in the presidency

TABLE 3.3
Continuity and Discontinuity among Zambian Foreign Policy Decision Makers

Date	Cabinet				UNIP Central Committee		
	Vice-President/ Prime Minister	Minister of Foreign Affairs	Minister of Defence	Minister of Finance	Secretary-General	Chairmen Foreign Affairs Committee	Chairmen Defence & Security Committee
1st Republic							
24 Oct. 1964	Kamanga	Kapwepwe	Kaunda	Wina	Chona (1961)		
7 Sept. 1967	Kapwepwe	Kamanga		Mudenda			
23 Dec. 1968		Mudenda		Kapwepwe			
26 Aug. 1969		Kaunda		Mudenda	Kaunda		
8 Jan. 1970			Zulu				
7 Oct. 1970	Chona	Mudenda		Mwanakatwe			
2nd Republic							
28 Aug. 1973	Chona (PM)	Mwaanga	Milner		Zulu	Mudenda	Kaunda
10 Dec. 1973		Banda	Kaunda	Chikwanda			
27 May 1975	Mudenda					Kamanga	
1 Dec. 1975				Mwananshiku			
3/10 May 1976		Mwale		Mwanakatwe			
20 July 1977	Chona						
16 June 1978	Lisulo				Chona		
12 Sept. 1978			Zulu*				Zulu
2 Jan. 1979		Chakulya		Lumina			

*Secretary of State for Defence and Security

since Independence, and Mark Chona has been Permanent Secretary for Foreign Affairs or special presidential assistant for foreign affairs continuously since April 1965.

The Foreign Affairs Committee of the Cabinet is composed of the incumbents of relevant portfolios— Foreign Affairs, Finance, Defence and Home Affairs— and other politically important ministers along with senior civil servants and others as the agenda requires. Despite the institution of a superior Central Committee subcommittee, the Foreign Affairs Committee has not been overshadowed or downgraded. The fact that it meets more frequently, continues to be chaired by the President, and includes the executive heads of the major ministries as well as the chairman and sometimes the vice-chairman of the party subcommittee is sufficient to ensure its continuing influence.

The dominance of State House, UNIP and the Cabinet in determining the foreign policy of Zambia is not complete. In particular issues or crises, other institutions within the system may be quite effective. The diplomatic community and multinational corporations in Zambia may condition Zambia's policies in specific issue areas such as towards international institutions or international exchange. The dependence of Zambia is not only a structural constraint on her foreign policy choices, it is also expressed from day to day through the influence of foreign diplomats and entrepreneurs in Zambia. Some maintain a close association with members of the national elite and participate informally in the direction of Zambia's foreign policy. Certain diplomatic missions in Lusaka may also provide Zambian officials with research and intelligence materials to advance their decision making on, say, domestic politics of the white-ruled states of Southern Africa. They may even suggest organizational reforms and regulations for the Ministry of Foreign Affairs itself. On occasion, various missions, especially East European ones, have had to be warned against indulging in unacceptable activities; in 1971, the East German trade office was even shut down for a period.[9] In addition, Zambia has claimed that there have been "many examples of South African financial and material support to opposition parties and groups in Zambia."[10] While she continues to reject pressures from the South, she is more receptive to inputs from elsewhere. Because the Zambian elite has sometimes been uncritical of cooperation with external interests, it has permitted the emergence of a nascent comprador class which depends on linkages with

TABLE 3.4
Diplomatic Representation in Zambia, 1965–1978
(in order of establishment)

	Status and Size					
	Sept. 1965	Aug. 1967	Nov. 1970	Oct. 1973	Jan. 1976	Jan. 1978
AFRICA (24)						
Zaire	E 4	E 4	E 5	E 5	E 7	E 10
Ghana	H 4			A*	A*	H 6
Egypt	E 3	E 4	E 4	E 4	E 4	E 5
Nigeria		H 3		H 6	H 6	H 5
Botswana		H 2	H 3	H 5	H 5	H 2
Guinea			A†	A†	A†	A†
Tanzania			H 5	H 6	H 7	H 9
Ivory Coast			A°	A°	A°	A°
Liberia			A*	A*	A*	A*
Senegal			A††	A††	A††	A††
Somalia			E 4	E 3	E 3	E 2
Ethiopia			A*	A*	A*	A*
Kenya			H 4	H 8	H 9	H 8
Swaziland				A*	A*	A*
Algeria				A†	A†	A†
Burundi				A†	A†	A†
Sierra Leone				A††	A††	A††
Malawi				H 4	H 4	H 4
Sudan				A*	A*	A*
Cameroon					A††	A††
Gabon					A°	
Madagascar						A†
Rwanda						A†
Angola						E 2
EUROPE (26)						
Britain	H 15	H 13	H 38	H 31	H 29	H 26
West Germany	E 2	E 3	E 6	E 6	E 5	E 6
USSR	E 6	E 9	E 24	E 22	E 16	E 11
France	E 2	E 5	E 10	E 10	E 8	E 10
Yugoslavia	E 1	E 2	E 6	E 7	E 9	E 9
Belguim	E 2	E 1	E 3	E 2	E 3	E 5
Sweden	C 1	E 1	E 3	E 11	E 11	E 11
Denmark	C 1	C 1	C 2	E 2	E 2	E 3
Norway	C 1	C 1	C 1	C 4	C 5	E 6
Czechoslovakia	E 1	E 3	E 8	E 6	E 9	E 4
Italy	C 2	E 2	E 9	E 6	E 5	E 4
Greece		C 1	C 2		C 2	C 1
Holy See		E 2	E 1	E 2	E 2	E 2
Ireland		C 1	C 2	C 2	C 2	C 2
Austria		C 1	C 1	C 1	E 5	E 3

TABLE 3.4 (continued)

	Sept. 1965		Aug. 1967		Nov. 1970		Oct. 1973		Jan. 1976		Jan. 1978	
					Status and Size							
Netherlands			E	2	E	4	E	4	E	3	E	3
East Germany			O	2	O	4			E	2	E	2
Finland					C	1	O	2	E	3	E	4
Switzerland					A†		C	2	C	2	A†	
Hungary					A†		A†		A†		A†	
Spain					A†		A†		A†		A†	
Rumania					A†		E	10	E	10	E	10
Poland					A†		A†		A†		A†	
Turkey							A*		A*		A*	
Bulgaria							A†		A†		A†	
Portugal											E	3
AMERICAS (9)												
USA	E	11	E	12	E	11	E	11	E	11	E	12
Canada			A°		A†		H	3	H	5	H	5
Chile			E	1	E	1						
Brazil							A*		A*		A*	
Peru									E	1	E	1
Jamaica							A††		A††		A††	
Cuba							A†		E	7	E	9
Guyana							H	6	H	5	H	4
Trinidad									A††			
ASIA AND PACIFIC (13)												
Israel	E	1	E	3	E	2						
India	H	3	H	3	H	3	H	12	H	11	H	7
China	E	5	E	5	E	19	E	28	E	30	E	31
North Korea					E	5	E	8	E	6	E	5
Syria					A†		A†		A†		A†	
Japan			A*		E	2	E	5	E	4	E	5
Pakistan							A†		A†		A†	
Sri Lanka							A*		A*		A*	
Australia							A†		A†		A†	
Iraq											A†	
Indonesia											A†	
Cyprus											A†	
Vietnam											A†	
INTERNATIONAL ORGANIZATIONS (13)												
UNDP	O	5	O	5	O	10	O	11	O	6	O	12
ECA	O	4	O	5	O	3	O	5	O	7	O	7
WHO	O	2	O	1	O	5	O	6	O	8	O	7
UNHCR			O	2	O	3	O	3	O	3	O	4

TABLE 3.4 (continued)

	Status and Size					
	Sept. 1965	Aug. 1967	Nov. 1970	Oct. 1973	Jan. 1976	Jan. 1978
Unesco	0 1	0 0				
ILO			0 2	0 2	0 2	0 2
UNICEF			0 3	0 4	0 4	0 3
FAO				0 1	0 1	0 4
Namibia				0 2	0 2	0 2
UNIDO				0 1	0 1	0 0
OAU				0 2	0 2	0 2
IBRD						0 1
UNFPA						0 2
EEC						0 5

E   Embassy; H   High Commission; C   Consulate;
          O   Office
A *   Accredited: resident in Nairobi
A †   Accredited: resident in Dar es Salaam
A †† Accredited: resident in Addis Ababa
A o   Accredited: resident elsewhere in Africa
Sources: List of Diplomatic, Consular and Trade
 Missions and International Organizations

external capital and groups. The transfer of foreign
tastes and technology, the dominance of the materialist ethic and the dilemmas of an import-substitution policy all reinforce Zambia's continued dependence on external actors, as noted in chapter 10.
    The diplomatic presence has grown rapidly in
Lusaka from eighteen accredited missions in 1965
to seventy in 1978 and twelve offices of international organizations (table 3.4). There are now
over 300 diplomats resident in Zambia, with the
most recent arrivals including missions from Angola,
Portugal and the EEC. This substantial diplomatic
community as well as visits by foreign delegations
and dignitaries are supervised by the Protocol
Division of the Ministry of Foreign Affairs. This
is headed by an under-secretary with the rank of
ambassador, and includes two senior and four ordinary
protocol officers, two of whom are normally in
attendance at Lusaka International Airport. The
chief of protocol and these officers supervise the
schedules and social activities of diplomats in
Zambia and so formally control their access to
decision makers. They limit the movement of the
diplomats outside of Lusaka in the interests

of state security: diplomats need to give forty-eight hours notice in seeking permission to travel outside the city or to the university campus. Protocol Division is informed of all changes in diplomatic personnel and issues identity cards to approved representatives. The chief of protocol communicates with the diplomatic community through the dean of the diplomatic corps, both of whom can apply social and legal sanctions against offending diplomats.

Protocol regulates the size of missions in Zambia and monitors their propaganda activities. It is particularly sensitive about direct relations between diplomats and Zambians and is meant to approve invitations to official diplomatic functions. It publishes the diplomatic list each year and makes arrangements for state and ministerial visits on the instructions of State House, where it coordinates events with the President's special assistants on international politics. It also arranges meetings for heads of missions with the president or minister of foreign affairs. It attempts to provide a conducive environment and suitable rules in which the resident diplomatic community can represent foreign governments to Zambia and contribute to the making of foreign policy. Yet, with a small youthful staff and a wide range of functions, the ministry sometimes succeeded in irritating the diplomatic corps without effectively monitoring their activities. Missions of both states and international organizations are located in Zambia not only to encourage bilateral relations but also as regional offices to gather information on Southern Africa. Diplomats in Zambia can readily communicate with the liberation movements, refugee organizations, and the UN agencies concerned with the region.

Although there are direct relations between foreign entrepreneurs and the Zambian economy, the international politics of trade and investment are concentrated within the Zambia Industrial and Mining Corporation (Zimco). The international relations of its major manufacturing branch, Indeco, are in turn centered in the group's technical services department. This centralization and coordination of Indeco's external relationships was undertaken to enable

> Indeco to use its size and procure the
> best terms possible whether dealing with
> foreign investors (as possible partners)
> or procuring goods and services. This
> aspect has become increasingly important,
> as the Group has had on occasions to appeal
> to international financiers for support

87

TABLE 3.5
International Relations of ZIMCO, 1977

ZIMCO Divisions and Subsidiaries	Foreign Ownership		
	Major Partners	Country	%
Copper mining			
Nchanga Consolidated Copper Mines (NCCM)	Minerals and Resources Corp. Ltd. (Anglo-American Corporation)	South Africa	40%
Roan Consolidated Mines (RCM)	American Metal Climax (AMAX)	Britain United States	49%
Mindeco			
Mindeco Noranda Limited	Noranda Mines	Canada	49%
Mokambo Development Co. Ltd.	Geomin	Rumania	49%
Zambian National Energy Corp. (ZNEC)			
Agip (Zambia) Limited	Agip	Italy	50%
Indeni Petroleum Refinery Co.	ANIC (ENI)	Italy	50%
Shell & BP Zambia Limited	Shell	Britain	49%
Tazama Pipelines Limited	Tanzania Government	Tanzania	33%
Indeco Chemicals Division			
Zambia Oxygen Limited	British Oxygen	Britain	49%
Kafironda Limited	ICI	Britain	46%
Kapiri Glass Products Limited	Coutinho Cara	West Germany	35%
Nitrogen Chemicals of Zambia	Kobe Steel	Japan	8%
Indeco Breweries Division			
National Breweries Limited	Lonrho	Britain	49%
*Duncan, Gilbey & Matheson	Duncan, Gilbey & Matheson	Britain	34%
Zambia Sugar Company Ltd.	Tate & Lyle	Britain	24%
Zambia Breweries Limited	Labatts	Canada	20%

TABLE 3.5 (continued)

Indeco Industrial Division			
*Dunlop Zambia Limited	Dunlop (and others)	Britain	77%
Kafue Textiles of Zambia Ltd.	Amenital/Textilconsult	Liechtenstein	22½%
	Commonwealth Development Corp./	Britain	22½%
	Barclays Overseas Dev. Corp.		
Kasama Vehicle Assemblers Ltd.	Daimler Benz/DeutscheGesellschaft	West Germany	25%
	Toyota	Japan	15%
Livingstone Motor Assemblers	Fiat/Intersomer	Italy	30%
Mansa Batteries Limited	Airam Oy	Finland	30%
Metal Fabricators of Zambia	Phelps Dodge Svenska Metallverken	US/Sweden	19%
(ZAMEFA)	Continental Ore	United States	10%
Motor Parts Distributors Ltd.	Grindlays Bank International	Britain	25%
Other Indeco subsidiaries			
National Milling Company Ltd.	Chartered Consolidated/Spillers	Britain	49%
Lusaka Engineering Company Limited	Piacenza/Intersomer	Italy	40%
Chilanga Cement Limited	Commonwealth Development Corp.	Britain	30%
National Import & Export Corp. (NIEC)			
NIEC Agencies Limited	J.L. Morrison & Jones	Britain	49%
Consumer Buying Corp. (ZCBC)	Booker McConnell	Britain	33%
National Transport Corp. (NTC)			
Zambia Tanzania Road	Tanzania Government	Tanzania	35%
	Intersomer/Fiat	Italy	30%
Medical & Pharmaceuticals Corp. (MEPCO)			
National Drug Company Limited	Booker McConnell	Britain	49%

Sources: Zimco & Indeco annual reports, 1977   *Associated companies

on certain projects.[11]

The Chairman has also asserted that it is
in the   field of international relations
that Indeco has begun to forge links which
are truly in line with our national policy
of non-alignment. Whilst long-standing
commercial relations have naturally existed
with British institutions, it is gratifying
to report the strengthening of the bonds
between Indeco and organizations in the
following countries: Australia, Canada,
People's Republic of China, Italy, Japan,
Germany, Israel and the United States of
America. Contacts with the United Nations
specialist agencies are also continuing.[12]

In 1976-77 on a group turnover of $487 million, Indeco
made a profit after taxation of $5.8 million (or 1.2%)
of which $2.4 million (or 40%) was attributable to
outside shareholders, foreign and Zambian. In the
case of the parent holding company in 1975-76, Zimco
absorbed a loss of $6.9 million whereas the outside
shareholders in its subsidiaries reaped a profit of
$7.6 million. Table 3.5 lists the major foreign
partners in Zambian parastatals.

UNIP and State House see the present parastatal
structures as transitional from foreign ownership to
local Zambian control. The party has not been critical of the compromise with external capital as it
foresees new structures involving Zambian management,
ownership, and control in designs for participatory
democracy. However, the socialization of the present
national management into the multinational system may
check further progress toward any devolution of control and responsibility. Protracted bargaining before the self-management of the copper mines was
finally settled in October 1974 (after fifteen months
of negotiations) is indicative of the problems associated with the transition from partial to full state
ownership. But self-management in Zambia does not
necessarily mean an end to dependence on foreign
capital, technology, skills and products. Although
the copper mines now have Zambian managers, the minority shareholders still provide services. Alitalia
lost the management contract for Zambia Airways when
it became self-managing; Aer Lingus now provides substantial technical and training services. Although
Zambian economic   relations are concentrated in
Europe, she has also begun to diversify her relations
with Eastern Africa. Bilateral ties with Tanzania,

90

for example, are processed very differently from relations with Britain or West Germany.

ZAMBIA, TANZANIA AND SOUTHERN AFRICA: HUMANISM AS PARTY POLICY

Zambia's bilateral links with Tanzania are close,
informal and distinctive. In comparison with other
dyads, the relationship is highly decentralized and
multiple. Although the two countries at independence
were back-to-back, looking south and east respectively,
their common interest in African development and
liberation led to a close relationship between their
presidents. The shared perspective of Kaunda and
Nyerere on the problems of unity, freedom and development led to an exchange of views which has produced
compatible policies in a number of areas, notably
state control, political participation and leadership codes. With UDI, the relationship widened into
functional cooperation, especially in communications,
with the building of the TanZam road and Tazama oil
pipeline, the establishment of Tanzania-Zambia Road
Services and the decision to build the Tazara Railway with Chinese assistance.[13] As the relationship
has developed it has also become more diffuse with
most contacts now at ministerial level. The presidents continue to meet regularly, but there are
also routine relations between ministries, not only
foreign and home affairs, but also transport, industry, finance, etc. Although bilateral integration
has yet to reach the level achieved at the peak of
the East African Community, the ties have become personal, pervasive and relatively free from protocol.
The primary actors in this bilateral community
are the two State Houses, ruling parties, ministries
of foreign and home affairs and high commissions.
Tanzania attaches considerable importance to her mission in Lusaka and, on one occasion, appointed a
former principal secretary of foreign affairs to
head the post. Successive high commissioners have
acquired a special status in the diplomatic corps,
with ready access to State House and ministries in
Lusaka. The regular interaction between the two
countries has led to an identity of views on many
issues, such as Southern Africa, Biafra, the Middle
East and China. Although there have been differences
of emphasis or timing, the foreign policies of Tanzania and Zambia tend to be mutually supportive. In
particular, State Houses and Foreign Affairs exchange
notes and ideas routinely, and usually manage to
pursue compatible and frequently coordinated policies

on crucial issues such as the liberation movements, the OAU and the nonaligned movement.

Foreign policy in both states is directed by the president, with the ministry serving to implement these orientations; in neither state is the party particularly dominant in external relations. Although the two states have distinctive histories, societies, structures and values, their development and international strategies have typically converged. A common political perspective and style has legitimized and stimulated functional relations. The two states and foreign policy systems are both interdependent and integrated. However, UNIP and other bodies in Zambia are determined never to become as dependent on one route for external trade as the inherited dependence on Rhodesia. Intimacy with Tanzania is checked, therefore, by a determination to diversify communications and links. The independence of Mozambique has advanced this concern and the reopening of the Benguela Railway through Angola will greatly augment Zambia's communication options and enhance her role as the core of Central Africa.

In addition to promoting her national interests, Zambia is an advocate of political change in Southern Africa. Her diplomacy includes the exertion of pressure on Western states and on international and transnational organizations to support the liberation movements in Southern Africa (see chapters 6 and 7). Zambia provides transit facilities for the freedom fighters under strict rules and participates in the formulation of Front Line State and OAU policy toward the movements. Responsibilities for these nationalist organizations lies with State House; the President has his own personal representative at the Liberation Center to monitor the activities of the parties permitted in Zambia. The OAU Liberation Committee also has a subregional office in Lusaka, headed by a Zambian, Mr. M. K. Simumba. The need for control was revealed with the assassination of Herbert Chitepo and factional feuding within ZANU in 1975; Zambia has taken risks of internal disorder in her support of the movements. She has also advocated the provision of support to the liberation movements and has encouraged humanitarian and educational assistance from the UN system and from Scandinavia, the Netherlands and Canada; Zambian officials participate in the administration of such aid to refugees in Zambia and of transit privileges to the liberated areas.

Zambia's crucial frontier-state role in the liberation struggle has implications for her foreign policy: she is constrained in her relations with

92

the West because of the history of Western association with the white regimes of Southern Africa; she
is unwilling to antagonize states which support the
movements; and she imposes, particularly in Zimbabwe,
conditions on her assistance to the parties. Political change in the region will have a profound impact
on the geopolitics of Zambia and increase her foreign policy options. The response of disengagement
from Southern Africa (see chapter 5) is central to
Zambia's foreign policy behavior and values. The
prospects of majority rule in most of Southern Africa
will permit Zambia to revise her regional policy and
renew links with the Southern African economic complex.
      The foreign policy of Zambia includes a set of
largely compatible values, all of which are incorporated in her national ideology of Humanism: nonalignment, pan-Africanism, nonracialism and anticolonialism
(see chapter 2). Zambia also advocates internation-
alism and nonviolence, but these notions tend to be
subordinate to ideas of confronting racism and inequalities. The preambles to both state and party
constitutions include a declaration on Zambia's
foreign policy:
      The Party pledges its support for all people
      waging just struggles for national liberation
      from colonialism, neo-colonialism, imperial-
      ism and racism, and . . . the Party shall
      work to enhance the development of Pan-Afri-
      canism, African Unity and non-alignment.14

The objectives of the party, in addition to the promotion of development, humanism and equality, include
cooperation with progressive movements to eradicate
"colonialism, racialism, neo-colonialism, imperialism
and discrimination and to strive for the attainment
of African Unity."15
      According to the ten-year plan of UNIP, which
is to operate from 1974 to 1984, the foreign policy
of the humanist state will continue to advance "justice, peace, freedom and prosperity at home and to
maximize our contribution to bridge-building in international cooperation in order to help to strengthen peace and security for mankind."16 The nine
points in the party's policies can be divided into
three groups: African considerations, international
diplomacy and foreign trade.17 In Africa, UNIP advocates a strengthening of both the east and central
African regions and the OAU; it sees the region as a
basis for interregional economic, technical and political cooperation on the continent, and the OAU as

an instrument for promoting African independence, development and a world image. UNIP will also continue to pursue the total liberation of Africa and will work for functional cooperation in the continent to advance its self-reliance and prosperity. Zambia's global diplomacy will advocate nonalignment, good neighborliness, noninterference and international peace and stability. UNIP sees these notions as a defense against imperialism and neocolonialism, advancing the sovereign equality of all nations, and leading to mutual understanding and international cooperation respectively. Finally, UNIP will pursue foreign trade and economic policy consistent with Zambia's interests and will maximize her international trade and economic cooperation as a basis for understanding and peace.

UNIP has attempted to incorporate a diverse range of interests into its foreign policy projections for the next decade. This is one response to the various demands made in the foreign system. It is an attempt to enhance the representativeness and control of the party. However, not all these policies are equally compatible; nor have they been ranked according to importance or implementation. As a result, the generality of party guidelines is not particularly helpful to ministries involved in international relations.

THE ROLE OF THE MINISTRY OF FOREIGN AFFAIRS IN ZAMBIA

The Ministry of Foreign Affairs has made a bid to exercise a monopoly on the conduct of Zambia's international relations. Yet the development of state structures has increased the number of units in the national bureaucracy with external linkages. The Ministry has not been able to control the flow of communications between this diverse range of institutions and the external environment; it aspires to act as the only channel of communications if it is to manage Zambia's external affairs properly and so control sufficient resources to implement changes in foreign policy direction. The Zambian Ministry of Foreign Affairs, however, like the foreign offices of many new states has a limited capacity for action. It is still rather small and inexperienced; it lacks the ability to effectively monitor issues and analyze trends let alone project or predict the future. It is rarely able to seize the initiatives, and this capability is largely a function of State House and the Cabinet Committee

94

rather than the Ministry (see chapters 4 and 6).

The dependence of Zambia is symbolized by an asymmetrical relations between her Ministry for Foreign Affairs and the foreign offices of large powers. There are almost twice as many foreign diplomats in Zambia as Zambians in the Ministry of Foreign Affairs, and Zambia receives far more visiting delegations than she sends abroad. Because of such limitations, the Ministry concentrates on a few issue areas — economic and political affairs — and on relations with a few states and organizations — leading African and international actors, the OAU, UN and Commonwealth. Even in these select relationships, its ability to monitor events — let alone to direct them — is limited. Senior officers are preoccupied with routine responses to demands and issues; there is little policy making below the level of the minister and State House. The President, his staff and the Minister of Foreign Affairs may take the initiative, as over relations with the East African Community or negotiations between Frelimo and the Portuguese regime or "detente" in Southern Africa, but the ministry is not organized to seize opportunities arising from routine interactions. At least in the past, it has lacked the experience or confidence to play a role other than on the instructions of other ministries or governments. It has neither the intellectual nor the technical resources to direct its missions abroad as effectively as it would wish and, at times, it has taken refuge in adopting policies by proxy, at the suggestion of other ministries, missions or international organizations. With insufficient staff, it is preoccupied with day-to-day matters and, therefore, cannot place sufficient emphasis on research to begin to rectify Zambia's inheritance of subordination to external ideas and interests.

East suggests that the lack of control by foreign ministries is typical of new states;[18] the growth of interministerial functional cooperation and the absence of a clear set of policy guidelines is a function of the smallness of foreign offices in such states. However, in Zambia one minister of foreign affairs tried to regain the initiatives and to reassert his ministry's pre-eminence in external relations. He criticized the propensity of certain public servants to undertake unnecessary foreign travel; he also complained that "most of the trips abroad have been arranged by ministries, departments of parastatal organizations who seem to run foreign ministries of their own in total disregard of the only Ministry of Foreign Affairs which is recognized by the House."[19]

95

To assert the dominance of Foreign Affairs in the
foreign policy system, the minister advocated greater
use of Zambia's diplomats overseas to advance Zambia's
interests and image in the interests of economy and
coordination: "The Ministry of Foreign Affairs,
therefore, must be viewed as a huge public relations
organ of the Government, which also provides the
framework through which Zambia conducts her international affairs."[20]

The minister demanded a larger role for his
Ministry in the control of Zambia's external affairs.
In addition to not being asked to brief delegations,
the Ministry has sometimes not even been informed of
certain external negotiations: "We have wasted a lot
of money in the past by sending delegations to go and
initiate agreements which could have been initiated
by our diplomatic representatives. If we do not allow
our diplomatic missions to perform this particular
function, then we can as well close them."[21] The
problems of coordination are revealed in the history
of Zambia's attempt to join the East African Community.
The growth of ambiguity over whether to become full
or partial members was reflected in uncoordinated comment and representation; Zambia's delegations changed
both membership and position often, and this contributed to the withdrawal of the application in 1972 after
five years of increasingly spasmodic bargaining.[22]

One response to the diversity of actors in the
foreign policy system and to the threat to the primacy of the Ministry of Foreign Affairs has been to
make its officers more professional. Vernon Mwaanga,
when foreign minister, revived plans to develop a
large and better trained Zambian diplomatic corps.
In particular, the Ministry attempted to create a
career foreign service, this would enhance its control over recruitment and promotions. It has also
expanded the number of senior posts to create flexi-
bility. By increasing the number of superscale positions in Lusaka, more heads of missions could return
to serve at headquarters, thus maximizing ministerial
influence:

> We are currently engaged in an exercise to
> overhaul the foreign service structure com-
> pletely. Government has decided to esta-
> blish a career foreign service, distinct from
> though part of the civil service, but in
> which officers will be expected to realise
> their careers. To achieve this, attempts
> have been made to provide opportunities
> through the creation of no less than twenty
> posts of Assistant Secretary level. To
> this will, I hope, be added other more

senior posts so that when completed new
recruits should find no difficulty in
realising their ability.[23]

Mwaanga hoped that the professionalization of
the Zambian diplomatic corps would lead to greater
efficiency and control through a reduction of interministerial transfers and greater continuity in
posts. The foreign service has lost many senior diplomats to both parliament and parastatals and, in
turn, has had to accept political appointments of
senior politicians or bureaucrats in decline. It
has been under pressure to recruit more women and
to provide a nationwide protocol service. The Minister has responded positively to these demands; improved training should also lead to better representation abroad. Now that the head of each ministry
division is an under-secretary of ambassadorial rank,
transfers within the ministry should be facilitated:
We have decided to establish a career
service to ensure that the people that
we do train stay and make a career in
the Ministry of Foreign Affairs . . . .
There will be a system of inter-change-
ability between officials in the Ministry
of Foreign Affairs and serving diplomats
abroad. What we have proposed to do, Sir,
is to establish and strengthen the departments within the Ministry of Foreign
Affairs which will eventually be headed
by people who will hold the rank of Ambassador so that if we have to transfer an
Ambassador, say, from Rome to the ministry
headquarters, it will be easier for us to
send a head of department from the Ministry
of Foreign Affairs to become an Ambassador
abroad.[24]

Related to the problems of circulation and re-
tention of officers is the issue of foreign service
training. During 1964, some Zambian foreign service
officers were attached to Commonwealth missions or
foreign offices to assure experience on the job.
Also the Dag Hammarskjold Foundation sponsored a
four-week foreign service seminar in Lusaka a few
weeks before Independence. Since then, relatively
little has been done to institutionalize training
procedures either within the country or with external institutions. The National Institute of Public
Administration in Lusaka arranged three courses for
new diplomats in the early 1970s but abandoned these

97

in 1974 in favor of an annual two-week seminar for
ambassadors and high commissioners. At these, each
generation of senior officials receives talks from
Central Committee and cabinet members and lecturers
from the university and Institute of Public Administration.[25] Middle-rank officers continue to be
trained at Oxford, Columbia and other centers of
diplomatic instruction on an ad hoc basis.

Successive ministers have pledged to improve the
performance of the Ministry, reduce inefficiency and
eliminate irregularities in the appointment of diplomats. Petitioners to the Chona Commission on the
establishment of a one-party democracy in Zambia,
were critical of the excessive number of Zambian missions and of the practice of MPs appointed to the
foreign service retaining their parliamentary seats.
They advocated the establishment of a career foreign
service and appointments below head of mission to be
made by the Common Services Commission; and they
demanded that all Zambian delegations to international
conferences should be knowledgeable and capable.[26]
The government response to these proposals was generally positive. Earlier in 1972, fifty-three diplomats had been recalled from overseas as an economy
measure. However, the government did not agree to
any decrease in the number of Zambian missions; it
considered any such reduction would "be imprudent if
cordial diplomatic relations were to be maintained".[27]

The average size of a Zambian mission is now
seven, down from ten in 1972. Typically, the mission
includes a head of mission (undersecretary),counsellor
(assistant secretary), first secretary (principal),
second secretary (senior executive officer), either
an accountant or communications officer, a personal
secretary, a typist and a receptionist. Between
1973 and 1974, the rank of principal was divided into assistant secretary and principal, with one assistant secretary being attached to each mission. This
change in the establishment facilitated the appointment of senior personnel in early 1974. The decline
of the establishment overseas has reduced the range
in mission sizes. Although the Zambia High Commission in London continues to be larger than any other
mission, it has been reduced from an establishment
of twenty-five to one of fifteen. The ranking of
missions according to size has changed little with
the reduction of staff abroad, except that Tanzania
now places second to London and Peking has pulled
even with Washington.

The decline in overseas posts has upset the
balance in the Ministry between staff abroad and in

headquarters. As indicated in table 3.6, 1974 was
the first time that staff in headquarters exceeded
those overseas. One of the problems confronting new
foreign offices in Africa has been the lack of coordination and control in the ministry. Zambia appears
to have begun to confront this problem by recalling
almost twenty percent of her overseas staff between
1972 and 1974. This has also led to a departure from
the characteristic distribution of senior officers
in African foreign ministries; typically, most are
located abroad, leaving insufficient experienced
staff to coordinate policies at headquarters. Again,
Zambia has begun to grapple with this difficulty;
maturation may be associated with this new balance of
staff at home and overseas.

The opening and closing of Zambian missions is
one indicator of the growth of relations between Zambia and particular countries. Overseas representation
by Zambia has developed rapidly, if spasmodically
(table 3.7). At independence in October 1964, the
first missions were opened in London, New York, Washington and, some months later, Moscow. The early weeks
after independence also saw the establishment
of a succession of offices across the continent: in
Cairo, Accra, Lubumbashi, Kinshasa and Dar es Salaam
and, early in 1965, in Lagos and Addis Ababa. This
distribution of African posts reflects Zambian interests in neighboring states, centers of African
diplomacy and, above all, countries in which UNIP
had maintained offices prior to Independence. Except
for the embassy in Bonn in 1966, there were no further additions to Zambia's resident representation
abroad until 1968, when the Peking post and three
more African missions were opened: Gaborone, Abidjan
and Nairobi. Two years later, offices were established in Italy and Malawi and, in 1973, in the capitals of three middle powers: Sweden, Canada and Yugoslavia. Since then, embassies have been opened in
France and in Belgium, following Zambian adherence
to the Lome convention with the European Economic
Community. The Portuguese coup has also led to
missions in Mozambique, Portugal and Angola. This
modest but steady expansion of diplomatic representation has been checked by the closure during these
years of posts in three African countries: Ghana in
1966 as a consequence of the military coup which toppled President Nkrumah, Nigeria in 1968 as a result
of Zambian recognition of Biafra and the Ivory Coast
in 1978 for economy reasons. Only the Lagos mission
has been restored; indeed, with the new economic and
political importance of Nigeria and the withdrawal

99

TABLE 3.6
Ministry of Foreign Affairs Establishment and Expenditure

Rank	Headquarters				Missions Abroad			
	1965-66	1970	1974	1978*	1965-66	1970	1974	1978*
Minister, Minister of State, Parliamentary Secretary	3	3	8	6	-	-	-	-
Permanent Secretary, Under Secretary	2	1	2	5	-	-	16	25
Assistant Secretary	5	5	5	8	10	14	20	18
Other personnel	36	96	127	n/a	79	115	92	n/a
Total	46	105	142	n/a	89	129	128	n/a
Recurrent expenditure (US$m)	$0.6	$1.2	$1.6	$1.3	$1.3	$3.7	$4.5	$8.7

* 1978 Estimates
Excludes contribution to international organizations etc. Based on K1=US$1.40.

Sources: Establishment Registers, Financial Reports and Estimates of Revenue and Expenditure.

from Abidjan, Lagos has emerged as a major center of Zambian diplomatic activity.

The structure of the Ministry of Foreign Affairs in Lusaka has evolved in response to new demands and changes in representation abroad. Nevertheless, it has maintained an essentially orthodox structure combining area and functional desks. It has typically been divided into three divisions: political affairs, administration and protocol (table 3.8). At the same time, the Ministry has grown in complexity as Zambia's international relations have developed and has taken on particular functions at certain times, such as the Bureau of International Conferences, established in 1969 to prepare for the 1970 Summit of Non-Aligned States in Lusaka. The structure has characteristically included an under-secretary or minister of state for protocol and for political affairs, and desks for Africa, international organizations and protocol. As the Ministry has grown, so have the sections to control its administration and to coordinate its policies in the several regions of the world. Political affairs and administration typically involve the largest number of senior officers; African affairs has a smaller staff because regional politics are coordinated in State House rather than in the Ministry.

The Ministry is characterized by a high turnover of staff, both at ministerial level and below, partially because of the paucity of experienced senior officers in government.[28] Table 3.3 provides information on the occupancy of the role of minister of foreign affairs in Zambia. In the most recent shuffle in May 1976, Dr. Siteke Mwale was brought back from Washington to succeed Rupiah Banda who had himself taken over from Vernon Mwaanga less than a year earlier. On average, foreign ministers in Zambia have held office for two years, accentuating problems of continuity and coordination. The turnover of "permanent" secretaries has been even more rapid.

Zambia has one of the larger foreign ministries in Africa, but one of the smallest in the Commonwealth. Expenditure on the Ministry of Foreign Affairs has risen rapidly, from under $2 million in 1965-66 to $10 million in 1978, with the major increase in the cost of foreign missions; the headquarters overhead has remained remarkably stable and in recent years, actually declined (table 3.6). The Ministry is responsible for only one percent of total government expenditure, a level which is characteristic of new states. Salaries account for forty

101

TABLE 3.7
Zambian Diplomatic Missions Abroad, 1978

Mission*	Date	Establish- ment	Non-resident Accreditation	Comments
London	1964	15	Ireland, Nether- lands, Vatican	Office of Commissioner for North- ern Rhodesia, 1947–64; UNIP office 1960–64
New York	1964	11		Permanent Mission to the UN
Washington	1964	8	Argentine, Brazil, Haiti, Mexico, Peru	UNIP office, Los Angeles, 1960–63; accreditation to Chile, 1970–73
Cairo	1964	7	Morocco, Sudan	UNIP office, 1960–64; accredita- tions to 6 Arab states and Iran have now lapsed.
Accra	1964	—		UNIP office 1961–64; mission closed 1966; non-resident accredi- tation 1975–78
Lubumbashi	1964	5		Consulate-General; UNIP office 1960–61; Zambian attached to British Consulate, 1964
Kinshasa	1964	5	Congo (B)	
Dar es Salaam	1964	13	Burundi, Madagascar Rwanda, Seychelles, Somalia	UNIP office, 1961–64
Lagos	1965	6	Benin, Cameroon, Gabon, Niger	Mission closed 1968–72
Addis Ababa	1965	6		Also accredited to OAU and ECA
Moscow	1965	7	Bulgaria, Czecho- slovakia, GDR, Hungary, Poland	

TABLE 3.7 (continued)

Bonn	1966	7	Austria	
Peking	1968	8	North Korea, Vietnam	
Gaborone	1968	6	Lesotho, Swaziland	
Abidjan	1968	—		Mission closed early 1978; formerly accredited to Gambia, Ghana, Guinea, Liberia, Mauretania, Senegal, Sierre Leone
Nairobi	1968	7		Accredited to Uganda, 1968-71
Rome	1970	7	Malta, Switzerland, Tunisia, Turkey	Non-residential representation from Bonn, 1968-70
Lilongwe	1970	6	Mauritius	Contingency Office retained in Blantyre
Stockholm	1973	5	Denmark, Finland, Norway	
Ottawa	1973	6	Bahamas, Barbados, Cuba Jamaica, Trinidad	
Belgrade	1973	7	Albania, Rumania	Previously represented from Moscow
Paris	1974	5	Algeria	Non-residential representation from Bonn, 1968-74
New Delhi	1975	5		
Maputo	1975	7		
Tokyo	1975	5		
Lisbon	1975	6		
Brussels	1977	6		Also accredited to EEC
Luanda	1977	6		

Sources: List of Diplomatic Missions   * by date of establishment

TABLE 3.8
Ministry of Foreign Affairs, 1978

Ministers	Ministry	Divisions	
Minister of Foreign Affairs	Permanent Secretary	Under-Secretary (Administration)	Administration
			Economic & Technical Assistance
Minister of State			Finance
			Treaties
		Under-Secretary (Political Affairs)	Africa & Middle East
			Americas
			Asia
			Europe
			International Organizations
			Research & Information
		Under-Secretary (Political Education)	
		Chief of Protocol	Protocol
			Communications

Sources: Government Directory, Ministry of Foreign Affairs Directory

percent of its expenditure, the rest going for administration, especially travel and accommodation, and for memberships in international organizations. The Ministry's salary scales are the same as those for officers in the Zambian civil service, supplemented of course, by allowances for overseas service.

Although the ministry has a modest budget, it regularly overspends its authorized expenditure. In 1972, for example, overexpenditure amounted to two-thirds of the authorized expenditure. Such overexpenditure is indicative of the lack of administrative and political control exerted by headquarters in Lusaka. The auditor-general is continually critical of the lack of budgetary control over expenditures by Zambian missions abroad. His annual reports typically include details of significant sums of illegal, irregular or unnecessary expenditure, such as excessive baggage allowances, extravagant use of medical practitioners, purchase of superfluous cars and furniture, wasteful renting of office and residential accommodation, unauthorized phone calls and large deficits on personal advances to officers. The overexpenditure includes accidents to official cars, the purchase of unsound or unnecessary buildings, and unjustified or unauthorized travel. The propensity to live well is shown in two purchases for the houses of heads of mission: in Blantyre, "an amount of $304 was spent on carpeting for the bathroom and toilet in the High Commissioner's residence,"[29] while in Washington costs for the new ambassador's residence included "the purchase of twenty-five lamps of various types for $2,811, thirteen plaques for $323 and seventeen ashtrays for $143."[30] In his 1974 report, the Auditor-General noted that, because of some four years' delay in the construction of a new chancery in Dar es Salaam, the building will be useless, as Tanzania's new capital is to be sited at Dodoma.[31]

In 1974, the Minister of Foreign Affairs appealed to members of parliament to understand the reasons why "their long suffering colleagues abroad" overspent their budgets with such regularity. While expressing determination "to bring unconstitutional expenditure in the ministry and missions abroad to and end," he asked for tolerance of Zambia's inability to control all the costs of her foreign representation.[32] Less attention was paid to the habits of conspicuous consumption which some Zambian diplomats, in common with diplomats around the world, have acquired. A further problem is that a few foreign service officers have apparently been unable or unwilling to meet the demands of the Leadership Code for an end to

entrepreneurial activity. Zambian diplomats, like
many of their professional colleagues, appear to
enjoy, and some even exploit, the privileges of the
diplomatic circuit.

Finally, reference should be made to the role
of the military and the Ministry of Defence in foreign policy decision making. For security reasons,
very little information is available on the nature
and extent of their involvement, but there are compelling reasons to believe that their influence is
growing. In the first place, the size of the defense
forces and especially the defense budget increased
dramatically during the 1970s (table 3.9). Secondly,
the President has deliberately sought to incorporate
the military into the political system, partly no
doubt as a precaution against the kind of takeovers
that have plagued much of the rest of the continent.
As a result, the defense and security forces are

TABLE 3.9
Zambian Armed Forces and Military Expenditure,
1964-1977

Year	Armed Forces*	Military Expenditure†
1964	9,000	$11m
1965	9,000	29m
1966	11,000	28m
1967	10,000	31m
1968	11,000	34m
1969	11,000	25m
1970	12,000	42m
1971	13,000	93m
1972	14,000	108m
1973	16,000	74m
1974	16,000	82m
1975	16,000	75m
1976	17,000	233m
1977	n/a	222m

*US Arms Control and Disarmament Agency, Military
Expenditures and Arms Transfers; The International
Institute of Strategic Studies' annual Military
Balance quotes lower figures, for example, 7,800 for
July 1976.
†SIPRI Yearbook, 1978. Figures are in US$ millions
at 1973 prices and the 1973 exchange rate.

directly represented at various levels in the party,
Parliament and the cabinet. In 1973, General Chin-
kuli was appointed Minister of State for Defence and,
since then, has been promoted Minister of Mines and
now Minister of Power, Transport and Communications.
In addition, defense attaches have been posted to
three Zambian diplomatic missions abroad. These are,
significantly, Belgrade, Dar es Salaam and Peking;
there is no longer a defense attache in the high commission in London. Thirdly, the Ministry of Defence
supervises and liaises with the growing liberation
armies in the country. Moreover, with the intensification of the armed struggles in Zimbabwe and Namibia,
the army's onerous operational responsiblities for
the security of the exposed Zambezi border have involved it directly in perhaps the most critical sphere
of external policy. Finally, the creation in 1973
of a separate Central Committee subcommittee on defense and security (whose relationship with the Defence Council set up at Independence is not entirely
clear: **see figure 3.1)**[33] and the appointment of Grey
Zulu, previously UNIP Secretary-General, as chairman
suggest a heightened awareness of the importance of
the military as an instrument of state policy and
the need for a coordinated response to external
threats.

CONCLUSION

This chapter is an attempt to lessen our lack of
information and understanding about the making of
foreign policy in African states. It has focused on
the range of actors involved in the foreign policy
system of Zambia and on the problems of its Ministry
of Foreign Affairs. In no sense is this work exhaustive. Nevertheless, it is hoped that the typology
of actors and data on the structure of the foreign
office will lead to comparative analysis and further
research on the process of foreign policymaking. It
is presented as a modest contribution to ending the
neglect of such institutions in Africa which Kirk-
Greene has noted: "To date the study of the foreign
service cadres has dramatically been the missing factor in the analysis of the foreign relations of African states."[34] This is as true of Zambia as it is
of other African states. Nevertheless, it is important to recognize the limitations of this and other
similar studies because the process of decision making within these structures is considerably more
difficult to discern than the institutions themselves.
This is particularly apparent, perhaps, in a relatively

youthful foreign policy system still in the stage of
maturation. As Benedict Mtshali noted in his study
of Zambia's foreign office, "the Foreign Service
emerges as an establishment which is still engaged
in finding its own feet." Moreover, the centers of
decision making may well lie outside of the Ministry
or even outside of the government or country. Consequently, "it is difficult to assess the contribution of the Foreign Service Establishment to the formulation and implementation of Zambian foreign policy.
The dynamics of this policy have to be explained
largely in terms of other variables."[35]

NOTES

1. Cf. Marion Bone, "The Foreign Policy of Zambia",
in The Other Powers: Studies in the Foreign Policy
of Small States, ed. Ronald P. Barston (London:
George Allen and Unwin, 1973), pp. 121-153 and Jan
Pettman, Zambia: the search for security (New York:
St. Martin's, 1974).

2. See Benedict V. Mtshali, "Zambia's Foreign Policy:
The Dilemmas of a New State, 1964-1970", (PhD. Thesis,
New York University, 1972), pp. 295-96.

3. Constitution of UNIP, Art. 12(1)(h).

4. Ibid., Art. 16(2)(b).

5. K. Kaunda, press conference, 16 June 1978.

6. The commission on the one-party state had recommended a single Foreign Affairs, Defence and Security
Committee, but the government decided to assign foreign affairs to the proposed Political, Constitutional
and Legal Affairs Committee. Report of the National
Commission on the Establishment of a One-Party Participatory Democracy in Zambia (Lusaka: Government
Printer, 1972), p. 46; Summary of Recommendations
Accepted by Government (Lusaka: Government Printer,
1972), p. 24.

7. Constitution of UNIP, Art. 12(3).

8. Vernon Mwaanga, N.A. Deb. no. 35, 13 February
1974, c. 1399.

9. Times of Zambia, 13 September 1971, p. 1

10.   Zambia 1964-1974:   a decade of achievement
(Lusaka: Zambia Information Services, 1974), p.6.

11.   "Chairman's Statement", Indeco Limited Annual
Report, 1973 (Lusaka, 1973), p. 4.

12.   Ibid., p. 7.

13.   See Martin Bailey, Freedom Railway: China and
the Tanzania-Zambia link (London: Rex Collings,
1976); Richard Hall and Hugh Peyman, The Great Uhuru
Railway: China's Showpiece in Africa (London: Victor Gollancz, 1976); and Kasuka S. Mutukwa, Politics
of the Tanzania-Zambia Railproject: a study of Tanzania-China-Zambia relations (Washington: University
Press of America, 1977).

14.   Constitution of UNIP; a similar wording is found
in the Preamble to the Constitution of Zambia.

15.   Constitution of UNIP, Art. 4(b).

16.   Zambia UNIP National Policies for the next Decade, 1974-1984 (Lusaka: Zambia Information Services,
1974), p. 68.

17.   Ibid., pp. 69-70.

18.   See Maurice A. East, "Foreign Policy-Making in
Small States: Some Theoretic Observations Based on
a Study of the Uganda Ministry of Foreign Affairs",
Policy Sciences 4 (December 1973):   491-508.   See
also Peter J. Boyce "Foreign Offices and New States",
International Journal 30, no. 1 (Winter 1975):   141-
161, and Christopher Clapham, "Sub-Saharan Africa",
in Foreign Policy-Making in Developing States: A
Comparative Approach, ed. Christopher Clapham (Farn-
borough, England: Saxon House, 1977), pp. 75-109.

19. Vernon Mwaanga, N.A. Deb. no. 35, 23 January
1974, c. 404.

20.   Ibid., c. 405.   A previous foreign minister had
complained that "Certain statements made on international issues [by unauthorized spokesmen] have not
only been embarrassing, but also contradictory to
government policy.   This is playing into the hands
of our enemies, who seize these opportunities to
confuse our people" (Elijah Mudenda, Zambia Daily
Mail, 8 June 1971, p. 1).

21. N.A. Deb. no 35, 13 February 1974, C. 1396.

22. See Frank C. Ballance, Zambia and the East African Community (Syracuse: Syracuse University Program of Eastern African Studies, 1971), pp. 48-61.

23. Vernon Mwaanga, N.A. Deb. no. 35, 23 January 1974, c. 406.

24. Ibid., 13 February 1974, c. 1385.

25. See Zambia Seminar Programme for Zambian Ambassadors and High Commissioners, National Institute of Public Administration and Ministry of Foreign Affairs, Lusaka, 1974. For details of earlier attempts at diplomatic training in Zambia, see Benedict V. Mtshali, "The Zambian Foreign Service, 1964-1972", African Review 5, no. 3 (1975): 306-314.

26. See Zambia Report of the National Commission, pp. 32-33.

27. Times of Zambia, 19 February 1972, p.1

28. For details of the "wastage" of trained and experienced Foreign Service Officers and on the "politicization" of the appointments process in the Ministry, see Mtshali "The Zambian Foreign Service", pp. 303-310.

29. Zambia Report of the Auditor-General, 1971 (Lusaka: Government Printer, 1972), p. 21.

30. Report of the Auditor-General, 1972, p. 24. For earlier instances of lavish or careless expenditures, see Mtshali "The Zambian Foreign Service", pp. 315-316.

31. Report of the Auditor-General, 1974, p. 20.

32. Vernon Mwaanga, N.A. Deb. no. 35, 23 January 1974, cc. 403, 405.

33. The Defence Act, 1964, section 8.

34. A. H. M. Kirk-Greene, "Diplomacy and Diplomats: The Formation of Foreign Service Cadres in Black Africa" in Foreign Relations of African States, ed. K. Ingham (London: Butterworth , 1974), p. 319.

35. Mtshali, "The Zambian Foreign Service", p. 316.

Part II
Zambia and Southern Africa:
Confrontation and Contact

4
The Anglo-Zambian Dispute over the Use of Force in Rhodesia, 1964-1969

Zambia's distinctive perceptions of the character and significance of the Rhodesian unilateral declaration of independence (UDI), and her preoccupation with the liberation of Southern Africa, are illuminated most clearly by the almost classic confrontation between President Kaunda and Prime Minister Wilson over the issue of employing force to crush the rebellion. Even prior to 11 November 1965, Kaunda was convinced that force offered not only the best prospect of resolving the conflict, but also the only viable option. UDI served to reinforce this belief, which he has continued to press ever since. Wilson, on the other hand, was equally adamant in categorically rejecting a resort to force as impractical, unnecessary and undesirable.

Subsequent developments have tended to confirm Kaunda's assessment. By unilaterally renouncing the threat or use of force in Rhodesia, Britain discarded the one deterrent that might have forestalled UDI and thus virtually ensured the failure of efforts to overthrow the illegal Smith regime. Admittedly, it is impossible to assert with absolute confidence that a military invasion would ultimately have been successful, let alone simple, swift, and painless as some Zambian advocates anticipated. Nor is there any conclusive evidence to dismiss Harold Wilson's alarmist warnings that the application of force in Rhodesia might have led Britain down the slippery slope into another Vietnam. Nevertheless, the refusal to employ force, or even seriously to contemplate its use, was undoubtedly "a missed opportunity of historically great significance"[1] for the whole of Southern Africa and beyond. Moreover, the continued inability to crush the rebellion by alternative means has meant that many of the dire consequences which some feared would accompany the use of

force have come about anyway, often in aggravated
form. Even the possibility of armed intervention
from overseas has not been precluded.
    The three principal strategies proposed for re-
solving the Rhodesia crisis were military force, economic sanctions, and political negotiations. The
term "use of force" as used here refers to the calculated deployment of military power, primarily by
Britain, to achieve desired political change in Rhodesia. The phrase can also be understood in a
broader sense to embrace any form of coercive military behavior, whether explicit or implicit, designed to influence the course of events within Rhodesia
or on its borders, positively or negatively. Accordingly, non-military measures, in particular economic
sanctions and diplomatic pressure, are by definition
excluded.

BRITISH FORCE

    Controversy concerning the use of force in
Rhodesia arose in three different contexts, corresponding to the three more or less distinct phases in
the Rhodesian crisis: the period prior to UDI, the
immediate aftermath of UDI, and the years since,
following the consolidation of settler support for
the Smith regime, and the failure of economic sanctions to "bring the rebellion to an end within a
matter of weeks rather than months."[2]

Pre-UDI Deterrence

    During the two years leading up to Rhodesia's
illegal seizure of independence, the British were
engaged in a desperate and ultimately counterproductive rearguard action designed to retain some
residual control in a rapidly deteriorating situation. Basic British strategy, under successive
governments both before and after UDI, was to avoid
driving the "moderate" European element into the
arms of the extremists. As "moderate" was a relative term which, in Harold Wilson's perception, embraced even Ian Smith,[3] this policy in practice resulted in a steady if reluctant capitulation to successive Rhodesian demands. However, as no compromise short of a complete sellout of British principles would appease the Rhodesian leaders, each concession succeeded only in weakening further Britain's
remaining leverage.
    Confronted with this situation, it is under-
standable why London concluded, possibly accurately,

114

that any hint of force would have alienated irre-
trievably whatever liberal European opposition remained in Rhodesia. Accordingly, the British
government gave scant consideration to the four opportunities available to it to exercise some military restraint on the political ambitions of the
Rhodesian government. Had these been intelligently
exploited, they might conceivably have served to deter Salisbury from its single-minded pursuit of independence.

Zambian leaders resisted British pre-UDI policy
at every stage, though they did acquiesce in the fatal decision on the disposition of the Federal armed
forces. This occurred during the delicate negotiations over the dissolution of the Federation of
Rhodesia and Nyasaland at Victoria Falls in July
1963,[4] prior to Northern Rhodesia achieving self-
government. There was no real dispute over the disposition of the army among the successor states.
Rather, controversy centered on the decision to allow the Royal Rhodesian Air Force, the most powerful
strike force in Africa south of the Sahara and north
of the Limpopo, to "revert" intact to Southern Rhodesia. Initially, Kaunda claimed half of the RRAF
for Northern Rhodesia on the grounds that it had
been largely financed from copper revenues. However,
he was persuaded to abandon this position, apparently without consulting all his colleagues,[5] by the
practical consideration that the RRAF was effectively "a Rhodesian force manned by Rhodesians and
stationed in Rhodesia" and that there was no airfield in his country at that time capable of han-
dling jet fighters. Further considerations were the
promise of financial compensation — which never
materialized[6] — to purchase more modern equipment,
and an overriding concern to avoid prejudicing
agreement on the primary objective of de-Federation.
Kaunda may also not have fully appreciated the strategic implications of the decision;[7] certainly, like
Tanzania's President Nyerere at that time, he attached much higher priority to the provision of resources for development than for defense.

By allowing the operational control of Rhodesian armed forces to remain in settler hands the original mistake of 1923 in surrendering control in
defense matters to the white minority was confirmed
and compounded. Admittedly, Salisbury would have
fiercely resisted any alternative arrangement.
Nevertheless, if London had exerted as much pressure
on the Rhodesian prime minister to accept a more
equitable distribution of RRAF assets as it did on

115

the Zambian leader to extract his reluctant consent to preserving the unity of the force, the decisions reached might have had less far-reaching consequences. Subsequently, the British Labour government was able to argue quite legitimately that this blunder, which the party had opposed while in opposition seriously constrained its freedom of action in Central Africa.[8]

An actual or threatened pre-emptive military strike, designed to frustrate any planned coup and pave the way for the introduction of democratic reforms, was a second possibility. This option was ruled out from the first. It is "not our intention to impose majority rule by force," the British Commonwealth Secretary warned the Rhodesian nationalist leaders at the time of the UDI crisis of February 1965. "Britain could not herself act unconstitutionally, whether by armed forces or otherwise, to change the constitution."[9]

Apart from general objections to a resort to force, the British government was particularly concerned to avoid any provocation that might wreck the prospects of a multiracial solution emerging by agreement among the various communities. Anything short of a categorical renunciation of force, far from deterring UDI, could well have precipitated it, especially as a threat of force would have divided British parliamentary and public opinion, and thus encouraged the reckless instincts of the "cowboy" element in Salisbury. Although we now know that there was never any chance of negotiated settlement, it was not unreasonable at the time to have done nothing to prejudice this possibility, if only for tactical reasons.

The same argument was used to justify rejection of a third strategy: the positioning of a British standby force in neighboring Zambia as an implicit deterrent. As early as February 1964 and at regular intervals thereafter, Prime Minister Kaunda offered the British base facilities in Zambia.[10] Subsequently, at the Commonwealth conferences of 1964 and 1965, his pleas were reinforced by a senior Canadian official, Arnold Smith, soon to become Commonwealth Secretary-General, who urged the British informally (though with the knowledge of Prime Minister Pearson) to station a paratroop battalion in Zambia, and to drop it on Salisbury if necessary to deter UDI. On each occasion, the suggestion was dismissed out of hand. Various unofficial proposals along similar lines were also advanced in Britain. Six months before UDI, a Liberal Party spokesman

116

pressed the government privately to send "about 2000 British troops to Zambia" and, shortly before the proclamation, the London Observer called for the dispatch of Commonwealth and American forces to Malawi as well as to Zambia.[12] The consistent response of the British government was, however, that any threat of force must be ruled out while even a slim possibility of avoiding UDI by other means remained.

What is inexplicable, and occasioned such utter dismay in Lusaka, was the Labour government's deliberately well-publicized undertaking not to resort to force even in response to rebellion. This was the fourth missed opportunity. The startling announcement was first made by Commonwealth Secretary Arthur Bottomley in the course of his West African tour in August 1965,[13] and was confirmed by Prime Minister Wilson during his eve-of-UDI mission to Salisbury in October. "If there are those," Wilson lectured ZAPU and ZANU leaders in Salisbury, "who are thinking in terms of a thunderbolt in the shape of the Royal Air Force, let me say that thunderbolt will not be coming."[14] Profoundly depressed, the spokesmen of the African majority were led back to their detention camps (where they remained for another nine years), while Wilson recounted to a delighted Smith how severely he had dealt with the prisoners.

Bottomley's indiscretion may have been prompted by a politically embarrassing report by the Defence Correspondent of the London Times, claiming that "serious thought is being given by the Government to the problem of planning for a possible military intervention in Rhodesia." Although quickly denounced as "irresponsible speculation," some contingency planning was undoubtedly underway at the official level;[15] it would have been scandalous if British defense chiefs had not, with or without prompting, prepared plans to meet every eventuality. The whole episode was a pathetic display of political weakness and an unhappy augury for the future, as well as immensely cheering for Ian Smith.

Wilson's clumsy tactics appear to have been dictated not only by fear of the effect of any talk of force on the electorate at home and in Rhodesia, but also by a curious belief that, by being "utterly frank," he could somehow compel Smith to shed his dangerous illusions concerning British determination to wage "economic war."[16] Unfortunately, the subtlety of Wilson's approach was lost on the simple mind of Mr. Smith who rightly interpreted this uni-

lateral concession as removing the last serious
obstacle to his venture.
    The consequences of this succession of blunders
was predictably disastrous. "I knew through my contacts with many white Rhodesians," Humphry Berkeley,
the maverick British Conservative MP who was in Salisbury at the time of Bottomley's pronouncement in
August, records, "that it was largely this statement that led the Rhodesian Government to plan for
UDI, involving moving most of Rhodesia's foreign
exchange from London." When Wilson repeated the no-
force pledge, Berkeley was incredulous:

> I could not understand why so intelligent a man
> could have given away his trump card in advance.
> Even if he believed that the British Army would
> have mutinied if ordered into Rhodesia, . . .
> why give the game away.

"It was his inability to leave even the possibility
of a threat on the table as a last resort," the
Times observed in an editorial review of Wilson's
memoirs, "that perhaps fatally weakened his hand in
negotiations." Certainly, in the opinion of one
other commentator, this represented "the last chance
Britain had to exercise real responsibility in Rhodesia."[17] We shall never know whether bluffing
would have deterred UDI but there are strong voices
within the Labour Party who feel in retrospect that
it might have. Uncertainty in the mind of an adversary is a vital ingredient in deterrence.
    In addition to giving the green light to Ian
Smith, the refusal even to be non-committal about
British intentions had three other unfortunate effects. It showed the European opposition in Rhodesia that it could count on little support from London beyond brave words; it let South Africa and
Portugal know that they could intervene with impunity; and it convinced Kaunda and many other Commonwealth leaders, that Wilson was at best insincere,
and at worst deliberately "giving rein to the white
minority government to achieve its objectives by
illegal means."[18] When,following UDI, the British
Prime Minister argued, possibly with greater justification, against any resort to force, his words
carried little weight.

Post-UDI Compellance

In one important respect, UDI made no appreciable difference; the British government was as determined as ever to avoid a military confrontation in Southern Africa. Within hours of the Salisbury proclamation, Prime Minister Wilson reaffirmed his continued opposition to "coercing even the illegal Government of Rhodesia into a constitutional posture."[19] Nevertheless, the military and political context within which the ensuing angry debate on the use of force took place had changed dramatically. One complication was that the problem was now one of "compellence" rather than deterrence.[20] It was no longer a question of merely threatening the use of force, but of having to initiate it. On the other hand, there was now no doubt whatsoever of Britain's clear constitutional and moral right, perhaps even duty, to intervene militarily; Smith had provided ample pretext. "For British troops to enter British territory is not an act of war," was Wilson's spirited retort to a Conservative challenge on this point.[21] Moreover, the options available to Britain had been narrowed. With the search for a negotiated settlement abandoned at least for the moment one of the political constraints on the employment of force had fallen away. Whatever Wilson's private reservations may have been, publicly he now appeared firmly committed to "no truck with this illegal regime or any compromise with it."[22] Finally, UDI generated a powerful international response in support of force. Britain faced sharply mounting world pressure demanding immediate decisive action.

During the next several years, bitter debates on Britain's military responsibilities in Rhodesia dominated the proceedings of the United Nations, the Commonwealth, and the Organization of African Unity (OAU), in each of which Zambia assumed a leadership role. These took the form of largely unproductive confrontations between a minority of states with the military capacity but not the political will to intervene, and the majority who, while unable themselves to contribute militarily or in many cases even to appreciate the logistical problems involved, were vociferous in clamoring for a British invasion. The cleavage between the camps, however, went deeper and was more dangerous than that. There were economic and racial as well as purely military dimensions to the division, with the rich, white, western nations pitted against the poor, ex-colonial, Afro-Asian bloc. The chief protagonists were Britain and

119

Zambia, with the battle frequently assuming the character of a personal duel between Harold Wilson and Kenneth Kaunda.

The British and Zambian governments approached the issue on the basis of almost totally incompatible assumptions concerning the aims of policy, the implications of military involvement, and the availability of acceptable alternatives (table 4.1). Wilson was fond of asserting that the controversy was confined to differences concerning means, not ends. Yet this was far from being the case. Zambia supported Britain's declared intention of ending the rebellion, but opposed the restoration of a legal, racist regime, especially one headed by Ian Smith. Similarly, British proposals for an interim period of direct rule were welcomed only if they paved the way for early independence on the basis of majority rule. Wilson, however, despite categorical assurances to the contrary, was never really reconciled to No Independence Before Majority Rule (NIBMAR).

The two countries also differed fundamentally in their long-term strategies. Britain's ultimate aim was political disengagement from the whole tiresome Southern African imbroglio. Accordingly, she sought to quarantine the UDI crisis. Zambia, on the other hand, saw Rhodesia as an integral part of the broader Southern African problem, perhaps the key to it. She hoped that internationalization of the issue would have spillover effects in neighboring white-ruled territories, thus drawing Britain and other western countries inexorably ever more deeply into the Southern African vortex. Whereas London neither wished nor could afford a military (or economic) confrontation with Pretoria, Lusaka was anxious to promote precisely that. In the end, South Africa proved to be the fatal deterrent to effective action against Rhodesia.

On the practicalities of mounting a successful military operation against Rhodesia, the Zambians were excessively optimistic and the British unduly pessimistic. The former insisted that a British invasion would be simple, short, and bloodless; the latter feared a long and bitter campaign. Curiously, the stands of the two countries on the use of force were the reverse of their expectations concerning the efficacy of economic sanctions. On the latter, Wilson indulged in incredible flights of fancy. Kaunda was more realistic and his lack of faith was fully justified. Zambia's arguments in favor of force might have carried more conviction if she had been prepared to concede the validity of the British

120

TABLE 4.1
Conflicting Zambian and British Assumptions
concerning British Military Action in Rhodesia

Issues	UK Assumptions	Zambian Assumptions
OBJECTIVES		
Short term	legality	majority rule
Long term	disengagement	liberation of SA
MILITARY ASPECTS		
Nature	offensive	defensive
Scale	full invasion	police action
Precedents	none (Boer War?)	routine colonial expeditions
Character	racial war	civil war (between Europeans)
Organization		
Forces needed	2-4 divisions	modest
Availability	unavailable	no problem
Logistics	extremely hazardous	relatively simple
Will to fight		
SR forces	loyal to rebels	loyal to Crown
UK forces	uncertain	fight unnecessary
Operations		
Duration	prolonged	brief
Intensity	heavy fighting	resistence unlikely
Casualties	heavy	almost bloodless
Outcome	uncertain	easy victory
Conflict Scope		
SA reaction	intervention	cautious neutrality
UK-SA confrontation	feared	welcomed
Retaliation by SR vs. Zambia	massive	possible even if unprovoked
POLITICAL IMPACT ON:		
British public opinion	Suez debate in reverse	no serious division
SR settlers	more united	more divided
"moderates"	rally to rebels	rally to British
racists	strengthened	replaced
Negotiations	hopes shattered	pre-empt a sellout
Racial tensions	exacerbated	racial war avoided
ECONOMIC CONSEQUENCES FOR:		
SR economy	mass disruption	limited or none
SR Africans	severe hardship	sharp but short
Zambia	total collapse	short crisis
Britain	severe strains, devaluation	briefer, less costly than sanctions

claim that Salisbury's autonomy in defense matters
since 1923 was of crucial importance in distinguishing Rhodesia from other colonies where force had
been used against non-European peoples. As it was,
reiteration of the "kith and kin" charge shifted the
focus of the debate away from the real issues on
which the British case was much more vulnerable. In
particular, Kaunda's warning that a British force,
far from precipitating a racial conflagration
throughout Southern Africa, was the best hope of a-
voiding such a disaster, regrettably failed to attract the attention it deserved.

Immediately following UDI, President Kaunda
pleaded earnestly with Prime Minister Wilson to intervene militarily in Rhodesia, and renewed his offer of bases in Zambia for that purpose.[23] However,
Zambian leverage was insufficient to undermine British determination to resist all pressures for force.
Zambia had two potential bargaining assets, in addition to her ability to mobilize international
opinion. In the first place, Zambia could have
chosen to withdraw her sterling reserves suddenly
from London; this would almost certainly have forced
a devaluation of the pound.[24] Even more crucial was
Britain's dependence on the Copperbelt for nearly
half her copper supplies. "Had they been cut off,"
Wilson recorded, "by a Zambia made sullen by our refusal to use force, we would have had two million
unemployed within a matter of months."[25]

In fact, Zambia wielded neither weapon. Apart
from a reluctance to embarrass the British government while it labored under a slim parliamentary
majority, Zambia had to rely upon Britain to rescue
her from the consequences of retaliatory sanctions
imposed by Rhodesia. The temptation to commit economic suicide, in a final desperate endeavor to confront Britain with a situation which would leave her
with no alternative but to intervene militarily, occasionally crossed Zambian minds. Yet, as the railway payments crisis of May-June 1966 indicated,[26]
there was no assurance that even this supreme sacrifice would have been sufficient to overcome British
inertia.

Following the failure of Lusaka's initial efforts to commit Britain to crush the Rhodesian rebellion by force, or at least to protect the Kariba
Dam, Zambian pressure on the British eased for a few
months, though the campaign was never abandoned.
Thus, at the OAU Council of Ministers meeting in
March 1966, Simon Kapwepwe urged patience on his fellow foreign ministers. He also cosponsored a

Tunisian resolution which, by omitting any reference to force, provoked Algeria and other radical states to walk out in protest.[27] Two reasons account for this shift in Zambia's tactics. The first was Wilson's assurance at the Lagos meeting of Commonwealth leaders in January 1966 that UDI would be over "within a matter of weeks," probably by mid-April. Although never convinced, Kaunda was nonetheless prepared to give Wilson the benefit of the doubt.[28] Secondly, Wilson misled Kaunda into believing that if the Labour Party were returned to power with a solid majority at the forthcoming general election, force might be used, perhaps to deliver the coup de grâce to a crumbling Smith regime. To reinforce the trust that Kaunda had in him, Wilson tipped "Kenneth" off in confidence concerning the date of the election, and promised to communicate his specific plans to him afterwards. With this assurance that the Labour government would "do the right thing at the right time," the President instructed his ministers to postpone their demands for force.[29] Yet, once Wilson had won his massive majority, he turned, not to tougher action but to negotiations, euphemistically termed "talks about talks," to circumvent his solemn promise to have "no dealings with the rebel regime."[30] To add insult to injury, Wilson failed to inform Kaunda in advance. As a result, instead of receiving Wilson's eagerly-awaited message, Kaunda learned of the British volte-face from the BBC.

Kaunda understandably felt a deep sense of personal betrayal. He reacted with anger and shock. In his frustration, he lashed out at Wilson's perfidy, spurned British contingency aid, threatened to quit the Commonwealth, and revived with greater insistence than ever his peremptory demands for an immediate resort to force. The culmination of this concerted campaign coincided with the Commonwealth conference of September 1966.

Since 1964, meetings of heads of Commonwealth governments had become a major forum of debate on the Rhodesian issue (table 4.2).[31] The first discussion in July 1964, just prior to Zambia joining the Commonwealth club, was somewhat muted, and the issue of force found no place in the final communiqué. Even a year later, when the issue was aired much more thoroughly and a determined African minority led by Presidents Kaunda and Nyerere pressed for pre-emptive military intervention, the public account of the debate merely recorded that the British Commonwealth Secretary "emphasized

TABLE 4.2

Commonwealth Advocacy of Use of Force by Britain in Rhodesia: 1964-1969

Policy	July 1964	June 1965	Commonwealth Conferences January 1966*	September 1966*	January 1969
Force Advocated					
Immediately†	0	5	5	6	3
In event of UDI	0	1	—	—	—
If sanctions fail	—	—	5	4	0
To enforce sanctions	—	—	3	9	0
Total	0	6	12††	15††	3
Force Not Advocated					
But approved	1	0	0	1	4
But not ruled out	2	0	3	3	5
Opposed	2	8	5	4	10
No opinion expressed	13	7	2	0	6
Total	18	15	10	8	25
Total Membership	18	21	22	23	28

* Includes known views of members boycotting conference
† Zambian position. Zambia was not a member in July 1964
†† Eliminates duplication

the dangers of the use of force."[32]

UDI proved to be a watershed. As a result, at Lagos, despite the absence of Nyerere and Nkrumah, a majority of delegation heads favored force in one form or another. Even Wilson accepted the carefully qualified statement in the communiqué that "the use of force in Rhodesia could not be precluded if this proved necessary to restore law and order."[33] The subsequent confrontation in September 1966 almost wrecked the Commonwealth. By that time, the illusion that economic sanctions alone could have an appreciable political impact on white Rhodesian opinion had been shattered. Consequently, two-thirds of the Commonwealth spokesmen joined Kaunda in expressing "their firm opinion that force was the only sure means of bringing down the illegal regime in Rhodesia." In view of British opposition, "most" of them were also convinced of the need for UN military action against sanction breakers, principally Portugal and South Africa. Only Australia and New Zealand, and Malawi "shared the British Government's objections to the use of force to impose a constitutional settlement," though even this hard core again conceded that force "was not ruled out where necessary to restore law and order."[34]

By the time the Commonwealth next met, disillusionment with Britain was complete. During the Fearless negotiations with Smith, Wilson had gone back on his earlier pledge to his Commonwealth colleagues to insist on NIBMAR. The 1969 conference, therefore, centered around this issue, with far less attention devoted to the question of force. In any case, many members were now reconciled to the fact that there was little they could do to compel Britain to undertake military action and, therefore, that is was pointless to expend scarce diplomatic resources on the attempt. Even President Nyerere did not formally renew his appeal for force. As a result, President Kaunda, whose young nation had suffered most from the disastrous consequences of British policies, was almost isolated. The conference report merely recorded that "some Heads of Government reiterated their call on the British Government to use force to quell the rebellion," and that the British prime minister explained why this was "wrong and impracticable."[35]

Since then, the issue of force has faded almost completely from the Commonwealth stage which it once dominated. Neither at Singapore in 1971 nor at Ottawa in 1973 did the communiqué mention the question. One reason for this was the widespread

125

recognition that, particularly with the return of a
Conservative government to power in London, moral
suasion was likely to be even less productive than
with Labour. In any case, Commonwealth energies
were soon consumed in countering the British threat
to resume arms sales to South Africa. Since then,
the emphasis has shifted to intensifying the indigenous armed struggle rather than waiting for the
British to do what they had made absolutely clear
they had no intention of doing.

A similar resigned acceptance of the inevitable
eventually crept over the United Nations, despite
persistent Zambian efforts to mobilize world anger
against Britain. Although the General Assembly did
not actually call on Britain "to employ all necessary measures, including military force" in Rhodesia
until the eve of UDI,[36] during the next four years
this demand became an annual ritual. Its promoters,
who invariably included Zambia, pressed their case
ever more insistently and piled up consistently impressive majorities.[37] Since 1970, however, the
General Assembly has abandoned any specific reference to force, though the implications of calling
upon Britain "to take all effective measures to
terminate the illegal racist minority regime" are
clear.[38]

Efforts to secure Security Council approval for
the use of force in Rhodesia were potentially more
significant, as it alone among UN organs has the
authority under Chapter 7 of the Charter to sanction
a resort to force. Zambia's UN spokesmen were particularly active. Although not a member of the
Security Council until 1969, in December 1965,
Zambia had been mandated by the OAU, along with Algeria and Senegal, to act on behalf of all African
states before the Council in Rhodesian matters. However, the results were not encouraging. Of the
eight attempts, two (November 1965 and May 1968)
were not pressed in the face of threatened vetoes,
four (April, May, and December 1966, and June 1969)
failed to command the necessary majorities in the
Council, and the last two (March 1970 and March 1973)
succumbed to vetoes.[39]

The Organization of African Unity was equally
ineffective in prodding Britain into military action.
Its most dramatic initiative was its threat on 3
December 1965 to sever diplomatic relations if Britain failed to "crush the rebellion and restore law
and order" within twelve days.[40] Although even
President Nyerere would undoubtedly have been satisfied with some unambiguous undertaking to employ

126

force if sanctions failed to topple Smith within a
reasonable period, Wilson was unable to provide that
assurance. Nevertheless, he did endeavor to put the
best possible gloss on his intentions, almost to the
point of being disingenuous.[41] The full impact of
the threat, however, was blunted when, on the expiry
of the ultimatum, only a quarter of the OAU members
complied with the unanimously agreed resolution.[42]
For the next several years, apart from caucus action
at the United Nations, the Organization confined itself to adopting increasingly strident bi-annual
resolutions asserting that the use of force by
Britain was "the only way to bring down the illegal
regime." Early in 1969, however, the OAU revised
its strategy and, since then, has argued that "armed
struggle is the only means of settling the Rhodesian
problem."[43]

INTERNATIONAL FORCE

Guerrilla warfare was not the only military alternative to a British invasion. During the early
months after UDI, a wide range of possibilities was
canvassed, among them an OAU army operating from
Zambia, UN enforcement measures, a Commonwealth contingent, an international mercenary force, and even
intervention by the Great Powers. Although, for a
time, the possibility of independent international
military sanctions against Rhodesia worried Wilson
greatly, in the end nothing came of any of these
schemes.[44]

An African Army

The idea of an OAU army was first mooted in
June 1965, though not considered seriously until the
Accra summit in October. There, the African heads
of state formally resolved "to use all possible means
including force to oppose" illegal independence in
Rhodesia. Their five-point plan, according to one
account, called for the massing of OAU forces along
Zambia's border with Rhodesia. If this failed to
deter Smith or pressure Wilson into intervening effectively, direct military action would follow. The
OAU also appointed a secret Committee of Five (Egypt,
Kenya, Nigeria, Tanzania, and Zambia) to undertake
the necessary contingency planning.[45]
When UDI finally occurred, African leaders reacted with shock, indignation and a spate of martial
oratory — "masturbation," Harold Wilson called it

crudely. Reaffirmations of solidarity, impassioned appeals for an immediate OAU military initiative, and assurances of moral and material support for any concerted action reverberated competitively around the continent. In Nouakchott, the Senegal River Basin states led by Sekou Touré called on all African states to "regard themselves in a state of war" and to despatch military contingents to Rhodesia. In Nairobi, Eastern African leaders coordinated their military planning. Emperor Haile Selassie pledged Ethiopia's determination to accept whatever military or other sacrifices were needed.[46] President Nkrumah announced that "Ghana is prepared here and now to place troops at the disposal of the United Nations, the Organization of African Unity or Britain, in order to restore law and order in Rhodesia." He also proposed a meeting of African defense ministers "to prepare concerted plans."[47] Only Malawi, and to some extent Madagascar and the Central African Republic, sounded notes of caution. On the eve of UDI, President Kamuzu Banda, with characteristic relish and scorn, upbraided his fellow presidents for indulging in "childish nonsense." The Rhodesian army he claimed, with doubtful validity, could overrun the whole of East and Central Africa within a week and the Rhodesian air force reduce every capital to "ashes and dust" overnight.[48]

Nevertheless, spurred on by the general mood of exhilaration, the OAU galvanized itself into action. The Committee of Five, hastily summoned into existence in Dar es Salaam, heard an appeal from its Tanzanian chairman to "deploy Africa's great might to rescue our brothers" in Rhodesia. "No power on earth", he asserted, "will stop us from a final duel with the forces of white racism in Southern Africa."[49] Early in December, the OAU Council of Ministers meeting in extraordinary session requested members to make available "military advisers . . . to study and plan the use of force to assist the people of Zimbabwe."[50] Two months later, following further deliberations of the Committee of Five and its military experts, a Reconnaissance Group headed by Major-General N.A. Aferi, Ghana's Chief of Defence Staff, visited Zambia to undertake a detailed appreciation of the military situation on the spot.[51]

Encouraging as these successive councils of war were, they could not obscure the fact that the momentum for militancy was already dissipating in the face of political disunity and sober assessments of military realities. The relief with which African foreign ministers seized upon diplomatic sanctions

against Britain as, in effect, a substitute for immediate military action, was indicative of their
growing hesitancy. The OAU's inability to maintain
a united front with respect to even this limited objective further undermined confidence in the Organization's capacity to act. The Aferi Report formally
sealed the fate of the projected OAU army of liberation. On the basis of an exhaustive analysis, the
mission reluctantly concluded that African states
were in no position at that time to mount a successful invasion of Rhodesia with conventional forces,
and could not hope to achieve a state of combat
readiness in less than four or five years. In the
meantime, it advocated a resort to guerrilla warfare.

Ironically, in the course of General Aferi's
oral presentation to the Committee of Five in Addis
Ababa, a tearful Diallo Telli interrupted the proceedings to announce the coup d'état in Ghana. The
overthrow of Kwame Nkrumah, on the eve of the sub-
mission by Ghana of a fresh set of "concrete proposals for joint action,"[52] has given rise to the myth
that, but for "Operation Cold Chop," an OAU army
might have materialized. Admittedly, fear of an imminent despatch of a Ghanaian contingent to Rhodesia
was one of the reasons the coup leaders gave for
their action.[53] In fact, the project was already
dead. In any case, it is not at all certain how
committed Nkrumah ever was to sending his army into
action in Rhodesia.[54]

It is scarcely surprising that, with Britain
protesting her inability to crush the Rhodesian
rebels militarily, African states should also find
the task beyond their capabilities. There were
three principal reasons for this: the strength of
Rhodesia's armed forces, the problem of mobilizing,
transporting, supplying, and financing a combat
force on the scale required, and the attitude of the
host state, Zambia. There was also the fact that
most OAU members were economically and militarily
dependent on external powers, including Britain.

Although comparatively small, Rhodesia's army
and air force were well-equipped, highly mobile, and
supported by substantial trained reserves.[55] Moreover, they benefited from the advantage of interior
lines and familiarity with the terrain. An African
army, on the other hand, would have comprised inexperienced troops, with inadequate and insecure base
facilities. It would also have had to contend with
all the inherent difficulties associated with coalition warfare — "a jigsaw of small contingents"
with different languages and military traditions,

non-standardized arms and equipment, and improvised joint command structures.[56] It is for these reasons that the OAU military mission had concluded that a 4:1 numerical superiority would be needed instead of the customary 2:1. This implied a force of three to four divisions, perhaps 40,000 to 50,000 men. Clearly, nothing approaching that number of troops was readily available.

Although the combined strength of African armed forces numbered nearly half a million,[57] only a fraction of this total could be released for OAU duty. In many cases, national armies were barely adequate to maintain internal security. Zaire was still recovering from its latest rebellion. The Sudan had a major civil war on its hands in the South. Ethiopia faced guerrilla challenges in Eritrea and the Ogaden. Kenya, like Tanzania and Uganda, had experienced army mutinies less than two years earlier and was now attempting to contain the Somali shifta. In Western Nigeria, law and order had almost completely broken down. The Entente states were more concerned with Ghanaian and Guinean subversion than with Southern Africa. Arab North African interest was focused on the Middle East; Egypt, in addition, was bogged down in Yemen. Few states, therefore, were able to back up their brave words with meaningful contributions. Rhetoric outstripped resources. Although two weeks after UDI, President Kaunda announced that "offers of troops are flowing in daily,"[58] few of these amounted to anything significant and none, it appears, was in a form that was immediately acceptable (table 4.3).

Ghana's proposed contribution was the most credible of any announced. Yet, even it scarcely constituted an effective fighting force. It is not necessary to accept at face value the accusation by Nkrumah's critics that the Ghanaian army had "virtually been reduced to a rabble" to recognize that its combat efficiency had deteriorated greatly.[59] In particular, the equipment abandoned in Zaire had never been properly replaced. Admittedly, President Nkrumah envisaged that, "if African armed forces are compelled to put down the Smith regime by force, then this will not be done by means of conventional warfare but by organizing a rising in mass by the people."[60] Nevertheless, the Ghanaian army was clearly in no positin to undertake any major military assignment beyond its borders. The People's Militia, which President Nkrumah decided to raise specifically for service in Rhodesia, was even less impressive militarily. It comprised unpaid volunteers who were

TABLE 4.3
Offers of Military Assistance for an OAU Force in Rhodesia, 1965

State	Total Armed Forces	Offers of Military Assistance				
		Troops	Combat Aircraft	Arms & Supplies	Transit & Transport Facilities
North Africa					
Algeria	48,000	Volunteers		yes	
Egypt	180,000	yes	?	yes	
Commonwealth					
Ghana	17,000	Army units People's militia			yes
Sierra Leone	1,360	yes			
Tanzania	1,800	600*			
Other					
Congo (B)	1,800	150+ Volunteers			
Ethiopia	35,000	yes	?		?
Guinea	5,000	Volunteers			
Zaire	32,000				yes

* for the defense of Zambia

to undergo training on a part-time basis. About
5,000 men and women, mainly from the ranks of the
unemployed, in addition to all 17,000 members of the
Worker's Brigade, rallied to the call, though it appears that no one was formally enlisted and no one
received any training.[61]

The only country formally to designate a unit
for service in Zambia and to draw up detailed operational plans for the move to the Zambezi was Tanzania.
"Operation Tembo (elephant)" provided for a battalion group of about 600 men equipped with Soviet
arms to stand by at Morogoro ready to respond
quickly in the event of Rhodesian aggression against
Zambia. The force was not to perform offensively
and, once the immediate threat passed, it disbanded.[62]

Equally daunting were the logistical problems.
With the lessons of the Zaire expedition of 1960 in
mind, President Nkrumah promptly assumed emergency
legal powers to "requisition Ghanaian aircraft,
ships, vehicles and other property necessary for
transporting armed forces."[63] However, Ghana's resources were inadequate to meet even her own supply
needs, and the position of other African states with
some modest air transport capability, notably Ethiopia and Zaire, remained uncertain. Moreover, the
availability of transit facilities in Zaire did not
compensate for the fact that Zambia's three international airfields would have been hard pressed to
cope with the additional traffic a military invasion
force would have entailed. A further crucial factor
was finance; General Aferi had estimated the cost of
fielding a single African battalion at $50 million
per year. "No African state or states," one Zimbabwean freedom fighter concluded, "could produce that
amount of money for a war in distant Rhodesia, when
they were failing to provide a million dollars in
one year to all the liberation movements."[64]

In addition to all the military constraints on
OAU action, there was the awkward political fact of
Zambia's firm opposition to the presence of an African army on her territory. Despite occasional ominous intimations that Zambia should be compelled to
cooperate, her veto could not easily be overridden.
Four weighty reasons account for Lusaka's reluctance
to host an invasion force. The first was fear of almost certain failure. Related to this was Zambia's
frightening vulnerability to retaliatory attack by
Rhodesia's superior air power. Thirdly, there were
serious questions of internal and external security
to consider if units not fully under Zambian command
were stationed along the Rhodesian border.[65] The

132

decisive factor in President Kaunda's thinking, however, was his determination to avoid a racial conflagration. Even prior to UDI, he had warned of the
dangers of OAU or UN (as opposed to British) military intervention for race relations, not only in
Rhodesia but throughout the continent, and not least
in Zambia. "I fear a racial and ideological war
would engulf the whole of Southern Africa," Kaunda
reiterated in public and private, "if such troops
were moved in . . . Only British troops can prevent
such a racial war occurring."66 This was the message conveyed to members of the OAU's Committee of
Five when they visited Lusaka shortly after UDI.
     In any case, within three months, the issue of
African military operations in Rhodesia had quietly
faded away. Since early 1966, it has been reviewed
only occasionally, and never seriously. Nigeria, in
particular, has taken the initiative in urging mobilization of an OAU force to defend the Front Line
States against Rhodesian aggression.67 The ebullient
General Amin has also proffered his services. "There
are thousands of volunteers in Uganda," he informed
President Kaunda in November 1973, "well-trained and
equipped, led by me, who are only waiting for a green
light to march into Zimbabwe."68 All such proposals
have, however, been firmly discouraged. Kaunda, like
Nyerere, has long realized that an African army or
high command is only a "dream". The liberation of
Zimbabwe would have to come about primarily as a result of the efforts of the people themselves.

UN Enforcement Action

     Zambia, along with other African states, also
pressed for UN military sanctions in accordance with
Article 42 of the Charter. There were two possibilities here: direct measures against Rhodesia, or
coercive action against sanction-breakers, principally Portugal and South Africa. In either case, a
Security Council "decision" formally declaring the
Rhodesian rebellion a "threat to international peace
and security" under Chapter VII was required. This
was not conceded until the adoption of selective
mandatory economic sanctions in December 1966.
     The British government was determined to block
the imposition of UN military sanctions against Rhodesia. Such a prospect was even more an anathema
than direct British intervention, as London could
expect to exercise only limited control over the
composition and role of any international operation.69
Prior to UDI, Harold Wilson had warned Ian Smith not

to count on the protection of a British veto. "It
was possible," he said, "that, either despite or because of the United Kingdom's unwillingness to use
force, the United Nations themselves would send in
troops." Yet, after UDI, he made it clear that
Britain would not hesitate to resort to the veto if
necessary.[70]

There were also practical constraints on the
UN's ability to mount an invasion. Which were the
member states both able and willing to take on another Korea or Vietnam? Britain would not, and
there was little enthusiasm in Scandinavian or in
Commonwealth countries outside Africa. Australia
and New Zealand were already committed in Malaysia
and Vietnam and, in any case, were sadly out of
sympathy with African aspirations. India, Pakistan,
and Malaysia were embroiled in local wars; and the
Caribbean countries, while outspoken in their demands
for force, could at best muster a token contingent.[71]
As for Canada, she had neither the independent military capacity nor the political will to act.

African efforts to ensure that UN economic
sanctions were "effectively supervised, enforced and
complied with by South Africa and Portugal" were
equally unsuccessful,[72] except in the case of the
Beira resolution. In April 1966, the Security
Council invoked Article 42 for only the second time
in its history to authorize Britain "to prevent, by
the use of force if necessary, the arrival at Beira
of vessels reasonably believed to be carrying oil
destined for Rhodesia."[73] The resolution resolved
the immediate crisis precipitated by the berthing of
the tanker <u>Joanna V</u> at the Mozambique-Rhodesia Pipeline Company terminal, but did nothing to plug the
major loopholes in the sanctions net, namely
Lourenco Marques (Maputo) and South African ports.[74]
As Foreign Minister Kapwepwe commented drily: "A
great power mobilizes the formidable resources of the
world organization — and succeeds in stopping one
miserable tanker."[75] Subsequent attempts by the
African members of the Security Council to broaden
the authority delegated to Britain to blockade the
whole Southern Africa coastline as well as commodities other than oil, failed. Britain objected to
being asked to accept sole and unlimited responsibility for the enforcement of UN sanctions.[76]

London fought a fierce rearguard action against
mandatory economic sanctions because it feared (quite
correctly) that to concede these would inevitably
reinforce demands for their enforcement against sanction-breakers. Nevertheless, the British government

was eventually compelled to abandon reliance on voluntary sanctions, first on a selective basis (December 1966) and later more comprehensively (May 1968). It was more successful in resisting the application of economic or military measures against Portugal and South Africa, despite their flouting of UN decisions. The reason Britain went to such great lengths to protect those primarily responsible for destroying the cornerstone of her Rhodesian policy, was economic rather than political. Given the parlous state of her economy, Britain could not risk a confrontation with South Africa. Thus the crucial contradiction in opting for economic sanctions in order to fend off pressures for military sanctions was exposed: the economic weapon could only be effective if enforced.

Great power intervention — with or without UN blessing — might appear to have offered the most promising prospect of successful international military measures against Rhodesia. Certainly, President Kaunda, driven to the point of exasperation by the British refusal to protect Kariba, intimated on several occasions that he might be compelled to invite in another friendly power.[77] Indeed, in December 1965, he despatched ministerial missions to Washington and Moscow to lobby for a UN force which would at least occupy the Kariba dam site. Both delegations returned disappointed.[78]

The United States was embroiled in Vietnam, and in any case, regarded the issue as falling within the British sphere of influence.[79] Communist military involvement appeared more credible as both the USSR and China had strong ideological, strategic, and political incentives for responding positively to African appeals for assistance. Hints by Kaunda that he might seek communist support[80] reinforced reports of concrete and tempting propositions emanating from Moscow and Peking. One inspired account alleged that, for a week in late November 1965, "it was touch and go whether Kaunda would accept the Chinese offer" of troops to take over Kariba.[81] This may have been the threat Prime Minister Wilson alluded to when he recounted to Parliament, presumably for domestic consumption, that "we have been within inches of very serious intervention by other countries." Certainly, he appeared to take "the prospects of a Red Army in blue berets" crossing the Zambezi very seriously indeed. He repeatedly warned that East and West were engaged in a "struggle for the soul of Africa," and that the communist powers who sought a "military foothold on the continent of

Africa" would welcome "the aura of legitimacy" UN
authorization would provide.[82]

What form communist military assistance would
take was never made clear. Possibilities ranged
from logistical air support to a full-scale expeditionary force. One suggestion advanced by Nkrumah
was that a great power guarantee should be sought to
deter Portugal and South Africa intervening in Rhodesia in opposition to an invading OAU army. The
Ghanaian President also hinted ominously at the recruitment of an international mercenary force. "Outside the African continent", he declared, possibly
in reference to communist countries, "there were
thousands — indeed hundreds of thousands — of individuals with p .tary training who are prepared to
fight against racialism . . . . We must consider
realistically how we can mobilize and equip them."[83]

In fact, Moscow seemed content at the time to
support the African cause from the side-lines. Soviet
leaders had no desire to get involved in a second
Zaire fiasco. Nor did they have much sympathy with
the African strategy of emphasizing British responsibilities. Russia had no intention of making sacrifices to restore British colonialism in Rhodesia, assure an uninterrupted flow of copper to the West,
protect foreign investments, or even support Zambia
which, initially at least, she regarded as a neocolonial dependency of a capitalist mining empire.

In any case, despite this occasional tactical
use of the specter of Red armies in Rhodesia to shake
British complacency, Kaunda was as concerned as Wilson to avoid an escalating ideological conflict
there. "The problems of a cold war", he declared
shortly before UDI, "are too vivid in our minds to
contemplate military action by the United States of
America or Russia."[84] Britain, therefore, remained
the key to the situation.

BRITISH MILITARY PRESENCE

Even before the collapse of Wilson's sanctions
policy became fully apparent, London had accepted
the inevitability of establishing some modest military presence in Central Africa, both to appease its
critics and to pre-empt action by others. Besides,
there were British interests there, notably Zambian
copper supplies and the substantial British communities north as well as south of the Zambezi, which
were regarded as sufficiently vital to protect by
force if necessary. Accordingly, four broad military

136

options, short of an actual invasion of Rhodesia, were explored: a "show of force," the stationing of British units in Zambia, the contingency use of force in Rhodesia, and a protective Commonwealth force for Kariba. All these alternatives, in varying degrees, would have helped sustain the loyalists in Rhodesia, and arrest the drift to de facto acceptance of the rebel regime.[85]

Show of Force

One imaginative scheme, attributed to Malcolm MacDonald's fertile mind,[86] called for a paratroop battalion to descend on Salisbury and prepare to defend itself but not attempt to seize control of the government. At the same time, a powerful emotional appeal would be made to the monarchical sentiments and "kith and kin" instincts of the European population. Princess Alexandra, or some other royal dignitary,[87] would land by helicopter in the garden of Government House, while the band of the Grenadier Guards would parade through the streets of the capital in full uniform, trumpets blaring, and playing patriotic tunes. This dramatic plan, if executed with dash and daring immediately after UDI, might well have succeeded in nipping treason in the bud. Unfortunately, the idea sparked no response among the cautious politicians in London.

Another bold proposal for limited military intervention involved aerial bombing of Rhodesia's oil import routes from Mozambique and South Africa, particularly the railway through the Malvernia desert and the road across the Limpopo at Beitbridge.[88] First promoted by Singapore's Prime Minister Lee Kuan Yew at the September 1966 Commonwealth conference, with encouragement from Secretary-General Arnold Smith, the suggestion quickly attracted support from Kaunda and other delegates, and was later taken up by Liberal party spokesmen in Britain.[89] The appeal of air power, as compared to ground troops, lay in its greater feasibility, economy in lives, and the hope that politically it could be justified as an extention of economic sanctions. The British government, however, dismissed the idea out of hand as risky, ineffective, and probably counter-productive. Even if the operation succeeded, it was argued, settler opinion in Rhodesia would be alienated, without achieving any lasting benefit. The interruption of border traffic would probably be brief and scarcely crippling, unless, of course, the exercise were repeated at regular intervals.[90]

British Forces in Zambia

In its search for a viable alternative to military intervention in Rhodesia, London's preferred option was the positioning of British ground and air units in Zambia. This seemed attractive on several counts. It represented a positive response to the chorus of critics who were denouncing British inactivity, without involving any commitment to crossing the Zambezi. Further, it offered Zambia a guarantee against aggression from Rhodesia. Although Britain did not rate this threat very highly, she did recognize that Zambia was vulnerable to air attack, that Smith's behavior was unpredictable, and that it was important to relieve President Kaunda's undoubted fears.[91] A peacekeeping force would also minimize the danger of a border incident escalating to the point where Britain could no longer avoid direct military involvement. In addition, British troops would have a stabilizing influence on Zambian domestic politics. London viewed Kaunda as a courageous statesman who was desperately trying to pursue sensible policies in the face of heavy pressure from his more radical, or at least rasher, colleagues. The presence of friendly forces could strengthen his hand, deter anyone tempted to exploit the crisis for personal advantage, and reassure the nervous expatriate community particularly on the Copperbelt.[92] However, the decisive consideration was that Britain, by preempting Zambian air space and military bases, could eliminate the threat of OAU, UN, or communist intervention. Wilson made no attempt to disguise this motive. "We should do everything in our power," he argued in Parliament, "to prevent the stationing of other air forces in Zambia, wherever they may come from."[93] Finally, a British contingent would serve to reinforce economic sanctions. As Arthur Bottomley explained some years later, the intention was "to compel Mr. Smith to keep his forces at maximum strength, at great cost to his economy."[94]

Presumably, the assumption underlying this proposal was that Smith could be bluffed into believing that British forces might at some stage actually invade Rhodesia. Yet Wilson assured Parliament categorically that any troops sent to Zambia would be "purely for defensive purposes," and he clearly meant it. "Short of an attack by Rhodesia on Zambia," he told the nation, "they would not be permitted to join in any offensive operations on or over Rhodesian soil."[95] This operational restriction led Kaunda to veto the proposal for ground forces. The only condition on which he was prepared to host British troops was that they invade Rhodesia.

The Zambian President was not unhappy — though for somewhat different reasons — at the exclusion of non-Commonwealth forces. He was also prepared to swallow his pride and, barely a year after independence from Britain, seek British protection. As Zambia's exposure to attack from the air was a direct consequence of British policy in handing over the Federal airforce to the Rhodesians, he considered he had legitimate claim to British air cover. However, he did not feel the same need for external assistance against invasion. "We are quite satisfied and very confident", he assured Parliament, "that our own troops can cope with any offensive attacks from Rhodesia."[96] Nor was he appealing for help for internal security or domestic political reasons. This suggestion Kaunda found particularly offensive and embarrassing, especially when articulated in crude and disparaging terms by rightwing Conservative spokesmen for the Rhodesia lobby. "I think we all know", Julian Amery explained,

> that troops would be sent to protect what is a reasonable and moderate government in Zambia against extremists at home and against Afro-Asian countries situated further away . . . . This is a strange commentary on the effects of majority rule in Zambia . . . . the only way in which a democratically elected government in Zambia can be maintained in a crisis may be by the intervention of British military forces.[97]

Two days after UDI, President Kaunda approached Prime Minister Wilson informally concerning the possibility of British military assistance. Wilson's response was distinctly cool. Two weeks later, following urgent consultations with his East African colleagues and an OAU defense mission to Lusaka, Kaunda formally appealed to Britain "to safeguard the integrity of Zambia's air space" and "to take immediate action to police and secure the security of the Kariba power installations" on the Rhodesian side of the border. On this occasion, London responded with such alacrity that Zambian suspicions were aroused. Over the next several days, a hectic series of negotiations took place as Wilson raced to establish a military presence in Zambia before the OAU Council of Ministers assembled in Addis Ababa on 3 December.[98]

Controversy centered chiefly on the conditions under which the Royal Scots battalion would operate within Zambia (table 4.4). While Wilson began by insisting that any British units should be "under unequivocal British command," he eventually acquiesced in a compromise arrangement providing for nominal Zambian control on the understanding that no unacceptable orders would be issued. Secondly, London conceded Lusaka's point that the presence of British forces should not "prejudice in any way Zambia's sovereign right to obtain assistance from any quarter should the need arise." In return, the British reserved the right to withdraw at any time. This was essentially a theoretical question as Zambia had no intention of inviting other countries to supply troops.[99]

On the issue of location, the British originally pressed, on logistical as well as political grounds, for a base at Lusaka airport, but eventually agreed to deploy their forces along the Kariba North Bank. This concession still did not satisfy Kaunda, who continued to insist that any base should be a springboard from which to seize the power installations on the South Bank. "We do not need troops to sit in Zambia," he declared, "We need them for Kariba." Accordingly, he would entertain a British offer only if he were given an early "date in writing" when troops would cross to Kariba.[100] Wilson was adamant; he considered that, quite apart from any political objections to the operation, a military assault on the powerhouse was the surest way to guarantee its destruction. Consequently, the Zambian cabinet, after further agonizing, finally declined the offer of ground troops. Nkrumah and Nyerere, among other African leaders, cabled Kaunda to express

TABLE 4.4
Hosting British Ground Forces in Zambia: Conditions

| Conditions | Position Adopted by: | |
	Britain	Zambia
Command	British	Zambian
Other foreign forces	excluded	not excluded
Location	Lusaka	Zambezi border
Role	defensive (protect Zambia)	offensive (protect Kariba)

congratulations and relief at the breakdown of negotiations.[101]

In concentrating his diplomatic guns, during
the early weeks after UDI, on the defense of Kariba
rather than the overthrow of the Smith regime, the
Zambian President was motivated by two principal
considerations. The first was a real and immediate
fear for the security of this vital power station.
Although jointly owned by the two countries, it was
physically controlled by the Rhodesian rebels who,
Kaunda was firmly convinced, were perfectly capable
of desperate and vindictive measures to sabotage the
Zambian economy. If Smith were to cut off Kariba
power or blow up the electrical installations, the
Copperbelt would quickly be crippled. Secondly,
Kaunda hoped that, by narrowing his target, he would
make the case for limited British intervention militarily more feasible and politically more acceptable.
He optimistically expected that the British Government's direct economic and financial stake in Kariba,
if not its clear moral and legal obligations to
Zambia, would provide sufficient incentive to galva-
nize it into effective action. Moreover, the military problems involved in investing Kariba were more
manageable than in the case of a full-scale invasion.
Naturally, the Zambian Government was also well aware
that successful British occupation of Kariba would
make the task of subduing the rest of the country
much easier, militarily and politically. Yet attractive as this prospect was, it was not the major
Zambian concern; the request for troops at Kariba was
not "a devious trick intended to lure the naive
British into an armed clash with the Rhodesian
rebels", as some Britons suspected.[102]

President Kaunda's decision to accept a squadron
of Javelin jet aircraft equipped with air-to-air mis-
siles, along with the appropriate radar environment
and a protective detachment of the RAF Regiment, was
a more satisfactory compromise from the British than
the Zambian point of view. Legally, Zambia's sovereign rights remained inviolate. Yet in practice the
RAF pre-empted all three international airfields in
the country and controlled Zambia's air space. This
effectively precluded intrusions by other powers,
whether Rhodesian, African, or communist.[103] Admittedly, high visibility of the RAF contributed
greatly to reassuring Zambian and expatriate opinion
during a tense period. In addition, it provided protection for the oil airlift. On the other hand, with
the British unwilling to neutralize Kariba, there was
not the same threat of retaliation from Rhodesia to

contend with. Moreover, powerful as the Javelins
were, they did not carry an air strike capability.
This was Kaunda's "main demand" and, when it was
finally refused, he asked the squadron to withdraw.[104]
As a result, in August 1966, the last shadow of a
British military presence on the Rhodesian border
faded away.

Lusaka's rejection of British conditions for the
deployment of troops in Zambia did not imply abandonment of its request for a protective force to guard
Kariba,[105] or of the British counter-proposal to
position a battalion in Zambia. Wilson revived the
latter at the time of his visit to Lusaka on 13 January 1966. He was convinced that the rebel regime
would collapse within a matter of weeks and was
anxious to have a military unit stationed close at
hand. Kaunda was skeptical but, as he did not wish
to discourage any development that might conceivably
lead to British military involvement in Rhodesia, he
agreed to receive a military mission led by Major
General J.E.F. Willoughby, GOC Middle East Land
Forces, the following week.[106] However, the terms of
reference of the mission were so restrictive politically that its report predictably ruled against any
attempt to seize the Kariba South Bank. There could,
therefore, be no question of Zambia accepting the renewed British offer.

In retrospect, one must ask whether Zambia was
wise to insist that the British government commit itself in advance to crossing the Zambezi on a given
day. Might not the presence on the Rhodesian border
of a substantial force with an offensive capability
have introduced an element of uncertainty into rebel
calculations? Moreover, with troops deployed along
the Zambezi, Wilson would have been able to act
quickly if political or military circumstances
changed. The Zambian cabinet reacted as it did
basically because Kaunda and his colleagues were convinced that Wilson would never resort to force in
Rhodesia. Nor is it easy to point to any occasion
since when London would have unleashed its forces had
they been conveniently located in Zambia. Certainly,
there was no serious consideration given to employing
the Javelins in a strike role to disrupt Rhodesian
communications. This is not to suggest, however,
that Wilson in his own mind ever finally ruled out
force in all conceivable circumstances.

Contingency Force

Harold Wilson's political style combined an attempt to keep all options open with wizardry with words and cleverly qualified phraseology which created the impression of specificity to obscure calculated imprecision. In the case of the contingency use of force, he hoped that, by hinting at but never seriously considering its employment, he would appease the African states and bluff Smith, without alienating the Conservative opposition. The two contingencies, in addition to overt Rhodesian aggression against Zambia, which Wilson indicated might justify the limited deployment of British forces in Rhodesia, were a breakdown of law and order, and interference with the supply of Kariba power to Zambia. In each case, a substantial British interest would be threatened.

In reassuring Parliament a few hours after UDI that "this problem is not one to be dealt with by military intervention," Prime Minister Wilson added: "Unless, of course, our troops are asked for to preserve law and order and to avert a tragic action, subversion, murder, and so on."[107] What was the significance of this exception? Kaunda and other African leaders assumed that the successful seizure of power by a band of traitors constituted convincing evidence of a fundamental breakdown of law and order; Wilson disagreed. Nor did he regard the systematic flouting of the rule of law as sufficient provocation. Even the political "murder" of five Africans in March 1968 merely evoked expressions of "abhorrence" and condemnation as "a grave breach of the rule of law."[108] Paradoxically, the law and order proviso reinforced repressive tendencies in Salisbury; to present a façade of domestic tranquility, Smith pressed ahead with instituting the full _apparat_ of a modern police state.

The remote prospect of British intervention also offered an incentive to Zimbabwean liberation movements to create chaos inside Rhodesia. When the British failed to react to the Sinoia massacre of ZANU freedom fighters in April 1966, Kaunda inquired pointedly: "Are they going to wait until thousands of people are killed?"[109] The events of August 1967 produced even greater bewilderment. By that time the internal security situation in Rhodesia had deteriorated to the point where South Africa recognized the need to move in paramilitary forces to restore law and order; Britain still stood idly by. The explanation is that Wilson's operational definition of a "breakdown of law and order," though never publicly articulated, was a serious threat to European lives or political control. In terms of the realities of British politics at the time, this was the limit of his maneuverability as he saw it. As a result, although his policy was certainly not racist in intent, it appeared close to that in practice.

Wilson did envisage the possibility that, if the Smith regime showed signs of crumbling under the effects of economic sanctions, a small British force might administer the coup de grâce. As he explained in great confidence to his Commonwealth colleagues at Lagos in January 1966 at the peak of his euphoria, "If the armed forces split, there would be no argument against UK troops moving in at once at the request of the loyalists."[110] Hence, the reference in the Conference communiqué to "the use of military force in Rhodesia" not being "precluded if this proved necessary to restore law and order," and Wilson's renewed appeal to Kaunda to accept British troops to enable London "to take quick advantage of a division within Rhodesia."[111] With the failure of oil sanctions and the abandonment of a "quick-kill" strategy, the opportunity of employing force as a supplement rather than as an alternative to economic sanctions evaporated. Even the idea of a British military presence in Rhodesia during the interim period after the end of UDI but prior to legal independence was abandoned.[112]

The second loophole Wilson allowed himself related to Kariba electricity. At the end of November 1965, he solemnly promised Kaunda that, "we shall not stand idly by if Rhodesia cuts off power supplies to the Copperbelt," as the result would be "to destroy the economy of Zambia, and indeed very seriously to disrupt our own economy." He added, under Opposition questioning, that he was prepared to "take whatever action was necessary . . . . If that did mean a limited operation we should be prepared to undertake that operation." Again, these brave words were skilfully chosen to convey more to Kaunda than Wilson really meant by them. As he explained privately to the Leader of the Opposition and hinted in public, this undertaking in no sense involved a commitment to force.[113] If Salisbury shut off Zambia's power supply, Britain could retaliate by simply infiltrating a single saboteur into the Kariba power station to deny power to Rhodesia, There was no assurance that the flow of electricity to Zambia would be restored. Obviously, neither Kaunda nor Smith was fooled by this feeble threat.

144

Commonwealth Kariba Force

In the wake of the OAU ultimatum to Britain in
early December 1965 and Lusaka's mounting bitterness
over Britain's refusal to guarantee the security of
Kariba, Prime Minister Wilson floated the idea of a
Commonwealth peacekeeping force. As originally conceived, the plan envisaged an army brigade comprising British, Canadian, and Australian battalions, deployed on the South Bank in agreement with Rhodesia
and Zambia to neutralize the Kariba installations.[114]
To avoid any implied recognition of the rebel regime,
the World Bank, as a major partner in the original
dam project, was approached to initiate the negotiations. World Bank sponsorship also had the advantage
of providing a measure of international legitimacy,
without incurring the political risks of direct UN
involvement.
British motives in promoting this scheme were
principally to protect Kariba against sabotage by
either rebels or freedom fighters (thereby meeting
Kaunda's genuine fears) and to preclude the possibility of intervention by others. London also appears to have hoped to boost Commonwealth prestige,
facilitate useful contacts with loyal elements in
the Rhodesian army, and perhaps pave the way to wider
political contacts with Salisbury. What incentive
there was to induce Salisbury voluntarily to surrender its strongest bargaining asset is not clear.
The whole idea, in fact, revealed incredible naiveté
concerning the ability of Britain to manipulate the
Smith regime.
Actually Smith had no opportunity to pronounce
on the short-lived proposal, as Australia, Canada,
and the World Bank all reacted negatively to it.
Canberra's response was predictable. Ottawa was
equally unenthusiastic, doubting the political feasibility of the scheme, and viewing the military risks
with something like horror. Ottawa also questioned
the appropriateness of a Commonwealth as opposed to
a UN peacekeeping mission, especially one confined
to white contingents.
The World Bank took the view that it was not in
the business of organizing paramilitary operations.
It did, however, agree to explore the possibility of
some more modest presence involving Bank inspection,
supervision or perhaps even management of the Kariba
complex. Accordingly, Burke Knapp, the Bank's Vice-
President shuttled between Salisbury and Lusaka in
search of some common ground on which the two partners could agree.[115] Smith was opposed to the Bank

assuming any operational role and was positively apoplectic at Zambian suggestions of a UN trustee-ship, but he was receptive to the presence of mere observers. For Kaunda, this was obviously inade-quate. In any case, he was at this point preparing to send missions overseas to promote the idea of a UN force to control Kariba. Consequently, the World Bank initiative came to nothing.

Prime Minister Wilson continued to cling to the hope that some Commonwealth military presence at Kariba might prove feasible. He revived the issue briefly in discussions with Lester Pearson in Ottawa in December 1965[116] and again in July 1966, and also advanced it rather hesitantly during negotiations with the rebel regime in September and December 1966. On the latter occasion, he seemed to regard the force as providing an external guarantee for the Tiger settlement, in addition to protecting the Kariba power installations. Smith rejected the proposal as totally unacceptable, arguing that the only threat to the dam came from "terrorist infiltration from north of the Zambezi," and that the risk of this would increase, not diminish, if a Commonwealth unit re-placed Rhodesian security forces.[117] Thus, all Wil-son's ingenious schemes to appear prepared to employ force without actually doing so finally collapsed.

FEASIBILITY OF FORCE

Apologists for British inaction have marshalled an impressive array of political, economic and mili-tary arguments to justify, or at least explain, the government's refusal to contemplate a military occupation of Rhodesia. Zambian spokesmen, on the other hand, consistently discounted or dismissed these constraints outright as mere excuses. One minister confidently asserted that it was all as easy as "crushing a louse"; military intervention, he claimed had the support of over ninety-five percent of British MP's, and would immediately split Rhode-sian white opinion, forcing Smith to surrender within twenty-four hours without blood being shed or even a fight.[118] How valid were those conflicting perceptions?

Military Constraints

There can be little doubt that the military prob-lems involved in mounting a successful assault on Rhodesian were formidable, and Zambian efforts to minimize and, on occasion, ridicule them scarcely inspired confidence in the military judgement of such critics. Nevertheless, Britain's Defence Minister Dennis Healey was indulging in some hyperbole when he contended that,

> Purely as a military operation, the defeat and destruction of the Rhodesian armed forces would have been one of the most difficult in history. The Rhodesian armed forces are roughly equivalent to those of Norway, but they are as difficult to get at as those of Laos.[119]

Geography and politics combined to prescribe the form of any invasion. Following paradrops on the airfields at Salisbury and Thornhill (Gwelo), the bulk of the troops would have had to cross the Zambezi somewhere along the difficult fifty mile stretch east of Lake Kariba. At the same time, it would have been necessary to wrest control of the air from the RRAF, possibly with the assistance of V-bombers based on Nairobi, and to protect vulnerable supply bases and other strategic targets in Zambia against retaliatory attack. The defense chiefs, understandably, were hesitant. Nevertheless, the operation was not as daunting as the politicians maintained.

Debate on the military feasibility of the scheme focused on five aspects: the availability of adequate forces, logistical support, the extent of Rhodesian resistance, the willingness of British troops to fight their "kith and kin," and the danger of South African intervention.[120]

Estimates of the size of the force required to occupy Rhodesia have varied from a battalion for a coup de main immediately after UDI, to a brigade assuming minimal resistance, to two divisions with ancillary troops and air support in the event of determined opposition. With full mobilization, Rhodesia might have been able to field an army of 20,000 Europeans, although she could not, for economic reasons, have sustained that level of effort over a lengthy period. The maximum commitment of British manpower needed would, therefore, have been in the order of 35,000, including an invasion force of 15,000. A brigade group would probably have sufficed, especially during the early weeks after UDI, to acquire control of the major centers in the country. Nevertheless, it would still have been necessary to have the balance of the force readily available in reserve to meet unforeseen contingencies, to ensure speedy success, and above all to maximize the psychological impact. The larger the British expeditionary force, the less resistance there would likely have been, the shorter the campaign, the fewer the casualties, and the less explosive the domestic political repercussions.

Britain's Strategic Reserve comprised two battalions on standby, and a third available on short notice. Beyond that, it was a matter of withdrawing units from elsewhere around the globe. This would not have been easy, militarily or politically, as Britain's dwindling military resources were already vastly overextended. In 1965, Aden and Malaysia in particular constituted a heavy drain.[121] Nevertheless, the necessary troops could have been mustered, though this would probably have meant the temporary detachment of units from the British Army of the Rhine.

Logistics posed an even greater challenge. Although President Kaunda had, since February 1964, repeatedly offered advance staging facilities in Zambia,[122] a British invasion force, would still have had to rely initially on Aden, 2,200 miles from Lusaka, and, after it was abandoned in November 1967, on Cyprus, 3,500 miles distant.[123] The question of adequate communications with the coast was even more serious. The nearest major port, Beira, seven hundred miles from Lusaka, was ruled out by the Portuguese. So suspicious were they of British intentions that they even refused permission for the RAF to operate an oil airlift out of Beira, as they suspected that the true purpose was to provide cover for an invasion of Rhodesia.[124] Tanzania also withheld landing rights to the RAF though for the opposite reason: Britain's refusal to entertain a direct military solution in Rhodesia.

Even in the best of circumstances, the task of airfreighting virtually all supplies a thousand miles inland from the coast was staggering. Besides, it was not simply a matter of providing military support; there was also the problem of sustaining the Zambian economy, as Rhodesia would certainly have severed all road and rail links with the South. Even with the copper industry placed on a care and maintenance basis, it would still have been necessary to ferry in vast quantities of oil, food, and other essential civilian supplies. Clearly, RAF Transport Command was incapable of providing sufficient airlift capacity. The only way to have met the air freight requirements would have been to commandeer a large armada of civilian aircraft, and perhaps also invite US participation.

148

Although it might have been feasible shortly after UDI secretly to have organized a coup de main using limited forces based on Aden, thereafter logistical difficulties ruled out the possibility of surprise. It would have taken a week to fly a single brigade into Zambia, and three months to build up a forward base. Yet, surprise was not necessarily an advantage in an operation which ought to have been as much political and psychological as military. The objective in confronting Rhodesia with a convincing demonstration of military superiority and political determination was to discourage resistance, in order to avoid the necessity of actually having to crush it.

How realistic was it to assume that armed opposition in Rhodesia would have been less than total? Or would there have been the long, bitter and bloody civil war that Labour government spokesmen freely predicted?[125] This was the crucial imponderable in the military equation. It seems reasonable to postulate that the swifter and more decisive the British military response, the less the resistance that would have been encountered. In the immediate aftermath of UDI, a single paratroop battalion would probably have met minimal opposition. Despite efforts to purge Rhodesian forces of "loyal" elements, the army and air force commanders were known to support the Governor. They would undoubtedly have been able to persuade a majority of regular force, as opposed to territorial, officers not to repudiate their oath of allegiance to the Queen. Even the British South African Police, though less reliable, would likely have acquiesced.

As the rebel regime consolidated itself, the prospects of a comparatively bloodless operation receded. Nevertheless, references to the "Dunkirk spirit" and the specter of a second Boer War are entirely inappropriate analogies. The Rhodesian whites were too urbanized to mount a credible threat of sustained guerrilla resistance. Admittedly, it would have been necessary, in the words of one senior British officer, to send in "an extremely large intervention force prepared to fight every bloody inch of the way against both soldiers and civilians."[126] Military commanders must plan for the worst. But this was not the most probable scenario. At no time would resistance have been negligible; neither would it have proved militarily unmanageable.

Would British troops have been prepared to fire on their "kith and kin"? A few highly publicized desertions to Rhodesia among RAF personnel in Zambia

lent substance to these fears, which in some minds
conjured up visions of the Curragh mutiny of 1914.
Yet, experience in Northern Ireland since suggests
that the danger of military indiscipline should be
heavily discounted.[127] British troops would undoubtedly have found their task in Rhodesia distasteful,
but it was not one they would have refused to undertake.

Fear of South African intervention presented a
final military constraint. Rhodesia was a difficult
enough nut for Britain to crack; to take on the rest
of Southern Africa was completely out of the question.
Zambians, predictably, argued that Pretoria would
intervene economically, but would not dare to do so
militarily.[128] The British, on the other hand, did
not expect South Africa openly to defy economic sanctions, but were convinced that she would not stand
idly by if Rhodesia were in danger of being overrun.
The Zambians were undoubtedly right on both counts.
There is no reason to believe that Pretoria would
have felt threatened by a British invasion of Rhodesia. The situation in August 1967, following
major ANC-ZAPU incursions into Rhodesia, which led
to the decision to move in "police", was very different; South Africa was clearly the next target. An
OAU army would have posed the same threat. But British military objectives were clearly limited in scope
and, moreover, direct British rule might have been
positively welcomed in so far as it strengthened
Rhodesia as a buffer against "terrorist" infiltration.[129]

Economic and Political Constraints

There is no doubt that a major military campaign
in Central Africa would have imposed a severe strain
on Britain's faltering and mismanaged economy. The
financial burdens of the operation and of a lengthy
period of occupation might have precipitated a disastrous run on the British pound. There was also the
threat to Kariba and hence to the supply of Zambian
copper, so crucial to Britain's export earnings.
Above all else was the fear of an economic confrontation with South Africa, a major trading partner. All
these possibilities were real and frightening, though
by no means inevitable or, in the short run, intolerable. Paradoxically, as Robert Good has pointed out,

only direct intervention . . . had any chance of
avoiding the risk of a critical confrontation
with South Africa always inherent in economic

sanctions. In fact a military solution in Rhodesia imposed directly after UDI was probably
the only available means for resolving the
crippling contradiction between Britain's economic stake in South Africa . . . and its political stake in Rhodesia . . . .[130]

Despite Wilson's denials, domestic political
considerations appear to have been the decisive constraint on British military action.[131] With a parliamentary majority of only one, although a moderately comfortable de facto majority, Wilson's overriding preoccupation was short-term political survival, not moral principles or long-term consequences.
He was anxious, in the interests of "national unity,"
to bend over backwards to appease the Opposition,
which on the issue of Rhodesia was united only in its
repudiation of any hint of force. Coaxing a reluctant Conservative front bench into acquiescing in
tightening the sanction screws step by step was politically more important than concessions to the
minority of backbench Labour militants pressing for
military sanctions. Moreover, only a handful of his
ministers felt strongly about Rhodesia, and few of
these were influential in 1965.[132] When, in 1968,
three of them, Judith Hart, Maurice Foley, and Lord
Walston, attempted to revive discussion in the cabinet of the use of force, it was too late.
    Public opinion was more worrisome. UDI was
never an issue that aroused the passions of the public. On the contrary, it became quickly bored with
the subject, and tended to react to it in personal
terms, such as the likely effects on workers' pay
packets. Successive public opinion polls revealed
only minimal popular support for a military solution
in Rhodesia.[133] On the other hand, this did not preclude the possibility that, with bold leadership
and careful conditioning, the reaction of the British
public to a short successful campaign in the weeks
immediately after UDI might not have been adverse.
    The individuals and groups in Britain prepared
to support military measures were less numerous,
vocal, and well connected, and less well organized
and financed, than the powerful Rhodesian lobby. The
case for the use of force was left to various pro-
African organizations, sections of the press such
as the Guardian and the Observer, and a few prominent
leaders, including the Archbishop of Canterbury, to
argue. The Guardian continued to press for force as
late as March 1968, much to the annoyance of the
Times, which dismissed the idea with scorn: "To

151

fight a war which the great majority of the country believe to be wholly mistaken is the proposal of a crank . . . . There is enough bloodshed in the world without the militarism of newspapers." In a spirited retort, the _Guardian_ concluded sadly that "the most material argument against action is that, in Britain, it is politically objectionable."[134]

The final argument against the use of force was that it would destroy all hope of a harmonious non-racial society emerging in Rhodesia. Force would trigger a racial holocaust that might engulf the whole of southern Africa and possibly the rest of the continent. Yet this was precisely why President Kaunda pleaded so earnestly and so often for early British military intervention. Only the British could prevent a prolonged racial war. To leave the Rhodesian problem to freedom fighters or to the African states to resolve would ensure the very disaster that the British government claimed it was seeking to avoid. Wilson's refusal to acknowledge this compelling argument, let alone face up to its implications, profoundly altered the course of Southern African history in general and Zambia's socio-political prospects in particular.

CONCLUSIONS

On the basic strategic issue of Rhodesia, Zambian instincts were essentially sound in suggesting that economic sanctions, at least as conceived in London, were bound to fail, and that only military force could end the rebellion. Where Zambians erred, was in underestimating the magnitude of the task, and misunderstanding British motives and concerns. British Guiana, Kenya, Antigua, and other instances of British military intervention, with which Lusaka was fond of comparing Rhodesia, were not landlocked territories in the center of a continent with a comparatively well-developed economy, an independent military capability and next door to a powerful patron (with strong economic and other links with Britain). Nevertheless , Britain's failure to employ force to suppress the Rhodesian rebellion is a sad tale of missed opportunities, naive optimism, faulty perceptions, political weakness, and sheer incompetence. Harold Wilson must shoulder a considerable share of the blame for the tragic course of events[135]

There can be little doubt that a British invasion of Rhodesia, with all its inherent difficulties, was militarily feasible and, if undertaken early enough, would have succeeded reasonably quickly and possibly easily. It seems indisputable in retrospect — though it was perhaps less clear at the time — that a serious miscalculation was made in not moving forces into Rhodesia immediately after UDI. Such a step would have been greatly facilitated if British troops had previously been stationed in Zambia. Indeed, there is a fair chance that this precaution alone might have sufficed to deter Smith from illegally declaring independence. Instead, he was offered prior assurance that no military action would be taken against him.

If, for domestic political reasons, it was deemed impossible to respond forcefully in November 1965, then it would have been reasonable to expect plans to be laid for military measures following the general election of March 1966.[136] This returned the Labour government to power with an overall majority of nearly one hundred seats. Admittedly, a coup de main was no longer possible; the operation would have had to be conceived on a considerably more ambitious scope. Nevertheless, the crucial considerations in the decision not to intervene were neither military nor economic.

Initially, the principal explanation advanced for refusing to entertain the use of force was that economic sanctions would topple Smith more swiftly, surely, and cheaply. Yet, as events quickly demonstrated, the assumptions on which this policy was based were doubly faulty. Economically, sanctions failed to bite deeply enough and, politically, they proved counter-productive as a means of reforming racial attitudes. European political opinions were not, in fact, determined by economic self-interest, at least not in the short run. Despite this, Wilson continued to profess unqualified faith in the ultimate efficacy of the economic weapon and to reject the alternative of force.

He did so for three reasons. To begin with, Wilson appeared convinced that he had discovered in sanctions a wholly new instrument which would revolutionize international relations, by providing an effective substitute for force in fostering social change. Secondly, although Rhodesia ranked high on his list of priorities, he remained supremely preoccupied with short-term domestic political implications. Confronted with the need to choose between political opportunism at home and his proclaimed principles abroad, he opted for the former. Finally, Wilson was anxious not to slam the door on a return to the conference table, which a recourse to force

153

would have precluded. Accordingly, he sacrificed
the use of force in the vain pursuit of an illusory
belief that the Rhodesian settlers in Rhodesia could
be persuaded by sweet reason voluntarily to surrender
their privileges. In fact, the attempt to reform the
Smith regime was a hopeless endeavor. The only basis
for agreement was a sellout.

The fundamental assumptions underlying Britain's
Rhodesia strategy were so wildly unrealistic that one
is bound to ask whether there were not some more sin-
ister explanation for Wilson's behavior. Three have
been suggested: first, that he was motivated by considerations of "kith and kin," second, that he conspired with Smith to perpetuate white rule in Rhodesia, and third, that he was protecting British capitalist interests in Rhodesia.137 None of these explanations on examination is adequate. Yet they continue to receive currency principally because the
real reason is so improbable. While events have
made a mockery of Wilson's solemn promises to deal
decisively with the rebels, the charge that can be
levelled against him is neither racialism nor treason
nor subservience to big business, but monumental incompetence.

Virtually all the dire predictions concerning
the spillover effects of a resort to force have in
fact materialized, but as a result of the failure to
employ force. A crisis which might have been resolved in a matter of weeks or months, has been prolonged for well over a decade. The cumulative economic costs of sanctions for Britain now greatly exceed the short-term financial burden military action
would have entailed. Similarly, the disruption of
the Zambian economy has been long and painful rather
than brief and dramatic. The misery of so many in
Rhodesia has been perpetuated unnecessarily, and the
toll of lives lost continues to mount. In addition,
the prospects for harmonious race relations have
been gravely prejudiced. Finally, the political
costs to Britain of her tarnished reputation in
Africa are incalculable. It is small comfort to
Zambians to recall that they warned the world about
these consequences, even if they proved helpless to
influence the course of events decisively.

NOTES

1. Robert C. Good, UDI: The International Politics
of the Rhodesian Rebellion (Princeton: Princeton University Press, 1973), p. 314.

154

2. Meeting of Commonwealth Prime Ministers, Lagos, 1966, Final Communiqué (London: HMSO, 1966), Cmnd. 2890.

3. Br. H. C. Deb., vol. 720, 11 November, cc. 352, 353, and 12 November 1965, c. 634; Harold Wilson, The Labour Government, 1964-70 (London: Weidenfeld, 1971), pp. 152, 162, 316, 312, 569; Humphry Berkeley, Crossing the Floor (London: Allen, 1972), pp. 112-13. See also, Arthur Bottomley, Times (London), 2 December 1974, p. 6.

4. Southern Rhodesia, Prime Minister's Office, Report of the Central African Conference, 1963 (Salisbury: Government Printer, 1963), C.S.R. 30-1963, pp. 11-12.

5. UNIP Press Release, Lusaka, 12 May 1963; NR Leg. Co. Deb., no. 108, 18 July, c. 370, and 24 July 1963, c. 548, Zambia N. A. Deb., no. 5, 9 December, c. 97 and 15 December 1965, cc. 231-32; Zambia Information Service (ZIS) Background, no. 50/65, 7 December 1965, p. 1; Manchester Guardian, 11 December 1965, p. 9.

6. "Zambia-Rhodesia: The Economic Ties and Their Financial Effects. The History of the End of Federation," mimeograph (Lusaka: Ministry of Finance, June 1968), pp. 14-18. The Northern Rhodesian government claimed $8,212,400 on the basis of assurances given in July 1963, but repudiated in November 1963. Zambia inherited only four veteran Dakotas and two Pembroke transport aircraft.

7. The Victoria Falls "agreement was a remarkable one because the Northern Rhodesians accepted that Southern Rhodesia should keep the RRAF intact . . . . Politics is the art of the possible, and what I found possible to achieve was the chance given to Southern Rhodesia to have a strong army and air force . . . ." (R.A. Butler, The Art of the Possible: The Memoirs of Lord Butler [London: Hamilton, 1971], pp. 229, 230).

8. National Executive Committee statement, 23 October 1963. Report of the Sixty-Third Annual Conference of the Labour Party, Brighton, 1964 (London: Transport House, n.d), pp. 13-14. "The Labour shadow cabinet had considered opposing the transfer, but after an exchange with . . . Kenneth Kaunda, we decided to withdraw our opposition on the ground that he had, albeit reluctantly, agreed to the transfer . . . ." (Wilson, Labour Government, pp. 21-22).

9. Arthur Bottomley, H. C. Deb., vol. 708, 8 March

1965, c. 36; British High Commission, Salisbury, Press Release, 3 March 1965.

10. Times, 5 February 1964, p. 10; NR Information Service, Press Release, no. 1109, 2 July 1964; ZIS Background, no 15/65, 15 April 1965, p. 5; New York Times, 23 June 1965, p. 3. The offer was formally withdrawn in 1976 (Zambia Daily Mail, 30 March 1976, p.1).

11. Times, 29 April 1975, p. 6; Ottawa Citizen, 5 May 1965, p. 29.

12. Times of Zambia, 28 May 1971, p. 1; H. C. Deb., vol. 761, 27 March 1968, c. 761; Observer (London), 3 October 1965, p. 10. The late Leonard Beaton argued at the time that the psychological effect of a massive show of military strength would have been to divide European opinion, not unite it. He advocated asking the United States to fly a Marine Brigade into its Wheelus Base in Libya, and deploying two British brigades in Rhodesia on the pretext of countering a communist threat to Swaziland (interview, 2 November 1970).

13. Simon Kapwepwe, Foreign Minister, UN General Assembly, Verbatim Records (A/PV.1339), 28 September 1965, p. 2; Africa Research Bulletin: Political, Social and Cultural Series (ARB:PSC), 1965, p. 352; Times, 18 August, p. 6 and 24 August 1965, p. 6.

14. Southern Rhodesia: November 1963 - November 1965 (London: HMSO, 1965), Cmnd. 2807, pp. 111, 131, 132; H. C. Deb., vol. 718, 1 November 1965, cc. 633-34; Times, 1 November 1965, p. 8.

15. Times, 4 August, p. 8 and 5 August 1965, p. 10; Br. H. L. Deb., vol. 269, 5 August 1965, c. 404; Good, UDI, p. 63; Andrew Skeen, Prelude to Independence (Cape Town: Nasionale Boekhandel, 1966), pp. 33, 41-42.

16. H. C. Deb., vol. 722, 1 December 1965, c. 1913; Southern Rhodesia: 1963-65, pp. 83, 113-14. Wilson did, however, warn Smith repeatedly that at the UN "pressures for military action" were "building up strongly" and might prove "irresistible, regardless of the United Kingdom's attitude" (Southern Rhodesia: 1963-65, pp. 82-85, 113-14). Smith was unimpressed. Bottomley had earlier hinted that he "would be prepared to risk [war] in certain circumstances" (Times, 18 August 1965, p. 6; UN General Assembly, Verbatim Records [A/PV.1340], 28 September 1965, p. 12).

17. Times, 6 July 1973, p. 16; 27 April 1971, p. 13, 25 May 1972, p. 18.

18. Kapwepwe, A/PV.1339, p. 2.

19. H. C. Deb., vol. 720, 11 November 1965, c. 361; also 12 November 1965, c. 538.

20. Thomas C. Schelling, The Strategy of Conflict (New York: Oxford University Press, 1963), p. 195. "The distinction is in the timing, in who has to make the first move, in whose initiative is put to the test."

21. H. C. Deb., vol. 721, 1 December 1965, c. 1437.

22. H. C. Deb., vol. 720, 12 November 1965, c. 633; also 11 November 1965, c. 354.

23. ZIS Background, no 12/66, 12 May 1966, p. 4.

24. Times of Zambia, 21 July p. 1 and 22 July 1966, p. 1. There was also a threat to inferfere with British investments in Zambia (ibid., 3 January 1966, p. 7).

25. Wilson, Labour Government, pp. 182-83; Foreign Report, no. 1025, 12 October 1967, pp. 4-5.

26. Richard L. Sklar, "Zambia's response to the Rhodesian unilateral declaration of independence," in W. Tordoff, ed., Politics in Zambia (Berkeley: University of California Press, 1974), pp. 327-32.

27. ZIS Background, no 56/65, 30 December 1965, p. 5 and no. 7/66, 10 February 1966, p. 4; Observer, 22 May 1966, p. 2.

28. Although not swept off his feet by the euphoric atmosphere of the Lagos conference, which he did not attend, Kaunda, according to Colin Legum, was convinced, during Wilson's brief visit to Lusaka on 13 January 1966, that "sanctions will do the job, more slowly but equally as well as British military intervention" (Observer, 16 January 1966, p. 2). Earlier, a Zambian minister had announced that the government had "reliable information" that "Ian Smith would soon collapse" (Times of Zambia, 5 January 1966, p. 1).

29. Richard Hall, The High Price of Principles: Kaunda and the White South (Harmondsworth: Penguin, 1973), pp. 135-36; Good, UDI, p. 155; Observer, 22 May 1966, p. 2. Wilson's memoirs omit any reference to these events.

30. H. C. Deb., vol. 720, 11 November, c. 354 and 12 November 1965, c. 633; vol. 722, 10 December 1965, c. 770; vol. 723, 25 January 1966, c. 48.

31. Information is based on public disclosures of private statements. Wilson's memoirs contain extensive summaries of the secret conference proceedings.

32. Commonwealth Prime Minister's Meeting, 1965, Final Communiqué (London: HMSO, 1965), Cmnd. 2712; Wilson, Labour Government, p. 109.

33. Meeting of Commonwealth Prime Ministers, Lagos, 1966, Final Communiqué (London: HMSO, 1966), Cmnd. 2890.

34. Meeting of Commonwealth Prime Ministers, London, 1966, Final Communiqué (London: HMSO, 1966), Cmnd. 3115.

35. Meeting of Commonwealth Prime Ministers, London, 1969, Final Communiqué (London: HMSO, 1969), Cmnd. 3115.

36. A/RES/2022(XX), 5 November 1965. Zambian was one of forty-three cosponsors.

37. The percentage of UN members voting for the annual Rhodesia resolution peaked in November 1967. 1965: 69.5% (61.0% on "force" clause alone); 1966: 73.6% (64.5% on "force" clause alone); 1967: 75.4%; 1968: 68.8%; 1969: 65.8%.

38. A/RES/3297(XXIX), 13 December 1974.

39. Zambia felt humiliated that her resolution in June 1969 was defeated by abstentions. As a result, in March 1970, a deal was struck with Spain over Gibraltar. This enabled the draft resolution condemning the persistent refusal of Britain "to use force and bring an end to the rebellion" to receive the necessary nine votes in the Security Council, thus compelling Britain and the USA to cast vetoes, the latter for the first time (Good, UDI, p. 290).

40. OAU Council of Ministers, Resolutions of Ordinary and Extra-Ordinary Sessions (Addis Ababa, n.d.), p. 91.

41. Humphry Berkeley urged Wilson to give Nyerere "a life-line." Following a visit to Dar es Salaam, he reported (9 December 1965) that, "I think it would suffice to spell out in greater detail the circumstances in which the British troops might enter Rhodesia" at the stage when "the Smith regime is crumbling" (Crossing the Floor, pp. 113, 115).

42. Algeria, Congo (B), Egypt, Ghana, Guinea, Mali, Mauretania, Sudan and Tanzania. Somalia had previously broken relations. OAU membership at the time was thirty-six.

43.   Council of Ministers, Resolutions, pp. 41, 95, 100, 116, 138, 154, 169.   In May 1969, a ZAPU official told the UN that, "We think it is time to put an end to the call on Britain to use force to topple its regime in Rhodesia" (Richard Gibson, African Liberation Movements [London: Oxford University Press, 1972], p. 168).   Following the decision to proclaim Rhodesia a republic, the OAU once again condemned Britain for "her consistent refusal to use force" (CM/Res. 207 (XIV), 6 March 1970).

44.   3 December 1965.   Cecil King, The Cecil King Diaries, 1965-1970 (London: Cape, 1972), pp. 43, 44.

45.   West Africa, 26 June 1965, p. 703; OAU Assembly of Heads of State and Government, Resolutions and Declarations of Ordinary and Extra-Ordinary Sessions (Addis Ababa, n.d.), p. 41, 25 October 1965; Daily Graphic (Accra), 10 November 1965, p. 3; Africa Report 10, no. 11 (December 1965): 36; Simon Malley, "Les Africains ont un plan," Jeune Afrique, no. 257, 28 novembre 1965, p. 12.

46.   Cecil King Diaries, p. 43; ARB:PSC, 1965, pp. 409-10; Daily Graphic, 15 November 1965, p. 1: West Africa, 26 November 1965, p. 1321; 1 January 1966, p. 25.

47.   Ghana Ministry of Information, Ghana Press Release no. 321/65, 12 November 1965, p. 1.   Nkrumah appears to have been the only African leader to appreciate that the OAU could not legally undertake "enforcement action", except in "self-defence", without specific Security Council authorization. He regarded the Security Council resolution of 20 November 1965 calling upon the OAU "to do all in its power to assist in the implementation of the present resolution in conformity with Chapter 7" of the UN Charter, as providing some legal basis for action.   Ghana Parl. Deb., vol. 41, 25 November 1965, cc. 2-3, 15.   See also Zdenek Cervenka, The Organization of African Unity and Its Charter (New York: Praeger, 1969), pp. 186-87.

48.   Malawi Hansard, 9 November 1965, p. 216.

49.   Times, 20 November 1965, p. 7.

50.   Council of Ministers, Resolutions, p. 92, 5 December 1965.   Algeria, Egypt, Ethopia, Ghana, Sierra Leone, Somalia and Sudan provided military experts. African states were also asked for "military and other contributions", but only for the defence of Zambia.

51. In addition, there were Algerian, Egyptian, and Nigerian members. The mission was in Zambia 6-12 February 1966.

52. Ghana Parl. Deb., vol. 43, 1 February 1966, c.6.

53. A. A. Afrifa, The Ghana Coup (New York: Humanities Press, 1966), pp. 13, 32, 104-5; A.K. Ocran, A Myth is Broken (London: Longmans, 1968), pp. 40, 61, 99; L.H. Ofosu-Appiah, The Life of Lt.-General E.K. Kotoka (Accra: Waterville Publishing House, 1972), pp. 71-74, 79; Peter Barker, Operation Cold Chop (Accra: Ghana Publishing Corporation, 1969), pp. 90-94, 121.

54. Sir Arku Korsah claimed that "at the time of his departure to Peking, [Nkrumah] was planning to send the whole Ghana Armed Forces to Rhodesia, thus leaving room for his notorious secret army trained by Russians and Chinese to tighten his totalitarian grip on the country" (Daily Graphic, 21 March 1966, p. 9). Geoffrey Bing, on the other hand, asserts that this matter "was never discussed at any of the many staff talks" (Reap the Whirlwind [London: MacGibbon & Kee, 1968], p. 425). See also Ruth First, The Barrel of a Gun (Harmondsworth: Penguin, 1972), p. 199.

55. David Wood, "The Armed Forces of African States", Adelphi Papers, no. 27 (April 1966):16-17.

	Army	Air Force	Para-Military Police	Total
Regular	3,400	900	6,400	10,700
Reserves	4,000 est.	——	28,500	32,500
Total	7,400	900	34,900	43,200

56. Ibid., p. 4.

57. North Africa: 315,000; Black Africa: 165,000 (ibid., p. 28).

58. ZIS Background, no. 49/65, 25 November 1965, p. 3. He added that the previous day, he had received the first offer from a non-Commonwealth country in Africa.

59. Afrifa, Ghana Coup, pp. 103-4. See also Barker, Operation Cold Chop, p. 94; Ofosu-Appiah, Kotoka, pp. 73-74.

60. Ghana Parl. Deb., vol. 41, 25 November 1965, c. 17.

61.   Ibid., c. 16; Ghana Press Release no. 12/66,
7 January 1966, p. 3.   Daily Graphic, 18 November
1965, p. 1; 3 January, p. 3; 7 January 1966, p. 1.
In joining up himself, the Ga Manche (paramount chief
of the Accra peoples) declared: "Osagefo has
sounded the trumpet, and we must all rally to the
call to finish Ian Smith once and for all" (Daily
Graphic, 1 December 1965, p. 16).

62.   A.D. McKay, "The Canadian Military Training and
Advisory Assistance Programme to Tanzania, 1965-1970"
(MA thesis, Carleton University, 1972), p. 78.   The
Tanzanian decision was taken following an East African summit meeting in Nairobi on 15 November 1965,
which Zambian Vice-President Reuben Kamanga attended.
Uganda and Kenya stated they were in no position to
provide troops. President Kenyatta had earlier
criticized his foreign minister for a belligerent
speech at the UN implying that Kenya might contribute
to an African force.

63.   West Africa, 4 December 1965, p. 1393.

64.   Nathan Shamuyarira, "National Liberation through
Self-Reliance in Rhodesia, 1956-1972" (PhD thesis,
Princeton University, 1976), pp. 430-31.

65.   Zambia was keenly aware of the problems created
by the presence of FLN units in Tunisia and PLO units
in Lebanon and Jordan as well as British troops in
Cyprus.

66.   ZIS Press Release, no. 1710/65, 23 October 1965,
p. 23 and Background, no. 50/65, 2 December 1965, pp.
2-3; Manchester Guardian, 12 December 1965, p. 9.

67.   Africa Report 17, no. 7 (July-August 1972):6;
West Africa, 30 June 1972, p. 815; Zambia Daily Mail,
14 June 1974, p. 1.

68.   BBC Summary of World Broadcasts, Part 4,
ME/4462/B, pp. 4-5, 28 November 1973; Zambia Daily
Mail, 1 January 1973, p. 3; Times, 29 June 1974, p. 4;
26 June 1977, p. 4.   Subsequently, Amin reported that
he had personally reconnoitered possible invasion
routes along the South African border (Sunday Times
of Zambia, 4 January 1976, p. 1).

69.   H. C. Deb., vol. 721, 23 November 1965, cc. 247,
252, 257.

70.   Southern Rhodesia: 1963-1965, p. 114, 29 October
1964; Wilson, Labour Government, p. 180.   The Observer claimed that "Wilson specifically warned Mr.
Smith that . . . Britain would not use its veto to
prevent UN action" (10 October 1965, p. 10).

71. Jamaica offered a "defence contribution, including men and material". Resolution of Jamaican
House of Representatives, 16 November 1965, UN Security Council (S/6969).

72. UN General Assembly, Resolutions (A/RES/2508
[XXIV]), 21 November 1969. The first General
Assembly resolution specifically to propose "sanctions" against South Africa and Portugal was A/RES/
2383(XXIII), 7 November 1968. Of the two attempts to
institute economic sanctions in the Security Council
against these two sanction-breakers, the first failed
to obtain majority support (24 June 1969, S/9270) and
the second was vetoed (17 March 1970, S/9696).

73. UN Security Council Resolutions (S/RES/221),
9 April 1966.

74. With the independence of Mozambique, massive
documentation on the international conspiracy to circumvent oil sanctions has come to light. See Martin
Bailey, and Bernard Rivers, Oil Sanctions against
Rhodesia (London Commonwealth Secretariat, 1977);
Jorge Jardin, Sanctions Double-Cross: Oil to Rhodesia
(Lisbon: Editorial Intervençao, 1978); and "Background to Zambia's Case against the Oil Companies",
mimeographed (Lusaka: Ministry of Legal Affairs, 1977).

75. Good, UDI, p. 149.

76. UN Security Council doc. S/7243, 6 April 1966;
S/7285, 23 May 1966; S/7630, 12 December 1966;
S/10928, 22 May 1973; Verbatim Records (S/PV.1340),
16 December 1966, pp. 43-45.

77. ZIS Press Release, no. 1710/65, 23 October 1965,
p. 23; no. 1857/65, 17 November, 1965, p. 1; ZIS
Background, no. 50/65, 2 December 1965, pp. 3-4;
Financial Times (London), 12 February 1966; Times of
Zambia, 4 November 1968, p. 1.

78. Times of Zambia, 20 December, p. 7; 22 December
1965, p. 1.

79. ZIS Background, no. 50/65, 2 December 1965, p. 2.
According to Richard Hall, "the US ambassador in
Lusaka, Robert Good, was convinced that force should
be used and worked unavailingly for American pressure
to be put on Britain to that end." (High Price of
Principles, p. 134). See also Relations between the
Rhodesian Government and the United Kingdom, November
1965-December 1966 (Salisbury: Government Printer,
1966), C.S.R. 49-1966, p. 99.

80. Two simulation exercises point to the benefits
for Zambia of a strategy of progressive involvement

of Soviet military power (Robert H. Bates, "A Simulation Study of a Crisis in Southern Africa," African Studies Review 13, no. 3 [September 1970] p. 264; J. Friedman and C. Stevens, "Anatomy of a Crisis," Millenium [London, Summer 1971], p. 81).

81. Ottawa Citizen, 6 December 1965, p. 1; Manchester Guardian, 26 November 1965. At his 25 November 1965 press conference, Kaunda inquired, "How many of you gentlemen realize how close we are here to the third world war? I personally realize this and only the British can stop this coming about" (ZIS Background, no. 49/65, p. 2).

82. H. C. Deb., vol. 722, 20 December 1965, c. 1700; vol. 720, 12 November 1965, cc. 632-37; vol. 72, 23 November 1965, cc. 249, 255; Wilson, Labour Government, pp. 181, 223; Manchester Guardian, 27 November 1965, p. 1.

83. Ghana Parl. Deb., vol. 41, 25 November 1965, cc. 15, 17.

84. ZIS Press Release, no 1710/65, 23 October 1965, p. 23, no 1924/65, 27 November 1965, p. 1; ZIS Background, no. 50/65, 2 December 1965, p. 2.

85. By advising loyal Rhodesians that it was the "duty" of public servants and others "to carry on with their jobs," but not to "assist the illegal regime," Wilson presented them with a "cruel dilemma" (H. C. Deb., vol. 720, 11 November 1965, cc. 355, 361-62). Only 36 of 12,000 civil servants resigned (Kenneth Young, Rhodesia and Independence [London: Dent, 1969], p. 319). See also, N. A. Deb., no. 5, 9 December 1965, c. 94.

86. MacDonald, who returned to London from Kenya on 5 November 1965, spent the next four years in Africa trying to undo the harm resulting from Wilson's failure to take his advice at the time of UDI.

87. Lord Mountbatten was also mentioned. Wilson had previously considered appointing him Governor of Rhodesia (Labour Government, p. 150).

88. Economist, 12 December 1966, p. 1225. Rhodesia's three rail outlets were to Beira, to Lourenço Marques (with a line to South Africa), and to Durban via Botswana. A direct rail route to South Africa was opened in September 1974. There are also main roads to Beira, and to South Africa via Beitbridge.

89. New York Times, 8 September 1966, p. 12; Wilson, Labour Government, p. 280; H. C. Deb., vol. 736, 10 November 1966, cc. 1574-76; vol. 761, 27 March 1968,

cc. 1622-23; Young, Rhodesia and Independence, p. 332n.

90. David Owen, The Politics of Defence (London: Cape, 1972), pp. 115; Richard Crossman, Diaries of a Cabinet Minister, 3 vols. (London: Hamish Hamilton, 1975), 1:879. Following the sabotage of the Luangwa Bridge in Zambia in June 1968, an emergency replacement was installed within seventeen days.

91. H. C. Deb., vol. 721, 1 December 1965, cc. 1433-35.

92. Africa 1965, no. 24, 10 December 1965, p. 2: H. C. Deb., vol. 721, 1 December 1965, cc. 1463-64.

93. H. C. Deb., vol. 721, 1 December 1965, c. 1433, Opposition MP Julian Amery summed up Government policy with brutal clarity: "We are afraid that if we do not send forces to do nothing other countries will send forces to do something" (ibid., c. 1472).

94. Sunday Times (London), 30 January 1972, p. 3.

95. H. C. Deb., vol. 721, 1 December 1965, c. 1430; Manchester Guardian, 2 December 1965, p. 1.

96. N. A. Deb., no. 5, 9 December 1965, cc. 95-96; ZIS Background, no. 50/65, 2 December 1965, p. 1.

97. H. C. Deb., vol. 721, 1 December 1965, cc. 1474-75.

98. Manchester Guardian, 3 December 1965, p. 1; 15 December 1965, p. 1; ARB:PSC, 1965, p. 408. N. A. Deb., no. 4, 9 December 1965, c. 95.

99. N. A. Deb., no. 5, 9 December 1965, c. 96; H. C. Deb., vol. 721, 1 December 1965, c. 1430; Manchester Guardian, 3 December 1965, p. 3; ZIS Background, no. 50/65, 2 December 1965, pp. 2, 4.

100. ZIS Background, no. 50/65, 2 December 1965, pp. 1-3; no. 52/65, 12 December 1965, p. 3; N. A. Deb., no. 5, 9 December 1965, c. 96.

101. Wilson, Labour Government, p. 182; Manchester Guardian, 3 December 1965, p. 1; H. C. Deb., vol. 722, 21 December 1965, c. 1917; Daily Graphic, 2 December 1965, p. 1. Wilson argued that "one civilian in a white coat could have pulled the switches before the power station could be occupied." If this was all that happened, an occupying force could presumably have easily rectified the situation. Bottomley later claimed: "I have little doubt that, if force had been used, Smith and his wild men would have blown up the Kariba Dam. After all, they had little to lose.

They had the Wankie coal mines to give them power"
(H. C. Deb., vol. 845, 9 November 1972, c. 1234).

102. Manchester Guardian, 15 December 1965, p. 1.

103. Ibid., 6 December 1965, p. 10.

104. Wilson, Labour Government, p. 182; ZIS Press
Release, no. 1557/66, 24 August 1966, p. 1. The cost
of maintaining the squadron in Zambia for the period
of nine months was $7,400,000, half of which was ac-
counted for by the cost of airlifting aviation fuel
into Zamiba (H. C. Deb., vol. 734, 20 October 1966,
c. 45).

105. ZIS Press Release, no. 1977/65, 6 December 1965,
p. 1; no. 2031/65, 14 December 1965, p. 1; Background,
no. 53/65, 12 December 1965, pp. 1-3.

106. Good, UDI, pp. 122-23; Daily Telegraph (London),
20 January 1966; Times of Zambia, 20 January 1966,
p. 1; ZIS Press Release, no. 154/66, 25 January 1966,
p. 1.

107. H. C. Deb., vol. 720, 11 November 1965, c. 360.
Next day, Wilson explained that the request would
have to come from the Governor (c. 538).

108. Ibid., vol. 761, 27 March 1968, cc. 1623-24,
1677-78.

109. ZIS Press Release, no. 773/66, 30 April 1966,
p. 1.

110. L.B. Pearson, Notes, 12 January 1966, p. 2,
L.B. Pearson Papers; see also the Sun (London) 5
January 1966.

111. Final Communiqué, Lagos, 1966; Pearson, Notes,
p. 2. Even Welensky is said to have favored threatening force "at an appropriate time" (Berkeley,
Crossing the Floor, p. 114).

112. Rhodesia: Documents Relating to Proposals for
a Settlement, 1966 (London: HMSO, 1966), Cmnd. 3171,
pp. 16, 49, 54-55, 70-71, 98; Good, UDI, p. 195.

113. H. C. Deb., vol. 721, 1 December 1965, cc. 1430,
1433-34, 1439-40; vol. 722, 21 December 1965, cc.
1921-23. The Lord Privy Seal was more explicit: "We
are not making any sort of military commitment here"
(H. L. Deb., vol. 270, 1 December 1965, c. 1274).

114. It was anticipated that Australia might only
contribute a company, in view of her Vietnam commitments. Smith's record of the Tiger talks a year
later quotes Wilson as having envisaged New Zealand

and Rhodesian participation. This is incorrect
(<u>Relations between the Rhodesian Government and the
United Kingdom</u>, p. 113). See also <u>Economist</u>, 11
December 1965, p. 117, and <u>Manchester Guardian</u>, 14
December 1965, p. 1.

115. IBRD Vice-President Burke Knapp and Hugh Scott
were in Salisbury (15-18 December), Lusaka (18-20
December) and Salisbury (20 December), p. 5, 23
December, p. 2, 29 December 1965, p. 7; <u>Financial
Times</u>, 9 December, p. 1, 16 December, p. 14,
23 December 1965, p. 12.

116. <u>Ottawa Citizen</u>, 20 December 1965, pp. 1, 3;
<u>H. C. Deb.</u>, vol. 722, 21 December 1965, c. 1923.
There were vague hints in April 1966 of a Zambian
approach to Ottawa for an all-Canadian Kariba force
but no request was ever made.

117. <u>Relations between the Rhodesian Government and
the United Kingdom</u>, pp. 40, 50, 113; <u>Rhodesia:
Documents</u>, 1966, pp. 16, 70.

118. Mainza Chona, Minister of Home Affairs, ZIS
<u>Press Release</u>, no. 1993/65, 8 December 1965, p. 1.

119. <u>Times</u>, 3 October 1967, p. 7.

120. Good, <u>UDI</u>, pp. 55-65; Bruce Reed and Geoffrey
Williams, <u>Denis Healey and the Policies of Power</u>
(London: Sidgwick and Jackson, 1971), pp. 189-91;
William Gutteridge, "Rhodesia: The Use of Military
Force," <u>World Today</u> 21, no. 12 (December 1965):499-
503; Neville Brown, "Military Sanctions against Rho-
desia," <u>Venture</u> 17, no. 2 (December 1965):9-12;
Robert Sutcliffe, "The Use of Force in Rhodesia,"
<u>Venture</u> 19, no. 4 (April 1967):5-8; Simon Clements,
"The Facts about Force," <u>Spectator</u>, 16 December 1966,
p. 770; "By Jingo if we do," <u>Economist</u>, 17 December
1966, pp. 1222-25.

121. Healey argued that, although Britain had about
one hundred military commitments, her resources permitted only one major campaign to be fought at any
one time (<u>Times</u>, 5 August 1965, p. 10). In 1965,
that campaign was in Borneo where 50,000 British
troops were tied down — more than were needed in
Rhodesia. The end of Indonesia's confrontation with
Malaysia in 1966 released two brigades of Gurkhas for
service elsewhere.

122. <u>Times</u>, 6 February 1965, p. 10. The offer was
publicly renewed four times prior to UDI, and at
least six times in the course of the next three years.

123. On 5 November 1965, the UN General Assembly, with all OAU members voting in favor, demanded "the immediate and complete removal" of the British military base at Aden (A/RES/2023 [XX]). Wilson complained that, "I could not understand [Labour Party] colleagues who pressed me to attack Rhodesia with force of arms and denied me the means in terms of essential bases" (Labour Government, p. 243).

124. Good, UDI, p. 134n; Economist, 18 December 1965, p. 1310; 17 December 1966, p. 1225.

125. H. C. Deb., vol. 722, 21 December 1965, c. 1914.

126. Reed and Williams, Denis Healey, p. 189.

127. Times, 4 August 1965, and 6 July 1973. A recent report claims that the British MI6 "now admit that it was a mistake to have advised Sir Harold Wilson not to send troops into Rhodesia immediately Mr. Smith declared UDI in 1965 on the grounds that they would not fire against their own kith and kin" (Manchester Guardian Weekly, 7 August 1977, p. 4). The reluctance of British troops to break the Protestant strike in Ulster in May 1975 suggests that there may be political limits to the employment of forces there.

128. K. Kaunda, "A Racial Holocaust in Central Africa?", Punch, 9 March 1966, p. 335; interview on Zambia Broadcasting Service, 24 November 1966.

129. Martin Loney, Rhodesia: White Racism and Imperial Response (Harmondsworth: Penguin, 1975), pp. 139-140. There was always, of course, a danger of South African volunteers flocking to Rhodesia (Good, UDI, p. 58).

130. UDI, p. 312.

131. Wilson, Labour Government, pp. 180-81, 189-90; Good, UDI, p. 64; Berkeley, Crossing the Floor, pp. 111, 122-23; Reed and Williams, Denis Healey, p. 190; Crossman, Diaries, 1:378, 407.

132. Crossman, Diaries, 1:378-79, 394, 406-407; Lord Wigg, George Wigg (London: Michael Joseph, 1972), pp. 325-26.

133. Eric Silver, "Mr. Wilson, the Public and Rhodesia," Venture 18, no. 2 (February 1966): 4-5; Economist, 17 December 1966, p. 1222. The most favorable poll, in mid-November 1965, reported 22% support for the use of force in compliance with a mandatory UN resolution.

134. *Observer*, 3 October, 10 October, p. 10; 5
December, p. 10, 19 December 1965, p. 8; *Manchester
Guardian*, 3 December, p. 12, 10 December 1965,
p. 10; 13 March, p. 8, 15 March 1968, p. 10; *Times*,
14 March 1968, p. 11.

135. Wilson's own characterization of his personal
leadership style on Rhodesia seems curiously misperceived: "There are different styles of captaincy
and premiership. History was full of top-rank
centre-forwards relegated to the reserves for failing
to try a shot at goal for fear of missing. I would
not mind the accusation of failure if my shots went
wide; rather that than be condemned for being afraid
to try" (*Labor Government*, p. 566).

136. David Owen, currently British Foreign Secretary, has written that, "sadly it has to be admitted
that the opportunity existed, following the return
of a Labour government in March 1966 with a large
majority, to enforce a genuine solution . . . ."
(*Politics of Defence*, p. 116).

137. Loney, *Rhodesia*, pp. 19, 146, 157-58.

5
Disengagement and Integration, 1964-1974: A Transaction Analysis

Few countries have undergone as deliberate and dramatic a reorientation in their external relations as Zambia during her first decade of independence. This chapter attempts (1) to assess the scope of Zambia's disengagement from the Southern African system and her integration with East Africa, (2) to compare the extent of change in different functional issue areas,and (3) to distinguish between behavioral patterns at the governmental and societal levels. The justification for focusing on this aspect of Zambian policy is that the search for an alternative to the inherited dependence on Southern Africa has constituted a central and continuing policy thrust. Almost everything else — relations with the rest of the continent and with countries overseas — has reflected the pervasive impact of this central national preoccupation.

Historically, Zambia formed an integral part of the Southern African regional system, principally because of the contribution of her copper to the region's wealth and her own landlocked condition. South Africa constituted the core of this constellation, economically, socially and to some extent politically, although Zambia's closest direct ties were with Rhodesia. Typically, Zambia interacted with South Africa only indirectly through Salisbury — known disdainfully as Bamba Zonke or "Grab All". To adopt a commercial analogy, Zambia was merely a local office of a Rhodesian branch plant of a South African parent company. Zambia also had long standing contacts with Angola and especially Mozambique, particularly in the field of transportation. This vast area embracing South Africa (and Namibia), Rhodesia and the Portuguese colonies — all subject to minority rule throughout Zambia's first decade — collectively comprise the Southern African subsystem for the purpose of this chapter.

The hardening of racial attitudes in the South coupled with the spread of African majority rule throughout Black Africa in the 1960s rendered the perpetuation in Zambia of any hegemonial relationship increasingly intolerable. A deeply-felt sense of economic grievance combined with a re-awakened ethnic pride reinforced the growing nationalist pressures for self-determination. Freedom from Britain and disengagement from Southern Africa, and especially Rhodesia, were seen as opposite sides of the same political coin. The initial phase of disengagement was political: the dissolution at the end of 1963 of the Federation of Rhodesia and Nyasaland, which, ironically, the British originally conceived of as a check on the infectious spread of apartheid ideas northward. This paved the way for Independence the following year and a shift in the focus of attention to the promotion of economic independence from the South. "We are embarking on very bold schemes," President Kaunda announced on the morrow of Independence, "which I hope very soon will lessen our dependence on Southern Rhodesia, South Africa, Angola and Mozambique."[1] Nevertheless, progress towards realizing that goal was comparatively modest during the new government's first crowded year in office. Rhodesia's Unilateral Declaration of Independence (UDI) in November 1965 transformed the situation dramatically. UDI supplied not only a powerful new political incentive to disengagement but also the economic compulsion. When Lusaka supported UN sanctions, Salisbury retaliated swiftly by cutting off completely the flow of oil to Zambia.

The corollary of the policy of disengagement was the political and economic reorientation of the country towards East Africa and especially Tanzania. In 1961, Zambia's United National Independence Party (UNIP) joined the Pan African Freedom Movement of East, Central and Southern Africa (PAFMECSA) and, the following year, Kenneth Kaunda became its chairman. Also, as early as 1962, UNIP called for a rail link with Tanzania.[2] "This railway is a political necessity," Kaunda declared. "Even after Rhodesia wins majority rule, there will be Mozambique and South Africa between ourselves and the sea."[3] Once independence had been achieved, Lusaka joined eagerly in UN Economic Commission for Africa efforts to promote economic integration within Eastern Africa. In April 1965, it sponsored an Interterritorial Conference on Trade Expansion between Zambia and East Africa and, in October 1965, hosted an ECA subregional Conference on Harmonization of Industry.[4] Yet, as with

disengagement, there were few concrete achievements
to record prior to UDI.

However, during the course of the next five
years, the Zambian economy underwent an unprecedented
structural transformation as the government struggled
to extricate itself from dependence on the South.[5]
Trade with Rhodesia in particular declined dramatically, as did reliance on Rhodesia Railways for copper exports. At the same time, important new links
were forged with Tanzania. Initially these were of
an emergency character but, with time, permanent new
infrastructures have emerged: an oil pipeline, a
modern highway and finally, in 1976, completion of
the railway. Moreover, in December 1967, Zambia formally applied for membership of the ill-fated East
African Community.[6]

The achievements of this period at the regional
level were all the more remarkable as they coincided
with the implementation of an impressive national
development program. In 1969 alone, the gross domestic product at factor cost recorded a phenomenal
23.2% increase.[7] Yet, within a year, the economic
outlook deteriorated drastically. A collapse of the
copper market sent world prices plunging from over
$1800 per tonne in April 1970 to under $1000 per
tonne nine months later.[8] Then, in September 1970,
a massive cave-in occurred at Mufilira, one of the
world's largest copper mines. The impact of these
twin calamities on export earnings and even more on
government revenues was devastating. Copper, which
in 1969 provided over half the country's net domestic
product, contributed less than one quarter in 1971.[9]
At the same time, a critical maize shortage following
the disastrous drought of 1970 compelled the country
to turn to foreign markets, including Rhodesia, for
massive supplies of its staple diet. With exports
declining and imports mounting, foreign exchange
reserves dwindled to one quarter of their value less
than two years earlier. In the circumstances, the
government had no alternative but to curtail imports
severely. At the same time, to ease dangerous in-
flationary pressures, it announced in February 1972
that henceforth importers would be encouraged to buy
from the cheapest source, which in many cases meant
South Africa.[10] For all these reasons, as well as
the intense frustration stemming from the continued
failure of the world community to deal effectively
with the Rhodesian rebellion, the momentum of disengagement slackened temporarily. Enthusiasm for
integration with East Africa also appeared on the
wane.

171

Negotiations with the East African Community opened in November 1968, but soon bogged down as Zambians came to appreciate the full implications of common market membership for an interior state with a high-cost economy. Active efforts to achieve even a limited form of associate membership ended early in 1971 following the Uganda coup, though this development was more a convenient pretext for suspending negotiations than an adequate explanation of Zambia's declining interest in Community participation. On the other hand, the strains which the emergence of Amin created within East Africa, as well as the growing realization in Lusaka that the primary concern was with improved communications rather than economic advantages, served to draw Tanzania and Zambia even closer together.[11]

In January 1973, relations with Southern Africa were again transformed with Rhodesia once more providing the catalyst compelling Zambia to turn her back on the South. Ian Smith's ill-considered action in suddenly closing the frontier along the Zambezi effectively cut off the flow of imports to Zambia from and through the whole of the southern part of the continent. At the same time, it provoked President Kaunda to respond with a ban on the export of copper through Rhodesia, and to refuse to resume trade across the border when Smith realized the magnitude of his miscalculation and sought rather clumsily to back down. From Rhodesia's point of view, the attempt at economic blackmail proved thoroughly counterproductive. Not only did the rebel regime lose in copper traffic a major source of foreign exchange, but it compelled Zambia to accept risks which until then she had not felt economically and politically able to run prior to the completion of the Tanzam railway. In the circumstances, the Zambian reaction to this formidable challenge was courageous — but predictable. No country could safely allow its lifeline to the sea to remain at the mercy of a malevolent neighbor if there was any conceivable alternative. As a result, the goal of total disengagement, at least with respect to Rhodesia, became a realistic possibility. The Lusaka-Dar es Salaam entente also reached new peaks of cordiality and mutual assistance. However, subsequent developments, notably the closure of the Benguela Railway in 1975 as a result of the Angolan civil war, a further and even more devastating collapse of the copper market following the record prices of 1974, and the continuing congestion in the port of Dar es Salaam aggravated by the closure of the Kenya-Tanzania border, have conspired to slacken

the pace in the final stages of disengagement and to
cast a slight shadow across the course of Zambian-
Tanzanian relations for the first time. This is a
theme to which we will return in subsequent chapters.
This chapter concentrates on the decade prior to the
collapse of Portuguese colonialism.

DISENGAGEMENT AND INTEGRATION

    Disengagement denotes a systematic reduction by
one actor in a system of the scope and intensity of
its positive interactions with other actors in that
system. Integration, on the other hand, can be defined as an intentional increase in the scope and
intensity of an actor's positive interactions with
other actors or with a system of actors.[12] Thus, the
two terms are essentially opposites. This is not to
suggest that the simultaneous pursuit by Zambia of
disengagement from Southern Africa and integration
with East Africa has been merely a matter of seeking
to replace one hegemonial relationship with another;
there is no intention of leaping from the frying pan
into the fire. Fortunately, there is little likeli-
hood of replicating the past as the two situations
are vastly different.
    To begin with, the element of dependence and
disparity is not as great. Every landlocked country
is to some extent at the mercy of transit states,
but the degree of Zambian dependence on East Africa
is bound to be far less and its scope more limited
than it was in relation to Southern Africa. The
latter exercised a predominant influence in the
spheres of investment and labor as well as trade and
communications. Similarly, the asymmetrical character
of the relationship is much less marked. By most
measures — population, GNP, trade, education, armed
forces etc. — Southern Africa commands five to fifty
times the resources and the corresponding benefits
available to Zambia, whereas the ratios of disparity
with East Africa range only from one to eight. The
relative imbalance is particularly striking when
Zambia is compared with South Africa and Tanzania
respectively. Clearly, East Africa lacks the capability, even if it had the inclination, to exploit
Zambia to the extent that Southern Africa has in the
past. There are now too many potential options
available to Zambia to allow history to repeat itself.
    Secondly, there is no ideological barrier to
cooperation with East Africa. On the contrary,

173

particularly in the case of Tanzania and Zambia, the personal philosophies and political programs of the leaders have been strikingly similar.[13] With respect to Southern Africa, on the other hand, racialism, colonialism and repression have rendered impossible any relationship based on equality and mutual respect.

A third distinction stems from the voluntary character of the partnership being forged with East Africa. Admittedly, following UDI, Zambia had only two alternative outlets to the sea through independent Africa: through Tanzania or through Zaire, and conditions in the latter were still too chaotic to offer a reliable lifeline. Nevertheless, Zambia eagerly seized on the necessity of appealing to Tanzania for assistance to foster a relationship it favored on other grounds. Clearly, the inducements to participation in the East African Community were predominantly non-coercive.[14] By way of contrast, Zambia's earlier "engagement" to the South was a colonial imposition. The Federation of Rhodesia and Nyasaland, in particular, arose out of a betrothal arranged between the parents and the groom over the fierce protests of the bartered bride.

This is not to suggest that the political and emotional incentives to integration have been anything like as powerful or sustained as the determination to disengage. Subordination to the South has been a searing experience that has left an indelible imprint on the Zambian consciousness, whereas the full implications of closer association with East Africa are still difficult to visualize. Moreover, nationalism reinforces the drive for disengagement, but inhibits enthusiasm for integration. This is the dilemma of the pan-Africanist that President Nyerere so clearly recognized when he warned that: "As each of us develops his own state, we raise more and more barriers between ourselves." He concluded that: "It is not impossible to achieve African unity through nationalism . . .[but] it is difficult."[15] Finally, the historical context in which the urge for integration with East Africa has emerged has ensured that Zambians view it at least as much as a means to the end of disengagement as an end in itself. On the other hand, disengagement is also in an important sense an instrumental value in that it constitutes a precondition for effective confrontation with the minority regimes south of the Zambezi. The Zambian government in general and President Kaunda in particular are firmly committed to political transformation in Southern Africa. Yet, to the extent that Zambia remains dependent on the White South, support for the liberation struggle is necessarily constrained.

The indicators employed to operationalize the concepts of disengagement and integration are principally transaction flows. The theoretical and practical problems inherent in this form of analysis are formidable. Apart from the complexities of the phenomena being measured, the empirical data available on developing African countries is frequently deficient, both quantitatively and qualitatively. Moreover, there is growing scepticism among scholars concerning the precise significance of transaction data.[16] To compensate for these liabilities, or at least to minimize them, a multi-indicator, multi-measurement, multi-dimensional approach has been adopted here. In the case of indicators, an effort has been made to tap as wide a range as possible in the hope that these might reveal some convergence, or at least that composite indices will prove less subject to error than single indicators. Inevitably, the principal focus is on trade, communications and migration but, where feasible, other measures including political transactions are utilized. As the approach is from the perspective of a single state, not a region, the comparative element in the data is provided synchronically (since Independence in 1964) rather than cross-sectionally.

Nye has argued persuasively in favor of disaggregating integration into its economic, social and political components, and others have emphasized the need to distinguish between societal and governmental actors.[17] These functional categories and levels of analysis are also relevant as dimensions of disengagement. Accordingly, they have been combined in the simple matrix in table 5.1. The essence of this study is to obtain appropriate indices for each of the boxes.

It is important to appreciate that, in the Zambian environment, "society" (conceived as the "attentive public") effectively excludes the bulk of the subsistence sector, comprising two-thirds of the population. The peasant masses are, for all practical purposes, outside the decision-influencing process on national issues and sufficiently independent of the money economy not to be greatly affected by, for example, increases in the cost of living resulting from disengagement. Moreover even the modern sector is far from homogeneous. In particular, recognition must be accorded to the realities of race even with a government dedicated to the ideal of nonracialism. Accordingly, allowance is made for the differential behavior patterns of Zambians and Europeans.

175

TABLE 5.1
Dimensions of Disengagement/Integration

Actor Level	Functional Dimensions		
	Political System	Society	Economy
Governmental	X	X	X
Societal:Zambian	———	X	X
Societal:Non-Zambian	———	X	X

INTERGOVERNMENTAL TRANSACTIONS

Common Services

The breakup of the Federation of Rhodesia and Nyasaland at the end of 1963 was preceded by prolonged negotiations on the nature and scope of the intergovernmental arrangements to replace it. In the past, Federal apologists had "tended to argue that where a low level of regional identity exists, the creation of strong central institutions is necessary to provide the framework for its growth."[18] When this failed to materialize, they retreated to a neofunctionalist position. The British in particular pressed for "effective new forms of collaboration between the territories" so that "the benefits of association might be preserved."[19] This aroused Zambian suspicions that, in Nye's words, "the neofunctionalists were federalists in functionalist clothing, pursuing federal ends through what appeared to be functionalist means." Or, more colorfully, neo-functionalism was "a strategy for attacking the castle of national sovereignty by stealth, with interest groups as mercenaries and technocrats as agents within the walls to open the gates quietly."[20] Ideally, Zambia would have preferred no formal ties with Rhodesia at all after Independence because of their potential harmful spillover effects on Zambia herself. Consequently, a Common Service Organization on the East African model (as proposed by the British) was out of the question. Even the revival of the purely consultative Central African Council which had served as a forum for functional cooperation from 1945 to 1953 was more than Zambian leaders were prepared to accept. At the same time, they were sufficiently realistic to acknowledge the need for some joint decision-making machinery to

176

maintain certain essential shared services, at least
during a transitional period. The Siamese twins
could not be surgically separated immediately. "You
cannot build a wall across Kariba like the Berlin
wall," Kaunda admitted. "We must have some tie-up
with Southern Rhodesia, whether we like it or not."[21]
    The British (and Rhodesian) negotiators consid-
ered that the "essential core" of any future association lay in "the shared economic arrangements, such
as the common market in goods and labor, and the
joint banking, credit, exchange and currency facilities." Yet, the most Lusaka would concede in the
financial sphere was "the possible need for interim
joint arrangements in such matters as currency."[22]
Accordingly, provision was made for the central Bank
of Rhodesia and Nyasaland to function for two years
beyond the end of the Federation.[23] In only four
fields — three commercial and one technical — was
Zambia prepared to contemplate continuing collaboration with Rhodesia, and then only on the basis of
strict equality of ownership and control and on the
understanding that the commercial enterprises would
be run as purely business operations. As a result,
joint statutory corporations were established for
Rhodesia Railways,[24] the Central African Power Corporation (Kariba),[25] Central African Airways (with
Zambia Airways as a jointly and wholly owned subsid-
iary),[26] and the Agricultural Research Council of
Central Africa.[27] The latter two were tripartite
bodies with Malawian participation. A number of
factors contributed to Zambia's willingness to compromise, among them respect for the expressed concern of the World Bank for protection of its rail and
power investments,[28] the realization that the headquarters and most of the shared assets and staff were
physically located in Rhodesia, and the opportunity
which membership offered of influencing political
developments in Rhodesia by promoting nonracialism
within the common services.[29] The decisive consideration, however, was political: anxiety not to prejudice or delay a breakup of the Federation in any
way. Acceptance of certain common services was a
price Zambia was prepared to pay to secure British
and Rhodesian agreement on defederation.
    Although dissolution of the common services was
always regarded as a possibility, it was nevertheless
confidently assumed even in Lusaka that the post-
Federal agreements would provide a mutually satisfactory basis for cooperation for the foreseeable future.
This did not prove to be the case (table 5.2). In
mid-1965, the Bank of Rhodesia and Nyasaland was

TABLE 5.2
Dissolution of Post-Federal Common Services

Common Service	Zambian Share	Zambian decision to withdraw	De facto dissolution	De jure dissolution
Bank of Rhodesia and Nyasaland	29.31%	28 June 1963	1 June 1965	30 June 1965
Agricultural Research Council	40.00%	30 March 1967	30 September 1967	30 September 1967
Rhodesia Railways	50.00%	8 November 1965	30 June 1967	——
Central African Airways	45.00%	30 August 1967	31 December 1967	——
Central African Power Corporation	50.00%	——	——	——

formally wound up, six months ahead of schedule. More significantly, as early as April 1965, the Rhodesian government proposed the breakup of the unified railway system, and Zambia agreed in principle three days before UDI.[30] But it was principally that rebellion which destroyed the basis for continued cooperation across the Zambezi. Even the comparatively innocuous Agricultural Research Council succumbed to the inexorable pressures in Zambia to disengage. The only common service to survive in recognizable form was the Central African Power Corporation, in part because of the physical difficulty of splitting the Kariba dam. Yet, even its long term future remained in some doubt. Until 1974, Zambia was still absolutely dependent for power on the jointly owned Kariba South generating station in Rhodesia. With the commissioning of the Kafue power stations (in 1972 and 1977) and the Kariba North installations (in 1976), Zambians are at last more than self-sufficient in electricity. The new Lusaka control center will also free Zambia from dependence on the Sherwood station in Rhodesia. Thus, the fate of the last constitutional legacy of the Federation awaits the outcome of current political developments in Rhodesia.

The major common services dissolved were the railways and the airways. Both ceased joint operations in 1967, though in neither case has a final agreement been achieved on the division of the assets and liabilities among the national successor organizations. Eventual dissolution of Central African Airways was perhaps predictable, in view of the prestige attached to national airlines. Nevertheless, the economic significance of Rhodesia Railways was much greater, and controversy concerning its operation correspondingly more intense. This accords with Nye's Law of Inverse Salience: "the more important the task by nature or impact, the weaker the authority of the organization will be."[31]

One measure of the extent of Zambian disengagement from intergovernmental cooperation with Rhodesia is the decline in the number of meetings of joint decision-making organs. The agreements establishing the common services typically provided for a policy-making Higher Authority (except in the case of the Agricultural Research Council) at ministerial level and a board of management composed essentially of civil servants.

Of the higher authorities, only that for civil air transport can be said to have functioned at all, and even it never met. Instead when higher authority

179

approval proved indispensable, business was transacted by circulating a resolution for signature — a form of conference by correspondence. Agreement on some practical arrangement was particularly important in the case of the Higher Authority for Civil Air Transport as it exercised "the powers of the Government of any Territory" in the matter of international air traffic rights. This contributed the only element of supranational political authority in any of the common service agreements, though it, too, was subject to the rule of unanimity.[32] The other committees of ministers were, at Zambian insistence, deliberately given minimal powers to ensure their meetings would be infrequent. In actual fact, only the Higher Authority for Railways ever met, and then only once — on 8 November 1965 on the eve of UDI, only to adjourn without issuing any policy directive.[33] Since UDI, no meeting of any higher authority has been held. As one Zambian minister explained, he "could not by virtue of the policies of this government sit on the Higher Authority for Civil Air Transport with the so-called rebel ministers."[34] In the case of the railway system, Zambia repeatedly urged the British Government "to appoint lawful members to the Higher Authority to act on behalf of Rhodesia" as had been done for the Reserve Bank of Rhodesia but, according to President Kaunda, "our requests were answered by a mixture of lies and evasion."[35] On one occasion shortly after UDI, the Railways Authority reverted to the practice of circular resolutions. However, on 25 February 1966, Zambia advised the Railways Board that this procedure was no longer acceptable.[36] This action finally ended any prospect of the Higher Authority for Railways ever functioning. In any case, with the de facto division of the railways (and the airways) the following year, the need for ministerial bodies in these fields lapsed. Only the Higher Authority for Power (HAP) maintains a tenuous and somewhat curious existence. In 1970, under pressure from Lusaka which was anxious to secure legal authorization to proceed with Kariba North, the British government abandoned its previous uncooperative attitude and agreed to appoint two members acceptable to the Zambian government to the HAP "in place of the ministers of the government of Southern Rhodesia."[37] Since then, the reconstituted HAP has adopted at least five resolutions, all by correspondence.

Although the Zambian government attempted to extend its ban on direct dealings with "ministers" of the illegal Salisbury regime to include relations between officials, this did not prove practicable. Contact continued at three levels: at policy conferences concerned with the future of the common services, at regular meetings of boards of management, and in periodic consultations at the operational level.

In July 1966, Lusaka approached London (rather than Salisbury) concerning the dissolution of the unitary railway system but, as in the case of membership of the Higher Authority for the Railways, the response was "a mixture of deceit and weakness, coupled with platitudes allied to evasion." Eventually, in November, President Kaunda presented the British with an ultimatum: either they agreed within seven days to negotiate the breakup or "we may be obliged to negotiate directly with the rebel regime in Rhodesia, unpalatable as that would be."[38] Needless to say, London merely protested its helplessness. Accordingly, talks between Zambian and Rhodesian officials commenced the following month. The agreement that finally emerged took the form of virtually identical letters, dated 22 May 1967, from the delegation heads to their respective governments.[39] Subsequently, similar discussions took place on the dissolution of Central African Airways.

Following UDI, the boards of the various common service organizations also continued to meet (table 5.3). Only with the breakup of three of them in 1967 did the frequency of meetings decline significantly. Nevertheless, Zambian qualms about acquiescing in anything that might imply recognition of the rebels necessitated resort to a variety of procedural devices. In the case of the Railways Board, the legal requirement of Higher Authority approval for deficit budgeting and capital expenditures was simply ignored. In letters to the two governments on 11 May 1966, the Board argued boldly that, despite the Higher Authority's persistent failure to function, the Board was still bound to carry out its statutory obligations — "making decisions where compelled to do so without Higher Authority approval."[40] The Central African Power Corporation (CAPC), on the other hand, adopted the subterfuge of a "Committee" composed of members of the Corporation to circumvent the awkward legal vacuum created by the expiration on 20 December 1965 of the appointments of the Rhodesian members. On one occasion in 1966, the Zambian members did overlook the illegality of the Rhodesian appointments and participated in a formal Corporation meeting.[41] Similarly, in November 1969, Lusaka acquiesced in a complete change in the Rhodesian

181

TABLE 5.3
Meetings of Boards of Common Services, 1964-74

					CAPC			Index 1964
Year	BRN	ARC	CAA	RR	Corp	Cee	Total	= 100
1964	10	3	11	16	11	—	51	100
1965	5	2	12	17	14	—	50	98
1966	—	3	10	14	1	9	37	73
1967	—	1	10	8	0	12	31	61
1968	—	—	—	3	0	8	11	22
1969	—	—	—	3	0	11	14	27
1970	—	—	—	4	1	12	17	33
1971	—	—	—	4	0	10	14	27
1972	—	—	—	3	0	11	14	27
1973	—	—	—	3	1	12	16	31
1974	—	—	—	3	1	12	16	31
Total	15	9	43	78	29	97	271	

BRN: Bank of Rhodesia and Nyasaland Board
ARC: Agricultural Research Council
CAA: Central African Airways Board (figures not pre-
      cise)
RR: Rhodesia Railways Board of Management
CAPC: Central African Power Corporation:
       Corporation (Corp) and Committee (Cee)

membership of the Railways Board,[42] no doubt because,
following the breakup of the Rhodesia Railways, the
amount of residual business to transact was minimal
though not unimportant. Nevertheless, these devi-
ations from political purity were exceptional. More
significant was Zambia's insistence in 1970 that the
Higher Authority for Power be reconstituted to provide a quorum of legal CAPC members.[43]
        Another indicator of the extent of Zambia's
institutional disengagement from Rhodesia is the size
of the common service bureaucracies as measured by
their administrative budgets and staffs (table 5.4).
After an initial buildup during the early years of
the organizations, a sharp decline in their human and
financial resources set in, particularly following
the breakup of the railways and airways in 1967. The
shrinkage is even more marked when compared to the
spectacular growth of the size of and expenditure on
the Zambian bureaucracy, or when allowance is made
for devaluation and inflation.

TABLE 5.4
Zambia-Rhodesia Common Services Bureaucracies,
1964-74

Year	Senior Administrative Staff	Administrative Expenditure* (US$)	Mean Index 1964=100
1964	529	8,310,000	100
1967	594	10,955,000	122
1968	31	872,000	8
1969	31	641,000	7
1974	31	1,088,000	9

*Year ended June 30. The increase after 1969 is principally a reflection of inflation. The Zambian Kwacha is converted in this and subsequent tables at the rate of K1=US$1.40, despite the devaluation of the dollar in 1972.

Sources: Annual reports of common services organizations.

At the time of Independence, there were no institutional links at governmental level between Zambia and East Africa. Various schemes had been proposed in the past, but consideration of these ended with the commitment of Northern Rhodesia to the Federation of Rhodesia and Nyasaland. UDI and the search for alternative routes, however, led to the emergence of a number of common services with East Africa and especially Tanzania. These have been of two types: public corporations and private limited liability companies (table 5.5). In addition, several intergovernmental standing committees exist at ministerial or official level to deal with common problems such as security and shipping.

The scale of operation of the three Zambia-Tanzania common services has expanded greatly in terms of numbers of employees and the value of their fixed assets, and has approached in size the three joint Zambia-Rhodesia organizations at their peak (table 5.6). As was the case with Rhodesia, the railway is by far the largest of the enterprises shared with Tanzania. Integration with the East African Community as a whole was less impressive. The relatively low level of linkage achieved prior to its demise contrasted sharply with the rhetoric of

TABLE 5.5
Zambia-East Africa Common Service Organizations

Common Service	Date Established	Head-quarters	Zambian Participation US$	%	Other Partners	Corporate Structure
Zambia Tanzania Road Services Ltd.	12 May 1966	Lusaka	980,000 (1966) 1,470,000 (1968)	35	Tanzania 2 Italian firms	Private company
Eastern Africa National Shipping Line Ltd.	28 June 1966	Dar es Salaam	280,000	17	Kenya Tanzania Uganda Southern Line	Private company
Tazara Pipelines Ltd.	8 Dec. 1966	Ndola/Dar es Salaam	467,000	67	Tanzania	Private company
Tanzania Zambia Railway Authority (TAZARA	3 Oct. 1968 (reconstituted Nov. 1972)	Dar es Salaam		50	Tanzania	Public corporation

TABLE 5.6
Scale of Operations of Zambian Common Services with
Rhodesia/Tanzania, 1964-74

	Employees		Fixed Assets (US$m)	
	Zambia-	Zambia-	Zambia-	Zambia-
Year	Rhodesia	Tanzania	Rhodesia	Tanzania
1964	30,424	———	439	———
1966	31,104	950	456	7
1968	654	2,300	205	60
1970	666	10,500	100	70
1972	708	43,000	228	200
1974	644	30,000	254	380

Sources: Annual Reports of Zambia-Rhodesia common
services, and of INDECO; Kasuka S. Mutukwa, Politics
of the Tanzania-Zambia Railproject (Washington:
University Press of America, 1977). Figures for
Zambia-Tanzania common services must be regarded as
only approximate.

government spokesmen. Although Lusaka continued to
profess an interest in eventual full membership of
the Community, no real progress was made towards even
the more limited objective of joining some of the
East African common services. In November 1968, Zambian negotiators indicated an interest in the Harbors
Corporation, the Posts and Telecommunications Corporation, the Research and Social Council and possibly
East African Airways — but not East African Railways.[44] Zambian interest in the East African Harbors
Corporation is obvious. This had been demonstrated
as early as 1967 when the government provided a grant
of $1,400,000 and a loan of $4,800,000 towards the
cost of development of the port facilities of Dar es
Salaam and Mtwara.[45]

Political Transactions

Interstate agreements, diplomatic exchanges and
heads of state contact provide further measures of
Zambian interaction at the government level with
Southern Africa and East Africa. During the final
months of the Federation and with the full concurrence

TABLE 5.7
Zambian Agreements with Southern Africa and East
Africa, 1964, 1969 and 1974

Year	Southern Africa	Rhodesia	Tanzania	East Africa
1964	10	11	4	4
1969	11	6	16	16
1974	20	5	17	17

of Zambian leaders, Northern Rhodesia concluded a
number of agreements with southern neighbors, notably
those with Rhodesia establishing common services.
However, the great majority of the international obligations Zambia inherited at Independence were originally incurred by the Federal or British governments.
Lusaka undertook to honor all of these (without being
quite certain what they were) pending a review to
assess their implications. As a result, half the
agreements with Southern Africa have since been abrogated — and only two new ones negotiated, in June
1968[46] and July 1971. Both of these involved undertakings by Portugal to cease "retaliatory" action
against Zambia in return for assurances concerning
guerrillas allegedly harbored on Zambian territory.

Of the ten agreements that are no longer in force,
two dealt with trade relations (with South Africa
and Portugal); Zambia has no trade agreement with
Rhodesia as, under the Federation, the two countries
formed a customs union and later, when Salisbury offered an agreement, Lusaka spurned it. Four agreements were in the communications field; these concerned
the railways and airways (and are in practice, if not
legally, inoperative), and membership of the (Southern) African Postal Union and the (Southern) African
Telecommunications Union.[47] In 1970, Zambia withdrew
from a third international organization, the International Red Locust Control Service in Mbala, following
the creation of a new body which excluded the Southern
African minority regimes from membership. Finally,
Zambia terminated the various arrangements with Rhodesia, South Africa and Portugal governing extradition and fugitive offenders.[48]

The pattern of treaty relations with East Africa
has been very different (table 5.7). At the time of
Independence, few agreements existed, but since then
their number increased steadily until the early 1970s.

A majority, reflecting Zambia's continual search for alternative routes, have dealt with communications. Most have also taken the form of bilateral arrangements with Tanzania, though several, mainly dealing with security matters, have been concluded with the East African states collectively. Curiously, there appear to have been no purely bilateral agreements with either Kenya or Uganda.

Apart from treaty relations, the scope for intergovernmental disengagement from South Africa and Portugal was much more limited than in the case of Rhodesia as there had never been the same degree of political integration. Until 1963, the jurisdiction of the South African Accredited Diplomatic Representative in Salisbury embraced Zambia, but this lapsed with the dissolution of the Federation. Shortly afterwards, in January 1964, Dr. Kaunda offered to exchange ambassadors with Pretoria provided the Zambian envoy was assured equality of treatment with other diplomats in South Africa.[49] This condition was evidently unacceptable as the initiative was ignored.

The only official Zambian representation in South Africa was the Government Labour Office opened in Johannesburg before the Second World War to deal with contract labor on the mines. In late 1965, following the South African decision to require all foreign Africans to carry passports, a Senior Passport Officer, with consular responsibilities limited to the issuing of travel documents to expatriate Zambians, was attached to the Johannesburg Office.[50] The Zambia Labour Department Representative (also a European) resident in Salisbury since 1938 assumed similar functions after UDI. Both offices were closed in 1968 (table 5.8).

With the end of the Federation, the Portuguese consul in Ndola was withdrawn. However, Lisbon continued to press Lusaka to exchange ambassadors, or at least accept a consular representative; Zambia consistently refused as long as Portugal clung to her colonies. The only regular forum for consultation with the Portuguese at an intergovernmental level was the monthly meeting of the Beira Port Traffic Advisory Committee composed of port users (including Rhodesian governmental and railway representatives). However, its deliberations were normally confined to technical issues. The so-called Mixed Luso-Zambian Commission which the Portuguese at one time claimed existed consisted simply of a series of four ad hoc meetings in 1968 and 1969 to investigate violations of Zambia's borders.[51]

187

The absence of direct diplomatic relations did
not entirely preclude high-level contact between
Lusaka and Pretoria or Lisbon (though not until late
1974 with Salisbury).[52] Yet, contact has at best been
sporadic and hardly qualifies as the "beneficial communication" spanning "a period of several years" that
Alker and Puchala consider the test of significant
transaction flows.[53] On the contrary, these encounters have been more comparable to the peaking of diplomatic exchanges during a disintegrating relationship prior to the outbreak of war. Between April and
August 1968, President Kaunda and Prime Minister Vorster engaged in a fairly extensive exchange of correspondence exploring Southern African issues, especially Rhodesia. Moreover, on five occasions between June 1968 and March 1971, the Zambian President
received South African emissaries, who appeared primarily interested in securing his consent to a meeting
with Vorster; the missions were uniformly unsuccessful.[54] Similar intermittent contact was maintained
with Lisbon. Dr. Kaunda corresponded on occasion
with successive Portuguese prime ministers and, in
March 1971, his Special Assistant on Foreign Affairs
visited Lisbon. The overthrow of the Portuguese dic-
tatorship in April 1974 produced a brief period of
intense interaction between Lisbon and Lusaka, culminating in 1975 in Kaunda's state visit to Portugal
and an exchange of diplomatic missions. In the case
of Mozambique in particular, Kaunda was highly instrumental in promoting a smooth and speedy transition to Independence.[55]

TABLE 5.8
Number of Official Representatives: Zambia and
Southern Africa/East Africa, 1964-1974

Year	Zambia-South Africa	Zambia-Rhodesia	Zambia-Tanzania	Zambia-Kenya
1964	1	1	0	0
1968	1	1	9	3
1969	0	0	9	3
1974	0	0	12	12

Sources: Diplomatic Lists and Government Directories

TABLE 5.9
Zambian-East African Heads of State Meetings, 1964-74

Year	Kaunda-Nyerere	Kaunda-Kenyatta	Kaunda-Obote/Amin	Eastern Africa Summits	Total*
1964-67	29	12	17	9	58
1968-71	23	7	10	3	40
1972-74	19	0	2	0	21
Total	71	19	29	12	119

*Summit meetings excluded to avoid duplication

Diplomatic linkages between Zambia and East Africa have evolved only gradually (table 5.8). Missions were first exchanged with Tanzania and then with Kenya, though in each case Zambia acted several years before the East African states reciprocated. No resident high commissioners have yet been exchanged with Uganda and even Zambia's non-resident representation established in 1966 lapsed following the Amin coup of 1971. One reason for the comparatively slow pace of development of official relations is paradoxically the very closeness of high-level political relations. These have been regarded as too important and too intimate to be entrusted to diplomats. The East African states have not yet opened missions in each other's capitals. Of greater significance, therefore, as indicators of political integration may be the summit meetings of the heads of state (table 5.9). Two trends are apparent here: President Kaunda has had much closer direct contact with President Nyerere than with the other East African leaders, and the frequency of personal encounters has tapered off since the peak year of 1967. The explanation of this decline is to be found in the passing of the immediate crisis engendered by the Rhodesian rebellion, growing preoccupation with domestic affairs, particularly since 1971, improved telecommunications and greater reliance on diplomatic channels. After the mid-1970s many presidential meetings were part of the broader, multilateral entente amongst the five Front Line States.

ECONOMIC TRANSACTIONS

The long and sorry history of Zambia's absorp-
tion into the Southern African economic empire in
general and the Rhodesian economy in particular
underlines the significance of economic indicators as
a measure of disengagement from the South. Two of
these have special relevance: trade (imports and exports) and energy (electricity, coal and oil).

Statistics on financial transactions might also
prove revealing if more data were available. A
qualitative assessment, however, suggests that considerable progress has already been made in reducing
Zambia's financial ties with Southern Africa. On
26 May 1965, national foreign exchange controls
were instituted in place of the federal regulatory
machinery which had continued to function for nearly
a year and a half following the dissolution of the
Federation. Also, overseas companies were urged to
establish "truly Zambian offshoots" in place of mere
order offices of their Southern African regional subsidiaries. The Government was especially anxious
that foreign businesses in Zambia should dissociate
themselves administratively from Rhodesia.[56] As a
result, most multinational corporations transferred
supervisory responsibility for their Zambian branches
to Nairobi or London. Finally, there was the series
of economic reforms announced between April 1968 and
November 1970. These led to agreements on 51% government participation in a large number of companies
ranging from the giant mining corporations to comparatively small-scale concerns. Admittedly, this
action was not directed specifically at foreign control emanating from any particular quarter. Nevertheless, the predominance of Southern African investments in Zambia ensured that the greatest impact
would fall on them. Zambianization of the economy
has been primarily at the expense of Rhodesian and
South African financial interests.

Trade

Table 5.10 demonstrates both the nature and the
extent of previous Zambian trade dependence on the
South, particularly with respect to imports, and also
the degree of disengagement so far achieved. Although at Independence Southern Africa provided a
market for only 12% of Zambian exports (mainly copper), nearly sixty percent of imports originated
there, with Rhodesia directly or indirectly providing
over three-fifths of this amount. (Imports of

190

TABLE 5.10
Zambian Trade with Southern Africa (by value, excluding electricity)

Year	Rhodesia		South Africa		Southern Africa		
	% imports	% exports	% imports	% exports	% imports	% exports	Index*
1964	36.1	4.1	21.9	7.8	58.2	12.0	100
1966	15.9	1.0	24.7	5.7	40.7	6.8	68
1968	2.4	0.2	24.5	2.1	27.4	2.4	44
1970	1.4	0.1	18.2	1.2	20.3	1.4	28
1972	1.4	0.2	15.0	2.0	16.7	2.3	32
1974	0.0	0.0	7.6	0.4	7.8	0.5	12

*1964 percentage of total trade = 100

Source: Annual Statements of External Trade

191

Rhodesian electrical energy have been excluded from all trade calculations as the Kariba generators, while physically located on the south bank of the Zambezi, are jointly owned with Zambia.)

During the first decade of Independence and especially since 1966, trade with the South was reduced by two-thirds in money terms and by nearly 90% in relation to total Zambian trade. If national income is used as a control, the dimensions of the decline are even more dramatically revealed. Aggregate indicators for Southern Africa as a whole, however, obscure some significant variations in the separate patterns of trade with individual countries. Even before the closure of the border in 1973, trade with Rhodesia, in terms of both imports and exports, had dwindled to the point that it was almost insignificant.[57] During 1971-72, a slight recovery occurred when, faced with a disastrous drought, Zambia was compelled to purchase substantial quantities of Rhodesian maize but this represented no more than a temporary setback. In any case, since January 1973, direct trade (except for Zairien transit traffic) has ceased.

The trade pattern with South Africa is more complex, particularly with respect to imports. During the Federal period, South Africa lost out relatively to Rhodesia which was able to exploit the tariff advantages of a customs union to expand greatly her markets in Zambia. Consequently, the proportion of imports from Rhodesia increased two-and-a-half times, while the proportion from South Africa fell by a quarter. The South African share continued to decline during the first year after Independence, though not as rapidly as Rhodesia's. However, following UDI, South African sales to Zambia recovered as Zambia shifted a portion of her purchases away from Rhodesia to South Africa. In practice, this often meant merely dealing with the Johannesburg head office instead of the Salisbury branch. In money terms, imports more than doubled between 1964 and 1967. Nevertheless, the extent of this reallocation of purchases within Southern Africa should not be exaggerated; the percentage of South African imports increased only modestly. In fact, as indicated in table 5.11, South Africa reaped only a fifth of the windfall from UDI.

The temporary relaxation of restrictions on trade with South Africa instituted in 1971 and formally acknowledged in February 1972 following the collapse of world copper prices, revived hopes in South Africa of a restoration of its profitable market

TABLE 5.11
Diversion of Zambian Imports from Rhodesia, 1965-67

| Years | Decrease in Rhodesia's % share of Zambian imports | Diversion of Zambian purchases to: | |
		South Africa	Elsewhere
1965-1966	15.3	4.2	11.1
1966-1967	9.3	0.0	9.3
1965-1967	24.6	4.2	20.4

Source: Annual Statements of External Trade

in Zambia. The results were disappointing to Pretoria,
and prospects were further seriously impaired the
following year when Rhodesia precipitately closed her
northern border. Despite a resort to circuitous routes,
initially through Angola and Malawi and then through
Botswana, the re-opening of Dar es Salaam to South
African goods designated as essential, and the improvisation of an airlift, the additional transport costs
incurred probably more than cancel out South Africa's
previous natural advantage of proximity. In any
case, the South African share of the Zambian market
has continued to decline steadily, and by 1974, was
only one-third of what it was ten years earlier.[58]
     The Portuguese colonies were never significant
Zambian trading partners. Annual trade never reached
the $3 million mark. Nevertheless, trade is now three
or four times what it was in 1964 and may grow further if suggestions about cooperation across Central
Africa, especially with Mozambique, materialize.
     Much oratory and considerable energy has been
expanded in promoting trade between Zambia and East
Africa. The inspiration behind this drive has come
from a combination of ideology and economic necessity:
it is conceived as both a practical expression of
pan-Africanism and a partial solution to the search
for alternative markets and sources of supply.
     The obstacles to closer economic collaboration
with East Africa — in ascending order of potency —
have been fiscal, physical, informational and structural. As early as February 1964, Zambia lowered her
tariffs on certain Kenyan and Zanzibari commodities.[59]

On the other hand, East Africa lost the competitive
advantage it had enjoyed under Commonwealth preferences when, in pursuance of her policy of nonalignment, Zambia introduced a single column customs
tariff at the beginning of 1966.[60] Nevertheless, the
Zambian tariff level is, for historical reasons, ap-
proximately half that prevailing in East Africa.[61]
Another positive manifestation of Lusaka's intentions
was the decision in September 1967 to admit goods of
East African origin under Open General Licenses. Unfortunately, for administrative reasons, this concession had to be revoked fourteen months later.[62]

Meanwhile, some of the communication problems
inhibiting expansion of interregional trade were
being overcome. Although Central African Road Services had pioneered a scheduled freight service to
Nairobi since 1957, as late as 1963 traffic on the
Great North Road to Dar es Salaam averaged only eight
lorries per week.[63] Yet, within a few months of UDI,
a fleet of over a thousand giant vehicles was plying
the route regularly. Under this punishment, the
route soon disintegrated into the "Hell Run" but, as
a result of a major reconstruction operation, a
modern hardtopped highway capable of withstanding the
massive tonnages using it now links Zambia with Dar
es Salaam.

Inaccessibility also bred ignorance of the potential for mutual exploitation of markets in Zambia
and East Africa. The initiative in exploring these
opportunities came from Lusaka. In 1964, the government mounted an exhibition at the Nairobi Agricultural Show.[64] The following year, it convened a
conference in Lusaka on interregional trade and despatched a trade mission to East African capitals.
Also, trade commissioners were appointed to Dar es
Salaam in 1967 and to Nairobi in 1970. In return,
beginning in 1965 a succession of Kenyan and Tanzanian trade missions descended on Zambia. (Uganda continues to evince little real interest in commercial
relations with Zambia or, for that matter, with Tanzania.) Although no formal trade agreements emerged
from these visits, imports from East Africa doubled
in 1966 and again in 1967 (table 5.12). As a result,
a substantial trade deficit developed with Kenya and
Tanzania. One reason for this was that, after UDI,
Zambia's most pressing need was for alternative
sources of supply, not new markets. It is not surprising, therefore, that the Zambian Industrial and
Commercial Association (ZINCOM) delegation that
toured East Africa in 1968 was more concerned with
imports than exports. In any case, the government

TABLE 5.12
Zambian Trade with Kenya and Tanzania, 1964-74 (in million $US, excluding oil)

Year	Kenya		Tanzania		East Africa	
	Imports	Exports	Imports	Exports	Imports	Exports
1964	$ 0.4	$ 0.6	$ 0.6	$ 0.4	$ 1.0	$ 1.1
1966	1.7	0.9	1.2	0.6	2.9	1.7
1968	5.4	0.7	2.4	0.3	7.9	1.1
1970	10.9	0.8	4.7	1.3	15.9	2.4
1972	10.4	1.3	3.0	1.1	13.4	2.7
1974	16.6	4.3	4.9	10.3	21.5	14.7

Source: Annual Statements of External Trade

TABLE 5.13
Trade Disengagement from Southern Africa and Integration with East Africa, 1964-74 (by value excluding "Rhodesian" electricity and "East African" oil)

Year	Southern Africa (US$m)		East Africa (US$m)	
	Total trade	% world trade	Total trade	% world trade
1964	177	26.1	2	0.3
1966	182	17.8	5	0.3
1968	137	11.4	9	0.8
1970	106	7.3	18	1.3
1972	110	8.4	16	1.2
1974	62	3.1	36	1.8

Sources: Annual Statements of External Trade

was eager to encourage businessmen in Zambia to break their traditional ties with Southern Africa. Gradually, under pressure, the structural orientation of the Zambian economy began to veer eastward, with Kenyan entrepreneurs doing markedly better than Tanzanians in exploiting the market opportunities opened up in Zambia, at least until the close of the Kenya-Tanzania border in 1977.

Nevertheless, the extent of economic integration achieved with East Africa must be kept in perspective. While the 17-fold increase in trade over the decade is impressive, the level of trade with East Africa as a whole is still only a fraction of Zambia's residual trade with Southern Africa (table 5.13). While Zambian trade with Southern Africa dwindled to thirty-five percent of its 1964 level, trade with East Africa was in 1974 only twenty percent of the level of Southern African trade a decade earlier. Expressed differently, by 1969 the East African Community had managed to fill less than nine percent of the market vacuum created by Zambia's policy of squeezing out imports from the South; since then, the East African share has actually declined, despite the pressures generated by the Rhodesian border closure. Success in diverting her exports eastward was originally even more modest (table 5.14). The big increase in 1974 has not been sustained partly because it can largely

TABLE 5.14
Diversion of Zambian Trade from Southern Africa
to East Africa, 1964-74 (by value)

	% Imports Diverted*			% Exports Diverted*		
Years	From Southern Africa	To East Africa	% Diverted to EA	From Southern Africa	To East Africa	% Diverted to EA
1964-69	-31.7	+2.8	+8.7	-10.8	+0.1	+ 0.7
1969-74	-18.7	-0.2	-1.1	- 0.6	+0.8	+13.7
1964-74	-50.4	+2.6	+5.1	-11.4	+0.9	+ 8.0

*As % of total imports/exports, excluding
   "Rhodesian" electricity and "East African" oil
Sources: Annual Statements of External Trade

TABLE 5.15
Stages in Zambian Disengagement from Rhodesian
Sources of Energy

Date	Oil	Coal	Electricity
Dec. 1965	Rhodesian oil embargo; UK-US-Canadian airlift (till October 1966)		
June 1966		Nkandabwe mine in production	
Sept.1966	Tazama pipeline from Dar es Salaam opened		
Nov. 1970		Maamba coal washing plants opened	
Oct. 1971		Wankie coal imports end	Kafue Stage 1
Aug. 1976			Kariba North Bank Stage 1

be explained by maize exports to meet a temporary
drought in Tanzania and also because of the closure
of the Kenya-Tanzania border. It seems unlikely that
East Africa can ever hope to provide an adequate alternative to Southern Africa as a trading partner.
Certainly to date, Europe not Africa has been the
principal beneficiary of disengagement (table 5.14).

Energy

At Independence, Zambia was dependent on Rhodesia for all her major sources of industrial energy.
The Kariba hydro-electric generating station, though
jointly owned, was situated on the south bank of the
Zambezi and outside Zambia's physical control; the
high grade coal and coke essential to the refining of
copper and lead came from Wankie; and oil for the
railways, road transport and the mines flowed through
the Beira-Umtali pipeline to the Feruka refinery.[65]
The rebellion in Rhodesia directly threatened
each of these pillars of the Zambian economy. With
the mining of the approaches to Kariba (and the refusal of the British to respond effectively), the
Salisbury regime acquired the capability of closing
down the Copperbelt with impunity at any time it
wished merely by pulling a switch — though for its
own reasons it chose not to do so. In the case of
coal, Ian Smith on 17 December 1965 suddenly boosted
the royalty a hundredfold from 14 cents to $14.00 a
ton and introduced a new export tax on coke of over
$22.00 a ton. Although he was forced to climb down
two weeks later when President Kaunda called his
bluff, the oil embargo instituted at the same time,
allegedly in retaliation against British sanctions,
continued.
The resulting oil drought was the most critical
energy problem confronting the Zambian Government.
The situation was compounded by the fact that the
international oil companies had conspired with the
Smith regime prior to UDI to reduce Zambian petrol
stocks to a minimum contrary to a 1962 agreement.[66]
Consequently, by 13 January 1966, gasoline supplies
in the country amounted to less than three days' consumption.[67] Nevertheless, the oil crisis proved the
easiest and quickest to resolve (table 5.15). As an
immediate palliative, an Anglo-American-Canadian airlift was mounted to ferry in oil from Kinshasa, Nairobi
and Dar es Salaam.[68] By the time it wound up in
October 1966, considerable progress had been made in
introducing alternative surface routes. Moreover,
strict rationing (over a period of thirty-three months)

198

ensured that available supplies were allocated to the most essential services. Finally, in September 1968, the oil pipeline, constructed from Dar es Salaam to Ndola in record time, was opened. Thus, within three years of UDI, Zambia had succeeded in completely overcoming the effects of the Rhodesian ban on transit traffic in oil.

The search for satisfactory alternative supplies of metallurgical coal proved more difficult. It was also a matter of increasing urgency as successive railway crises interfered with normal Wankie traffic. So serious did the shortage become that in October 1966 the mines were forced to cut back production by one quarter for a period of seven months. To meet the immediate situation, small quantities of coal were imported at great expense through Lobito from South Africa and West Germany, but the final answer lay in discovering a dependable domestic source. Exploration began even before UDI and in anticipation of it, but it was mid-1966 before the first mine was in production. Even so, output was disappointing, costs were high and the quality was low. Gradually, however, the numerous difficulties were surmounted. In addition, mine demands were reduced by partially converting to heavy fuel oil. As a result, imports dwindled from a massive 1.2 million tonnes in 1965, to less than 50,000 tonnes in 1971, before being eliminated entirely.[69] On the other hand, dependence on Wankie coke continued; here, there was no immediately-available alternative domestic source. As a result, the financial and logistic problems of securing supplies from elsewhere (principally West Germany at nine times the cost) constituted one of the most serious consequences for Zambia of the closure of the Rhodesian border in January 1973.[70]

While oil imports through Rhodesia were cut off almost overnight as a result of UDI, and Wankie coal imports declined to zero over a period of eight years, imports of "Rhodesian" electrical power — the major energy resource at the time of Independence — increased sharply until 1972 (table 5.16). Only with the expansion of the capacity of the Victoria Falls power station in 1969 and especially the completion of Kafue Stage One in 1971 has the trend been reversed. In fact, by 1974, Zambia had ceased to be a hostage to Kariba South, and had become a net exporter of electricity — before power from Kariba North came on stream in 1976.

East Africa has not offered an alternative source of supply for either electrical power or coal. Extensive deposits of coal exist in the Ruhuhu Valley within 100 miles of the Great North Road, but these

TABLE 5.16
Zambian Dependence on Rhodesia for Energy, 1964-74 (by quantity)

Year	Oil via Rhodesia		Wankie Coal		Kariba Electricity (net)	
	Million gallons	% total oil imports	1,000 tonnes	% total supply	million KWH (net)	% total consumption
1964	40.2	100.0	974.3	99.6	,831	67.1
1965	52.7	99.8	1,157.5	99.7	2,011	68.9
1966	0.6	1.2	878.4	85.7	2,076	69.6
1967	—	—	979.3	70.8	2,621	81.1
1969	—	—	668.0	61.9	2,868	78.9
1971	—	—	48.3	5.6	2,035	62.1
1973	—	—	0.6	0.1	1,732	33.6
1974	—	—	—	—	—	—

Sources: Annual Statements of External Trade; Monthly Digest of Statistics

will remain unexploited until branch lines from the Tanzam railway and a general industrial infrastructure in that region are completed. Tanzania did, however, replace Rhodesia quickly and completely as a supply route for Zambia's rapidly growing imports of oil.

A comparative analysis of the sources of Zambia's energy supplies highlights the extent and rapidity of the structural changes that have occurred since Independence (table 5.17). Reliance on Southern African energy sources, once virtually total except for electricity, has now ended in all fields. With respect to the country's primary energy requirements, complete disengagement from the South — once considered an impossible dream — is now a reality. Two developments have made this radical restructuring of the national energy position possible: import substitution (in the case of coal and electricity) and alternative routes (for oil). Whereas in 1964 domestic resources provided only one-quarter of Zambia's consumption of electric power and none of her other energy needs, a decade later she was 90% self-reliant in coal and coke, and could boast of surplus capacity in hydro-electricity. Moreover, the abandonment of thermal power generation has meant that electricity production is much more economical.

The one area of continuing concern is oil, though here the inherited dependence on Rhodesia has been shifted to Tanzania. As a result, East Africa has assumed crucial new importance in Zambia's national energy policy. In terms of her total requirements, reliance on Tanzanian routes has grown dramatically from zero at Independence to over 60% within a decade. In fact, with the skyrocketing costs of oil, Zambia in 1974 was, in value terms, more dependent on the East for her energy than she had ever been on the South.

COMMUNICATIONS

All countries aspire to assured, efficient and economical means of international communication but, for Zambia, this is a condition of national survival. It is not simply the fact of being landlocked geographically and hemmed in on three sides by hostile neighbors. Equally important is the heavy export-orientation of the country's economy. Zambia's economic and political viability as a state rests on her ability to deliver her copper to the markets of the world.

Transit Traffic

Zambia's traditional outlet to the sea had been the southern route through Rhodesia to Mozambique and South African ports. From the first, political

201

TABLE 5.17
Sources of Zambian Energy, 1964-74

Year	Source (% value)			Source (% quantity)		
	Southern Africa	East Africa	Domestic	East Africa (oil)	Domestic (coal/coke)	Domestic (electricity)
1964	46.1	–	50.0	–	–	25.1
1965	50.8	–	46.5	0.2	–	22.1
1966	39.7	8.7	44.4	59.8	10.8	19.9
1967	46.8	24.3	28.3	81.8	27.4	18.6
1969	50.1	26.6	22.1	99.9	35.2	18.9
1971	41.9	29.7	24.5	99.9	84.9	26.9
1973	16.7	40.9	40.7	99.9	94.0	65.9
1974	–	62.2	33.4	99.7	89.6	100.0

*Percentages of values of total energy supplies (oil, coal and coke, electricity).
Expressing energy in value terms, though necessary for comparative purposes, is
partially misleading because the excessive costs of thermally generating relatively
small amounts of electricity in Zambia during the early years, and the huge
increases in oil and coal prices in 1973 obscure the basic trends.

Sources: Annual Statements of External Trade; Monthly Digest of Statistics; Central
African Power Corporation Annual Reports.

and commercial interests conspired to ensure that
Zambia and especially the Copperbelt were tied in
tightly to the Southern African transport network.
Any outside challenge, even from the Lisbon-based
Benguela Railway, was fiercely resisted by a combination of subtle pressures and ingenious economic
inducements in the form of railway freight rate and
ocean shipping tariff penalties and concessions.[71]
     Whereas, with respect to trade with Southern
Africa, imports have always exceeded exports, in
terms of transit traffic, the opposite is the case.
In 1964, 41% of Zambia's imports and 87% of her exports transited Southern Africa. Moreover, the volume of the transit trade in monetary terms increased
steadily until 1969, reflecting the rapid expansion
of the Zambian economy. On the other hand, the proportion of total imports and of exports passing
through Southern Africa was by then below the levels
prevailing at the time of Independence. In practice,
it has been easier to divert exports, mainly copper,
to alternative routes than imports, principally because port facilities at Lobito and especially Dar
es Salaam were less versatile than at Beira.
     Aggregate data on regional transit traffic ob-
scures the fact that Lusaka considered the use of the
Zaire-Angola and Malawi-Mozambique routes less objectionable than the traditional outlet through Rhodesia. On the Zambian scale of political acceptability, the Rhodesian route ranked lowest and the
Tanzanian route highest, while the Portuguese east
and west coast ports fell somewhere in between.
Lobito and Beira were welcome short-term expedients
pending completion of the TAZARA railway and the
development of adequate port capacity in Dar es
Salaam.
     When transit traffic through Rhodesia is ex-
tracted from that of the Southern African region as
a whole (table 5.18), its crucial importance to Zambia is readily apparent. In 1964, 61% of imports and
95% of her exports used the southern route. Yet, by
1970, Rhodesia Railways was carrying considerably
less than half Zambia's trade. Thus disengagement
was fast becoming a reality well before the cutoff
in January 1973 finally ended reliance (apart from
some residual road traffic) on this historic artery.
     The corresponding increase in dependence on East
African ports is dramatic. Whereas, prior to UDI,
transit traffic through Tanzania was virtually non-
existent, by 1974, 40% of imports and nearly 50% of
exports travelled this route (table 5.18). Since

TABLE 5.18

Zambian Transit Traffic through and Trade with Rhodesia and Tanzania, 1964-74

Year	% Imports and Exports through:				% Trade through and with:			
	Rhodesia		Tanzania		Rhodesia		Tanzania	
	Imports	Exports	Imports	Exports	Imports	Exports	Imports	Exports
1964	60.7	95.0	0.0	0.0	96.8	99.1	0.3	0.1
1965	65.1	95.6	0.0	0.0	96.0	98.4	0.3	0.2
1966	60.3	69.4	1.2	10.0	76.0	70.4	1.5	10.1
1967	50.8	52.0	14.0	28.2	57.1	52.4	14.2	29.1
1968	54.7	41.4	16.9	34.6	57.1	41.6	17.4	34.7
1969	51.2	51.2	17.9	31.7	53.2	51.3	19.0	31.9
1970	42.9	43.3	23.2	35.5	44.3	43.4	24.3	35.6
1971	42.5	47.1	20.9	32.8	44.7	47.2	22.3	33.0
1972	45.4	50.1	20.7	27.3	46.8	50.3	21.2	27.5
1973	8.4*	5.4*	29.8	41.0	8.6	5.4	30.3	41.2
1974	0.7	0.0	39.1	46.0	0.7	0.0	39.8	46.8

*Despite the closure of the border in January, there was a substantial volume of transit traffic through Rhodesia reported for 1973 because the import data refers to goods cleared during the calendar year (especially coke imported in bond in 1972), and data on copper exports is recorded at the time of shipment from port. 72

Source: Annual Statements of External Trade

then, with the blocking of the Benguela Railway and the inauguration of TAZARA, Dar es Salaam's share of Zambia's transit traffic has increased to the point where Tanzania's near-monopoly is rivalling Rhodesia's pre-UDI stranglehold.

The radical reorientation of export routes for Zambian copper provides, in perhaps the most sensitive sphere of all, a further measure of the extent of disengagement from the South. Prior to UDI, all copper was exported through Rhodesia. Yet, by 1968, her share had been reduced to less than one-third of the total. Another third reached world markets through Angola, and the balance — the "largest third" — was trucked over the Great North Road to Dar es Salaam. When Lusaka attempted to increase Lobito's quota even further at the expense of Rhodesia, Salisbury reacted in November 1968 with a prohibitive 50% surcharge applicable whenever shipments of copper across the Victoria Falls Bridge fell below 25,000 tons per month (later 75,000 tons per quarter). As Zambia was not yet in a position to dispense with the southern route entirely, she was compelled to comply with Rhodesia's stiff demands. Hence, until 1973, nearly half of Zambia's copper continued to be exported through Rhodesia.

Border Traffic

The altered character of Zambia's external communication links is further illuminated by isolating indicators of Zambia's trade with and through Rhodesia and Tanzania, the two neighbors with whom she has the closest contact (table 5.18). In 1964, virtually all Zambia's external trade crossed the Zambezi border with Rhodesia, whereas six years later only half of it used this route and, since January 1973, effectively none. Trade across the Tanzanian border, on the other hand, developed from almost nothing to over 40% of the total. Expressed differently, the proportion of Zambian trade wholly outside white minority control has within the decade risen spectacularly from under 1% to nearly 50% and, with the independence of Angola and Mozambique, the percentage is now considerably higher.

The final abandonment of the southern route in January 1973 has merely accelerated and completed the process of disengagement from Rhodesia. Admittedly, Zambia has once again been compelled to bear a much higher economic cost to preserve her political freedom of action than if the path had been more

orderly. Nevertheless, the country was in a far
stronger position to meet this challenge than during
the precarious months following UDI. Whereas the
attempt to dispense with the use of Rhodesia Railways failed in 1966,[73] it succeeded in 1973. On
the other hand, part of the price of independence
from Rhodesia was much greater dependence on Angola.
   During the period of Portuguese rule, this was
politically distasteful; nevertheless, it represented
the lesser of two evils. What could not be predicted
was that in 1975 this route too would be closed.
This squeezed Zambia severely, especially prior to
the opening of the railway to Dar es Salaam the following year. It also put Zambia in the position
once again of being unduly dependent on the ability
and goodwill of one neighbor, however benevolent at
the moment, to service Zambian traffic safely,
speedily, and cheaply. As a result, there was some
unease in Lusaka that the country might be in danger of replicating its perilous pre-UDI position of
having all its transportation eggs in one uncertain
basket.

Air Communications

Air travel has long superceded rail and even road
transportation as the major means of communication
between Zambia and neighboring states, especially
for the expatriate and business communities. Moreover, politics appears to have had a less lasting
effect on the flow of traffic than might have been
expected. Certainly, there has been no complete
severance of all air connections, as once seemed
likely. In 1964, Zambia Airways flights to South
Africa were withdrawn and, following the breakup
of Central African Airways at the end of 1967, all
direct flights between Zambia and Rhodesia ceased.
However, more circuitous and expensive routes through
Malawi and Botswana and, until 1973, by bus between
Livingstone and Victoria Falls airports were quickly
devised, often serviced by larger and faster aircraft.
Also, an increasing number of private companies acquired their own planes or patronized air charter
firms. The government even offered UTA and Alitalia
fifth freedom privileges in 1967 to operate between
Lusaka and Johannesburg, partly to cater for children attending South African schools, and encouraged
Botswana to schedule convenient connections at Gaborone and Francistown for through passengers. Nevertheless, the frequency of flights across the Zambezi

TABLE 5.19
Scheduled Air Connections between Zambia and Southern
Africa/East Africa, 1964-74

Year	Rhod-esia	Tanz-ania	Southern Africa	East Africa
1964	49	2	52	8
1966	53	2	54	10
1968	26	10	30	26
1970	14	10	22	17
1972	25	9	31	25
1974	20	10	36	29

Source: ABC World Airways Guide

has been reduced substantially, especially in the
case of Rhodesia (table 5.19). Moreover, since
"Zambian" traffic through Malawi and Botswana is
only a fraction of the total, the degree of disengagement is greater than the data might suggest.
The significance of the volume of air traffic
between Zambia and East Africa is also difficult to
gauge as many passengers are merely in transit.
There has, however, been a quite dramatic increase
in the frequency of flights, particularly between
Lusaka and Nairobi, except for a period during 1966
and 1967 when Zambia Airways planes were banned from
East Africa (and Zaire) in accordance with an OAU
resolution.[74]   As a result, direct flights to East
Africa are now almost as numerous as the indirect
links with Southern Africa, and passenger capacity
is considerably greater (table 5.19).
In other aspects of air communications, disengagement from Rhodesia has been virtually complete.
This is particularly true of air traffic control
which previously had been centered in Salisbury.
Zambians, not unnaturally, found it intolerable that
the RAF Javelin squadron, invited in after UDI to
defend the country against a possible Rhodesian air
strike, should be subject to rebel operational control.
Even prior to this, the government had pressed for
its own Flight Information Centre in Lusaka and,
despite fierce resistance within ICAO, this was
achieved at the beginning of 1967.[75]

TABLE 5.20
Foreign Radio Listenership in Zambia, 1971

Radio Station	% of Zambian Population Listening to Foreign Broadcasts: "music only" listeners:	
	Included	Excluded
Southern Africa		
South Africa	8.3	5.4
Rhodesia	3.6	2.7
Mozambique	2.7	1.4
Angola	0.8	0.4
Independent Africa		
Zaire	15.3	4.5
Malawi	10.1	6.7
Tanzania	8.9	3.7
Total listenership*	24.2	

*Excludes duplication

Source: Graham Mytton, Listening, Looking and Learning: Report on a National Mass Media Audience in Zambia (1970-73) (Lusaka: Institute of African Studies, University of Zambia, 1974), pp. 93-96.

Information

Information flows represent another element in communications. Unfortunately little data is available on broadcasts across Zambia's borders, and none over time. What evidence does exist suggests that a quarter of the adult population, or half of all radio listeners, tune in to foreign stations. Radio Tanzania Dar es Salaam's overall popularity rating is slightly higher than that of Radio South Africa but, when those whose interest is confined to music are excluded, the rankings are reversed (table 5.20). Moreover, in border areas of the country where ZBS reception has been poor, reliance on Southern African sources for news and opinion has been heavy. With the introduction of the powerful new Chinese transmitters in April 1973, Zambia is in a much

stronger position to compete effectively with foreign broadcasts both inside the country and in neighboring states.

If flow of books, periodicals and newspapers is
easier to measure, their significance is more difficult to interpret. Nevertheless, it seems reasonable
to assume that the level of literature imports is
primarily an indicator of the extent of European
societal interaction at least with respect to Southern
Africa. The data suggests (table 5.21) a somewhat
erratic pattern, principally because during 1968 and
1969 the introduction of import route controls temporarily disrupted normal commercial channels. Since
then, Southern Africa has never succeeded in recap-
turing its previous share of the Zambian market which,
in 1964 amounted to nearly 20%. Rhodesia never recovered and has virtually ceased to serve as a source,
while in relative (though not absolute terms) South
African publishers retain only one-third of their
former market.

In the case of East Africa, no simple conclusions emerge from the confusing data available. In
the base year 1964, the value (though not the weight)
of imports actually exceeded that of imports of
Southern African origin. Moreover, the nationality
of consumers of East African literature in Zambia is
by no means clear. What can be said is that East
Africa and, above all, Kenya continues to corner a
substantial share of the Zambian market and that,
since Independence, the increase in the value (and
weight) of imports has been significant — even if
less dramatic than the drying up in the flow of print
from across the Zambezi.

PEOPLE

The flow of persons across boundaries is evidence of societal interaction, though not necessarily cooperation. Yet it represents more than this.
Data on population movements record not only the
cumulative effects of the decisions of individuals,
but also the influence of government policy expressed
in terms of visa requirements, taxation, restrictions on recruitment, currency regulations and tourist promotion. It is not always easy, therefore, to
decide precisely what migration measures. In the
case of Zambia, the analysis is further complicated
by the need to disaggregate flows in terms of race
and nationality.

TABLE 5.21

Source of Imported Books, Periodicals and Newspapers, 1964-74 (US $ thousand)

Year	Rhodesia		South Africa		Tanzania		Kenya	
	Value	%	Value	%	Value	%	Value	%
1964	$56.3	9.1	$62.5	10.1	$6.0	1.0	$158	25.4
1966	16.7	1.0	143.4	8.3	3.2	0.2	210	12.2
1968	2.4	0.2	12.4	1.2	44.2	4.3	105	10.3
1970	2.2	0.2	59.8	5.8	19.5	1.9	274	26.5
1972	1.8	0.1	79.7	4.8	3.4	0.2	194	11.8
1974	0.0	0.0	63.9	3.4	3.6	0.2	317	16.9

Source: Annual Statement of External Trade

TABLE 5.22
African Population of Zambia Born in Southern Africa
and East Africa

	Foreign-born Africans				
Place	1963 census		1969 census		
of					Index
Birth	no.	%	no.	%	1963=100
Southern Africa	130,430	57.2	99,675	39.9	76
Rhodesia	52,230	22.9	57,781	23.1	110
South Africa	600	0.3	5,002	2.0	834
Angola/					
Mozambique	77,600	34.0	36,892	14.8	48
East Africa			22,833	9.1	
Tanzania	12,990	5.7	22,423	9.0	173
Kenya			292	0.1	
Uganda			118	0.0	
Total Alien					
Africans	228,130	100.0	249,637	100.0	109

Sources: Census returns

African Migration

Alien Southern Africans[76] constitute a tiny and
declining proportion (2.5%) of the Zambian population. Nevertheless, except for the Angolans, they
have, at least in the past, played a more important
part in the economy of the country than their numbers
might suggest. A comparison between the 1963 and
1969 censuses (table 5.22) indicates that the size
of the foreign-born African community declined by
one-quarter during the intervening years. This is
more than accounted for by the reduction in the mi-
grant peasant population from neighboring Portuguese
territories. At the same time, a modest increase in
the number of Rhodesians was recorded along with the
emergence, for the first time, of a sizable South
African alien community, many of whom are more or
less refugees who fled northwards in the exodus of
the mid-1960s. This should not be interpreted as

TABLE 5.23
Estimates of Zambian Africans Resident in Southern
Africa, 1962-74

| Year (December) | Resident in: | | |
	Rhodesia	South Africa	Southern Africa
1962 (April-May)*	69,740		
1964	61,500	15,500	77,000
1969 (March)*	44,510		
1970	40,000	6,000	46,000
1974	33,000	5,000	38,000

*Rhodesian censuses; estimates from other years cal-
culated on bases of migration statistics.

Sources: Rhodesian census returns, 1962, 1969 and
Migration Reports for Rhodesia; G.M.E. Leistner,
"Foreign Bantu Workers in South Africa", South Afri-
can Journal of Economics 35 (1967): 47, 49; South-
ern African Data (Pretoria: Africa Institute, 1970),
"Labour", p.10.

evidence of any significant strengthening of societal
links with the South. On the contrary, quite apart
from the smallness of the numbers involved, the growing public demand for Zambianization of the jobs of
non-citizens indicates that alien Africans are under
increasing pressure. This is as true of Tanzanians,
the only significant East African community in Zambia,
and even the miniscule but highly visible group of
Kenyan traders as it is of Southern Africans. As
indicated in chapter 6, Zambia is now acting as host
to a growing number of refugees and exiles from the
continuing regional liberation struggle.
    More significant as a measure of Zambian socie-
tal sentiment towards Southern Africa is the decline
in the number of Zambians living south of the Zambezi.
During colonial days, Zambians regularly migrated
south in search of employment. No reliable figures
exist as to the magnitude of this movement, but the
evidence suggests that at the time of Independence
at least 75,000 Zambians resided in Southern Africa,
80% of them in Rhodesia (table 5.23). Since then,
these communities have dwindled to little more than

212

TABLE 5.24
Zambian Contract Labor in Southern Africa, 1963-1967

| | South Africa (WENELA) | | | Rhodesia | |
Year	Recruit-ment	Repatria-tion	Net	Farm Contracts	Total Recruits
1963	5,451			1,392	6,843
1964	5,438	4,158	-1,280	387	5,825
1965	5,991	4,546	-1,445	0	5,991
1966	4,572	5,481	+ 909	0	4,572
1967	0			0	0

Sources: Department of Labour Annual Reports; Department of Civil Aviation, Quarterly Statistical Returns.

half their former size, and even less in the case of South Africa.

Many of those lured south had been recruited on contract specifically to work in the South African gold mines or on Rhodesian farms. With the coming of Independence, the Zambian Government intervened to end what it considered an unacceptable form of indentured labor. Arrangements had already been made to terminate the Rhodesian labor draft in 1964, and, in September 1964, the recruitment agreement with the Witwatersrand Native Labour Association (WENELA), which had operated in the Western Province since 1938, was abruptly abrogated (table 5.24). However, the inability of the authorities to provide adequate alternative employment opportunities immediately produced a minor political backlash that contributed to the government's electoral setback in that province in 1968.[77]

This might seem to suggest that the attempt to sever societal ties with the South was not universally welcomed. Certainly, a fair proportion of those who ventured south on their own, particularly those who settled in Rhodesia, appear to have established roots there, and are unlikely to return until they retire.[78] Nevertheless, the incentive in the migratory labor system has always been more economic than social. In any case, the link was primarily of regional significance within Zambia. It is now of little importance and is becoming steadily less so.

TABLE 5.25
African Business Visitors to Zambia

Nationality	1966	1968	1974* no.	index
Southern African	2,717	1,301	489	18
South African	1,013	642	261	
Rhodesian	890	580	137	
Angolan/				
Mozambican	814	79	91	
East African		18,532	2,755	101
Tanzanian	926	15,916†	2,213	
Kenyan		2,510	445	
Ugandan		106	97	

* May include some non-Africans. For index, Southern Africa 1966=100.

†Appears to reflect truck traffic on Great North Road.

Source: Migration Statistics. Figures of 1966 are based on August-December data.

        A similar decline has occurred in the number of Zambians employed in Tanzania.[79] This has been particularly marked since 1964 following the abolition of contract recruitment of foreign labor and the widening of the disparity in living standards in the two countries. The recruitment of Zambians to work in Tanzania on the construction and operation of the Tanzam railway represents a temporary reversal of the trend but even here the numbers involved are far smaller than originally anticipated.
        Another dimension of interaction comprises private Zambian economic ties with neighboring states. In the past, little interest has been evinced in this, partly no doubt because of its supposed limited scope, but also because of the colonial legacy of generally underrating all African economic activity. As a result, the data that exists is quantitatively sparce and qualitively uneven (table 5.25). What statistics are available suggest that business contacts with Southern Africa have diminished greatly, while links

TABLE 5.26
European Population of Zambia, 1961 and 1969

Country	By Citizenship		By Place of Birth	
	1961	1969	1961	1969
South Africa	19,417	4,006	25,211	5,779
Rhodesia		434	5,856	1,352
Southern Africa		4,785	31,530	7,474
Zambia		4,343	16,127	7,274
East Africa		90	311	417
All	75,549	43,390	74,549	43,390

Sources: Census reports for 1961 and 1969

with East Africa have expanded steadily. At the same
time, a group of Zambian business executives associated with companies with South African connections
has emerged since the late 1960s who find it expedient to retain personal contact with their head offices in Johannesburg.

European Migration

The most dramatic change in the expatriate community in Zambia since Independence has been the reduction in both the numbers and the proportion of
white Southern Africans (table 5.26). Although the
total European population declined by 42% between
1961 and 1969 —from roughly 2% of the country's
population to 1% — the numbers of those born in South
Africa or Rhodesia fell 76%. This amounts to a major structural transformation in the composition of
the European sector. On the one hand, Rhodesian
railway workers and South African miners and commercial farmers trekked south and, on the other hand,
a small but significant number of Europeans were recruited overseas on contract to assist with the expansion of the public service, the secondary schools
and industry. The number of East African Europeans
in Zambia has remained infinitesimal.

Immigration statistics provide additional evidence of the altered pattern of European migration.
The heavy net outflow of whites mainly to the South

began in 1963 and in fact peaked before Independence. Nevertheless, during the next couple of years, substantial numbers of European immigrants continued to arrive from the South: 670 from Rhodesia and 1,060 from South Africa during Independence Year, 1964. Within five years, this flow had been reduced to a trickle. As with several other indicators, the fall off from Rhodesia came sooner and was more severe than for Southern Africa as a whole. One factor in this was government policy on the recruitment of skilled labor from the South. Although the Minister of Home Affairs insisted in 1967 that there was no discrimination against Rhodesians and South Africans in the issuance of visas and employment permits, and certainly there appear to have been no formal instructions issued to companies, "employers were advised to recruit elsewhere if possible."80 As a result, as early as 1965, the two mining companies ceased entirely to seek employees in Rhodesia and turned to South Africa only for highly specialized personnel.

As a consequence of these changes, the European community's close societal ties with the South were progressively attenuated. A larger proportion of the expatriate population felt a genuine, though in most cases only a short term commitment to the country.81 Moreover, by 1969, ten per cent of Europeans had acquired Zambian citizenship. Nevertheless, the level of personal contact remains high, as is quickly apparent whenever a threat arises to the seasonal mass movement of expatriate schoolchildren across the Zambezi. In the case of South Africa, a similar trend has occurred (table 5.27) with the fall off in the volume of holiday traffic being particularly striking. Yet, if account is taken of the dwindling size of the European population of Zambia, it is evident that the level of interaction on a per capita basis actually increased (until 1973) especially in the case of businessmen. Certainly, the southward flow of visitors is still many times greater than that heading eastward. Although visits to East Africa have more than doubled since Independence, their number has yet to reach 4,000 a year.

A final measure of migration trends is the flow of Southern African visitors to Zambia. Statistics here are not entirely reliable. Nevertheless, it is clear that a dramatic drop in numbers had occurred even before the border closure in 1973 (table 5.28). This appears to have been especially pronounced among Europeans. Once again, Rhodesia has led the way in terms of time and percentage reduction. Statistics on business visits by Southern African whites suggest

TABLE 5.27
Zambian Visitors to South Africa by Motivation,
1964-74

Year	Business	Holiday	Education	Total
1964	1,297	26,825	2,366	30,488
1966	1,847	28,021	4,219	34,087
1968	2,229	23,855	3,386	29,470
1970	2,445	16,905	2,543	21,893
1972	1,132	13,661	1,715	16,508
1974	1,367	6,367	1,157	8,891

Source: South African Tourist Corporation Annual
Reports

TABLE 5.28
Visitors to Zambia by Country of Last Permanent
Residence, 1964-74

Year	All Visitors	Rhode-sians	South Africans	East Africans
1964	92,099	35,093	14,622	3,400*
1966	108,469	15,000*	19,000*	4,200*
1968	96,696	11,512	5,237	30,723†
1970	48,970	8,988	3,388	8,841
1972	61,638	10,429	4,240	6,188
1974	44,265	1,031	981	5,936

*Estimates based on incomplete data

†Appears to reflect heavy truck traffic on Great
North Road

Sources: Migration Statistics

217

a remarkable 79% decline between 1966 and 1968, and a 85% decline in the case of Rhodesians.[82] However, this data is based on nationality, not residence, and fails to reflect the fact that many Rhodesian and South African businessmen are British, or dual citizens who, with the connivance of their governments, travel on British passports.

One category of visitors has presented Zambia with an acute dilemma. The Government has been anxious to exploit the country's unrivalled tourist potential much more fully than in the past in order to boost foreign exchange earnings, generate employment, and diversify the economy. Yet, it is confronted with the unwelcome fact that, for geographical reasons, the most obvious target group is the white community in Southern Africa. As late as 1966, as many as eighty percent of tourists visiting Victoria Falls came from the South,[83] and the prospects of increasing the flow were good. Nevertheless, Lusaka resisted the temptation and even took positive steps to discourage holiday visitors from the South. When, in November 1966, a system of tourist visas available at the port of entry was introduced, this facility was specifically denied to South Africans, Rhodesians and Portuguese tourists on political and security grounds.[84] As a result of these and other measures, the tourist trade was practically wiped out. In the first five years of independence, the total number of Southern African visitors to Zambia plummetted from 50,000 to 10,000 with the collapse of tourist traffic proportionately even more devastating. Livingstone, the tourist capital of the country and already suffering from the effects of UDI, was particularly hard hit, and 1973 dealt it a final blow; in 1974, only 270 residents of Southern Africa visited Zambia on holiday. Nevertheless, this was the price the government was prepared to pay to promote economic and social disengagement. In this connection, the increase in East African visitors has served as only a marginal compensating factor. Although numbers have almost doubled, they remain small, and in the case of tourists, almost negligible — totally only 359 in 1974.

CONCLUSIONS

Having surveyed the major indicators of Zambian disengagement from Southern Africa and integration with East Africa, it remains to assess their various dimensions in terms of the model previously postulated

218

(table 5.1). Inevitably, the process of selecting factors and constructing composite indicators based on simple unweighted arithmetical means is somewhat arbitrary and the resulting indices rather crude. Nevertheless, they are suggestive of trends, even if not precise measures of them. Wherever possible, comparisons are drawn between Southern Africa and East Africa. The conclusions are summarized in table 5.29.

Governmental Level

The evidence confirms the conventional wisdom that success in political and administrative disengagement from Rhodesia has been substantial and that progress towards integration with Tanzania has, in relative terms, been considerable. In fact, positive Zambian interactions with the Tanzanian political system are now broader and more intense than they were with Rhodesia during the early post-federal period. Available indicators on collaboration with the Southern African and East African regions as a whole reveal similar, if less pronounced trends. The momentum towards a closer and more institutionalized relationship with the East African Community has, however, ground to a halt, and summit meetings of Eastern African heads of state no longer take place (table 5.9).

In protest against racial practices south of the border, Lusaka has intervened effectively to minimize certain — mainly European — societal contacts across the Zambezi. In addition to terminating the recruitment of contract labor, it has banned sports activities, entertainment functions, and occasional films and publications. Moreover, stricter frontier formalities and restrictions on transportation services, especially with Rhodesia, have been introduced, though no general ban on travel, telecommunications or postal services has been imposed.[85] At the same time, there has been active official encouragement of strengthened social ties with East Africa. No reliable measure of the vitality of these links is available, but it is doubtful if they are yet as strong as past relationships with the South, except in the field of sport.[86]

In the economic sphere, firm government directives have transformed Zambia's traditional trade patterns and transportation routes. On the other hand, the crucial area of trade is paradoxically the one in which the least progress has been made in developing closer economic ties with East Africa. Moreover, by most measures, residual economic dependence

219

TABLE 5.29
Dimensions and Degrees of Disengagement from Southern
(1974 indices based on Southern Africa 1964=100)

	Functional Dimensions of Zambian Political System		
		S	E
GOVERNMENTAL	Common services*		
	meetings	31	–
	bureaucracies	9	?
	scale	30	93
	Agreements	50	85
	Representation†	0	57
	Summit meetings††	–	100
	Mean	24	84

SOCIETAL: Zambian

SOCIETAL: Non-Zambian

† Full mission complement assumed to be seven
†† Based on East Africa 1964=100

TABLE 5.29 (continued)
Africa and Integration with East Africa, 1964-1974

Interactions with Southern (S) and East (E) Africa

Society	S	E	Economy	S	E
Contract labor	0	0	Total trade	35	20
Sport	0	?	% total trade	12	7
			% energy	0	135
			% transit imports*	1	64
			% transit exports*	0	48
Mean	0	?	Mean	10	55
Alien African population**	76	18	African business visitors	18	101
Zambians abroad	49	?			
Immigrants	?	20			
Visitors	4	12			
% literature	?	89			
Mean	43	35	Mean	18	101
Air flights	69	56	Air flights	69	56
European population**	24	1	Business visitors	6	?
			Business visits (to SA)	105	–
Immigrants	12	?			
Visitors	4	12?			
Visits (to SA)	29	–			
% literature	18	?			
Sport	0	?			
Mean	22	23	Mean	60	56

*Indices are for Rhodesia/Tanzania
**Population censuses, 1961-1969

221

on the South remained until 1973 more significant
than the new links being forged with the East. However, the closure of the Rhodesian border and the
Lobito route as well a completion of the TAZARA railway have radically altered the relative importance
to Zambia of these two regions.

Societal Level

The principal indicators of societal interactions
between Zambians and Africans in Southern Africa and
East Africa are changes in the size of the respective foreign communities on either side of the borders
(tables 5.22-24). Although the resulting indices do
not inspire great confidence, they do suggest a considerable measure of social disengagement from the
South — though rather less in the case of Rhodesia —
and a corresponding increase in social integration
with East Africa and especially Tanzania. Nevertheless, on balance, relations at the African societal
level still appear to be closer with the South than
with the East.

Assessments of private Zambian economic ties
with neighboring countries are even more speculative.
The most that can be deduced from the sketchy data
available (table 5.25) is that contacts between
African businessmen are expanding with East Africa
and diminishing with Southern Africa, and that the
former are now much more extensive than the latter.

Indicators of social interaction between the
European community in Zambia and the South are more
readily available and more reliable. These suggest
that a remarkable degree of disengagement has already
been achieved, especially with respect to Rhodesia.
In fact, the weakening of links across the Zambezi
may have been proportionately greater among Europeans
than among Africans, though clearly the cohesiveness
of the former was far more marked at the time of Independence than in the case of the latter — and
probably still is. On the other hand, business contacts remain close, at least as far as visits to
Johannesburg are concerned. In relations with East
Africa, the expatriate factor is less relevant as a
measure of integration. Yet, to the extent that the
frequency of air flights is a gauge of European commercial involvement, it appears that, despite the
growing closeness, East Africa still ranks below
Southern Africa in importance. Moreover, Nairobi
rather than Dar es Salaam is the focal point of business interest in East Africa.

The transaction flow analysis developed in this chapter points to the following conclusions:

1. The Zambian Government's determined efforts to disengage from the South and especially from Rhodesia have been remarkably successful, even in the critical economic sphere — so much so that a final break with Rhodesia in January 1973 proved feasible.

2. East Africa and especially Tanzania have partially succeeded in appropriating Southern Africa's historical role as an outlet to the sea for Zambia. Reorientation towards East Africa is least apparent in the field of trade — which may help to explain Zambia's caution concerning membership of the East African Community. Political and administrative ties with Tanzania are now closer than with Rhodesia at the time of Independence.

3. Societal contacts are diminishing with Southern Africa and increasing with East Africa, though links with the former still appear in many spheres to be closer than with the latter, even for Zambian Africans.

4. The reduction in the scope and frequency of European interaction with the South is largely a function of the altered size and composition of the expatriate community in Zambia. Business contacts have suffered least.

5. In general, disengagement and integration have proceeded further at the governmental level than at the societal level, and in the political sphere as compared with the social and economic spheres.

6. Indices of Zambian interaction with Rhodesia are generally lower than with Southern Africa as a whole, and higher for Tanzania than for East Africa.

7. Disengagement from Southern Africa has achieved more progress than integration with East Africa, partly no doubt because nationalist pressures reinforce the former but not the latter.

8. The real turning point in the structural reorientation of Zambia's political, economic and social relations with her neighbors was UDI, not Independence.

223

NOTES

1. Press Conference, 25 October 1964. Zambia Information Services (ZIS) Background, no. 27/64, 18 November 1964, p. 2. See also, Central African Mail, 19 June 1964, p. 5.

2. UNIP Policy (Lusaka: UNIP, [1962]), pp. 9, 65. "One of the projects to receive priority will be the railway line from Kapiri Mposhi to Tanganyika." When UNIP Becomes Government (Lusaka: UNIP, 1963).

3. To Richard Hall 1963. Africa Digest, 15, no. 1 (February 1968): 6.

4. ZIS Press Release, no. 210/65, 11 February, no. 233/65, 16 February, no. 564/65, 12 April, and no. 1600, 6 October 1965.

5. Kenneth D. Kaunda, A Humanist in Africa: Letters to Colin M. Morris (London: Longmans, 1966), p. 127.

6. Frank C. Ballance, Zambia and the East African Community (Syracuse: Program of Eastern African Studies, Syracuse University, 1971), p. 1.

7. Economic Report 1971 (Lusaka: Ministry of Finance, 1972), p. 55.

8. Mindeco Limited, Annual Report 1971, p. 9.

9. Mindeco Mining Year Book of Zambia 1971 (Kitwe: Copper Industry Service Bureau, 1972), p. 24.

10. Times of Zambia, "Business Review", 11 February 1972, p. 8.

11. Ballance, Zambia and the East African Community, pp. 51-61; Times of Zambia, "Business Review", 25 June 1971, p. 8.

12. The conscious promotion of cooperation is a much broader definition of integration than many currently in use. Ernst Haas restricts the term to "The process whereby political actors in several distinct national settings are persuaded to shift their loyalties, expectations and political activities to a new center whose institutions possess or demand jurisdiction over the pre-existing national states." The Uniting of Europe: Political, Social

224

and Economic Forces, 1950-1957 (Stanford: Stanford
University Press, 1958), p. 16. Richard W. Chadwick's
formulation of integration as "The intensity of organized, cooperative activities of two or more nation-
state systems" is closer to that employed here. "A
Brief Critique of 'Transaction Data and Analysis:
In Search of Concepts' by Barry B. Hughes", International Organization 26, no. 4 (Autumn 1972): 681.

13. President Amin of Uganda represents a significant exception. His emergence provided a significant
brake on the momentum of integration in Eastern
Africa and contributed to the collapse of the Community.

15. Hayward Alker and Donald Puchala advance this
as a condition for community formation. "Trends in
Economic Partnership: The North Atlantic Area,
1928-1963", J. David Singer, ed., Quantitative Politics: Insights and Evidence (New York: Free Press,
1968), p. 289.

15. "The Dilemma of the Pan-Africanist", Zambian
Papers no. 2 (1967), pp. 4,5.

16. Barry B. Hughes, "Transaction Data and Analysis:
In Search of Concepts", International Organization,
26, no. 4 (Autumn 1972): 672-74.

17. J. S. Nye, Peace in Parts: Integration and
Conflict in Regional Organization (Boston: Little,
Brown, 1971), pp.26-27; Donald J. Puchala, "Integra-
tion and Disintegration in Franco-German Relations,
1954-1965", International Organization 24, no. 2
(Spring 1970): 184; Hughes, "Transaction Data and
Analysis", p. 679.

18. Nye, Peace in Parts, p. 44.

19. Southern Rhodesia, Prime Minister's Office,
Report of the Central African Conference Victoria
Fall Hotel, July 1963 (Salisbury: Government Printer,
1963), C.S.R. 30-1963, pp. 8-9; R. A. Butler, The
Art of the Possible: The Memoirs of Lord Butler
(London: Hamish, Hamilton, 1971), pp. 216-24.

20. Peace in Parts, pp. 51, 54.

21. ZIS Press Release no. 395/63, 5 April 1963, p.2.

22. Report of the Central African Conference, pp. 9-10.

225

23. Rhodesia and Nyasaland Federation, The Federation of Rhodesia and Nyasaland (Dissolution) Order in Council 1963, S.I. 1963/2085, 20 December 1963, sec. 70(1).

24. Ibid., sec. 71; "Agreement between the Government of Southern Rhodesia and the Government of Northern Rhodesia relating to the Rhodesia Railways", 10 December 1963, Northern Rhodesia Government Gazette, 53, no. 70, 11 December 1963.

25. Federation of Rhodesia and Nyasaland (Dissolution) Order in Council, sec. 36; "Agreement between the Government of Southern Rhodesia and the Government of Northern Rhodesia relating to the Central African Power Corporation", 25 November 1963; Northern Rhodesia Government Gazette 53, no. 63, 26 November 1963, pp. 725-29.

26. Federation of Rhodesia and Nyasaland (Dissolution) Order in Council, sec. 50; "Agreement between the Government of Southern Rhodesia and the Government of Northern Rhodesia relating to the Central African Airways Corporation", 4 December 1963, Northern Rhodesia Government Gazette 53, no. 67, 5 December 1963, pp. 797-803.

27. Federation of Rhodesia and Nyasaland (Dissolution) Order in Council, sec. 61. Zambia rejected proposals to retain common meteorological, statistical, film and tourist services.

28. UN Treaty Series, vol. 551, pp. 119-27; vol. 568, pp. 215-31.

29. Central African Mail (Ndola), 24 January 1964, p. 4; Zambia N.A. Deb. no. 2, 12 January 1965, c. 17.

30. ZIS Press Release no. 1404/66, 29 July 1966, p. 3; no. 2049/44, 14 November 1966, p. 1. President Kaunda claimed that the British Government had insisted in 1963 on joint operation of the Rhodesia Railways system, "despite the wish expressed by this country and Rhodesia that the railways should not be run on a unitary basis" (ibid., no. 2049/66, p. 1).

31. Peace in Parts, pp. 23-24.

32. Federation of Rhodesia and Nyasaland (Dissolution) Order in Council, sec. 48. Under the Federation of Rhodesia and Nyasaland (Dissolution) Order

in Council (Amendment) Act, 1967, Zambia revoked this power. The CAPC agreement also contained a potentially supranational element; if the Higher Authority for Power is "unable to render a decision or finding", it is obliged to submit the issue to binding arbitration. A similar procedure applies in the event of disagreement between the two governments ("Agreement ... relating to the Central African Power Corporation", Art. 20).

33. Rhodesia Railways, 17th Annual Report 1966, p.3. The Committee of Finance Ministers set up to administer the Bank of Rhodesia and Nyasaland also never met.

34. N.A. Deb., 14 July 1967, c. 148.

35. ZIS, Press Release, no. 2049/66, 16 November 1966, p.1.

36. Rhodesia Railway, 17th Annual Report 1966, p.2.

37. Southern Rhodesia (Higher Authority for Power) Order 1970 (London: HMSO, 1970), S.I. 1970/892, 12 June 1970 (six days before the Labour Government defeat), N.A. Deb.,no.23, 23 September 1970, cc. 35-36. The two "Rhodesian" members were Sir Evelyn Hone, last Governor of Northern Rhodesia, and James C. Morgan, a retired Foreign and Commonwealth Office official who had participated in the Federal dissolution exercise in 1963.

38. ZIS Press Release, no. 2049/66, 14 November 1966, p. 2.

39. Rhodesia Railways, 18th Annual Report, 1967, p. 6.

40. Ibid., p. 8.

41. Central African Power Corporation, Annual Report and Accounts, 1966, p. 2; 1967, p. 1.

42. Rhodesia Railways, 21st Annual Report, 1970, p. 5.

43. See note 37 supra. The CAPC was composed of three Zambian and three Rhodesian members plus a chairman and one other appointed by the HAP. The two appointees (who were reappointed in 1970) with the three Zambian representatives constituted a

legal quorum of five. The Corporation met in 1970, 1973, 1974, and 1976 (CAPC Annual Report and Accounts, 1971, p. i; 1973, p. 28; 1974, p. 32; 1976, p. 28.

44. Ballance, Zambia and the East African Community, pp. 31-38, 51-52. Lusaka and Dar es Salaam were determined to have the Tanzam railway administratively independent of both Zambia Railways and East African Railways. In the case of East African Airways, Zambia was anxious to ensure that airline facilities would not be concentrated in Nairobi to the same extent as Central African Airways facilities had been centralized in Salisbury.

45. ZIS Press Release, no. 88/68, 12 January 1968, p. 1.

46. UN Security Council, Verbatim Records (S/PV. 1486), 18 July 1969, pp. 2, 11; (S/PV. 1488), 23 July 1969, p. 4.

47. Withdrawal from the APU (and ATU) took effect on May 31, 1966, but the concessionary postal rates continued until September 1967. First Report of the Auditor-General on the Public Accounts for the financial year ended 31st December 1967 (Lusaka: Government Printer, 1968), p. 26.

48. N.A. Debates, no. 2, 20 January 1965, c. 394; no. 7, 21 September 1966, c. 2335; no. 13, 27 August 1968, c. 444; "The Fugitive Offenders (Southern Rhodesia) Order, 1966", Statutory Instrument No. 371 of 1966, 11 October 1966, Supplement to the Republic of Zambia Government Gazette, 17 October 1966.

49. Central African Mail, 24 January 1964, pp. 3-4. See chapter 7 for a fuller account of the rationale behind this initiative.

50. N.A. Deb. no. 7, 11 August 1966, c. 582; Ministry of Labour, Annual Report of the Department of Labour, 1968, p. 1.

51. UN Security Council, Verbatim Records (S/PV 1486), 19 July 1969, pp. 2, 9, 11, 12; (S/PV 1488), 23 July 1969, pp. 4-5.

52. Zambia ignored repeated Rhodesian requests for meetings at ministerial level (Ian Smith, Salisbury broadcast, 18 January 1973).

53. "Trends in Economic Partnership", pp. 288-89.

54. Dear Mr. Vorster ...: Details of exchanges between President Kaunda of Zambia and Prime Minister
Vorster of South Africa (Lusaka: Zambia Information
Services, 1971). For the resumption of contacts in
late 1974, see chapter 7.

55. The critical Portuguese-Frelimo negotiations
took place in Lusaka, 5-6 June and 5-7 September 1974.
On the earlier "Lusaka Programme" (12 September 1973)
drawn up by President Kaunda and Jorge Jardim, the
Mozambican businessman and Malawi consul in Beira,
see Jorge Jardim, Moçambique: Terra Queimada (Lisbon: Editorial Intervenção, 1976), pp. 77-135
and annexes.

56. ZIS Press Release no. 1529/65, 23 September 1965,
p. 2; no. 1971/65, 6 December 1965, p. 2; N.A. Deb.
no. 2, 19 January 1965, cc. 314-16.

57. Following the breakup of the Federal common market, imports of Rhodesian goods became subject to
Zambian tariffs. For the first six months, duties
were suspended, but this suspension was withdrawn
for most goods (except foodstuffs) on 27 June 1964
and for the remaining goods on 24 March 1965. However, to offset a rise in the cost of living, a general suspension of duty was introduced for a variety
of goods. Two days after UDI, Commonwealth preferences for Rhodesian goods were withdrawn and in December 1965, import controls were introduced. These
are now the major instruments for controlling Rhodesian trade. Report of the Controller of Customs
and Excise, 1964-65 (Lusaka: Government Printer,
1966), p. 2; 1965-66, p. 2.

58. Imports from South Africa dwindled further in
1975 to 6.8% of the total, but rose to 7.5% in 1976
(despite an absolute decline in the value of imports
from South Africa).

59. Northern Rhodesia, Leg. Ass. Deb. no. 1, c. 162,
11 March 1964.

50. Report of the Controller of Customs and Excise,
1965-66, p. 2.

61. Ballance, Zambia and the East African Community,
p. 104.

62.   Annual Report of the Ministry of Commerce, Industry and Foreign Trade, 1967 (Lusaka Government
Printer, 1968), pp. 5-6; ZIS Press Release no. 1952/
68, 31 Ocotber 1968, p. 1.

63.   Marion Bone, "Zambia's Relations with Tanzania",
mimeographed (Lusaka: University of Zambia, May
1968), p. 2.

64.   In addition, Zambia has exhibited in Dar es
Salaam each year since 1968.   The East African governments have also had stands at the Ndola Trade Fair:
Kenya since 1965, Tanzania since 1967 and Uganda,
1968-70.   Rhodesia was represented at Ndola in 1964,
and South Africa planned to participate but subsequently withdrew.

65.   The pipeline was opened in December 1964 and
the refinery in May 1965.

66.   Under clause 18 of the Construction and Refining
Agreement (16 February 1962) with the former Federal
government, five oil companies undertook "to maintain
in the Federation stocks of petroleum products at
normal commercial levels which are customarily sufficient to ensure against reasonably foreseeable
risks of interruption of supplies." Apparently, UDI
was delayed a month to allow gasoline stocks to be
built up from 24 days consumption (16 October) to
three months consumption (11 December). During the
same period, Zambian stocks of gasoline were deliberately run down from 1,525,000 gallons (23 days
supply) to 894,000 gallons (13 days) while stocks of
other fuel dropped from 610,000 gallons (11 days)
to 438,000 gallons (8 days). ("Background to Zambia's Case against the Oil Companies", mimeographed
[Lusaka: Ministry of Legal Affairs, 1977], pp. 14,
31; Peter Kellner, "Tiny's Oil War with Ian Smith",
Sunday Times, 12 June 1977, p. 63).

67.   ZIS Press Release no. 638/66, 15 April 1966, p.1.

68.   British airlift: Nairobi/   5,400,000 gallons
      Dar-Lusaka/Ndola (19 Decem-
      ber 1965 - 31 October 1966)

      Canadian airlift: Kinshasa-   1,100,000 gallons
      Lusaka/Ndola (27 December
      1965 - 30 April 1966)

<u>American airlift</u>: Kinshasa-   3,200,000 gallons
Lubumbashi (4 January - 30
April 1966)

69. Imports (18,000 tonnes) were resumed briefly in
1972.

70. The cost of German coke was $280 per tonne com-
pared with $31 for Wankie coke. Coke was needed for
the Ndola lime works (which decided to convert to
fuel oil) and the Kabwe lead mine (which commissioned
a fine-coke plant in 1977 to provide coke breizer
from local coal at $110 per tonne for its new Waeltz
kiln). Bank of Zambia, <u>Annual Report, 1974</u>, pp. 27,
44; George K. Simwinga, "The Copper-Mining Industry
of Zambia: A Case-Study of Nationalization and
Control", <u>Sage Yearbook in Politics and Public Pol-
icy</u>, 1 (1975): 89; <u>Africa Research Bulletin: Economic, Financial and Technical Series</u>, 1977, p. 4175.

71. Edwin T. Haefele and Eleanor B. Steinberg,
<u>Government Controls of Transport: An African Case</u>
(Washington: Brookings Institution, 1965), pp. 10-
23; Elliott, <u>Constraints on the Economic Development
of Zambia</u>, pp. 329-327.

72. <u>Annual Statement of External Trade</u>, 1973, p. G1.

73. R. L. Sklar, "Zambia's Response to UDI", <u>Mawazo</u>
1, no. 3 (June 1968): 20-25.

74. Council of Ministers, ECM/Res. 13 (VI), 5 December 1965; ZIS <u>Press Release</u> no. 157/66, 25 January
1966. Zambia Airways aircraft were registered in
Rhodesia.

75. <u>Report of the Fourth Africa-Indian Ocean Regional
Air Navigation Meeting, Rome, 23 November - 18 Decem-
ber 1964</u>. ICAO Document 8477, AFI/IV, pp. 8-2/3;
Supplement no. 1, p. 5.

76. In Zambian parlance, an alien is normally a non-
Zambian African, whereas an expatriate is a non-African, generally a European. Non-African Zambian
citizens are also sometimes loosely classified as expatriates.

77. Thomas Rasmussen, "Political Competition and
One-Party Dominance in Zambia", <u>Journal of Modern
African Studies</u>, 7, no. 3 (October 1969): 26-27.

78. The South African government has provided alternative and considerably lower estimates of the size of its Zambian population:

	1969	1970	1971	1972	1975	1976
Zambian residents	1463	1290	754	638		
Zambians registered at labor bureaus					903	766

South Africa House of Assembly Debates, "Questions and Replies", vol. 45, 14 June 1973, c. 1010; South Africa, 1976 (Pretoria: Government Printer, 1976) p. 466.

79. The number of Zambian males employed in Tanzania was as follows:

1962	3254
1963	2643
1964	2524

Tanzania, Annual Report of the Labour Division, 1964-1965 (Dar es Salaam: Government Printer, 1969), pp. 17, 51.

80. Zambia Mail, 25 May 1967, p. 4; Ministry of Home Affairs, Annual Report, 1965 (Lusaka: Government Printer, 1967), p. 17.

81. The Lusaka cell of the notorious Afrikaner Broederbond was reportedly disbanded in 1966. (Sunday Times of Zambia, 17 December 1972, p. 11).

82. Migration Statistics, 1966, 1968; 1966 statistics available only for August to December. In 1974, 47% of Rhodesian and 37% of South African visitors (by residence) came on business (ibid, 1974).

83. Zambian Information Services, Press Release no. 172/67, 9 February 1967, p. 1.

84. Ministry of Home Affairs, Immigration Department Annual Report, 1966, p. 2.

85. Mail bearing rebel stamps was for a time surcharged. Passenger train service across the Victoria Falls Bridge ended in September 1969, but the express bus service between Lusaka and Salisbury was greatly improved. Even when in December 1972 Rhodesian buses were banned from crossing into Zambia, steps were

taken by the government-controlled United Bus Company
of Zambia to provide connecting services at the border. These arrangements were overtaken by events.
Since January 1973, virtually no one has been allowed
to cross the border.

86. Bone, "Zambia's Relations with Tanzania", pp. 10-
11.

6
Zambia and Southern African Liberation Movements 1964-1974

Zambia is the most strategically positioned and dangerously exposed host state engaged in the liberation struggle in Southern Africa. Not only is she the only landlocked country fully committed to the cause, until 1974 she was surrounded on three sides by target regimes.[1] This gave her borders with Southern Africa that were far longer than those of any other state—more than 1600 miles in all. Moreover, she abutted four of the five major theaters of guerrilla activity: Tete province, the Zambezi valley, Caprivi and Eastern Angola; no other host state has been involved on more than one front. A further complicating factor is Zambia's unique copper wealth. While this has been a major source of strength, it has also meant that her vital lines of communication and industrial installations have provided inviting targets for retaliatory action by hostile neighbors.[2]

Although Southern Africa has constituted the central focus of Zambian foreign policy, direct support for liberation movements has formed only one element in a broader strategy. The key to this has been Zambia's determination to develop her economic, political and military capabilities as rapidly as possible in order to provide the requisite freedom of action for an effective role as a host state. Accordingly, there have been sustained efforts to disengage from the South, to strengthen and diversify the country's economic infrastructure, and to foster national unity, as in the 1973 enactment of a One-Party Participatory Democracy.

In addition to embarking upon a substantial internal restructuring of the country and experimenting with regional diplomacy (chapter 7), Zambia sought to mobilize international support for the confrontation with Southern Africa. Here, the attitude of the Western powers was seen as crucial. For this reason, a major effort was devoted to persuading and pressuring them, directly and through the UN and OAU as well as through nongovernmental channels, to intervene decisively in favor of justice in Southern Africa. However, as faith in the power of reason diminished, the complementary policy of supporting armed struggle came to assume enhanced importance. Nevertheless, it remained only one instrument, admittedly a vital one, in a coordinated Zambian strategy designed to effect a political transformation in Southern Africa. The individual liberation movements, and especially their leaders, were regarded as means to this end, and not ends in themselves. As Vice-President Simon Kapwepwe commented in 1968, guerrilla warfare is not "the only means of solving the Rhodesian problem."[3]

There were compelling reasons for Zambia's outspoken support for the liberation struggle in Southern Africa. Morally, the case for self-determination and racial equality was unanswerable. Ideologically, the Government was committed to the Nkrumah dictum that independence is "meaningless unless it is linked up with the total liberation of Africa."[4] An element of "kith and kin" sentiment was also present in the understandable concern expressed for the fate of "our brothers." A further motive for Zambia's policy was her concern to project a pan-African image; accordingly, she was keenly sensitive to any suggestion that she was not responding as positively as she might to OAU initiatives. However, there were even more fundamental explanations solidly rooted in Zambia's domestic and regional interests. The political transformation of Southern Africa was the ultimate answer to the country's dependence on the minority regimes to the South. Moreover, the perpetuation of racial conflict there threatened not only to inflame the whole subcontinent but to engulf Zambia as well. At stake were her economic prosperity, her fragile experiment in nonracialism, her political stability, her internal and external security, and perhaps even her independence. With respect to the latter, government spokesmen were outspoken in articulating their grave suspicions concerning the ultimate aims of South Africa's "outward looking" foreign policy.

At the same time, the liberation struggle in Southern Africa confronted the government and people of Zambia with a series of moral and political dilemmas concerning the means by which their commitment to "the total liberation of Africa"[5] should be translated into concrete measures of support. In

addition to initial doubts concerning the legitimacy
of a resort to violence and of Zambian government
involvement in it, there was uncertainty concerning
the extent to which a host state should concern itself in the domestic affairs of liberation movements.
Finally, the government had to face up to the implications for its internal and external security of
offering hospitality to freedom fighters.

Support for the liberation movements poses several difficulties for Zambia relating to both domestic and foreign policy. As indicated below, support
entails not only regulation and supervision of the
movements themselves, but also increased surveil-
lance of sensitive border and refugee settlements.
Moreover, because a host state is seen by external
enemies to be partisan in the struggle, its own security may be threatened; consequently, its own
defense preparations and budget inevitably increase.
Externally, association with the nationalist movements becomes a factor in relations with a range of
other states and coalitions outside Africa, with the
Second and Third Worlds tending to be supportive,
and First World critical of such assistance. Once
again, the potential difficulties for Zambia are
considerable as socialist states may disregard her
national interests in extending support to the freedom fighters, while some Western powers may wish to
include links with the liberation movements as one
issue when bargaining over aid or trade. In other
words, the price of principles has been—and continues to be—high, involving both internal and external costs and complications.

The delicate position of a host state deeply
committed to the cause of liberation is rarely fully
appreciated either by "microphone revolutionaries"
who can safely indulge in ringing calls for sacrifice from the security of their distant capitals,
or by the freedom fighters themselves who understandably press for open-ended undertakings of support and a complete free hand to pursue their goals.
How Zambia has sought to reconcile her revolutionary
idealism with the realities of her exposed position
on the front line of freedom in Africa is the theme
of this chapter.

LIBERATION SUPPORT

According to a Government spokesman, "Zambia's
policy since Independence has consistently remained
one of rendering every possible assistance to the

liberation movement in Southern Africa within the framework of the decisions of the OAU."[6] Yet, what did "rendering every possible assistance" mean in practice? The spectrum of options available to Zambian authorities to express their solidarity with Southern African liberation movements ranged from simple moral encouragement to overt military intervention. It is scarcely surprising that the employment of Zambian armed forces directly in a liberation role has never been seriously contemplated, except possibly in the form of aerial retaliation against Southern African capitals in the event of bombing attacks on Zambian towns.[7] Yet, at one time, even the granting of moral support posed a problem.

Acceptance of the legitimacy of armed struggle was a particularly painful personal decision for President Kenneth Kaunda. As a Gandhian pacifist by nature and conviction, he was long firmly committed to the resolution of conflict by nonviolent means. During Zambia's struggle for independence, he had consistently urged moderation upon his more militant followers, and had largely succeeded in confining their agitation to peaceful channels.[8] Moreover, initially he had even opposed the creation of a Zambian army, except for purely ceremonial purposes. As late as 1961, he had resisted the despatch of army cadets to Britain for training. Yet, under the ineluctable pressure of events in Southern Africa, the President gradually reconciled himself to the necessity of armed resistance to minority oppression.[9] In April 1964, he was offering ZAPU "every possible moral and material aid short of military aid"; and in December he declared before the United Nations: "I do not call for violence."[10] Even his insistent demands that the British over- throw the rebel regime in Rhodesia by force were attempts to pre-empt large-scale racial violence. The turning point in Dr. Kaunda's outlook came in late April 1966 following Prime Minister Wilson's announcement of the proposed "talks about talks" with Ian Smith, and the Sinoia massacre two days later when seven ZANU freedom fighters were killed by Rhodesian security forces.[11] Thereafter, all ambiguity in his attitude to the instrumental use of violence fell away, though he continued to regard it as a necessary evil. The authoritative Lusaka Mani- festo of 1969, with its appeal for negotiations but its acceptance of war as the only alternative, accu- rately reflected his thinking (see chapter 2).[12]

Yet it was one thing to approve of freedom fighting and quite another to sanction Zambian in- volvement in it. Decision makers in Lusaka have

237

TABLE 6.1
Southern African Liberation Movements in Zambia: 1964-1974

Liberation Movements (founding dates)	Formal Recognition by OAU	Formal Recognition by Zambia	Lusaka Office (status)*	Guerrilla Operations Initial Front	Guerrilla Operations Zambian Front
ZIMBABWE					
Zimbabwe African People's Union (ZAPU) (1961)	1964	1964-75	1963-75 H	Wankie 12 Aug 1967	Wankie 12 Aug 1967 30 Aug 1972
Zimbabwe African National Union (ZANU) (1963)	1964	—	1963-66 R 1966-75 H	Zambezi 29 Apr 1966	Zambezi 29 Apr 1966 Centenary 21 Dec 1972
Front for the Liberation of Zimbabwe (FROLIZI) (1971)	—	—	1971-75 H	Zambezi 17 Feb 1973	Zambezi 17 Feb 1973
African National Council (ANC) (1971)	Jan 1975	Dec 1974	1975-76 H†	northeast 1975	
SOUTH AFRICA					
African National Congress of South Africa (ANCSA) (1912)	1964	1965	1964- R		Zambezi 13 Aug 1967
Pan-Africanist Congress of South Africa (PAC) (1959)	1964	—	1964-68 R		Tete June 1968
Unity Movement of South Africa (UMSA) (1943)	—	—	1967- R		

238

TABLE 6.1 (continued)

NAMIBIA						
South West African People's Organization (SWAPO)(1959)	1964	1965	1965–	H	Caprivi 26 Aug 1966	Caprivi 26 Aug 1966
South West Africa National Union (SWANU)(1959)	1964–65	—	—			
ANGOLA						
Popular Movement for the Liberation of Angola (MPLA)(1956)	Nov 1964	1965	1965–68 R / 1968–74 H / 1974–76 R		Luanda 4 Feb 1961	Moxico 18 Mar 1966 / Luanda May 1968
National Liberation Front of Angola (FNLA)(1957)	Aug 1963	1975	1962–66 S / 1974–76 S		north 15 Mar 1961	
National Union for Total Liberation of Angola (UNITA)(1966)	Jan 1975	1975	1966–67 H / 1968–76 S		Moxico 1 Mar 1966	Moxico 1 Mar 1966
MOZAMBIQUE						
Mozambique Liberation Front (FRELIMO)(1962)	1964	1965	1964–75 R		Cabo Delgado 25 Sept 1964 / Tete 24 Oct 1965	Tete 8 Mar 1968 / Tete 24 Oct 1965
Mozambique Revolutionary Committee (COREMO)(1965)	—	—	1965–74 H		Tete 24 Oct 1965	

* H: headquarters   R: regional office   S: suboffice
† external headquarters

239

naturally been concerned to avoid providing the minority regimes with legal pretexts for engaging in hot pursuit or pre-emptive strikes. Accordingly, every effort has been made to minimize the extent of direct Zambian assistance.[13] This has had the paradoxical consequence of lending credence to contradictory accusations: first, that Zambia has not been as supportive of freedom movements as she might have been and, secondly, that she has been far more deeply implicated in "terrorism" than has actually been the case.

Recognition

A necessary preliminary to the provision of administrative or operational assistance to liberation movements is some measure of recognition (table 6.1). Initially, this was a Party function, but since Independence it has become the responsibility of Government. During the period under review, recognition has, in practice, taken three forms: official designation (as with ZAPU, FRELIMO, MPLA, ANCSA, SWAPO and later the ANC in Rhodesia), de facto acceptance (ZANU, FNLA and FROLIZI briefly, COREMO until 1974, and UMSA), and passive toleration (UNITA). The PAC of South Africa enjoyed second category status until August 1968, when it was banned and its leaders expelled.[14] The previous year, the entry permit of the UNITA leader had also been withdrawn. However, his party continued to maintain an unofficial, though on occasion highly visible, presence in Lusaka. Following the Portuguese coup, it was gradually restored to grace. Similarly, FNLA which had long been inactive in Zambia was once again accorded de facto recognition for a short period. On the other hand, SWANU lapsed permanently into oblivion and, with it, any status it may once have claimed.

Several criteria have governed decisions on recognition. Perhaps the most important has been OAU policy, which in turn was based on popular support, military activity and commitment to total liberation.[15] Zambia has followed the OAU lead in all cases except with respect to ZANU, FNLA and, since 1968, PAC. On the other hand, COREMO, the Unity Movement, FROLIZI and UNITA, none of which had, at least until the early 1970s, any official standing with the OAU Liberation Committee, have been accorded varying degrees of recognition. Where there were divided movements, the decisive consideration has been the Government's judgment as to which

faction commanded majority support at home. In the
case of Rhodesia, President Kaunda early asserted
that, "Africa must do as was done in Zambia and support the majority—and clearly ZAPU commands the
majority."[16] Quality of leadership, personal
friendships and demonstrated operational effectiveness, all of which might be thought to have favored
ZANU over ZAPU and, to a lesser extent, PAC over ANC
(though not FNLA over MPLA), proved less significant.
Dar es Salaam, on the other hand, assessed these
conflicting considerations differently and, hence,
backed ZANU rather than ZAPU, and welcomed the PAC
leaders deported from Zambia. This is one issue on
which Presidents Kaunda and Nyerere agreed to differ.
One incidental consequence of this was to make it
more difficult for them to wield a credible threat
jointly to withhold (or withdraw) recognition as a
means of imposing unity on warring liberation groups.
As one Zimbabwean nationalist concluded: "If Tanzania and Zambia . . . had both supported only one
party in the period 1964-71, it is almost certain
that the other party would have died a natural death
because of the lack of a secure sanctuary near
Rhodesia."[17]

Administrative and Financial Assistance

     Recognition, whether formal or de facto, en-
titled "foreign nationalist parties" to the administrative facilities of the African Liberation Center
established in 1965 on the outskirts of Lusaka, to
the use of Zambian travel documents, and to various
other minor material perquisites including the inclusion of the names of six leaders on the State
House protocol list. Six of the eight Southern
African liberation movements long recognized by the
OAU, as well as three splinter groups, have maintained offices in Zambia. Nearly half at one time
or another had their external headquarters in Lusaka.
The only significant party no longer located there
is the banned South African PAC.
     Apart from equipping and maintaining the Center
and making available certain other services in kind,
Zambia provides only limited and essentially ad hoc
financial assistance to liberation movements on a
bilateral basis. She prefers, on principle, to have
all administrative and operational support funnelled
through the OAU Liberation Committee's Special Fund
(and has urged other OAU members to do likewise).
In 1963, UNIP had been one of the Committee's earliest beneficiaries[18] and, since then, Zambia has been

among its most loyal contributors. Although her
assessment amounts to only a modest percentage of
the total budget, the record of most OAU members—
at least until recently—in supporting the liberation struggle with anything more than ringing rhetoric and resounding resolutions has been so deplor-
able that Zambia's contribution has in some years
constituted more than a quarter of the funds actually received. In 1969, she was one of only five
member states not in arrears in her payments.[19]

Radio Propaganda

One sphere in which a distinction has usually
existed between the privileges accorded movements
which were officially recognized and those which
were not, was external broadcasting. Prior to
Independence, Dr. Kaunda denied any intention of
allowing radio facilities to be used to broadcast
propaganda to Rhodesia.[20] UDI changed that. Within
a few days of the Declaration, and in advance of an
OAU request on the subject, ZAPU was granted the use
of Radio Zambia to mobilize its supporters across
the Zambezi. The principal purpose was to precipitate British military intervention in Rhodesia by
promoting a breakdown in law and order.[21]
The results were disappointing. Initially, the
programs were hastily produced, poorly conceived,
frequently crude, and generally of a low quality.
It was not simply that the language employed was inevitably pretty uncompromising. ZAPU leaders were
desperate men who had been publicly ridiculed and
accused of betrayal by President Kaunda (and others)
for being "stupid idiots" in doing nothing to resist
Smith.[22] The more frustrated they felt, the more
virulent their vernacular appeals became.
The broadcasts proved partially counterproductive. The response from the Zimbabwean masses,
while far from negligible, was less than the promised uprising. The Smith regime, however, reacted
strongly, skilfully exploiting nationalist excesses
to embarrass the British government to whom both
sides looked for salvation. In two widely distrib-
uted pamphlets entitled "Britain's Part in the
Incitement of Murder, Arson, Sabotage and Destruction in Rhodesia" and "Murder by Radio,"[23] the
Rhodesian rebels catalogued in extravagant terms the
sorry tale of alleged British complicity in the ZAPU
broadcasts. Although there was no substance to the
charges, Salisbury's formidable propaganda offensive
was undoubtedly damaging. Whether for this or other

reasons, in 1966, political broadcasts to Zimbabwe were curtailed. Thereafter, ZAPU broadcasters were confined to reading the news in Shona and Sindebele three times daily (until March 1971, when the announcer was restricted, along with other party leaders) and producing news commentaries on world affairs (until July 1972 when the person involved was ordered deported).[24]

The fading of the voice of Zimbabwe did not end political broadcasts to Southern Africa. In January 1971, MPLA instituted a daily 45-minute program, "Angola Combatente," which quickly acquired a wide audience. Then in May 1973, Zambia formally inaugurated its new External Service—"the war of words channel"—with the aid of powerful new Chinese transmitters. FRELIMO, ZAPU/ZANU, MPLA, ANC and SWAPO were each allocated an hour a day. As a result, Radio Zambia blanketed the subcontinent for more than forty hours a week in twenty-two languages, with the liberation movements accepting responsibility for almost all the content.[25] This constituted assistance on a massive scale, and undoubtedly had a significant impact on African opinion throughout Southern Africa.

Operational Facilities

The really delicate issue for Zambia is the provision of operational assistance to freedom fighters, as this could have serious implications for the country's internal and external security. Basically, the liberation movements have sought five concessions from host states: transit rights, transit camps, training camps, operational bases and finally rights of sanctuary. Granting freedom of transit was the easiest for the government to rationalize; there seemed nothing improper in permitting Southern Africans to return home, bearing their arms, to carry on the struggle inside their own countries. Certainly, there has been no attempt to deny that freedom fighters are crossing Zambia, with official approval, on their way south. "Zambia," one minister explained, "is doing no more than giving these people from abroad the right of way into the country they are fighting for."[26]

Yet, in practice, the problem proved more complicated than this. It was not always feasible to insist on uninterrupted passage of cadres through to the battle zones, particularly during periods of comparative inactivity or where, as in the case of Rhodesia until recently, no liberated area existed.

Accordingly, the need for transit camps arose. Eventually, Lusaka concluded that these too could be safely sanctioned, provided the length of stay of the visitors was limited to a few days, or a week at the most.[27] However, even these less stringent regulations proved difficult to enforce. While instances have occurred of individual freedom fighters being jailed for lingering too long, in most cases there appeared to be no alternative to further extensions in the period of grace.

Nevertheless, the Zambian government continued to treat all freedom fighters, apart from designated party officials and certain transport personnel, as transients. Accordingly, they acquired no rights to residence or to freedom of movement; nor were they entitled to pursue their normal activities. In particular, they were forbidden to engage in military training; on this, the government was insistent—at least until 1974—despite frequent allegations to the contrary.[28] "We have no training camps in Zambia," President Kaunda declared categorically, "none whatsoever."[29] So confident was the government of its innocence in this regard that it publicly invited the South African government and anyone else to undertake a tour of inspection. "We are ready to take them to every inch of Zambia," the Foreign Minister promised. One South African journalist accepted the challenge, but failed to confirm his suspicions.[30] Admittedly, a certain amount of informal training was carried on clandestinely, but it appears not to have been militarily significant. Certainly, there has been nothing comparable to the major training centers in Tanzania and Algeria. Nor is it easy to understand why these would be necessary in view of the availability of superior facilities elsewhere. Yet, despite this, critics have continued to confuse training camps, which were not authorized, with transit camps which are.

Zambia was equally adamant that neither operational bases from which attacks could be launched against neighboring countries nor privileged sanctuaries to which freedom fighters could return were authorized on her soil. "It has always been the policy of my Government," President Kaunda asserted as late as 1971, "not to allow 'freedom fighters' or any other type of military or paramilitary unit to operate from Zambia against or within neighboring territories. . . . Zambia cannot and does not tolerate the use of its soil as a base for military or paramilitary operations."[31]

244

The principle of a liberation struggle waged
inside the target territory rather than by raiding
parties from staging points outside is sound revolutionary theory, but it has not always been consistent with OAU rhetoric on the responsibilities of
host countries, to which Zambia claimed to subscribe.
As a result, an inevitable element of ambiguity has
crept into her public pronouncements. When, at the
1972 OAU Summit Conference, King Hassan called on
all border states to "accept military bases" and,
with them, "all the inconveniences, such as the
right of pursuit and reprisals . . . even if they
are bombed day and night by the enemy," as happened
to Morocco during the Algerian war, President Kaunda
felt constrained to respond somewhat equivocally
that the decisions taken on the basis of the King's
"reported statement" would be implemented in the
"spirit of Rabat."[32] The Rabat conference also concluded that "the proposed Combat Posts within Member
States" were "unnecessary at present."[33] This was
no doubt a welcome relief to the Zambian government
which was anxious at this time to avoid a public
commitment to a policy so obviously calculated to
provoke reprisals—at least until the country was in
a better position to defend itself. Nevertheless,
it is only realistic to assume that, even prior to
1974, some two-way freedom fighter traffic across
Zambia's borders occurred that the authorities
either were unaware of, or unable to control, despite attempts to supervise it and keep it within
reasonable limits.

CONTROLS

From the outset, the Zambian government was
determined to ensure that it exercised adequate control over freedom fighter interactions with each
other, with the Zambian population, and even with
the Southern African regimes. With respect to the
activities of liberation movements within Zambia,
there was understandable concern with the implications for internal and external security of the
presence in the country of even modest numbers of
armed and not always fully disciplined cadres.
Although the units involved were in no way comparable, quantitatively or qualitatively, to the
Palestine liberation armies in Jordan and Lebanon,
in relation to Zambia's small and already overextended defense forces, they represented a serious
potential threat. In the case of guerrilla

245

operations in the field, economic as well as security considerations dictated the need for constraints.

The ultimate weapon at the disposal of the government was the power to bestow or withdraw recognition, and with it the privilege of operating in and from Zambia. However, this was a blunt instrument that could only be wielded in exceptional circumstances, especially as there was always a risk of incurring the displeasure of either the OAU or other front line states. In any case, the government was anxious not to take sides in quarrels between or within exile parties. Accordingly, it sought as far as possible not to promote its own ideological line or to influence the course of the constant internecine struggles for power. Such restraint was never easy and, on occasion, proved impossible.

The one "domestic" issue that the government considered was its legitimate concern was disunity within the ranks of the liberation movements. This manifested itself in two forms: the failure of rival parties to form common fronts and intraparty conflict.

Common Fronts

Zambia has been less doctrinaire than many OAU members in her approach to the thorny problem of unity among national liberation movements. The reason for this is rooted in her own nationalist experience: UNIP was itself a breakaway party. There was less inclination, therefore, to condemn secession in all circumstances. On the other hand, Zambian leaders recognized the utility of their own tactical coalition with the opposition ANC during the transitional period 1962 to 1964. And, in the much more difficult struggle Zimbabweans faced, unity was considered even more essential; Algeria, not Zambia, was the appropriate model.[34] Besides, Zambia had every interest in avoiding chaos on her borders. There was, therefore, a predisposition in Lusaka to favor the single party system of Tanzania (and subsequently Mozambique) as it appeared to offer greater prospect of an orderly transfer of power in Rhodesia and Angola than the multitude of parties with which Zaire embarked on Independence.

Zambian involvement, through UNIP, the government and the OAU, in efforts to reconcile divided liberation groups dated back before Independence (table 6.2). Not surprisingly, the earliest, and most intimate contacts were with ZAPU and ZANU. Many of their leaders were friends and colleagues of

246

Zambian leaders from school and university days or during the struggle against the Federation. In the case of nationalists from Angola, Mozambique and other territories, there was not the same history of personal collaboration; besides, a language barrier frequently intervened.

In April 1964, after months of agonizing appraisal, UNIP formally declared its support for Joshua Nkomo and ZAPU rather than Ndabaningi Sithole and ZANU.[35] Although the timing of the announcement—three days after Nkomo's restriction—may not have been entirely coincidental, the decision was based principally on evidence supplied by UNIP branches throughout Rhodesia that ZAPU was overwhelmingly the majority party.[36] This was a political judgment that Zambians felt uniquely qualified to make, and explains their consistent support of ZAPU ever since, despite the strong pro-ZANU sentiment in other African states, notably Tanzania. Nevertheless, in practice, the Zambian attitude has been more evenhanded than this firm commitment suggests, partly no doubt because ZANU managed to establish close personal and political relations with an influential minority in the Cabinet. In any case, the government and the Party have never ceased to seek unity.

Efforts to heal the breach began shortly after the split in August 1963, with both Kaunda and Sipalo, UNIP's Secretary for Pan-African Affairs, attempting to bring the two sides together.[37] Then, the following August, Lusaka hosted an OAU meeting at which the Tanzanian and Malawian foreign ministers offered their good offices to bring about a "united front." As both ministers were ZANU sympathizers, the presence of Zambian spokesmen in the wings helped to restore the balance—and, incidentally, reinforce ZAPU intransigence.[38] A year later, the depressing routine was repeated in Nairobi where a Special OAU Commission of six "neighboring" states headed by Zambia, and subsequently a subcommittee of three including Zambia, again failed to record any progress towards a "common front."[39] A similar fate befell the efforts of the Reconciliation Committee established at the OAU Summit Conference in Accra in October 1965.[40] Thereafter, OAU pressure on the warring factions slackened, partly out of a sense of frustration but mainly because of UDI. Although in March 1966 Presidents Kaunda and Nyerere were asked to mediate the dispute,[41] and informal conciliation attempts continued, the general feeling was that the two liberation movements should be allowed to

TABLE 6.2
Zambian Efforts to Promote Unity Among Southern African Liberation Movements: 1964-1974

| Dates | Meeting Place | Initiative | Good Offices | Liberation Movements | | Comments |
				Zimbabwe	Angola/ Mozambique	
1964						
Jan-Feb	Lusaka	UNIP	Kaunda, Sipalo	ZAPU/ZANU		
Aug 14	Lusaka	OAU	Malawi, Tanzania	ZAPU/ZANU		Zambia was host
1965						
March	Lusaka	Zambia	Foreign Min Kapwepwe		all but FRELIMO	COREMO formed June 1965
July 20-22; Aug 27-29	Nairobi	OAU	Zambia, Tanzania, Kenya Uganda, Ethiopia Malawi	ZAPU/ZANU		Subcommittee: Zambia, Kenya, Tanzania
October	Accra	OAU	Zambia, Tanzania, Ghana, Sierra Leone	ZAPU/ZANU		
October	Lusaka	Savimbi	Kaunda		FNLA/MPLA	Meeting not held
1966						
February	Dar es Salaam	OAU	Zambia, Tanzania plus 3	ZAPU/ZANU		Reconciliation Committee Appt. March 1966
Sept	Lusaka	OAU Kaunda	Kaunda, Nyerere Kaunda	ZAPU/ZANU	FNLA/UNITA	
1968						
		OAU	Zambia, Zaire, Congo B Egypt		FNLA/MPLA	Committee of 5 appt. Sept 1967
		OAU	Zambia, Ghana, Tanzania, Kenya	ZAPU/ZANU		Appt. Sept 1968

TABLE 6.2 (continued)

1972						
Sept 9	Dar es Salaam	OAU	Zambia, Tanzania, Zaire, Congo B		FNLA/MPLA	Appointed June 1971
Dec 13	Kinshasa	OAU	Zambia, Tanzania, Zaire, Congo B		FNLA/MPLA	Kinshasa Agreement
1973						
March 14-17	Lusaka	OAU	Zambia, Tanzania, Kenya, Ghana, Cameroon	ZAPU/ZANU		Political Council & Joint Military Command agreed
May 31-June 1	Kitwe	Mulungushi Club	Kaunda, Mobutu, Nyerere		FNLA/MPLA	
October 27-29	Mwanza	Mulungushi Club	Kaunda, Mobutu, Nyerere		FNLA/MPLA	
1974						
May 7-9	Dar es Salaam	OAU	Zambia, Tanzania, Zaire, Congo B		FNLA/MPLA	
May 25-26	Lusaka	Kaunda	Kaunda, Mobutu (Nyerere)		FNLA/MPLA/UNITA	
July 27-28	Bukavu	OAU	Kaunda, Nyerere, Mobutu, Ngouabi		FNLA/MPLA factions	Bukavu Agreement
August 12-21	Lusaka		Zambia, Tanzania, Zaire, Congo B, Somalia		MPLA factions	Observers at MPLA Congress
Sept 1-3	Brazzaville	OAU	Kaunda, Nyerere, Mobutu, Ngouabi		MPLA factions	Brazzaville Agreement
Nov 7-10	Lusaka	Kaunda	Kaunda, Nyerere, Khama, Machel	ANC/ZAPU/ZANU		Nkomo & Mugabe present
Dec 4-7	Lusaka	Kaunda	Kaunda, Nyerere, Khama	ANC/ZAPU/ZANU/FROLIZI		Zimbabwe Declaration of Unity

demonstrate their relative military capabilities inside Rhodesia before a decision was reached.

When the long promised masterplans[42] failed to
unfold, disillusionment deepened. Dr. Kaunda had
already given vent to his feelings in a remarkable
outburst three days after UDI, when he bitterly denounced the leaders of both parties as "chicken-in-
the-basket" freedom fighters who, through their high-
living, arrogance and inactivity, had betrayed Zambia
as well as their own people. "The only reason why I
have tolerated the presence of these idiots," he
said, "is that I respect the four million Africans
and Europeans . . . in Zimbabwe."[43] Eighteen months
later, he reverted to the same theme in more measured
tones. "The situation calls for real unity," he
declared. "I don't want to be harsh here, but every-
one concerned with the welfare [of ZAPU and ZANU] is
getting very much upset by the inability of the
nationalists even in their divided form to be effective in the situation in Rhodesia."[44] Concerted
action, therefore, was essential. ZAPU redeemed its
reputation temporarily when, jointly with the South
African ANC, it launched its incursion into the
Wankie area in August 1967, shortly before the
Kinshasa OAU Summit.

Nevertheless, disquiet at the continuing disunity among Zimbabwean freedom fighters and frustration at the apparent helplessness of the African
states to do anything about it persisted; as Nathan
Shamuyaria notes sadly: "In African capitals and at
international or regional conferences, the leaders
of ZANU and ZAPU devoted more time to their interparty rivalry than to the fight against the common
enemy."[45] Despite this, the OAU continued to go
through the annual ritual of appealing to ZAPU and
ZANU to close ranks. In September 1968, Zambia,
Kenya and Tanzania were again asked to use their
good offices to effect a "united front,"[46] but the
results were invariably and predictably nil. In
fairness, however, it must be admitted that political
and ideological divisions within the OAU as well as
Soviet opposition were contributing factors in the
Organization's inability to impose unity.[47]

In 1971, a new approach was attempted. By then,
ZAPU was so rent by internal strife as to be organi-
zationally immobilized,[48] whereas ZANU had successfully restructured itself operationally (and ideologically). The Zambian government took advantage of
this altered power relationship to encourage those
elements within both movements which favored the formation of a new organization embracing the existing

parties but not necessarily under the same leadership. President Kaunda made it abundantly clear that ZAPU and ZANU had "got to choose between coming together or forfeiting Zambia's readiness to accommodate them."[49] Out of this confusion, FROLIZI emerged in October 1971. Zambia eagerly promoted its claims to OAU recognition but, before this could be formally accorded, the most promising effort to date to reincarnate a united Zimbabwean nationalist movement lost momentum.

Faced with the threat by angry OAU members of withdrawal of recognition (and, for ZAPU, a possible switch in Soviet policy), the two factions signed the Mbeya agreement in March 1972 establishing a Joint Military Command.[50] From the first, it proved a dead letter. A year later, five African foreign ministers meeting in Lusaka under the chairmanship of Zambia's Elijah Mudenda managed to extract a new agreement,[51] but only after Lusaka had reportedly threatened ZANU—now the stronger partner militarily—with expulsion. Nevertheless, after two attempts to set up the Joint Military Command, even the façade of unity was quietly abandoned. As the OAU Liberation Committee at its October 1973 meeting in Mogadishu reported with resignation, "regarding unity, the Committee again noted the usual lack of progress."[52]

The Portuguese military coup in April 1974, and the subsequent promises of early independence for Mozambique and Angola, compelled all actors in the Southern African drama radically to rewrite their Rhodesian scenarios. Dr. Kaunda was among the first to recognize the dramatic new possibilities opening up. Using Prime Minister Vorster as an intermediary, he secured the release of Joshua Nkomo, Ndabaningi Sithole and other Zimbabwean leaders who had been under restriction or detention in Rhodesia for more than a decade. Then, at historic meetings in Lusaka in early November and early December 1974, the Front Line presidents finally secured the firm agreement of ZAPU and ZANU (as well as of the FROLIZI rump) to "unite" under the banner of Bishop Muzorewa's African National Council which, as the sole legal nationalist organization in Rhodesia, all undertook to recognize as the "unifying force of the people of Zimbabwe."[53] It was a remarkable, though shortlived, achievement.

The Zambian government has been far less deeply embroiled in Portuguese African emigré politics. Its initial excursion into the Mozambique field was not an entirely happy experience. In March 1965,

251

Foreign Minister Kapwepwe convened a conference in Lusaka to forge a united nationalist movement out of the array of splinter groups scattered through neighboring countries. From this, COREMO emerged[54] but, as FRELIMO boycotted the meeting, the unintended consequence was to polarize divisions. The continued hospitality Lusaka extended to COREMO also cast a minor shadow over Zambian-FRELIMO relations that took several years to fade. In June 1974, however, on the eve of FRELIMO's takeover in Mozambique, Zambia pressed COREMO to dissolve itself and join the ruling party. When it declined to do so, Lusaka finally expelled its leaders.

In October 1965, at the suggestion of Dr. Jonas Savimbi and following the dismissal of Congo Premier Tshombe,[55] President Kaunda tried unsuccessfully to bring the MPLA and FNLA leaders together in Lusaka. A year later, however, he managed to arrange a meeting between Holden Roberto (FNLA) and Savimbi, who had now emerged as leader of UNITA.[56] Unfortunately, nothing came of this initiative and, on the two occasions when further meetings were organized, Roberto failed to show.

Attempts to reconcile MPLA and FNLA were complicated by conflicts between their principal patrons—the two Congos—as well as by the impact of international ideological forces. The Committee of Five on Angola, which the OAU established in September 1967 and of which Zambia was a member, found itself unable even to meet until the following June.[57] Three years later, in June 1971, the OAU designated the foreign ministers of four member-states, including Zambia, to assist in the task of reconciliation.[58] The following year, the two parties concluded the Kinshasa Agreement of December 1972 which provided for joint political and military institutions. Unhappily, it was never implemented.

During the next two years, Presidents Kaunda, Mobutu and Nyerere at their periodic meetings as members of the informal "Mulungushi Club" of Central African heads of state, strove valiantly to resurrect something from the wreckage of the Kinshasa accord. The Portuguese coup served as an incentive for a further series of conciliation initiatives culminating in yet another illusory agreement at the Bukavu summit meeting in July 1974. By this time, the problem had been greatly complicated by the internal divisions renting MPLA. In the end, the most that could be attained was agreement on a "common political platform" hammered out largely as a result of the diplomatic skill of Dr. Jonas Savimbi, the UNITA

leader.[59] This modest success was greatly welcomed
in Lusaka. Unfortunately, it too proved shortlived.

Although Zambia was, during this period, a firm
supporter of MPLA's claim to represent the Angolan
people, her overriding concern was not ideology but
the promotion of nationalist unity both to strengthen
the hand of the freedom fighters in their struggle
with the Portuguese and to ensure an orderly transition to majority rule. Zambians hoped to avoid a
repetition of the Zaire situation along their western border and astride their vital rail outlet to
the Atlantic.

Interparty and Intraparty Conflict

Freedom fighters in Zambia, in common with
exile groups everywhere and throughout history, have
inevitably suffered from feelings of insecurity,
anxiety and frustration. These have frequently
found expression in maladaptive behavior. This has
been apparent not only in a characteristic reluctance to collaborate with rivals, but also typically
in the marked propensity to indulge in bitter conflict both within and between parties.[60] Zambians
did not always fully appreciate the psychological
roots of these periodic violent releases of tension;
hence their frequent expressions of impatience. At
the same time, the Zambian government could not
afford to tolerate such counterproductive activity.
Its concern here was not simply with preserving law
and order. Equally important were the consequences
of internal strife for the military effectiveness of
the movements. PAC, ZAPU and MPLA were all in this
way, at different times and in varying degrees,
seriously weakened as fighting organizations.

In Zambian experience, Zimbabweans have been
the most frequent offenders. Armed clashes between
ZAPU and ZANU supporters were particularly prevalent
during the first year after their 1963 split. The
following year, UNIP recognition of ZAPU signalled
a fresh outbreak of fighting. This compelled the
government to issue a "stern warning" that it was
"not prepared to allow Northern Rhodesia to be a
fighting ground between members of political parties
of other countries," and that it would not hesitate
to close down party offices or deport those responsible. Government recognition "did not entitle members of ZAPU to eliminate their rivals by methods
which disturbed the peace of the country."[61]
Nevertheless, interparty violence remained a recurring feature of the Zambian scene.

More serious, however, was the succession of volcanic eruptions within liberation movements. The first victim was the Pan-Africanist Congress of South Africa. It had long suffered from personal and ideological rifts. In August 1968, it was banned and forty-five of its members deported to Tanzania for illegal entry, "contravening regulations" governing nationalist organizations, and "indulging in detentions and counter-detentions within their party."[62] There were also allegations of plots to assassinate Zambian ministers.[63] Consequently, the government decided to take no chances.

The internecine strife that has riven ZAPU was pursued at times with a passion befitting a religious crusade. Its roots lay in a combination of personality feuds, power struggles, ideological, strategic and generational differences, tribal rivalries and accusations of spying; but above all it was a reflection of the years of tension, isolation, deprivation and disappointment that the leaders had endured. The event that first compelled direct Zambian intervention was an armed assault in April 1970 on a ZAPU hostel in a Lusaka suburb where Shona supporters of the Chikerema faction apparently attempted to eliminate three Ndebele members of the party's war council. In the ensuing gun battle, three persons were wounded, one of whom is alleged to have died later.[64] A presidential ultimatum, demanding that the warring groups either patch up their differences or face expulsion, succeeded in restoring some semblance of unity, but only temporarily.

The following March, the Chikerema wing succeeded in kidnapping over twenty of its opponents at gunpoint.[65] This time, government patience was exhausted. In a major security operation, it rounded up the cadres of both groups, placed them under restriction in a remote bush camp, and impounded their arms and property. When, after several months, no progress had been made in effecting a reconciliation and, in addition, the rebels were displaying increasing defiance of the government, the President detained the more prominent among them, including the thirty-nine so-called "militants." Shortly afterwards, nearly 120 lower echelon supporters, some of them suspected spies or deserters, were (after consultation with the OAU) deported to Rhodesia where most of them were promptly arrested and three have since been sentenced to death.[66] Even this drastic action failed to instill a sense of sober realism into the ZAPU leadership. In October 1971, the party formally split on the issue of FROLIZI, with the Chikerema faction joining the new movement and the rest remaining aloof. The only beneficiary of this tragic upheaval has been the Smith regime; from 1970 to 1972, ZAPU was for all practical purposes militarily incapacitated.[67]

MPLA also experienced internal dissension (chapter 8). By early 1973, the split in party ranks inside Angola had reached Zambia, with armed clashes flaring up in transit camps.[68] Although the fighting appears not to have posed a serious security problem, it did adversely affect military operations against the Portuguese. This was deeply distressing to the Zambian government, especially as it had accorded more unqualified support to MPLA than to any other liberation movement.

Despite inspired reports alleging Zambian complicity in various plots to topple MPLA President Agostinho Neto in favor of Vice-President Daniel Chipenda, leader of the "Eastern Revolt," Lusaka did not in fact take sides in the dispute, other than to provide Chipenda and Neto with police protection.[69] At the same time, it struggled desperately to head off a final rupture. Apart from hosting MPLA's first congress near Lusaka in August 1974 (which unfortunately failed to forge party unity but instead ended in Dr. Neto walking out), President Kaunda was personally deeply involved in sustained Zambian efforts to reconcile the warring factions. In addition, he participated along with the presidents of Congo(B), Tanzania and Zaire in two major meetings of the OAU conciliation commission at Bukavu in July and Brazzaville in September. The latter encounter appeared to have resolved the conflict with Chipenda accepting Neto's leadership, but three months later the rift re-emerged, resulting in Chipenda's expulsion from MPLA.

Isolation

The Zambian government sought to isolate foreign nationalist parties from close contact with Zambian society and especially from members of their own communities resident in Zambia. This is consistent with the Zambian conception of freedom fighters as essentially transit visitors who were entitled to a corridor through the country, but not into it. The principal motive for this policy, however, was a desire to minimize the risk of direct or indirect alien involvement in domestic politics.

255

In implementing this approach, the first requirement was adequate supervision of liberation movement activities. This was the responsibility of a small secretariat within the Office of the President.[70] In addition, UNIP acted as a watchdog. Since 1971, there has also been a Sub-Office of the OAU Liberation Committee in Lusaka.[71] When this was first mooted, there appears to have been some concern felt in Zambia that it might undermine the government's authority. These fears were subsequently dispelled; the director is a Zambian, appointed by Zambia and fully acquainted with government policy (see chapter 3).

In January 1965, the government issued a directive "curtailing the activities of foreign African nationalist movements in Zambia."[72] The resemblance of this to earlier instructions governing embassy operations in Zambia was not entirely coincidental, as initially the government regarded the offices of recognized liberation organizations as having quasi-diplomatic status. Under these regulations, liberation movements were required to close their branches outside Lusaka, to confine their activities to the capital, and not to travel beyond ten miles from the center of the city without government permission. In addition, they were forbidden to campaign for funds, and the number of resident officers allowed was limited to six designated officials.

The Lusaka Liberation Center, where the administrative offices of liberation movements are located, was until 1972 in the care of the President's Personal Representative, the idiosyncratic Mukuka Nkoloso, also known for his exploits as the self-styled Director-General of the National Academy of Science, Space and Astronautical Research. The shepherding of the various organizations into a single compound under government supervision has not always been regarded by the freedom fighters as an unmitigated blessing. The Zimbabwean parties, in particular, have resisted centralization, and have managed to retain the downtown offices they had acquired before Independence. In all other cases, the government's wishes have prevailed.

The injunction against direct interactions with Southern African communities within Zambia was intended to ensure that the liberation movements did not develop the kinds of domestic political bases that gave Palestine liberation organizations at times an almost unchallengeable leverage with the governments of Lebanon and Jordan. In the case of Zimbabweans and Angolans, the local communities were substantial (table 6.3). Accordingly, firm steps

256

TABLE 6.3
Southern African Communities in Zambia

| Alien Africans | Refugees (1 Jan. 1970) | Total Populations (1 Sept. 1969) | |
		By Citizenship	By Birth
Angolans	8,192	8,405	28,919
Mozambicans	3,124	4,338	8,699
Zimbabweans	—	34,549	57,781
South Africans	284	1,490	4,246
Namibians	838	398	756
Total	12,438	49,180	100,401

Sources: UNHCR, Report on Current Operations, 1970, Annex II/A (i); Zambia Census, 1969. The refugee population appears to have been included in the census returns.

were taken to insulate as far as possible the refugee camps from contact with freedom fighters by moving them well away from the borders. In addition, party political activities were curtailed. Occasional meetings have, however, been allowed to commemorate important anniversaries, and these have sometimes been addressed by ministers or top UNIP officials.[73]
    Two other related problems have occasioned Lusaka some embarrassment. The first concerned individuals who found the "psychic tensions" of life as a guerrilla intolerable, and sought to escape its rigors by integrating with Zambian society. A number of Rhodesians, for example, have acquired taxis.[74] The government has attempted, fairly successfully, to prevent this by imposing a ban on freedom fighters (or even refugees) settling in the country or engaging in any form of business. In this endeavor, it has had the full support of the nationalist leaders who, however, have pressed the government to go much further and permit them to recruit cadres from within their own communities in Zambia. This it has not been prepared to do. In fact, from the first, all foreign recruitment was banned. Moreover, when the liberation movements, under pressure from the OAU to expand their military operations, resorted to compulsion to swell their

ranks, the Zambian reaction was swift and severe. In September 1968, in a circular letter to all UNIP regional officials, the Party's National Secretary appealed for assistance in reporting any "illegal recruitment," and spelt out government policy in unmistakable terms:

> No Nationalist Organization is permitted to recruit Freedom Fighters in Zambia and no Zambian resident should take part in any Foreign Nationalist Organization's activities. They are not even allowed to become members of Foreign Nationalist Organizations. They can only take part in political parties which are Zambian and the Minister of State for Presidential Affairs has put a complete stop to Nationalist Organizations recruiting within Zambia. Action has been taken whenever Nationalists have been found engaged in this illegal recruitment.[75]

A month later, nearly sixty Zimbabweans responsible for "kidnapping and abduction" were deported to Tanzania.[76] Whether these stern measures succeeded in stamping out pressganging completely is not clear; certainly, the liberation movements continued to argue with considerable logic though with less political realism, that conscription in wartime is both legitimate and necessary.

Operational Restrictions

The calculation of the risks incurred in Zambia's commitment to the liberation of Southern Africa is most critical in the case of the operational activities of cadres, whether in transit through Zambia or in action in the field. Figure 6.1 represents an attempt to conceptualize the problem on the basis of relative indices of host state support for liberation activities (S) and vulnerability to economic and military retaliation (V). These are quantified on a purely judgmental basis and can only be regarded as suggestive, not empirically tested. It is also assumed that the risk of retaliation is a function of V and S, and that a risk threshold (T=VS), beyond which the threat of retaliation may be actualized, exists. On this basis, Tanzania is judged to have struck a rational balance in the early 1970s between vulnerability and support, whereas Zambia (alone among African states) was clearly exposed to serious risk of reprisals from

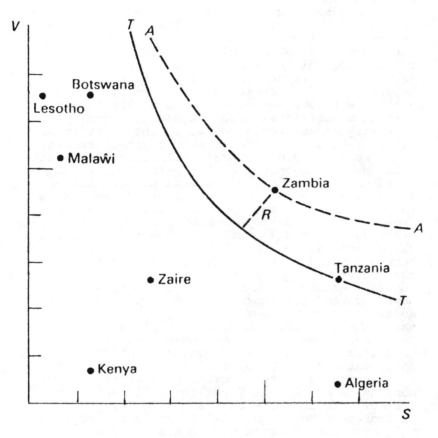

V = vulnerability to retaliatory action
S = extent of liberation support
T = risk threshold (= VS)
A = acceptable risk
R = risk of retaliatory action

FIGURE 6.1 The Risk Threshold in Southern Africa
  in the Early 1970s

the South. The extent of this risk is measured by R.
The task of Zambian decision makers, therefore, has
been to ensure, with respect to each individual
Southern African regime, that R did not exceed acceptable limits (A).

The Zambian government indicated its willingness to pay a substantial price as its contribution
to the liberation struggle. In fact, a measure of
martyrdom might have incidental benefits in assist-
ing in the mobilization of international opinion.
Nevertheless, if the level of conflict escalated
beyond occasional exemplary punishment, Zambia had
either to reduce her exposure or to strengthen her
defense capabilities. To subject the country to
crippling damage would not be in the interest of
either Zambia or   the freedom fighters themselves.

The history of Zambia's relations with Southern
Africa since Independence has been one of constant
maneuvering to maintain a viable balance between the
level of provocation and the means of deterrence on
the one hand, and between the threat of retaliation
from and degree of dependence upon the South on the
other hand. This is not the place to detail the
range and scale of hostile acts to which Zambia has
been subjected in the past. Suffice it to say that
these have embraced elements of economic and psychological warfare as well as military measures, and
have included blockades, economic blackmail, rumor-
mongering, aerial leaflet raids, subversion, sabotage, assassination, border incursions and bombings.

Precautions taken to control the logistical
operations of liberation movements inside Zambia
have centered on the supervision of arms shipments
in transit and on the avoidance of concentrations of
men and material that might invite pre-emptive
strikes. In the case of transit camps, these have
deliberately been kept small, mobile and scattered.
The arms traffic issue was more serious as it confronted the government with a policy dilemma:
whether to pretend it did not exist or whether to
attempt to regulate its flow, thereby according it a
measure of legitimacy. There was no third alternative; even if it had disapproved of gunrunning,
there was no way it could hope to eliminate it
completely.

Initially, Zambian authorities were tempted
simply to tolerate the "illegal" activities of the
liberation movements, but this quickly led to abuses
and a rash of arrests.[77] Moreover, as the scale of
operations increased, the government became alarmed.
Efforts were then made to suppress the traffic

completely. "While it should be understood and very clearly too," President Kaunda declared shortly before UDI,

> that we in Zambia support the struggle against colonialism in Africa, I believe it is my duty to warn participants in that struggle that the use of our country as a transit route for the transport of arms must cease. In the interest of Zambia and its people, we cannot tolerate the presence of unsupervised arms in the country. It is highly dangerous and, therefore, I would wish it to be clearly understood that from now on it is government policy that this traffic should be stopped. I have given fair warning to organizations who indulge in this activity of Government's policy and . . . they will contravene this at their own peril. . . . no country whatsoever anywhere in the world can allow free traffic of arms within its country.[78]

Predictably, this approach proved ineffective.

UDI, in "legalizing" resistance to the Rhodesian rebel regime, led to some relaxation of Zambia's stringent arms regulations. Nevertheless, the problems persisted. In the end, therefore, the government reluctantly concluded that it had no alternative but to assume much more direct responsibility for the control and transit of arms through its territory to ensure that they were neither diverted not stockpiled. Even so, it would be surprising if the liberation movements always cooperated fully with the authorities in adhering strictly to established procedures. If the number of court cases is any indication, a fair amount of unauthorized smuggling continued.[79]

Limitations on the operational freedom of action of liberation movements within Zambia requires no justification. What may be surprising is the extent to which Lusaka felt constrained to influence the conduct of guerrilla operations beyond its borders. It was not a question of Zambia directing the military campaigns of the liberation organizations, but rather of advising them what she would prefer that they not do. Three factors entered into Zambian thinking: humanitarianism, economic interest, and military security.

Zambian spokesmen have repeatedly made it clear that they strongly disapproved of the indiscriminate killing of Europeans in Rhodesia—on humanitarian

261

as well as pragmatic grounds. In chiding the Zimbabwean parties for their inactivity, President
Kaunda added, "I don't mean they should go cutting
people's heads off. They could be very effective
indeed . . . by weakening [the rebel regime] in many
fields which touch the purse."[80] On an earlier
occasion, in criticizing ZAPU broadcasts, he argued
that, "It is stupid to shout from the comforts of
Zambia, 'We are going to kill all white men'. How
does that help?"[81] Similarly, following the death
of a Rhodesian farmer, and accusations by Salisbury,
a government spokesman asserted that "Zambia does
not support killing by anyone. Murder is condemned
no matter whether this is perpetrated by rebels or
freedom fighters."[82] In other words, terrorism as
such was rejected.

Pending the reorientation of her economy and,
in particular, completion in 1975 of the TAZARA
railway to Dar es Salaam, Zambia had a vital economic interest in preventing freedom fighters from
disrupting her residual lines of communication
through and sources of supply in Southern Africa.
This meant insisting on no interference with
Rhodesia Railways (until 1973) and the Benguela
Railway,[83] with Kariba electricity and with Wankie
coal (until 1972). When, on Christmas Eve 1966 and
later in March 1967, UNITA forces blew up sections
of the Lobito route, Lusaka retaliated by refusing
to renew Dr. Savimbi's residence permit.[84]

Security was the major concern compelling Zambia to urge operational restraints on liberation
movements. In an attempt to avoid offering excessive or unnecessary provocation, she argued that
military operations must be initiated from within
Southern Africa, preferably well away from the
border, and that cadres should not seek sanctuary in
Zambia, thus risking violations of Zambian territory
by Southern African forces in "hot pursuit." Nor
have liberation movements been authorized to airlift
supplies into liberated areas. These conditions
were reasonably well respected but, as even Ian
Smith has admitted, there were definite limits to
the extent to which Lusaka could enforce its writ
throughout its vast and generally remote and scan-
tily populated border areas, let alone beyond them.

CONCLUSIONS

The first conclusion to which this analysis
points is that there was a steady evolution over

262

time in the Zambian government's commitment to the cause of Southern African liberation. British failures to act decisively in Rhodesia immediately after UDI, and again six months later following the Labour Party's election victory, marked significant stages along the way (see chapter 4), but even more crucial were the massive economic disengagement from the South and the buildup of defense capabilities (see chapter 5). The inevitable caution that characterized the early independence era gave way to a new confidence and bolder policies. In terms of figure 6.1, as vulnerability (V) diminished, liberation support (S) increased correspondingly without the risk of retaliation (R) exceeding acceptable limits (A).

Nevertheless, vital Zambian national interests, which ultimately the liberation movements also share, dictated the imposition of some constraints. This poses two questions: to what extent have these been unreasonable, and have they prejudiced the success of the liberation struggles?

Zambian guidelines on the behavior of liberation movements can be summarized in the following code of conduct:

(1) The priority task of freedom movements is to liberate their homelands; anything that detracts from that purpose should be discouraged and anything that contributes to it merits support.

(2) Liberation movements must not interfere in the domestic affairs of the host country, or add to its internal security problems.

(3) Liberation movements must abjure actions that harm the host country substantially more than the target country.

(4) The level and character of military activities in both the host country and the target country must not be such as to provoke retaliation against the host country on a scale that exceeds acceptable limits.

None of these restrictions is inherently unreasonable. In fact, the last two in particular imply substantial sacrifices on the part of the host country. In practice, Zambia has generally accorded the liberation movements all the assistance that could reasonably be expected in the circumstances. Moreover, as Zambia's capabilities have increased, so has her measure of support. Nevertheless, Zambian policies have necessarily involved an element of restriction, however justifiable. What effects has this had on the course of the liberation struggles?

There is no easy answer to this question, but a few comments may be pertinent. In the first place, a major constraint on the effectiveness of liberation forces was the endemic disunity between and within the movements. The empirical evidence suggests that the greater the degree of unity in a national liberation movement, the greater its success in the field. It is difficult to see any way in which Zambian restrictions contributed to this fragmentation. On the contrary, major resources of time, energy and emotion have been expended to try to bridge the divisions within the nationalist movements.

A second handicap affecting the liberation movements was shortage of trained manpower, modern equipment and supplies. Again, it is possible to formulate a proposition which has some empirical support, namely, that progress towards the end is proportional to the availability of the means. Here, too, these deficiencies cannot be attributed to Zambian actions. Nothing could have been achieved through training camps in Zambia that could not have been done, certainly more safely and probably more efficiently in a number of countries farther from the front line. Similarly, the supply situation depended on external, not Zambian, sources. Finally, Zambian restrictions, though sometimes irritating, did not seriously impede FRELIMO's progress. There is no good reason, therefore, to suspect that they were significant factors in the more limited successes of guerrilla forces elsewhere.

The physical hardships and psychological strains that are the inevitable lot of freedom fighters are sufficiently daunting to deter all but the most dedicated among them. It is understandable, therefore, that they should resent and resist any constraints at all on their freedom of action. Nevertheless, Southern African liberation movements were fortunate that the most strategically positioned host state in independent Africa proved so willing and able to be both sympathetic and sacrificial in its support.

NOTES

1. For developments since 1974, when circumstances and Zambia's response were in some respects very different, see chapters 7 and 8.

2. See Douglas G. Anglin, "The Politics of Transit

Routes in Landlocked Southern Africa," in <u>Landlocked
Countries of Africa</u>, ed. Z. Cervenka (Uppsala:
Scandinavian Institute of African Studies, 1973),
pp. 104-11, 129.

3. Zambia Information Service (ZIS) <u>Press Release</u>,
no. 1488/68, 21 August 1968, p. 1.

4. <u>Axioms of Kwame Nkrumah</u> (London: Nelson, 1967),
p. 52.

5. Preamble, Constitution of Zambia, 1973.

6. ZIS <u>Press Release</u>, no. 1518/68, 24 August 1968,
p. 1.

7. <u>Sunday Times of Zambia</u>, 17 September 1972, p. 1.

8. Fergus Macpherson, <u>Kenneth Kaunda of Zambia</u>:
<u>The Times and the Man</u> (Lusaka: Oxford University
Press, 1974), pp. 308-10, 314; <u>Black Government</u>
(Lusaka: United Society for Christian Literature,
1960), pp. 99-102; Kenneth D. Kaunda, <u>Zambia Shall
Be Free</u> (London: Heinemann, 1962), <u>passim</u>; Ali
Mazrui, <u>The Anglo-African Commonwealth</u> (Oxford:
Pergamon Press, 1967), pp. 14-17.

9. "Rhodesia and the World," in B.V. Mtshali,
<u>Rhodesia: Background to Conflict</u> (New York: Hawthorn
Books, 1967), pp. 6-7.

10. <u>Times</u> (London), 20 April 1964, p. 12; UN General
Assembly, <u>Verbatim Records</u> (A/PV. 1291), 4 December
1964, p. 2.

11. Robert C. Good, UDI: <u>The International Politics
of the Rhodesian Rebellion</u> (Princeton: Princeton
University Press, 1973), p. 235.

12. <u>Manifesto on Southern Africa</u> (Lusaka: Government
Printer, 1969), pp. 3-4. The liberation movements
were profoundly disturbed by the Lusaka Manifesto
which they interpreted as "abandoning the struggle"
(Nathan Shamuyarira, "The Lusaka Manifesto on Southern Africa," <u>African Review</u> 1, no. 1 (March 1971):
77).

13. ZIS <u>Press Release</u>, no. 1724/67, 27 August 1967,
p. 1.

14. Ibid., no. 1518/68, 24 August 1968, p. 1.

15. Nathan Shamuyarira, "National Liberation through Self-Reliance in Rhodesia, 1956-1972" (Ph.D. thesis, Princeton University, 1976), p. 490.

16. 4 August 1965, Africa Research Bulletin: Political Social and Cultural Series (ARB), 1965, p. 353.

17. Shamuyarira, "National Liberation through Self-Reliance in Rhodesia," pp. 495-96.

18. UNIP received $238,000 prior to the January 1964 general elections.

19. Minutes of the Fifteenth Session of the Co-ordinating Committee for the Liberation of Africa, Dakar, July 1969, cited in B.V. Mtshali, "Zambia's Foreign Policy: The Dilemmas of a New State, 1964-1970" (Ph.D. thesis, New York University, 1972), pp. 286-88.

20. Confidential News Report (Salisbury), 14 January 1964, p. 5.

21. ECM/Res. 13 (VI), 5 December 1965, para. (5); Shamuyarira, "National Liberation through Self-Reliance in Rhodesia," p. 513.

22. 14 November 1965, ZIS Background no. 47/65, p. 4.

23. Activities of the Zambian Broadcasting Corporation: Britain's Part in the Incitement of Murder, Arson, Sabotage and Destruction in Rhodesia (Salisbury: Government Printer, February 1966); and Murder by Radio (Salisbury: Ministry of Information, Immigration and Tourism, July 1966); see also, Kenneth Young, Rhodesia and Independence (London: Dent, 1969), pp. 352-53.

24. Saul Ndhlovu, Times of Zambia, 15 August 1972, p. 1.

25. Programmes (Lusaka: ZBS, September 1973).

26. Mainza Chona, Minister without Portfolio, ZIS Press Release, no. 681/68, 15 April 1968, p. 1; Star (Johannesburg), 3 October 1968. When, in 1968, Kaunda was asked if "these guerrillas pass through Zambia on their way down to Rhodesia and South Africa," he replied: "Certainly. Going and coming back to their own country, they pass through Zambia" (US News and World Report, 2 December 1968, p. 65).

27. Economist, 10 May 1969, pp. 31-32.

28. E.g., S.L. Muller, cited in Africa Contemporary Record (ACR), 1968-69, p. 249; France-Soir (Paris), 20 June 1970, p. 8; "Secret bases in Zambia," To the Point (Johannesburg) 2, no. 3 (10 February 1973):25-29.

29. ZIS Background, no. 31/67, 22 October 1967, pp. 7, 9; see also Times of Zambia, 25 October 1967, p. 1; Zambia N.A. Deb., no. 11, 17 October 1967, c. 34.

30. ZIS Press Release, no. 2114/67, 7 October 1967, p. 1; Times of Zambia, 12 April 1968, p. 1; Zambia News (Ndola), 27 October 1968, p. 1.

31. ZIS Background, no. 25/71, 22 March 1971, p. 3; Zambia Mail (Ndola), 17 December 1965, p. 1.

32. Sunday Times of Zambia, 18 June 1972, p. 2; Times of Zambia, 22 June 1972, p. 7.

33. Organization of African Unity Special 9th Summit (Addis Ababa: OAU, September 1972), p. 39.

34. Guardian (London), 30 May 1967, p. 8.

35. Times, 20 April 1964, p. 12.

36. Central African Mail (Ndola), 12 June 1964, p. 12.

37. Ibid., 26 March 1964, p. 1; Africa 1964 (London), no. 5, 6 March 1964, p. 3.

38. "Visit of Foreign Ministers," press statement, Lusaka, 15 August 1964; Central African Mail, 21 August 1964, p. 12.

39. Immanual Wallerstein, Africa: The Politics of Unity (New York: Praeger, 1968), pp. 166-67.

40. Rhodesia Herald, 22 October 1965, p. 1.

41. Daily Graphic (Accra), 4 March 1966, p. 19; ARB, 1966, p. 483.

42. See ZANU's "Call to All Africans of Zimbabwe" (June 1963) in N. Sithole, African Nationalism, 2nd ed. (London: Oxford University Press, 1968), pp. 41-42.

43. ZIS Background, no. 47/65, 14 November 1965, pp. 4-5. A general strike centered on Bulawayo was quickly crushed, 22-23 November (Good, UDI, pp. 82-83).

44. Guardian, 30 May 1967, p. 8; Zambia Mail, 29 April 1966, p. 12.

45. "National Liberation through Self-Reliance in Rhodesia," p. 554.

46. OAU resolution CM/Res. 153 (XI), para. 12.

47. Shamuyarira, "National Liberation through Self-Reliance in Rhodesia," pp. 485, 493, 495.

48. Richard Gibson, African Liberation Movements: Contemporary Struggles against White Minority Rule (London: Oxford University Press, 1972), pp. 169-73.

49. Zambia Daily Mail, 17 August 1971, p. 7.

50. ACR, 1972-73, p. C41.

51. Times, 19 March 1973, p. 4; Saul G. Ndlovu, Zimbabwe: Some Facts about Its Liberation Struggle [ZAPU: n.p., 1974], p. 59.

52. Shamuyarira, "National Liberation through Self-Reliance in Rhodesia," p. 494.

53. Lusaka agreement, 7 December 1974, ACR, 1974-75, p. B512.

54. Wallerstein, Africa: The Politics of Unity, p. 165.

55. When, in response to an earlier Kaunda invitation, Roberto had attempted to leave the Congo on 25 January 1965, Tshombe's secret police prevented his departure (Ernest Harsch, Angola: The Hidden History of Washington's War [New York: Pathfinder Press, 1976], p. 37).

56. Christian P. Potholm and Richard Dale, eds, Southern Africa in Perspective (New York: Free Press, 1972), p. 197.

57. Africa Confidential (London), 1967, no. 21, 20 October 1967, p. 8; OAU resolutions, CM/Res. 137 (X), para. 10 and CM/Res. 151 (XI), preamble; ACR, 1971-72, p. C20.

58. ARB, 1971, p. 2128.

59. Daily News (Dar es Salaam), 21 December 1974, p. 1.

60. For a sympathetic and insightful discussion of the "perceptual and behavioral problems of exile politics," see John Marcum's analysis in Potholm and Dale, Southern Africa in Perspective, pp. 270-72. He identifies "four types of dysfunctional behavior" as normal psychological impediments of exile: "personal aggression, regression, apathy, and compulsive repetition." See also, Ndlovu, Zimbabwe, p. 49.

61. Information Department, Northern Rhodesia Government, Press Release, no. 695, 12 May 1964, p. 1; Central African Mail, 20 March 1964, p. 6.

62. ZIS Press Release, no. 1518/68, 24 August 1968, p. 1 and no. 1536/68, 28 August 1968, p. 1.

63. Africa Confidential, 1968, no. 18, 6 September 1968, p. 5.

64. Shamuyarira, "National Liberation through Self-Reliance in Rhodesia," pp. 556, 560; Zambia Mail, 25 April 1970, p. 1; Observer, 26 April 1970, p. 5; AFP Africa no. 1676, 15 May 1970, p. 23. The Minister of Home Affairs insisted that the victim had died from a dog bite, not gunshot wounds.

65. Times, 15 March 1971, p. 6; Observer, 28 March 1971.

66. Government Gazette (Lusaka), 7, no. 76 (24 June 1971):569; John Hatch, "Zambia Under Stress," Venture, 23, no. 9 (October 1971):10-11; ARB, 1971, pp. 2295-96.

67. In June 1971, the OAU Secretary-General reported that the crisis within ZAPU was "so serious that it could affect for a long time the liberation struggle" in Rhodesia (ARB, 1971, p. 2124). Accordingly, OAU aid to ZAPU was suspended during 1971-72 (Shamuyarira, "National Liberation through Self-Reliance in Rhodesia," pp. 491, 495). In August 1972, ZAPU guerrilla operations resumed on a modest scale.

68. For text of MPLA Note of 3 June 1973 to the Zambian government, see ACR, 1973-74, pp. C74-75; also Sunday Times of Zambia, 4 August 1974, pp. 1, 4.

69. Ruth Weiss, "Factionalism delays Angolan independence," Montreal Gazette, 14 September 1974, p. 8; ZIS Background, no. 18/76, pp. 13-15. The ready acceptance of the belief in a Zambian commitment to Chipenda appears to have been due to the fact that he resided in Lusaka, that his faction was militarily more active than Neto forces at least along Zambia's western border, and that he happened to accompany Kaunda to Bukavu in the same way that Neto, Andrade and Holden Roberto arrived with their respective patrons, Nyerere, Ngouabi and Mobutu.

70. Government Gazette 3, no. 19 (3 March 1967), p. 158; ZIS Background, no. 35/68, 10 May 1968, p. 2.

71. Zambia Daily Mail, 29 June 1971, p. 4 and 16 October 1971, p. 5.

72. Radio Zambia, 29 January 1965 (ARB, 1965, p. 229).

73. E.g., Times of Zambia, 5 February 1972, p. 7; Zimbabwe News: Official Organ of ZANU (Lusaka) 7, no. 9 (September 1973):6-7.

74. Potholm and Dale, Southern Africa in Perspective, p. 385. n.82; Times of Zambia, 17 August 1971, p. 7.

75. Mainza Chona, "Recruiting Freedom Fighters from Zambian Residents," 8 September 1968. He added that: "Our worry, as Freedom Fighters, is that it is a pity that our comrades [in] ZAPU and ZANU are forcing people to be recruited. There can be no such person as a forced Freedom Fighter."

76. ZIS Press Release, no. 1782/68, 8 October 1968, p. 1 and no. 1899/68, 22 October 1968, p. 1. Forty-one ZAPU and seventeen ZANU members were involved (Times of Zambia, 26 October 1968, p. 1). The Minister of Home Affairs argued that, "Government could not tolerate a situation whereby the liberty and fundamental human rights of Zambian residents and citizens were infringed or violated in a most disgraceful manner" (Press Release, no. 1782/68, p. 1).

77. Central African Mail, 13 March 1964, p. 1; Times of Zambia, 10 September 1965, p. 1.

78. 9 September 1965, ZIS Background no. 35/65, pp. 1, 4, 5; see also Background no. 47/65,

16 November 1965, p. 4. Kaunda also announced that three weeks earlier the Portuguese had lifted their ban on Zambian arms in transit through Mozambique, following assurances that they would not be diverted to FRELIMO.

79. E.g., Times of Zambia, 30 April 1966, p. 6, 11 November 1967, p. 1, and 14 August 1970, p. 1; Zambia Mail, Magazine, 30 December 1966, p. 6.

80. Guardian, 30 May 1967, p. 8.

81. 14 November 1965, ZIS Background no. 47/65, p. 5.

82. ZIS Press Release no. 1080/66, 14 June 1966, p. 1; Observer, 22 May 1966, p. 2.

83. Africa Diary, 1970, p. 4932; Daily Times (Lagos), 31 December 1971, p. 13; Daily Telegraph (London), 17 January 1973.

84. Economist, 30 May 1970, p. 4; David M. Abshire and Michael A. Samuels, eds., Portuguese Africa: A Handbook (New York: Praeger, 1969), p. 397. It has since been argued that FNLA rather than UNITA was responsible (Charles K. Ebinger, "External Intervention in Internal War," Orbis 20, no. 3 [Fall 1976]:682).

7
Zambia and Southern African "Detente"

The tide of independence that swept, seemingly irresistibly, southward across the continent of Africa beginning in the mid-1950's came to an abrupt halt along the Zambezi in the mid-1960's. For nearly a decade, a political stalemate gripped Southern Africa, as independent black Africa and the white minority regimes struggled to control the fate of the more than forty million people of the subcontinent. As the years passed and little progress towards liberation was apparent, the high hopes of Africans began to fade, while the confidence of the ruling minorities in their ability to contain the pressures for change revived. The prospects of majority rule appeared to be receding ever further into the future, and chances of a peaceful transfer of power virtually disappearing.

The decisive rejection in 1972 of Smith's "final" terms of settlement with Britain provided a brief glimpse of the suppressed feelings of Rhodesian Africans. However, it was the Portuguese military coup in April 1974 which finally destroyed the pessimistic assumptions (or comfortable illusions) on which previous scenarios had been based. Within a matter of months, transitional governments were set up in Mozambique and Angola, and firm dates for early independence fixed. Then, in November 1974, South Africa narrowly escaped expulsion from the United Nations. Confronted with these disconcerting developments, Pretoria reacted remarkably rapidly, realistically and even ruthlessly. The result was a radical revision of its previous strategy for survival. In a desperate endeavor to cut its losses and recapture the diplomatic initiative, the South African government signalled its willingness to sacrifice Rhodesia and possibly Namibia on the altar of Southern African détente. The solidarity of the White South had been shattered. In the final analysis, it seemed kith and kin counted for very little.

President Kenneth Kaunda of Zambia was the first African statesman to appreciate the full potentialities for political penetration which the loosening of the Southern African logjam opened up. His response was prompt and imaginative. It was also courageous, for the risks were as great as the stakes were high. In agreeing to dialogue with the devil, Kaunda was exposing himself deliberately and dangerously to blackmail. Prime Minister Vorster of South Africa could at any time, as he did in 1971, pull the rug out from under the Zambian leader. A second Vorster doublecross would almost certainly have destroyed the Zambian President's credibility in the eyes of the rest of Black Africa, where already scepticism and even outright opposition were spreading. Nevertheless, Kaunda decided to gamble with his own reputation in the hope that he could use Vorster to further African objectives in Rhodesia.

While majority rule in Rhodesia within an acceptable time scale was not conceded let alone implemented during the "détente" interlude, the initial dividends from Zambian contacts with South Africa were moderately encouraging. A year earlier, few would have thought such developments possible. The first public intimation of the diplomatic thaw was the remarkable exchange of compliments between the two leaders in late October 1974. Of particular importance was Dr. Kaunda's startling characterization of Vorster's rather prosaic pledge to work for "peace, progress and development" in Southern Africa as "the voice of reason for which Africa and the world have waited for many years."[1] This bombshell at a time when Zambia along with other OAU members was mounting a campaign to drive South Africa out of the UN[2] may in part have been conceived as a Trollope ploy designed to nudge Pretoria into conceding more than it intended. Nevertheless, the rapidity of the response suggests careful orchestration.[3]

These verbal bouquets were quickly followed by more concrete actions. On three occasions, the presidents of the four Front Line States (FLS)[4] conferred secretly in Lusaka with Rhodesian government officials and/or Zimbabwean political leaders, who were released (at first only temporarily) after more than a decade in detention (table 7.1). Moreover, in early December 1974, Zimbabwean nationalist organizations agreed to reunite under the umbrella of the African National Council. In addition, a somewhat

273

TABLE 7.1
Meetings of Front Line States, 1974-1975

Dates	Place	Participants	Zimbabweans	Rhodesians	South Africans
1974					
Oct. 21-25	Lusaka	Kaunda Nyerere Machel Khama Mobutu	Moyo Chitepo		Oppenheimer Luyt
1.Nov. 7-10	Lusaka	Nyerere Kaunda Machel Khama (Neto)	Nkomo Mugabe Gabellah		
2.Dec. 4-7	Lusaka	Nyerere Kaunda Machel Khama	Muzorewa Nkomo Sithole	Gaylard A.Smith O'Neill	Fourie (Dec.9)
1975					
3.Jan. 19	Mbala	Nyerere Kaunda Machel Mogwe	Gabellah Chavunduka		
4.Feb. 7	Dar es Salaam	Nyerere Kaunda Machel Khama	Muzorewa Nkomo Sithole		
Feb. 9	Lusaka	Kaunda Malecela Mogwe	Muzorewa Nkomo Sithole	Gaylard A.Smith (Feb.4)	Muller Fourie
May 11	Dar es Salaam	Nyerere Kaunda Machel			
5.July 5-8	Dar es Salaam	Nyerere Kaunda Machel Khama (Karl I Bond)	Muzorewa Nkomo Sithole		
Aug. 25-26	Victoria Falls	Kaunda	Muzorewa Nkomo Sithole	I.Smith Wrathall De Kock Gaylard van der Byl	Vorster Muller Fourie van den Bergh
6.Sept. 13-15	Lusaka	Nyerere Kaunda Machel Khama			
7.Dec. 15-16	Dar es Salaam	Nyerere Kaunda Machel			

shaky ceasefire in the rapidly escalating guerrilla warfare being waged in Rhodesia was concluded to coincide with the partial restoration of political rights and the opening of "talks about talks" in Salisbury between the Smith regime and the liberation movements concerning the modalities of a constitutional conference. Equally significant was the partial disengagement from active duty of Pretoria's paramilitary police in Rhodesia, and the assurance of their complete withdrawal at an early date. Finally, there was the unprecedented flurry of secret shuttle diplomacy which was the distinctive feature of this "détente" interlude: Mark Chona's successive missions to Cape Town, Pretoria and Salisbury as well as to London and Washington, Hilgard Muller's series of flying visits to Zambia, and Johannes Vorster's penetration of West Africa on two occasions to confer with the presidents of the Ivory Coast, Liberia and Senegal. The culmination of this extraordinary spate of diplomatic interaction across the Zambezi was the historic encounter in August 1975 between the Rhodesian rebels and the Zimbabwean nationalists. This took place in the South African president's private railway carriage symbolically positioned at the precise midpoint of the Victoria Falls bridge across the divide between Black and White Africa. In an adjacent coach, the two sponsors — President Kaunda, on behalf of his fellow FLS colleagues, and Prime Minister Vorster — anxiously awaited the outcome. Despite their initial optimism, the conference quickly foundered. Thereafter, things rapidly fell apart; within six months, the momentum behind the "détente" initiative had petered out. Although there were subsequent, ineffective efforts to revive it, for all practical purposes Ian Smith had once again eluded the trap set for him. Accordingly, the Front Line States reverted with renewed conviction to a reliance on the armed struggle.

This chapter traces the Zambian roots of FLS attempts to enlist South African support to compel Salisbury to negotiate in good faith, and assesses the significance of this strategy of selective contacts for the liberation of Southern Africa. Zambia's actions, dramatic as they were, did not constitute a complete departure from past policy. Rather, they represented the consummation, after years of failure and frustration of intermittent efforts by Dr. Kaunda to convince white leaders in Southern Africa through quiet diplomacy that a peaceful resolution of the conflicts on the basis of justice and

equality was the only alternative to a bloody racial
holocaust that they were bound to lose in the end.
Zambian explorations of the potentialities of contacts with Pretoria fall into three periods. During
1964, Dr. Kaunda sought to barter Zambian diplomatic
and military concessions in return for specific modifications to South African domestic policy. This
proved unproductive. In 1968 and again in 1974-75,
Lusaka's strategy was to enlist South African support
in coercing the Smith regime in Rhodesia into conceding majority rule. In none of these instances
was any compromise with the principle of apartheid
involved. On the contrary, the entrenched racialism
of South Africa remained the ultimate foe.

DIPLOMATIC SUBVERSION

        In January 1964, on the eve of his election as
first Prime Minister of Northern Rhodesia, Dr. Kaunda
initiated an abortive attempt to exchange ambassadors
with South Africa.[5] His purpose was to effect "a
change of heart" there and thus transform apartheid
into "something better." He was not the first African statesman to adopt this strategy. During the
early years of Ghana's independence, President Nkrumah made a determined effort to court Pretoria in
the optimistic expectation that "the multiracial example of Ghana" would serve as an instrument to reform apartheid. In addition to publicly undertaking
not to interfere in South Africa's internal affairs,
Nkrumah actively promoted closer diplomatic, political, trade and cultural contacts. South Africa was
officially represented at Ghana's Independence celebrations and was invited to (but declined to attend)
the first Conference of Independent African States
in Accra in 1958. As late as October 1959, Foreign
Minister Louw was pressed to visit Ghana as part of
an exchange of ministerial delegations which hopefully would lead to agreement on reciprocal diplomatic representation. All this changed, however,
following the Sharpeville massacre in 1960 and the
withdrawal (which Nkrumah regretted) of South Africa
from the Commonwealth the next year. Subsequently,
Nkrumah bitterly assailed Kaunda's efforts to emu-
late his earlier example.[6]
        Apartheid touched Kaunda much more personally
than it did Nkrumah. "I find myself obsessed with
the tremendous problem of South Africa," the Zambian
leader confessed in early 1964. "If bloodshed really
does begin in South Africa, it will have a ghastly
effect, not only within the Republic itself, but

throughout the whole continent of Africa." Accordingly, he searched his heart for "a new approach to help all South Africans to solve their problem peacefully." In his opinion, the present was "the most critical psychological moment to show that there is understanding and sympathy for the people of South Africa."[7]

In publicly proposing an exchange of ambassadorial missions with Pretoria, Dr. Kaunda emphasized that he would insist on Zambian diplomats and their families (expected to number 30 to 40) receiving equal treatment with representatives of other states. "We will not have them pushed around as Kaffirs," he warned.[8] This condition proved a major stumbling block. "It must be very clear to representatives of other countries in South Africa," Prime Minister Verwoerd declared three months later, "that, while we shall act in their countries in accordance with their customs, we . . . expect them to act in South Africa in accordance with South Africa's customs."[9]

Apart from this one indirect allusion to the Zambian offer, the official response of the Pretoria regime was embarrassed silence. Clearly, the government was intensely irritated at what it regarded as at best a mischievous propaganda stunt and at worst a calculated act of subversion. As one South African commentator reported:

> If Dr. Kenneth Kaunda . . . had offered
> to send a force of saboteurs to South
> Africa, he could not have created a
> bigger stir than he has done by offering
> to exchange ambassadors . . . . Dr. Kaunda's suggestion has angered, rather than
> appeased South African leaders. They
> clearly suspect that he wants to smuggle
> a Trojan horse into the country in the
> shape of a black diplomat . . . . For this
> reason, they interpret Dr. Kaunda's offer
> as a threat. From the diplomatic mission
> which his ambassador would establish in
> Pretoria, they foresee a force of guerrilla
> fighters emerging — trained not to use
> guns and explosives, but to undermine at
> public banquets and at social gatherings
> the whole structure of the color bar on
> which apartheid is founded.[10]

This scenario, while grossly exaggerated, was not entirely misperceived. When challenged to reconcile his proposal with OAU policy, Dr. Kaunda denied there was any inconsistency: "It is just another way of fighting the same battle." The difference lay in the means, not the ends. Diplomatic immunity was conceived as an instrument to penetrate the South African laager and pierce the armor of apartheid.

Diplomatic relations with the South were perceived in Lusaka as a special case of exercising influence by moral precept. President Kaunda preferred that white racists should repent of their sins and be saved than that they should be destroyed. While his expectations in this regard were never as great as those of Malawi's Dr. Banda, he did consider the attempt at moral conquest might still represent a worthwhile endeavor. "We hope that by forming a good government here," a UNIP spokesman explained before Independence, "we will influence these [Southern African] countries to realize that what is possible here is possible there."[11] Hence the emphasis in Zambia on setting an example of racial harmony and exporting the image wherever possible. One redeeming feature of the residual common services reluctantly retained with Rhodesia following the breakup of the Federation was that they would enable Rhodesian whites to learn to work on a basis of equality with Zambian blacks.[12] The same faith in the persuasive potential of the Zambian experiment in nonracialism also underlay the invitations, in the heady atmosphere of 1974 and 1975, to leaders of white opinion in Southern Africa to see Zambia for themselves. As a result, a Rhodesian parliamentary delegation, prominent South African businessmen, a SABC television team and two Rhodesian farmers as well as Sir Roy Welensky toured the country. No doubt, their experiences contributed to challenging some common misconceptions of Zambia, but whether they made a significant impact on entrenched white racial stereotypes in Southern Africa is less certain.

By publicly declaring his interest even before Independence in establishing direct diplomatic relations with South Africa, Dr. Kaunda was clearly flying a kite. This explains his resort to the medium of a press interview with a Rhodesian journalist. Subsequently, he announced that he would be communicating an official offer to Pretoria within a few months. This was never sent. The negative reaction of the South African Government (and perhaps also that of Nkrumah and other African critics) deterred Kaunda from further formal action. Nevertheless, he continued to promote the idea periodically in public pronouncements in the course of the next six months, and only reluctantly abandoned "this last chance of helping to solve" South Africa's complex racial problem.

In the meantime, Pretoria had rebuffed two private Zambian initiatives during this period.[13] On the first occasion, Kaunda wrote President Swart appealing to him "very quietly," as the UN Secretary General had done publicly, to commute the death sentences handed down on three freedom fighters convicted in March 1964 of sabotage and murder. Swart did not bother to reply, or even acknowledge the letter and, in due course, the men were executed. Later, in June 1964, following the sentences of life imprisonment passed on Nelson Mandela and seven other ANC leaders, Kaunda cabled Swart to ask that these and other South African nationalists, including PAC leader Robert Sobukwe, be sent to Zambia in return for an undertaking that Zambia would not be used as a base for subversion against South Africa. This amounted to offering a kind of nonaggression pact. Again, there was no acknowledgement. Kaunda was understandably upset. "I am beginning to wonder," he declared, "whether in fact I am not being treated like a fool in my serious attempts to try and help, genuinely help, in this very serious problem." Accordingly, he decided that this would be "the last serious attempt to try and establish contact with that country."

Three years later, following Vorster's accession to power and the enunciation of the "outward looking" foreign policy, Pretoria revised its stand on black diplomats. But Zambia, unlike Malawi, was no longer interested. In the intervening period, the domestic racial policies of the South African regime had hardened further, and Kaunda could no longer see how Zambian diplomats could "in any way help in that situation." He also commented caustically that he hoped African ambassadors would not be required to wear "rings around their necks to announce the arrival of their excellencies."[14]

CONFIDENTIAL CORRESPONDENCE

Although, by the time of Independence in 1964, Zambia had largely abandoned hope of promoting internal reforms in South Africa through persuasion and example, UDI in Rhodesia provided an incentive to seek Pretoria's cooperation in ending the rebellion, or at least to secure guarantees of its neutrality. With the failure of UN economic sanctions to topple Ian Smith "within a matter of weeks rather than months" — or years, and the refusal of Britain to employ force, South Africa became the key to the survival of the Salisbury regime. She alone possessed

the leverage to dictate the fate of the rebel cause.
Admittedly, Portuguese Mozambique also connived fully and profitably in Rhodesian strategems to circumvent international sanctions. Nevertheless, South
Africa remained the major collaborator in sanction-
busting; in the critical matter of oil imports, her
role was decisive. Equally significant were Pretoria's actions in supporting the Rhodesian dollar
artificially by continuing to accept it at par and,
after August 1967, in openly intervening militarily
to bolster the hardpressed Rhodesian security forces.
     The South African government also gradually be-
gan to reassess its attitude towards Zambia. After
its initial blunder in spurning Kaunda's spontaneous
gestures of goodwill, Pretoria came to recognize more
clearly the crucial significance of Zambia for its
evolving strategy towards its African hinterland.
This was not merely a matter of the potential threat
which Zambia's geopolitical position as a host state
for liberation movements operating against Southern
Africa posed. On the positive side, her relative
wealth and political stability marked her out as an
attractive target for trade and investment. Moreover, Zambia's progressive policies and dynamic
leadership contributed greatly to her credibility
in OAU circles as a "militant" pan-African state;
this constituted an important asset in any South
African scheme to penetrate the continent. In a
very real sense, Zambia stood politically and geographically at the gateway to Africa. As a result, she
came to be perceived by policymakers in Pretoria as
the real prize, all the more so for being elusive.
Although publicly far greater attention was showered
on Malawi, this was faute de mieux and not because
of any intrinsic importance she possessed.
     Preliminary South African probing of Zambian
receptivity to suggestions for improved relations
began even before UDI, but intensified following Verwoerd's assassination and Vorster's assumption of
power. The primary thrust behind the drive was a
call for a personal meeting between Kaunda and Vorster at which mutual cooperation over a wide range of
functional issue areas could be discussed. Although
Lusaka apparently did not reject the idea on principle, it always found the specific dates Pretoria proposed "inopportune." Later, as a result of the escalation of guerrilla activity in Zimbabwe during
1967 and 1968, the question of Rhodesia was added to
the South African agenda. While publicly Pretoria
continued to pretend that UDI was purely a domestic
issue, it was increasingly concerned to see it

settled speedily. Accordingly, Lusaka was asked for
its views on suitable terms for a compromise settlement, and invited to join with rebel representatives
in tripartite talks.[15]

Zambia studiously ignored South African feelers
for the first two years or so.[16] However, she was
interested in exploring Pretoria's intentions concerning Rhodesia. Accordingly, in April 1968, President Kaunda addressed a lengthy personal letter
to Prime Minister Vorster detailing frankly but un-
emotionally the ideological and political impediments
to cooperation. He concluded:

> I am convinced beyond doubt that you per-
> sonally, Mr. Prime Minister, hold the key
> to the future insofar as finding peaceful
> solutions to problems confronting the whole
> of Southern Africa is concerned.

In an equally frank but somewhat less honest reply
a month later, Vorster denounced Kaunda's letter as
being "as presumptuous as it is uninformed." However, he concluded with an appeal for assistance in
widening the circle of cooperation in the subcontinent. "You, Mr. President", he acknowledged,
" . . . hold the key to the extension of this cooperation to all countries in Southern Africa."[17]

The following month, perhaps encouraged by Zambia's recognition of Biafra, Vorster despatched a
high-ranking emissary to Lusaka who again pressed
unsuccessfully for a meeting between the two leaders.[18]
Then in August, during the flurry of consultations
concerning Rhodesia leading up to the Fearless talks,
Kaunda wrote two further letters to Vorster, and received a second South African emissary.[19] Thereafter,
the correspondence ceased.

In his initial letter,[20] President Kaunda identified three factors — one general and two specific
— which accounted for the deterioration in relations
between the two countries to "about their lowest
ebb," despite the "vast potential" for "unlimited
cooperation" that existed. The root cause of the
difficulty was "the offensive nature of the preju-
dices of the South African authorities against Africans." This constituted "the only obstacle to a
much happier relationship between South Africa and
Zambia . . . . nothing else stands in the way of
the achievement of this objective." Consequently,
until Pretoria was prepared to treat all human beings
on a basis of equality, justice and mutual respect,
any form of cooperation would amount to "dishonesty
if not hypocrisy." At the same time, Kaunda expressed confidence that Vorster had "the necessary

courage and foresight" to enable him "to do within
South Africa" what he was doing "in cooperation with
certain independent African states." In his hard-
hitting reply, Vorster angrily repudiated any suggestion that apartheid involved a denial of human
rights or implied any notion of racial superiority.
In any case, "our domestic policy is our concern."
"What the world, and Africa in particular need today,"
he lectured Kaunda, "are leaders who mind their own
business."

Secondly, President Kaunda protested against
Vorster's publicly articulated threat in October
1967 that, in the event of an attack on South Africa,
he would "hit Zambia so hard that she will never forget it." Three times in the course of his letter,
Kaunda reiterated that:

> We in Zambia have nothing against the
> white people in South Africa as such.
> We have never adopted a policy of
> "Driving the white people into the
> sea" — this would in fact be unima-
> ginable, unrealistic and unChristian.

Vorster replied that his "timely warning" had not
been "a threat but a plain statement of fact," necessitated by "repeated statements by representatives
of Zambia . . . about the use of force against South
Africa and the putting of Zambian territory at the
disposal of terrorists." He then added ominously:
"That, to say the least of it, is to play a very dangerous game and you will do well to think it over
very carefully."[21] Kaunda was indignant at this further misrepresentation of his position. Although he
ignored the reference to "terrorists," he insisted
"with respect" in his response in August 1968 that,

> it is just not true that Zambia has
> advocated the use of force against
> South Africa. We have always, and
> ever since UDI, made a clear distin-
> ction between the problem in Rhodesia
> and the problem in your country. I
> want to reaffirm the fact that at no
> time has my Government or its repre-
> sentatives advocated the use of force
> against South Africa . . . . In ac-
> tual fact, nobody, at least in this
> part of the world, has considered the
> question of lumping together South
> Africa with the rest of the minority
> regimes. It is only South Africa's
> apparent decision to throw in her lot
> with the rebel regime in Rhodesia which

has brought her into the full focus
of criticism by the rest of the international community. We are perfectly
aware in Zambia that the solutions
which are being proposed for Rhodesia
are not applicable to the situation in
South Africa. It is important to understand, therefore, that at no time have
we considered that force is the answer
in South Africa.[22]

This assurance was somewhat less categorical than it
appeared. In particular, it blurred the distinction
which Kaunda undoubtedly made in his own mind between a conventional military invasion, such as he
had been advocating that the British should undertake
in Rhodesia, and external support for guerrilla action by South Africans. Also, he conveniently ignored Vorster's second specific charge of putting
"Zambian territory at the disposal of terrorists
who were trained by communists and others to murder South African citizens and to subvert the state."[23]

Rhodesia was the third obstacle to better understanding between Zambia and South Africa. Kaunda
sought to persuade Vorster that he was acting contrary to his own national interest in continuing to
shore up Smith. This was not only perpetuating op-
pressive racial policies, but promoting instability
and insecurity throughout Southern Africa. In any case,
the odds against the survival of the rebel regime
were "overwhelming." Instead, Pretoria should withdraw its economic and military assistance prepara-
tory to the restoration of direct British control
and the progressive introduction of majority rule.
Vorster remained totally unconvinced. "I am not
aware," he snapped back sharply, "that Rhodesia seeks
to harm or destroy Zambia . . . . It might just,
therefore, be worth your while to reconsider your own
attitude."[24]

Nevertheless, some weeks later Vorster intimated through an intermediary his willingness to discuss a settlement in Rhodesia on the basis of eventual majority rule. In mid-August 1968, on his return from overseas, Kaunda proposed that, as a first
step, there should be "a full and free referendum"
to test the true opinions of the people of Rhodesia.[25]
This idea evidently struck a responsive chord, for
Vorster quickly despatched a second envoy to Lusaka
to probe Kaunda's thinking on the subject more
fully.[26] Whether this sudden interest was prompted
by the recent flare up in guerrilla activity in Rhodesia (and the death of the first South African

policeman) or simply the impending visit to South Africa of Prime Minister Wilson's personal representative, Lord Goodman, is not clear. Certainly, it signified recognition by Vorster that any lasting settlement in Rhodesia would require Kaunda's seal of approval.

In amplifying on his referendum proposal, Dr. Kaunda stipulated that it should be countrywide in scope, that political detainees should be released and fundamental freedoms restored, that the nationalist parties should in return foreswear violence, and that the whole operation should be subject to international supervision. For this latter purpose, he suggested a commission comprised of Britain, Canada, India, Kenya and Sweden as well as South Africa and Zambia.[27]

In the end, nothing came of this initiative, possibly because by then the freedom fighter offensive had lost its momentum. In any case, Vorster drew back and declined to intervene effectively in the Anglo-Rhodesian negotiations. As a result, Smith and Wilson were left to battle themselves to a stalemate on board HMS Fearless in October. Nevertheless, Vorster continued to exude optimism. Publicly, he repeatedly assured Zambia of his fervent desire for friendship and, privately, he confidently predicted that, faced with the realities of Zambia's continuing economic dependence on the South, Kaunda would in due course "come around."[28] As Derek Ingram commented perceptively in November 1968:

> The most immediate priority in South Africa's foreign ministry today is the wooing and seduction of Zambia and its president, Dr. Kenneth Kaunda. The South Africans have made an exhaustive study of the president, his personality, style of government, and the political situation in Zambia. They have reached the conclusion that it should be possible to "neutralize" Zambia by persuading it to adopt a more friendly attitude to South Africa. It is all part of a masterplan which . . . aims at creating a buffer swathe right across Africa's waist so that the penetration of militant black Africa can be kept well at bay . . . .
>
> Thus it is Zambia that is the key to the South Africa masterplan . . . . So important does South Africa consider the seduction of Zambia it is reported to have offered President Kaunda a bodyguard

of 12 men to protect him from personal
harm if Zambia changes its policy.
Pretoria believes that the president
is more malleable than any other potential leader in Zambia.[29]

This strategic appreciation of the Zambian situation indicated a fundamentally faulty assessment
of Kaunda's character, reflecting apparently an
easy equation of Christian humanism with political
softness. In any case, President Kaunda's response
was to reiterate publicly what had previously been
spelt out in secret correspondence concerning the
conditions on which cooperation would be possible.
While welcoming Pretoria's expressions of friendship
and emphasizing that Zambia had never declared any
hatred for whites nor any intention of chasing them
into the sea, he explained on the eve of the Fearless talks that
       nothing stands between South Africa and
       Zambia in fostering friendship and coop-
       eration except for that government's
       policy of apartheid . . . . For South
       Africa . . . to court friendship with us
       under the prevailing conditions within
       that country amounts to asserting that
       we in Zambia are superior Africans to
       the Mandelas and Sobukwes.[30]
Despite this, Vorster remained convinced that Kaunda's
objections to South Africa's racial policies were
due simply to inaccurate information and that, if
only the two leaders could meet, these misunderstandings would quickly be dispelled. Following
persistent requests, discussions concerning the possibilities of a summit meeting took place in Lusaka
in February 1969, in Johannesburg the following
month, and in Munich in May 1970. In each case, the
talks ended inconclusively. As Vorster lamented
later, there was "always some excuse" why Kaunda
could not attend.[31]
       Meanwhile, in April 1969, the summit Conference
of East and Central African States meeting in Lusaka
issued a Manifesto on Southern Africa which was subsequently adopted by both the OAU and the UN General
Assembly.[32] Presidents Kaunda and Nyerere were its
principal authors (see chapter 2). This historic
document affirmed that on "the objective of liberation" there could be "neither surrender nor compromise." Nevertheless,
       we would prefer to negotiate rather than
       destroy, to talk rather than kill. We

do not advocate violence; we advocate an end to the violence against human dignity which is now being perpetuated by the oppressors of Africa.

Moreover, self-determination did not necessarily imply immediate majority rule. Not only was "some compromise on the timing of change" possible, but the institutions of self-government might, at least initially, take account of minority fears and "group self-consciousness." The Lusaka Manifesto also sought to reassure White Africans that:

> Our stand towards Southern Africa . . . involves a rejection of racialism, not a reversal of the existing racial domination. We believe that all the peoples who have made their homes in the countries of Southern Africa are Africans, regardless of the color of their skins, and we would oppose a racialist majority government.

The response from Pretoria was disappointing. While welcoming this evidence of "greater realism" on the part of African states, Foreign Minister Muller regretted that much of the document was based on misconceptions. In particular, its authors "falsely believe that there is racial discrimination in South Africa." Their refusal to accept at face value South Africa's repeated assurance of her commitment to the principle of human dignity, enshrined in the doctrine of apartheid, meant they were blocking the dialogue they claimed to favor. South Africa also complained that the Lusaka Manifesto was never officially submitted to it. Nevertheless, her attitude was clear; the African offer to seek peaceful political change in Southern Africa as an alternative to violence was spurned. Instead, in October 1969, Pretoria launched operation "dialogue" to convince Black Africa, in return for economic benefits, to "accept us as we are." This amounted to an attempt to internationalize apartheid by elevating the concept of "separate development" to the level of state actors.[33]

DIALOGUE

Dialogue with South Africa has proved the most contentious issue in OAU politics since UDI in 1965. Not that any African state supported Pretoria's version of dialogue; even its most outspoken advocates justified dialogue as a positive contribution to the eradication of racialism rather than acquiescence in it. Nor was the issue in dispute whether

286

to negotiate, but rather when and under what conditions. Admittedly, some Zimbabwean and South African nationalist leaders did, in practice, come close to repudiating negotiations in principle in favor of unrelenting armed struggle and unconditional surrender. However, other liberation movements, notably those in the Portuguese colonies, as well as the front line states not only accepted the desirability of meaningful negotiations but urged them as the preferred solution. In fact, all OAU members, by endorsing the Lusaka Manifesto, were formally committed to this approach. On the other hand, attitudes quickly polarized around the issue of whether to initiate exploratory contacts at that time, and what precise preconditions to insist upon. Despite considerable differences in emphasis within the "dialogue club",[34] all shared a common conviction that the armed struggle had failed or, as in the case of Dr. Banda, was counterproductive, and should be abandoned or at least supplemented by an alternative strategy. Accordingly, they favored responding positively to Pretoria's appeal for cooperation between black and white governments. They stipulated no prior conditions; there was no insistence on a domestic dialogue within South Africa, or even on the inclusion of apartheid among the agenda topics. Yet, these were the points Zambia and a majority of OAU members contested.

A further cause of controversy was the composition of the "dialogue club." It comprised an ill-assorted group of conservative (and generally anti-communist) African states, most of whom were economically heavily dependent on South Africa or her friend, France. The neocolonial image they projected was enough to discredit the whole idea in the eyes of many African radicals. The liberation movements were particularly suspicious, as they feared that dialogue implied:
(1) negotiations conducted between the minority regimes and independent African states over the heads of the indigenous peoples;
(2) a sellout, that is, a settlement on terms which, politically, fell short of immediate or assured majority rule and, economically, opened the door to neocolonialism; and, most disturbing of all,
(3) the possibility of a transfer of power to African representatives other than the freedom fighters — who, not surprisingly, felt that they alone had earned the right to inherit the political kingdom.

President Banda of Malawi was the pioneer proponent of dialogue. As early as December 1967, he

287

had exchanged diplomatic missions with South Africa, and in May 1970 welcomed Vorster to his country. Both actions aroused widespread criticism in Africa. Yet it was not until President Houphouet-Boigny of the Ivory Coast championed the cause that the dialogue debate assumed continental proportions. In November 1970, following assiduous courting by Pretoria (and discreet encouragement by Paris), he proposed a "peace mission" to "help the South African whites to enter into dialogue with their own blacks." Further fuel was added to the fire with his widely publicized declaration some six months later that, "after due consideration," he had concluded that dialogue was now "possible." The controversy peaked at the OAU summit in June 1971. There, dialogue was overwhelmingly repudiated, except where "designed solely to obtain for the enslaved people of South Africa their legitimate and inherent rights and the elimination of apartheid." Even in such cases, it should be "commenced only between the minority racist regime of South Africa and the people they are oppressing, exploiting and suppressing." It was a notable victory, but the price paid was considerable; nearly a third of the OAU membership either openly opposed the resolution, abstained, or walked out.[35]

Zambia was firmly in the majority camp. Despite the apparently flourishing friendship between Kaunda and Houphouet-Boigny that developed during the Biafran conflict, their approaches to South Africa were diametrically opposed. Zambia fiercely denounced any contact that might accord a measure of respectability to apartheid. "The philosophies of Zambia and South Africa on the question of the dignity of man are so divergent," an official statement explained, "that it would be impossible on Zambia's part to imagine any possibility of dialogue with South Africa." The Zambian foreign minister summed up the situation even more trenchantly: "No matter what an African's position, he would be just a nigger to Vorster."[36]

Following the failure of its initial efforts in 1968 to enlist Zambian participation in a Southern African coprosperity sphere, Pretoria attempted to bring Lusaka into line indirectly by mobilizing support for dialogue among African states farther afield. Eventually, this strategy too proved counterproductive but, in the process of promoting it, Vorster stooped to blackmail and character assassination. Early in 1971, following President Kaunda's return from the stormy Commonwealth Conference in

Singapore where he had played a leading part in opposing the resumption of British arms sales to South Africa, Vorster threatened to expose Kaunda as a "double-talker".[37] When this evoked no panic response from Lusaka, he despatched an envoy to Zambia (on 27 March) to reiterate his warning. Kaunda's reaction was that Vorster was free to publicize their contacts if he so wished. Accordingly, on 21 April — a week before Houphouet-Boigny's planned announcement on dialogue and two weeks before the opening of a critical UNIP Party Congress in Zambia — Vorster delivered a blistering personal attack on Kaunda. After quoting selectively from their 1968 correspondence, and extrapolating at length, he reached his peroration:

> Here one has the president of a country who, on the one hand, tells the African states . . . "Under no circumstances must you have a dialogue with South Africa . . . . " But ever since 1968 he himself has been having a dialogue with us. Here one has the president of a country saying, "It is pernicious to trade with South Africa, and you may not do so." But he himself trades with South Africa. Here one has a man who, on the one hand, . . . says that we want to attack him . . . . But in the same breath he tells us that others want to destroy him and that we must help him. Here one has a man who, on the one hand, tells the world outside that we are colonialists and, on the other hand, tells me that he has never said this about us. Here one has a man who, on the one hand, advocates the use of force against us morning, noon and night, and then tells me, "Nobody, at least in this part of the world, has ever said such a thing."

Vorster concluded by stating rather patronizingly that, although he was "making many allowances" for Kaunda, exposure of him was necessary "for the good of Southern Africa." He then issued an open invitation to Kaunda "to honor that promise of talks," adding, however, that: "I hope and trust that this double standard, this double-talking, will now stop once and for all."[38]

The immediate impact was devastating. Vorster had clearly set out to destroy Kaunda's credibility and authority in the eyes of the Zambian people and of the OAU, and it appeared that he had succeeded. "Goodbye, Dr. Kaunda" crowed the Afrikaans newspaper

Rapport in its banner headline.[39] Yet, once Kaunda
responded by promptly publishing the full text of
the four letters exchanged, the tide of opinion began
to shift. Vorster was now exposed as having misrepresented the facts for purely political purposes.
Moreover, in allowing his emotions to get the better
of his judgment, he committed what the London Times
in an editorial entitled "A Funny Way to Run a
Dialogue," termed an obvious "diplomatic blunder."[40]
Even President Houphouet-Boigny, who had a vested
interest in personal communications remaining confidential, publicly reprimanded Vorster for his gross
indiscretion. In the end, far from being discredited,
Kaunda emerged as a realistic and responsible state-
man rather than as the unreliable and unprincipled
extremist that Vorster had tried to portray him.
        Serious discussion of dialogue petered out by
the end of 1971, as Pretoria's relations with black
Africa plummetted to a new low. Even in the case of
the neighboring dependent states of Botswana and
Lesotho, the level of conflict escalated sharply.
Besides, the focus of attention in Southern Africa
was shifting to Rhodesia and the Pearce Commission's
test of acceptability of the British Conservative
Government's settlement terms. Nevertheless, within
three years, dialogue had been restored to the center
of the political stage. Despite the past history
of their relationship, Kaunda and Vorster, as the unchallenged leaders of the major black and white
states in the region were "condemned to live together" (as President Boumedienne has said of Algeria and France). Their fates were inextricably
interlocked in an interdependent community of conflict. As a result, "dialogue" re-emerged disguised
as "détente." Majority rule in Rhodesia was the
immediate issue of common concern that brought the
two antagonists together.

"DETENTE"

        The overthrow of the Portuguese government in
April 1974, and the military and political successes
of FRELIMO in central Mozambique which precipitated
it, transformed the Southern African political scene.
By September, a provisional government headed by a
FRELIMO prime minister had been installed in Maputo,
only forty miles from the South African border, and
an independence date set for the following June.
This dramatic turn of events presented Pretoria with
an acute dilemma: whether to intervene massively to
shore up the crumbling edifice of white minority rule

290

in Southern Africa, or to attempt an orderly strategic retreat behind its own politically and militarily
defensible borders. Confronted with this harsh
choice, the laager mentality successfully reasserted
itself. The decision to accept reality and adapt to
the new environment appears to have been taken as
early as June 1974 following the first meeting in
Lusaka between the Portuguese Foreign Minister and
FRELIMO President Machel, but the real test of sin-
cerity came in September at the time of the white
settler revolt in Mozambique. Pretoria's firm refusal to assist in any way, or to permit mercenaries
to mount a rescue operation, sealed the fate of the
uprising.

Rhodesia, as the most exposed outpost of the
Southern African defense perimeter, was clearly
marked out as the first victim of the new order.
The growing strength of the Zimbabwe African National
Liberation Army (ZANLA) operating under ZANU direction in northeastern Rhodesia since December 1972,
and the lengthening list of South African police
casualties, had already led Pretoria to reassess
its commitment to the Salisbury regime, especially
as South African liberation movements were no longer
active in Rhodesia — the original pretext for direct military intervention. The South African Government's own deep forebodings were amply confirmed
when General William Yarborough, retired head of
US Special Warfare Training, reported, following
secret missions to forward areas in Rhodesia early
in 1974, that Southern Africa had the "makings of
another Vietnam."[41] That was prior to the Portuguese
coup. Even then, the mounting guerrilla threat in
Rhodesia was confronting Pretoria with a fateful
decision whether to escalate the level of its involvement in Rhodesia by buttressing its police units
with regular troops. The collapse of Portuguese
power in Mozambique settled the matter. Rhodesia
was now clearly indefensible; militarily, she was
hopelessly outflanked and, economically, she found
her major rail outlets to the sea threatened. Moreover, the Limpopo river barrier, which for South
Africans was the psychological equivalent of the
Maginot Line, had been breached. Southern Africa
could never be the same again.

South Africa's initial approaches to Zambia in
February 1974 — three months before the coup in
Lisbon — were studiously ignored.[42] Kaunda was understandably reluctant to invite a repetition of the
shabby treatment he had received three years earlier.
Nevertheless, when the probing persisted and especially when, following the Mozambique revolution,

291

Pretoria indicated a willingness to discuss Rhodesia seriously, Kaunda finally decided to respond; South Africa might prove helpful in the "crusade" Lusaka was intent on launching to clear up the "unfinished business of liberation" in Southern Africa.[43] Accordingly, after a series of strategy sessions with neighboring African states, and urgent consultations in August with British Foreign Secretary Callaghan in Geneva and Secretary of State Kissinger in Washington, Zambia presented Pretoria with her three "minimum and urgent" demands.[44] These were in rough order of priority a "definite commitment" not to interfere "directly or indirectly" with decolonization in Mozambique or Angola, a timetable for the withdrawal of South African police units from Rhodesia, and "real self-determination and independence" for a united Namibia. Lusaka also let it be known — though this was played down publicly — that ultimately there would have to be a progressive liberalization of racial policies in South Africa herself. It was a formidable list, but not one that was so impossible that it would be dismissed out of hand. When, therefore, Vorster refrained from intervening in Mozambique's UDI crisis in September 1974, Kaunda was sufficiently encouraged to explore the possibilities of concerted action to resolve the Rhodesian issue. "If South Africa is interested in moving towards us," the Zambian foreign minister announced, "we are prepared to help by paying a price to achieve peace in the region."[45] In the course of the next four months, the two governments held bilateral discussions in Cape Town, Pretoria, Lusaka and Salisbury on at least fifteen occasions.[46]

At these sessions, an early understanding was reached on the goal of a peaceful transition to majority rule in Rhodesia and on a coordinated strategy to bring this about. This involved a de facto division of diplomatic labor: Pretoria undertook to drag Smith to the conference table for meaningful negotiations on the attainment of majority rule within a reasonable period of time, provided Lusaka succeeded in convincing the liberation movements to suspend the armed struggle, form a united front, and negotiate in good faith. Neither of the principals found the task of persuasion easy. The Zimbabwean leaders appear to have assumed that the battle had already been won and that it only remained to decide who would wear the crown. When the Zambian and Tanzanian officials first visited Salisbury prison in early November 1974, they were somewhat shaken to

292

learn not only that Ndabaningi Sithole was not
speaking to Joshua Nkomo, but also that he had been
deposed as ZANU leader by Robert Mugabe three weeks
earlier. Moreover, as soon as the detainees were
united with their wings in Lusaka, the power struggles within and between the rival factions resumed.
It was only with the greatest difficulty that the
frontline presidents, and notably Nyerere who used
his fierce temper to good purpose, succeeded in
jolting the four nationalist leaders into agreeing
on 7 December to a Declaration of Unity which papered
over the cracks temporarily.[47] Vorster, too, experienced difficulty disciplining his client. Ian Smith
was still not convinced that all was lost; in particular, he was counting on nationalist disunity to
save him once again. When, therefore, negotiations
between the Rhodesians and Zimbabweans appeared on
the point of success, he abruptly rejected the Lusaka Agreement which provided for a ceasefire in
return for political concessions and a constitutional
conference. Thus confronted with a challenge with
consequences "too ghastly to contemplate," Vorster
intervened swiftly and decisively. Smith thereupon
executed a skillful tactical retreat and, verbally
at least, fell into line.[48] Thereafter, the Front
Line States and South Africa were in a race against
time to maintain the momentum of "détente" and prevent the fragile consensus from dissolving. It was
a race they eventually lost.

     Throughout the first half of 1975, the shaky
edifice of Rhodesian "détente" was constantly threatened with collapse by a series of crises arising
out of deliberate provocation by Smith, Sithole's
intransigence, Mugabe's hostility to Kaunda and Nkomo's bid for ANC leadership, Kaunda's plain speaking
on South Africa at the White House in Washington
and at the Commonwealth Conference in Jamaica, propaganda battles between the protagonists in the
press,[49] and growing unease among militant and some
moderate OAU members at the implication of cooperating with South Africa even for the purpose of liberating Zimbabwe. Eventually, it was resolved to
make one final, supreme effort to secure a peaceful
settlement. Accordingly, following two secret visits
by Brand Fourie, the South African Secretary for
Foreign Affairs, to Lusaka in July, Mark Chona conferred with Vorster and Smith in Pretoria on 9 August.
The resulting Pretoria Agreement, to which the other
FLS presidents gave their formal support, provided
for a three-stage procedure: a preliminary conference "without any preconditions" on the Victoria

Falls bridge, detailed negotiations in committees "within Rhodesia," and a further formal conference to ratify the terms of settlement. In addition, a secret annex called for an end to the "infiltration of terrorists" in return for a promise of "no new detentions" during the committee stage. Finally, the four FLS governments "expressed their willingness to ensure" that the ANC implemented the Agreement; in return, Pretoria undertook to guarantee Salisbury's compliance.50

Unfortunately, the ANC, although closely consulted on the agreement, was not a signatory of it, and declined to be bound by it. Nevertheless, after further clarification concerning the right of ANC leaders to confer freely with their colleagues in Zambia, the Victoria Falls conference convened on 25 August. There, the symbolism of the bridge and the brooding presence of Kaunda and Vorster proved insufficient to impel the two parties "to publicly express their genuine desire to negotiate an acceptable settlement."51 The rebel regime remained blind to the political opportunities open to it and oblivious to the military realities confronting it.

Although Kaunda strove mightily to keep hopes of a nonviolent solution alive, the fracturing of the ANC and the South African invasion of Angola effectively undercut the foundations on which his earlier endeavors had been based. He actively encouraged the Smith - Nkomo negotiations for a genuine internal settlement (15 December 1975-19 March 1976) and furnished diplomatic, material and personnel support.52 Yet, even before the final collapse of the talks, he had concluded that Vorster was clearly unwilling and possibly unable to intervene forcefully enough to ensure their success.53 South Africa remained the key to a peaceful transition to majority rule in Rhodesia, but a key that Pretoria in the last analysis was not prepared to turn. On 8 February 1976, therefore, the Front Line States signalled the end of the "détente" exercise. Henceforth, in fulfillment of the Lusaka Manifesto of 1969 and the Dar es Salaam Declaration of 1975, liberation would be sought through intensified armed struggle. "Due to Smith's intransigence," Kaunda declared sadly, "Zambia has reached the end of the road regarding negotiations as an instrument of change. We have discharged our obligations under the OAU Manifesto on Southern Africa."54 A month later, following the failure of the Salisbury talks, the President was even more outspoken:

Even at this late stage, we allowed
peaceful change to have an opportunity
in Zimbabwe. The total breakdown of
constitutional negotiations in Rhodesia
has now demonstrated to all and sundry
that nothing can be gained by a peace
strategy as an approach to ending racism and colonialism . . . . We have
left no stone unturned in our determination to achieve majority rule by
peaceful means. We invested a lot in
the peace program as an instrument of
beneficial change. This has failed.[55]

While he placed the blame "squarely on the shoulders"
of Smith, Kaunda was bitterly critical of Vorster
for having "failed us badly"[56] over Rhodesia: "If
he wanted it tomorrow, the rebels in Rhodesia would
be on their knees and there would be majority rule.
But Mr. Vorster has continued to prop up the rebel
regime."[57] As for suggestions that he might meet
Vorster again, Kaunda was categorical that he would
"never" agree to this.[58] Within the Front Line
States, Kaunda had become the "leader of the war
party," whereas a few weeks earlier he had been the
"leader of the peace party."[59]

DEBATE OVER "DETENTE"

Controversy over the desirability of seeking
South African assistance in achieving a negotiated
settlement in Rhodesia led to the emergence of two
tacit coalitions[60] of disparate forces for and
against peaceful change (table 7.2). Opposition
to this strategy came from those who rejected any
contact with the apartheid regime of South Africa on
principle, from those who objected to the qualification "peaceful" and, at the other end of the political spectrum, from those who continued to resist
"change" itself. The doves were linked informally
by channels of communication which, to some extent
enabled them to act in concert. The hawks, on the
other hand, were not only totally unstructured
but sharply divided along racial lines into rival
black militants and white diehards. Each perceived
the other as its implacable foe, and would have in-
dignantly denied that they shared anything in
common. Certainly, their goals were diametrically
opposed — as were the ends pursued, though not the
means employed by the uneasy bedfellows in the dove
camp. At the same time, the hawks shared an interest in frustrating a settlement. Moreover, their

TABLE 7.2
Tacit Coalitions for and against Southern African
"Détente," 1974-1976

Domain	Doves	Hawks
South Africa	Vorster verligtes[61]	ANCSA verkramptes
Rhodesia	Businessmen ANC	Smith ZANU
Black Africa	Front Line States OAU moderates	Algeria, Guinea Somalia, Uganda OAU militants
Global	Britain, US Multinationals Soviet Union	China

efforts to sabotage a "sellout," though in no sense
coordinated, proved mutually supportive. Thus ZANU's
repudiation of the December 1974 ceasefire assisted
Smith, just as the re-arrest of Sithole in March
1975 strengthened ZANU's case for continuing the
armed struggle.

African critics of détente raised a host of objections to Zambian contacts with Southern Africa
regimes. Some opposed them on ideological grounds
as implying abandonment of force. Certain African
governments as well as many of the liberation movements had never fully accepted the Lusaka Manifesto
with its explicit preference for peaceful change.
Instead, they subscribed to the Maoist doctrine of
uninterrupted revolution as the only way of ensuring
not merely formal political independence but a subsequent socialist transformation as well.[62]

Zambia endeavored to reinsure herself in advance against accusations from the left of selling
out the African revolution, by involving the presidents of Tanzania, Botswana and FRELIMO at every
stage in the evolution of policy. The Front Line
States also kept other OAU members in the picture.
"When the first hopeful sign reached us," President
Kaunda recalled, "I contacted our . . . current OAU
Chairman, General Siad Barre" of Somalia. Shortly
afterwards, the foreign ministers of Zambia, Tanzania

and Botswana, between them, visited all other African states to brief their governments on developments.[63] Nevertheless, at the OAU Council of Ministers' meeting in February 1975, the FLS ministers found themselves on the defensive, with even tiny Lesotho — for her own domestic reasons — levelling charges of "softness." In the end, a resolution was adopted condemning contacts with the Pretoria regime as long as it refused to release and dialogue with its own nationalist leaders. Moreover, at Algerian insistence, it was agreed to convene a special conference in Dar es Salaam in April to plan how to counter Vorster's diplomatic offensive. There, the attack was finally beaten back — once it was firmly established that there was no intention of abandoning the guerrilla war option and, indeed, that the struggle would be intensified in order both to support negotiations and to offer a credible alternative in the event of their failure. With this assurance, most member states happily reaffirmed support for the Lusaka Manifesto, and expressed their determination to "capitalize" on the "unprecedented opportunities and challenges" opening up to them in Southern Africa, provided that, in any contacts with Pretoria, the agenda was confined to the question of the transfer of power to black majorities in Zimbabwe and Namibia.[64]

ZANU leaders also had their own personal and party reasons for wishing to opt out of the Lusaka Agreement. They alone commanded the military resources to continue the armed confrontation with confidence. Moreover, military victory offered the advantage not only of removing any threat of "false decolonization," but also of eliminating nationalist rivals and ensuring for ZANU a monopoly of political power after independence. As has been demonstrated repeatedly elsewhere in Africa, the real struggle in the final stages of colonialism is often the conflict among competing contenders for the right of succession. From a narrow partisan point of view, therefore, continued guerrilla warfare combined with fierce denunciation of all rivals represented a rational strategy for ZANU; at least, it was consistent with Riker's prescription for success: the systematic pursuit of the "minimum winning coalition."[65]

In addition to the opposition on ideological grounds to "détente" with South Africa, there were grave misgivings within the OAU concerning the political morality of any negotiations with the chief apostle of apartheid. The Zambian response was to

297

argue that the situation in Southern Africa differed
from that elsewhere on the continent (including Angola and Mozambique) in that there was no external
colonial power.   "The colonial power in Namibia and
to intents and purposes in Rhodesia" as well, President Nyerere explained, is South Africa and it is
with her that Africa must deal.[66]   The Zambian Foreign Minister also countered at Dar es Salaam with
the charge that a number of OAU militants "were not
being entirely honest."   Not only had these "microphone revolutionaries" gained their own independence
by peaceful means, but they were themselves in contact with Pretoria "with objectives contrary to the
furtherance of the objectives of the liberation
struggle in Southern Africa."   Provided Vorster was
genuinely prepared to talk decolonization, he argued,
there could be no objection to exploiting this ave-
nue to press for specific concessions.   (This was
the essential distinction between the strategy President Kaunda was pursuing and that of President
Banda of Malawi.)   On the other hand, "if negotiations fail and [the Zimbabweans] decide to fight,"
Foreign Minister Mwaanga added, "we will support
them," despite the fact that

> when the chips are down, we know that
> few around this table will come to
> our aid when we face the consequences
> of the armed struggle.   History bears
> us out.   The people of Zambia know it.
> Those who are not guilty of careless
> handling of truth also know it.[67]

A further complaint, voiced principally by the
liberation movements and especially ZANU spokesmen,
was that Zambian contacts with minority regimes in
Southern Africa constituted "foreign" interference
in their affairs, contrary to a 1971 OAU injunction
against dialogue, except on the initiative of the
liberation movements concerned.   Lusaka vigorously
denied it had in any way behaved improperly; on
the contrary, it had assisted the two sides in Rhodesia to come together around the conference table.
Certainly, its role here was crucial.   Nevertheless,
Zambia did not confine herself simply to offering
her good offices; she was a major actor in developments at every stage.   Her motives for involving
herself so actively were primarily idealistic;
although Zambia clearly had a material stake in a
satisfactory resolution of the conflict in Southern
Africa, her deep commitment to the liberation cause
was even more fundamental.

The decision to concentrate on independence for Rhodesia and Namibia also came under attack as effectively postponing the liberation of South Africa and thereby perpetuating apartheid rule. Yet, this step-by-step approach was nothing new. The OAU Liberation Committee had long operated on the basis of carefully worked out priorities; as Nyerere pointed out, it had "quite rightly given priority to the nationalist movements in the Portuguese colonies."[68] This had proved not only an effective strategy but also one with beneficial spillover effects on adjacent territories.

Finally, there were those OAU members who were not so much opposed to contact in principle as sceptical of its efficacy as a means of dislodging entrenched minority regimes. To counter this, Zambia pointed to a number of concrete achievements, notably Ian Smith's release of the detained nationalist leaders in Rhodesia, his acceptance of the Lusaka Agreement in December 1974 (after first rejecting it three days earlier), his willingness to sit down in conference with the authentic leaders of Zimbabwe whom he had previously denounced as "terrorists," his release of Sithole in April 1975 (after Sithole's reincarceration and reconviction), and, above all, the withdrawal of South African "police" from forward combat zones in Rhodesia in February and their repatriation south of the Limpopo in August 1975. In view of Smith's known propensity for prevarication and evasion, this was a creditable record of success, and justifies Kaunda's public testimony that Vorster had shown a "good deal of common sense" in dealing with Rhodesia.[69] "We would be less than honest," Foreign Minister Mwaanga declared in April 1975 at the OAU ministerial meeting in Dar es Salaam, "if we did not acknowledge that Mr. Vorster . . . had honored his word." As for the future, he confidently asserted that Pretoria had both the will and the ability to impose its policy on Rhodesia and Namibia. Since Vorster had now accepted "the inevitability of majority rule" in these territories, African states could rest assured that "peaceful change to majority rule in Rhodesia and full national independence in Namibia" would result.[70]

This prediction proved excessively optimistic. The task of "taming Smithy" was more intractable than Vorster had anticipated. The Rhodesian leader, as successive British governments have come to learn from bitter experience, was a notoriously slippery character. Consequently, Pretoria was compelled to intervene ever more openly in Rhodesian affairs until, eventually, the price proved more than it was prepared to pay. Besides, the South Africans were beginning to have serious doubts as to whether "détente" was serving their purposes as opposed to the aims of African liberation.

ASSESSMENT

Much of the misunderstanding within the ranks of the OAU and elsewhere stemmed from South Africa's success in winning almost universal acceptance for the use of the term détente to describe FLS policy. Although Kaunda and his colleagues objected vehemently to this designation—preferring such expressions as contact, talks, or even negotiations— Pretoria's label stuck. The distinction was more than a terminological quibble, for it went to the heart of the sharply contrasting expectations of the two sides. Kaunda conceived the contacts as a strictly limited exercise designed to release the grip of the minority on Rhodesia; they carried no implication of peaceful coexistence with apartheid itself. If détente is defined as "a reduction of conflictual interactions," then there was no détente with South Africa on domestic policy. Vorster, on the other hand, envisaged "détente" as opening up the possibility of an entirely new era of harmonious relations with Black Africa. "Give South Africa six months' chance," he announced exuberantly. "You will be surprised where we will then stand."[72] The surprising (and ill-founded) confidence Vorster exuded alarmed the critics and reinforced their existing reservations regarding "détente." It was widely assumed in OAU capitals and elsewhere (including Pretoria) that in any bargaining bout with South Africa, the Front Line States were bound to be bested. This profound distrust of their intellectual capabilities, diplomatic skills, and moral integrity was deeply resented by those who were bearing the burden of the battle.

Vorster's grounds for optimism rested on two dubious assumptions. The first was that, in the final analysis, economic self-interest would prevail over political ideology. In the case of South Africa, pursuit of an illusory Southern African economic community was undoubtedly a powerful incentive reinforcing the drive towards détente. With Zambia, on the other hand, economic rewards and constraints are an inadequate explanation of her search for a peaceful resolution of the Southern African con-

300

flict.[73] Admittedly, the continuing congestion in
East African ports following closure of Zambia's
border with Rhodesia in 1973 and especially the collapse of world copper prices occasioned great concern. Yet, if material considerations had been decisive in determining Kaunda's behavior, he would
have succumbed to the South's blandishments and in-
timidation much earlier. The dramatic shift in the
balance of power in Southern Africa consequent upon
the Portuguese coup, rather than Zambia's economic
fortunes, accounts for the moves towards "détente."
    Secondly, Pretoria was convinced that, by sa-
crificing Rhodesia and Namibia, it could save itself.
Not only would the major obstacles to détente be
removed, but the diplomatic credit thus earned with
African states would enable South Africa to buy immunity or, at the very least, deter neighboring
states from offering hospitality to South African
freedom fighters. Détente, therefore, was conceived
as an alternative to the necessity of dismantling
apartheid, not as a consequence of it. Moreover,
the spillover effects of successful collaboration
in one limited sphere of external policy were expected to temper the sharpness of conflicts in domestic
issue areas, as the African players became socialized into habits of cooperation. In this way, the
initial modest contacts with Black Africa might, in
due course, ripen into full détente with the continent, and hence restore South Africa's legitimacy
with the rest of the world.
    It was a seductively simple solution to Pre-
toria's international predicament; it would enable
South Africans to reap economic benefits and escape
diplomatic isolation without the necessity of making
painful political sacrifices. The weakness of the
scheme was that the FLS leaders had no intention of
allowing events to take this course. Gradually,
even Prime Minister Vorster came to doubt the feasibility of his grand design. Accordingly, as rein-
surance, he increased his 1975 defense budget by
more than one-third; détente and deterrence went
hand in hand.
    The South African scenario contained a final,
more fundamental flaw. Even if the target states
had been prepared to coexist peacefully with the
Pretoria regime, it is inconceivable that the regime
could successfully insulate its African population
from developments beyond its borders. Despite all
the apparat of a modern police state at its command,
South African society is simply not that impervious
to external penetration. The emergence of black

301

governments in neighboring states would inevitably
have accentuated the existing pressures for change
building up inside the country and exacerbated domestic tensions dangerously. In Southern Africa,
at least, the domino theory could appear to have
some applicability. This conclusion provides additional support for the Zambian thesis that the spillover effects of independence in Zimbabwe and Namibia
for the liberation of black South Africans were certain to be profound. It also reinforces Lusaka's
contention that its willingness to negotiate with
racist regimes represented merely a shift in tactics, not a reversal of strategy. This is the distinction Zambia drew between contact which it favored and détente which it did not.

Ultimately, FLS efforts at "détente" failed in
the immediate sense that Vorster proved unable or
unwilling to compel Smith to negotiate for majority
rule in good faith.[74] While diplomatic negotiations
to effect a peaceful transfer of power in Rhodesia
have continued, they have not taken the form of direct contacts between Lusaka and Pretoria. Instead,
successive Anglo-American teams have shuttled around
Southern African capitals. On the other hand, none
of the dire consequences critics feared from "détente" came to pass. Although the FLS leaders were
unable to manipulate Vorster for their own purposes,
he proved unable to manipulate them. On the positive side, it can be argued that the liberation
cause has emerged from the experience morally invig-
orated and materially strengthened. This is the
ultimate test by which "détente" must be judged: to
what extent did it further FLS goals, and at what
cost?

NOTES

1. Vorster addressed the South African Senate on
23 October 1974. Kaunda's reply, three days later,
was in part a response to Foreign Minister Botha's
promise to the UN Security Council (24 October 1974)
that "we shall do everything in our power to move
away from discrimination based on race and color."

2. "The acceptance of an offer that has not been
made, in order to induce the adversary to accept the
acceptance" (Coral Bell, The Conventions of Crisis
[London: Oxford University Press, 1971], p. 74).

3. Mark Chona, Kaunda's perambulating Special

302

Assistant on Foreign Affairs, appears to have first
visited Vorster in Cape Town on 5 October 1974.

4. This informal alliance of small, like-minded
states—Zambia, Tanzania, Mozambique and Botswana—
emerged out of a felt need to coordinate policies on
Rhodesia. It first met in Lusaka on 7 November 1974.
Machel was accorded head of state status from the
first, even before Mozambique achieved independence.
Angola's Neto did not join until nearly two years
later, long after the collapse of "détente."

5. Confidential News Report (Salisbury),
14 January 1964, p. 5. Subsequent statements appear
in Thomas Patrick Melady, ed., Kenneth Kaunda of
Zambia (New York: Praeger, 1964), pp. 239-40; Star
(Johannesburg), 22 January 1964, pp. 1, 5; Central
African Mail (Ndola), 24 January 1964, pp. 3-4.

6. W. Scott Thompson, Ghana's Foreign Policy,
1957-1966 (Princeton: Princeton University Press,
1969), pp. 28, 32, 42-43, 96-98; Sir Robert Menzies,
Afternoon Light (London: Cassell, 1967), pp. 200-
201, 206-207; Olajide Aluko, Ghana and Nigeria,
1957-70 (London: Rex Collings, 1976), p. 117.n.108;
Star, 7 January 1960, p. 1.

7. Star, 22 January 1964, p. 1.

8. Melady, Kenneth Kaunda of Zambia, p. 239.

9. South Africa H.A. Deb., 23 April 1964, c. 4831;
22 April 1971, c. 4994.

10. Central African Mail, 14 January 1964, p. 5.

11. Aaron Milner, Deputy Secretary General, Star,
8 January 1964, p. 16.

12. Kaunda, 25 January 1964. Colin Legum, ed.,
Zambia: Independence and Beyond (London: Nelson,
1966), pp. 67-68.

13. Zambia Information Services (ZIS) Press Release,
no. 1109/64, 2 July 1964, p. 6; ZIS Background,
no. 27/64, 18 November 1964, p. 4.

14. ZIS Press Release, no. 2082/67, 5 October 1967,
p. 8. There have been journalistic suggestions
that, if in the euphoric atmosphere of October 1974,
Vorster had offered to exchange diplomatic missions,

Kaunda might have accepted.

15. Dear Mr. Vorster . . . : Details of exchanges between President Kaunda of Zambia and Prime Minister Vorster of South Africa (Lusaka: ZIS, 1971), p. 1.

16. On the other hand, characteristically Kaunda did "feel compelled as a Christian" to cable Mrs. Verwoerd to offer his "personal sympathy" following the assassination of her husband in 1966 (ZIS Press Release, no. 1641/66, 9 September 1966).

17. 1 April and 2 May 1968. Dear Mr. Vorster, pp. 4, 6. The Kaunda letter was delivered by a Zambian envoy, reportedly a Zambian businessman (H.A. Deb., 21 April 1971, c. 4929).

18. An earlier meeting scheduled for 24 May was cancelled by Vorster as "a waste of time" in view of Kaunda's "very vicious remarks against South Africa" in a speech in Gaborone the previous day. Vorster later alleged, rather unconvincingly, that Kaunda "subsequently informed me that I was not to take that speech too seriously, that it was intended for the consumption of other people" (c. 4935). Vorster also claimed this meeting had been arranged at Kaunda's request (cc. 4934, 4935). This is categorically denied by Zambia (Dear Mr. Vorster, p. 10).

19. The South African emissary met with Kaunda on at least five occasions: 22 June 1968 (Lusaka), 29 August 1968 (Lusaka), 15 February 1969 (Lusaka), 3 May 1970 (Munich), and 27 March 1971 (Chipata). Vorster also reported a sixth meeting on 21 January 1969 in Zambia as well as visits by a Zambian envoy, to Pretoria in April 1968 and March 1969 (H.A. Deb., 21 April 1971, cc. 4934-38, 23 April 1971, c. 5080).

20. 1 April 1968, Dear Mr. Vorster, pp. 2-4.

21. 2 May 1968. Ibid., p. 5.

22. 15 August 1968. Ibid., p. 7.

23. Ibid., p. 5.

24. Ibid., pp. 4, 5.

25. 15 August 1968. Ibid., p. 8.

26. 29 August 1968. Foreign Minister Muller was visiting Malawi that day.

27. 29 August 1968. Ibid., p. 9.

28. Robert C. Good, UDI: The International Politics of the Rhodesian Rebellion (Princeton: Princeton University Press, 1973), p. 279. The day after Vorster received Kaunda's letter of 15 August 1968, he publicly predicted that the number of black diplomats in South Africa would increase. In mid-October 1968, at a time when an early end to UDI seemed possible, Vorster bet Lord Walston, a former junior minister in the British Labour government, a golf ball that South Africa would have a trade commission in Lusaka before the end of 1970. He lost.

29. Managing Editor, Gemini News Service, Citizen (Ottawa), 21 November 1968, p. 6.

30. Zambia N.A. Deb., no. 16, 2 October 1968, c. 6.

31. H.A. Deb., 21 April 1971, c. 4936. The sharp reaction in Africa to Vorster's visit to Malawi (two weeks after the May 1970 meeting) effectively ruled out any chance of Zambian agreement, though Vorster claimed (but Lusaka denied) that there was "a definite appointment for November 1970." At the March 1969 discussions between officials, the Zambian envoy evidently mentioned the fears Kaunda had voiced publicly that Rhodesia and Portugal were planning pre-emptive strikes against guerrilla transit camps in Zambia. Vorster interpreted this as an appeal for help (which Zambia insists it was not). Nevertheless, he flatly refused to intervene with his allies as he dismissed the invasion threats as "absolute nonsense" (ibid., c. 4937).

32. Manifesto on Southern Africa (Lusaka: Government Printer, 1969); UN General Assembly (A/RES.2505 [XXIV]), 20 November 1969. Portugal and South Africa voted against it, and Malawi (and Cuba) abstained.

33. Africa Research Bulletin: Political Social and Cultural Series (ARB), 1969, p. 1543; H.A. Deb., 21 April 1971, c. 4940.

34. South Africa's first use of the term "dialogue" in this context was in Muller's UN speech of 20 November 1969 (UN General Assembly Verbatim Records,

305

A/PV. 1815, p. 16).

35. Colin Legum, "Dialogue: the Great Debate," Africa Contemporary Record (ACR), 1971-72 (London: Rex Collings, 1972), pp. A66-82; also pp. C3-4.

36. Dear Mr. Vorster, p. 1; Sunday Times of Zambia (Lusaka), 20 June 1971, p. 1.

37. A decision to concert political and economic pressure on Kaunda appears to have emerged from the meeting of South African, Rhodesian and Portuguese intelligence chiefs in February 1971. South African news reports suggest that Pretoria thought that a coup d'état in Lusaka was imminent (Times [London], 25 April 1971, p. 4, 25 June 1971, p. II).

38. H.A. Deb., 21 April 1971, cc. 4939-40.

39. Rapport (Johannesburg), 25 April 1971, p. 1.

40. Times, 23 April 1971, p. 17.

41. Sunday Times (London), 15 December 1974, p. 13.

42. David Martin, "The Angolan Connection," New Statesman, 30 January 1976, p. 119.

43. Africa (London), no. 39, November 1974, p. 52.

44. Vernon Mwaanga, Sunday Tribune (Durban), 3 November 1974, p. 1. In a second interview the following day, Foreign Minister Mwaanga declared: "The minimum—I would call them fundamental—changes which could open the way to peace are South Africa's complete disengagement in Rhodesia—and termination of her illegal occupation of Namibia" (Rand Daily Mail [Johannesburg], 4 November 1974).

45. Sunday Tribune, 3 November 1974, p. 1.

46. ARB, 1975, p. 3522.

47. Colin Legum, "Southern Africa: The Secret Diplomacy of Détente," ACR, 1974-75, pp. A11-13, B512. The Zimbabwe African Peoples Union (ZAPU) led by Joshua Nkomo, the Zimbabwe African National Union (ZANU) which, under Ndabaningi Sithole, broke away from ZAPU in 1963, and the Front for the Liberation of Zimbabwe (FROLIZI), a splinter group headed by James Chikerema agreed to merge with Bishop Abel

Muzorewa's African National Council (ANC), then the only nationalist party still legal in Rhodesia.

48. <u>ACR, 1974-75</u>, pp. A13, B511.

49. Kaunda repeatedly cautioned the ANC "to refrain from public dialogue with Smith in the Press" (<u>Times</u>, 16 May 1975, p. 7); see also <u>Manchester Guardian Weekly</u>, 14 December 1974, p. 6; <u>Zambia Daily Mail</u> (Lusaka), 18 December 1974, p. 1.

50. <u>ACR, 1975-76</u>, p. C75.

51. Nkomo and Smith did sign a "Declaration of Intention to Negotiate a Settlement" (ibid., pp. C77-78). A revised version of this was signed on 1 December 1975.

52. Zambia seconded Leo Baron (a former Smith detainee and, at this time, Deputy Chief Justice of Zambia), Peter Kasanda, a State House official of ambassadorial rank, and two other officials and four secretaries to the Nkomo delegation (<u>Times</u>, 11 December 1975, p. 7).

53. <u>Observer</u> (London), 8 February 1976, p. 9.

54. Ibid., 15 February 1976, p. 1.

55. <u>Times of Zambia</u>, 20 March 1976, p. 1. The day before the final collapse, Nkomo flew to Lusaka for urgent consultations with Kaunda.

56. <u>Zambia Daily Mail</u>, 26 April 1977, p. 1.

57. <u>Rand Daily Mail</u>, 14 August 1976, p. 1. This interview was a year after the Victoria Falls summit, two months after Soweto, and a month after a major border incident involving South African troops operating from Namibia.

58. Ibid. He repeated this pledge in March 1977 (<u>Times</u>, 1 April 1977, p. 8.), but on two other occasions was slightly less categorical. Although he considered that talks at that time would be useless, he implied that this might not necessarily be the case if the FLS believed something was really moving in South Africa (<u>Zambia Daily Mail</u>, 26 April 1977, p. 1; <u>Citizen</u>, 1 December 1976, p. 7).

59. Colin Legum, "Capital Report," Canadian Broad-

casting Corporation, 4 April 1976.

60. A tacit coalition is a form of variable sum mixed motive cooperative interaction involving two or more actors pursuing independent but parallel paths for different and often irreconcilable reasons; no element of coordination or collusion need be present, or even any recognition of tacit support. It falls short of the degree of purposeful collaboration implied by such terms as "marriage of convenience" or "supping with the devil"—diplomatic behavioral responses characteristic of actors, such as Biafra, driven to extremities.

61. The governing Nationalist Party in South Africa is loosely divided into verligte (enlightened) and verkrampte (narrow-minded) wings. The terms are relative.

62. Peking (which backed ZANU) denounced "reactionary double tactics" until 13 September 1975, when it reversed itself and gave its blessing to "dialogue" as an instrument of liberation. Meanwhile, Moscow (which backed ZAPU) was shifting from support for a negotiated settlement to exclusive reliance on an armed struggle (ARB, 1975, p. 3752; ACR, 1975-76, p. A105).

63. Africa, no. 42, February 1975, p. 11.

64. "Dar es Salaam Declaration on Southern Africa," 10 April 1975, ACR, 1975-76, p. C74.

65. William H. Riker, The Theory of Political Coalitions (New Haven: Yale University Press, 1962), p. 32. In a characteristically vitriolic statement issued in Stockholm on 3 April 1975, one wing of ZANU denounced the "treacherous and counter-revolutionary . . . Kaunda-Vorster détente," accused Kaunda, among other sins, of "collusion" with Smith in the re-arrest of Sithole and the assassination of Chitepo, and called for "the hybrid of Kaunda's humanism and Vorster's and Smith's fascism" to be "exposed, denounced and neutralized."

66. 9th (Extraordinary) OAU Council of Ministers, Dar es Salaam, 7 April 1975. Nyerere consistently associated himself with and publicly defended Kaunda's "détente" efforts (e.g., Observer, 7 March 1976, p. 2).

67. 8 April 1975, Daily News (Dar es Salaam),
9 April 1975, p. 4.

68. 9th (Extraordinary) OAU Council of Ministers,
Dar es Salaam, 7 April 1975.

69. New York Times, 20 April 1975, p. 3.

70. Daily News, 9 April 1975, p. 4. For Mwaanga's
balance sheet of successes and failures, see N.A.
Deb., no. 38, 18 March 1975, cc. 2796-98.

71. Times of Zambia, 3 May 1975, p. 1, 30 March
1976, p. 1; N.A. Deb., no. 38, 18 March 1975,
c. 2999. Mwaanga argued forcefully that "Zambia and
her friends have not been engaged in dialogue with
South Africa. After all, one can [only] dialogue
with a friend. The term détente is not in our
vocabulary" (Daily News, 9 April 1975, p. 4).

72. 5 November 1974, Star (weekly), 9 November 1974,
p. 5.

73. Observer, 15 February 1976, p. 3.

74. "Vorster's missed chance," Economist,
23 September 1978, p. 22.

8
Zambia and the Angolan Civil War

No Zambian foreign policy action has generated
such fierce controversy, domestically or externally,
as Lusaka's response to the outbreak and internationalization of the Angolan civil war of 1975-76. Of
all the actors in that tragic conflict, there was
none—with the possible exception of China—whose behavior occasioned more surprise and bewilderment than
Zambia. For a time, President Kaunda, long recognized as one of the foremost fighters for Southern
African freedom, appeared threatened with isolation
from the mainstream of African progressive thought.
This role of "odd man out" was not one which he,
unlike President Banda of Malawi, either sought or
relished. It seems reasonable to assume, therefore,
that, in his mind, there were compelling reasons of
national interest or political morality which drove
him to cling so tenaciously to a policy stance which,
whatever its intrinsic merit, proved not only unpopu-
lar in radical circles in Africa and overseas but, in
the end, untenable. With a view to clarifying the
confusion surrounding Zambian policy, this chapter
seeks to ascertain precisely what that policy was
and, secondly, the reasons for it.[1]

This is no easy task. Any objective assessment
of Zambia's actions and motives is inhibited not only
by imperfect knowledge or at least contradictory
claims, but also by the emotional atmosphere in which
the debate has been conducted. Admittedly, the factual basis for judgement is now somewhat firmer than
at the peak of the crisis when conflicting propaganda
accounts flooded the media, confounding any real possibility of arriving at an independent verdict.
Nevertheless, there are still too many crucial issues
still in dispute to risk firm and final conclusions
concerning Zambia's involvement.

If the information gap has gradually been narrowed, the passions the controversy aroused have by
no means completely cooled. As in the case of the

subsequent invasions of neighboring Shaba, there has
been a tendency to force friends and foes alike into
neat "ideological" pigeonholes in accordance with the
observer's own political predilections. Admittedly,
the escalating conflict in Southern Africa has[2] at
various conjunctions produced tacit coalitions of
curiously incompatible bedfellows, notably China and
South Africa with their ingrained fears of Soviet
intrusion, ZANU and Ian Smith who shared a distrust
of détente, and MPLA and the remnants of Tshombe's
gendarmerie in their common opposition to Mobutu.
Yet, it is critical for an appreciation of the dynamics of the evolving situation in the subcontinent
not to be misled by ideological preferences and
stereotypes into attributing undue significance to
these shifting liaisons. To the extent that they had
any substance, they constituted contradictions in the
system rather than core components.

Despite the obvious hazards involved in seeking
even an interim assessment of Zambia's role in the
Angolan imbroglio, it should now be possible to sift
through the mounting accumulation of partisan opinion
and unsubstantiated assertions and, at least, isolate
the critical assumptions and issues which perpetuate
the sharply differing interpretations which continue
to prevail. Hopefully too, it should prove possible
to reach some tentative conclusions on the basis of
the available evidence. To begin with, however, it
is necessary to sketch briefly the broad outlines of
the conflict as a background to an examination of
Zambia's part in it.

EXTERNAL INTERVENTION

It is not possible to pinpoint with precision an
exact moment in time when the liberation struggle
against the Portuguese in Angola ended and the civil
war among the contending parties to inherit power
began. Even prior to the April 1974 military coup in
Portugal, political and even armed conflict among the
rival claimants inside and outside Angola—sedulously
fostered by both the colonial authorities and foreign
patrons—constituted an unhappy and costly diversion
from the primary target of the freedom struggle.
Throughout 1974, and especially after Lisbon recognized the right of independence in July and negotiated ceasefires with the liberation movements in
October, battles flared in the streets of Luanda and
other centers. Certainly by early 1975, the war of
succession was in full swing. The Alvor concordat in

January, although paving the way for an all-party transitional government, failed to usher in the promised era of political cooperation, ideological tolerance and national unity. Instead, it signalled a fresh phase of heightened violence which speedily escalated into open warfare.[3]

It is equally difficult to document the course of foreign intervention in the civil war. The Soviet Union with OAU sanction had, of course, actively supported Agostinho Neto's Popular Movement for the Liberation of Angola (MPLA) since the early 1960s, but the military requisites of a guerrilla campaign were modest compared with the demands of large-scale conventional warfare. After a period of decline beginning in 1972 while MPLA sorted itself out internally, Soviet assistance resumed in August 1974 when the first consignment of a $6 million shipment reached Dar es Salaam.[4] However, the really massive injection of modern Soviet military hardware, including modern tanks, missiles and jet aircraft, began only in March 1975.[5] By that time, US interest in the confrontation—and, even more, French concern—had also been aroused. Two months earlier, Washington had allocated an initial $300,000 to Holden Roberto's National Liberation Front of Angola (FNLA) "for political action, not weapons"; the meagre amount invested suggests that it could only have been intended as a symbolic gesture of diplomatic support for Mobutu.[6] In July, however, following the MPLA seizure of Luanda, the US government reversed its earlier decision not to provide military support to any faction and authorized $14 million in covert aid to FNLA and Jonas Savimbi's National Union for the Total Liberation of Angola (UNITA). By the end of the year, when Congress fearful of any repetition of the slide into war in Vietnam and preoccupied with Watergate and CIA scandals imposed its veto, total direct US assistance had increased to some $31.7 million.[7] In addition, undisclosed but substantial quantities of military supplies were funnelled through Zaire by the simple expedient of replenishing stocks of equipment transferred by Kinshasa to FNLA forces. Nevertheless, the scale of American involvement never approached that of the Soviet Union in either quantity or quality; the one incontrovertible fact on which all are agreed is that, in this arms race, Moscow's client clearly emerged the victor.

Less certainty surrounds Cuban[8] and, to some extent, South African[9] and Zairien intervention. Nevertheless, by all accounts, the Cuban units constituted the largest and, in the end, the decisive external military force. According to Havana, the decision to despatch an expeditionary army ("Operation Carlota") overseas was not taken until 5 November 1975—the day the South African battle group captured Benguela ("Operation Zulu"). Yet, Havana also admits that a month earlier, even before the big South African push began on 14 October, three troopships had arrived in Angolan ports with "instructors" who, within a very short time, were actively embroiled in the fighting.[10] Moreover, the first 230 Cuban military advisers had arrived the previous spring to set up four training centers. Meanwhile, President Mobutu had committed several battalions of regular troops to the FNLA advance in the north.[11]

Much energy and oratory has been expended on attempting to establish who intervened first in Angola in order that blame might be assigned for the internationalization of the civil war. This exercise is as pointless as it is futile. What transpired was a classic instance of a positive feedback process. At least up to the end of 1975, each increase in the military commitment of one external actor stimulated a like response in rival actors. This, in turn, reinforced the perceptions of hostility which had generated the initial action. Nevertheless, an underlying assumption of Zambian policy was the belief that Soviet intervention came first, and that the Americans, and even the South Africans, were merely reacting to it.[12]

In the end, the outcome of the war of succession was decided largely by external factors. Militarily, the balance of power was tipped in favor of the MPLA by the asymmetrical scale of foreign intervention and by the revolt in the American Congress. Nevertheless, the diplomatic battle for recognition waged in the OAU between the rival governments of the People's Republic of Angola (MPLA) and the Democratic Popular Republic of Angola (FNLA-UNITA) was also important. Although no African state formally recognized the latter, most OAU members, in compliance with OAU policy, delayed choosing sides pending clarification of the situation. Nigeria's role here was crucial; she had been the foremost advocate of a "government of national unity" and had even argued, on the eve of independence, for a three week delay to allow time for one final attempt to bring the warring parties together. Yet, once Lagos—reacting as much to domestic pressures as to Pretoria's intervention—reversed itself on 25 November and came out in support of Neto,[13] it was only a matter of time before a majority of African governments, and therefore the OAU as an organization, followed suit (on

313

11 February 1976). On 22 January, South Africa, shunned in Africa and overseas, by those she had optimistically expected to rally to her side as allies, began the humiliating retreat southward; this ended on 25 March when the last convoy of armored cars rolled back across the Cunene River into Namibia. Thus, Pretoria's disastrous gamble officially came to an inglorious end, though its consequences lived on.

ZAMBIAN-MPLA RELATIONS

The Zambian government was embarrassed as much by the unsolicited praise her Angolan policies elicited from apologists for South Africa as by the blanket condemnation of its radical critics. Groups with widely divergent ideological predilections have, for their own reasons, tacitly combined to present an interpretation of Zambian motives and behavior which deviated sharply from Lusaka's own perception of the path it was pursuing. In particular, Zambian policy was widely characterized by both left and right as embodying four features: hostility to an MPLA government, overt material support for UNITA including the provision of transit facilities, intercession with foreign governments to procure military supplies for these movements and, most damaging of all, connivance in South Africa's invasion of Angola. To what extent is there evidence for any of these allegations? Or, as Zambian spokesmen have charged, are the accusations of anti-MPLA bias and subservience to Pretoria part of a propaganda "campaign to isolate Zambia from those countries with whom she has stood in the battle to liberate Southern Africa"?[14]

Zambian relations with the MPLA evolved through three overlapping phases. The years of armed struggle beginning in the mid-1960s were followed by a period of internal party dissension in the early 1970s, culminating in the postcoup struggle for power and in international intervention.

Throughout the long years of armed resistance to Portuguese colonialism, Zambia accorded MPLA consistent, substantial and virtually exclusive moral and material support. Denied permission to operate from or through Zaire, Neto turned to Zambia for host state facilities. Kaunda's response was prompt and generous, despite his domestic preoccupation with the economic consequences of Rhodesia's UDI.[15] From March 1966, western Zambia became the principal operational base, "the logistical bridgehead", for guerrilla activities inside Angola. The price Zambians paid for

their commitment to the MPLA cause was high in terms
of lives lost and property destroyed. The fiercer
the struggle became, the more savage the reprisals
the Portuguese wreaked along Zambia's borders, east
and west. Between February 1966 and July 1969 alone,
there were at least 38 Portuguese incursions into
Zambia by land and 27 by air, in addition to a number
of instances of subversion and sabotage, notably the
dynamiting of the Luangwa bridge. Even more damaging
was the subtle and not so subtle economic pressure
Lisbon was able to exert by virtue of its control of
Zambia's two major outlets to the sea—Beira and
Lobito. No other African state, no other frontline
state, sacrificed as much for the sake of the MPLA
in this period as Zambia.[16]

Diplomatically too, Lusaka threw its full weight
behind Neto. Shortly after Independence, the MPLA
was authorized to open a regional office in Lusaka,
whereas the small FNLA office was allowed to fold in
early 1965 and Jonas Savimbi was expelled in June
1967, ostensibly for disrupting vital copper traffic
on the Benguela Railway. At the OAU, Zambian spokesmen consistently championed MPLA claims to sole recognition, and successfully opposed continued OAU designation of Holden Roberto as head of a provisional
Angolan government in exile (GRAE). Although Roberto
achieved a reconciliation with Nyerere in 1973, which
led to an invitation to Dar es Salaam and the opening
of an office there as well as the channelling of
Chinese military aid to FNLA, no comparable rapproche-
ment occurred with Kaunda.[17] Only in 1975, following
OAU recognition of UNITA in January and MPLA acceptance of the other two parties as full partners in the
transitional government, did Zambia accord equality
of status to all three movements.

Nevertheless, beginning in 1972, relations deteriorated considerably following the emergence of an
open split within MPLA ranks in Zambia between
Agostinho Neto and Daniel Chipenda, Vice-President and
military commander of the dissident Eastern Revolt.
(A third "tendency" within the movement, the Active
Revolt led by Joaquim Pinto de Andrade, operated out
of Brazzaville.) Neto's supporters in Africa and
overseas quickly accused Kaunda of siding with
Chipenda in the dispute. The evidence for this charge
was basically that Zambia did not allow the Neto faction a free hand to deal with "counterrevolutionary
currents" within the party. The critics' case rested
on four specific complaints, all characteristic of the
uneasy relationships which typically prevail when host
states offer hospitality to exiled liberation movements.

To begin with, Chipenda was for a time accorded special protection to forestall any possibility of assassination at the hands of his rivals. With both factions evidently bent on exterminating their opponents physically, this was clearly a prudent precaution.[18] Had Neto been in the country at the time, he too would have received similar protection. Secondly, fresh restrictions were reportedly imposed on the transit of war materials to the front. Although undoubtedly irritating, these measures appear to have been motivated by an understandable concern to ensure that imports of arms and ammunition were used for the purposes intended. Again, Lusaka was accused of detaining certain loyal Neto cadres in October 1973, while at the same time allowing Chipenda a free hand to deploy his units against his political opponents. These MPLA charges of discrimination inspired the first of a series of international campaigns in which liberation support groups around the world were mobilized to flood State House with telegrams of protest. Although the facts in this case have not been fully established, what limited evidence is available suggests that the MPLA claims are at best exaggerated and that the action taken may have been fully justified in the interests of internal security.[19] Finally, Zambia was held responsible for the decision of a rump MPLA congress, convened near Lusaka in August 1974, to oust Neto as president in favor of Chipenda. The truth is that UNIP leaders struggled for fully two weeks to reconcile the feuding MPLA factions at the Congress.[20] Nevertheless, when these efforts failed and Chipenda carried out his coup, the Zambian government refused to recognize his bid for leadership because of the undemocratic methods employed (though it did continue to provide him with police protection). As a result, he quit Zambia and has not returned since. The following month in Brazzaville, Kaunda and the other frontline leaders reinstated Neto as head of a (temporarily) reunited party.[21]

Throughout this unhappy period, the Zambian government (unlike the Zambian press on occasion) did its best to maintain its neutrality.[22] The official line in Lusaka was that who led the MPLA was entirely a matter for the party to decide. Nevertheless, Zambia did have a legitimate interest in encouraging an early and peaceful resolution of the leadership crisis. In the first place, the possibility of further armed clashes between rival factions posed a threat to internal security. More important, the internal upheaval was adversely affecting the party's

military effectiveness in the field. Even Dr. Neto
conceded in 1973 that there had been "a considerable
retreat of our forces inside" Angola.[23] This, in
fact, is what had led Moscow the previous year to cut
back and eventually cut off its material assistance
to MPLA, and even, for a time, to shift its support
to the rebel Chipenda.[24] So concerned, too, was
President Nyerere at the relaxation of pressure on
the Portuguese (which allowed them to transfer
troops to Mozambique) that he appealed to the Chinese
to reinvigorate FNLA as the best way of intensifying
the struggle. This they agreed to do following
Mobutu's pilgrimage to Peking in January 1973 and
Roberto's in December.[25] As a result, when the
Portuguese collapse came, the MPLA found itself politically and militarily in a relatively weak position.[26] This partly accounts for the OAU's willingness to accord equal status to all three liberation
movements and to urge them to unite in a government
of national unity.

The fact that Chipenda managed to command the
loyalty of the bulk of MPLA forces on the eastern
front, and appeared more receptive than Neto to the
unity appeals of the frontline states,[27] may have in-
clined Lusaka at one stage, for purely pragmatic reasons, to look with favor on him. If so, sympathy for
Chipenda was shortlived. Following his exclusion
from the transitional government, he joined FNLA and
transferred his base of operations to Zaire. By March
1975, disenchantment in Lusaka with him had become so
great that Zambia was urging Zaire to keep Chipenda
under firm control lest he precipitate a civil war.

President Kaunda's endeavors to promote unity
between as well as within Angolan parties date back
before Zambian independence. Despite calculated
snubs initially by Roberto and later by Neto, he per-
severed in his efforts—through OAU mediation, the
good offices of "Mulungushi Club" members, and personal diplomacy—to forge a common nationalist front
in the interests of minimizing interparty feuding and
maximizing military effectiveness.[28] The most promising of these initiatives culminated in the Kinshasa
Agreement of December 1972 between MPLA and FNLA,
but, like all subsequent reconciliations, it quickly
evaporated as soon as the summit leaders dispersed.
Although the Portuguese coup added new urgency to the
task, the smell of power and disarray within the
ranks of the MPLA rendered success even more elusive.
As a result, nothing of substance was ever achieved.
In any case, by this time the focus of concern was on
the piecing together of a national government. Here

too, Zambia was in the forefront in arguing the absolute necessity of a coalition government embracing
all three nationalist movements to take Angola into
Independence, or at least through the period of national elections provided for in the Alvor agreement.[29]

Throughout the long years of the liberation
struggle and up to 1975, there was little in Zambian
behavior that MPLA partisans could legitimately com-
plain of—apart from the periodic friction and minor
misunderstandings inevitable in a situation in which
two autonomous political authorities with somewhat
different priorities and asymmetrical regulative
capabilities sought to cohabit on the same territory.
On the contrary, Zambia had proved a strong, reliable
and indispensable ally whose record of support and
sacrifice for the MPLA cause was second to none. If,
after the Portuguese coup, Lusaka's commitment was
less exclusive than in the past and, to that extent,
fell short of MPLA aspirations, in practice the movement often continued to receive preferential treatment. Thus, it alone among Angolan parties had
access to Radio Zambia's External Service, a facility
which it used to beam a daily one-hour programme
"Angola Combatente" to Angola in some nine languages.[30] Admittedly, with the acquisition of operational bases in and supply routes through west coast
ports, the MPLA was no longer dependent on the long,
arduous haul from Dar es Salaam across Zambia into
eastern Angola. Nevertheless, the host state privileges it had enjoyed remained available to it. Even
later, at the height of the civil war, the MPLA continued to maintain an office in Lusaka. That conflict was, however, to open up a serious rift between
the former close collaborators.

GOVERNMENT OF NATIONAL UNITY

Early in 1975, a broad consensus emerged within
the OAU, as well as among the liberation movements
themselves, on a power-sharing formula to permit a
peaceful transfer of Portuguese power. The key to
the strategy was recognition of all three parties as
the sole, legitimate and equal representatives of the
Angolan people, pending the outcome of national elections. However, the MPLA—like the FNLA, but not the
weaker UNITA—never fully reconciled itself to a
status of mere equality. Accordingly, it set about
to establish itself as the dominant military force in
the country. This open challenge to the uneasy

318

equilibrium, enshrined in the Alvor and Nakuru accords, cast an increasingly ominous shadow over MPLA-Zambian relations in the months leading up to Independence in November 1975, and culminated in a serious confrontation following the increased internationalization of the civil war.

Controversy concerning Zambia's role in this conflict has centered on two competing perceptions of her involvement. Critics have portrayed Lusaka as promoting an anti-MPLA crusade in collaboration with Pretoria, out of fear of radical social change at home and in neighboring countries, and as a result of its neocolonial links with the South. Zambian spokesmen, on the other hand, have protested vehemently that the government was merely insisting on the right of the Angolan people to decide their own destiny free of domestic and external dictation. Far from departing from the "basic principles of Pan-Africanism," Zambia took her stand firmly on the twin pillars of OAU policy: no intervention by foreign powers in African affairs and no interference by OAU members in the internal affairs of other independent states.[31] In practice, neither principle proved easy to apply consistently. In operational terms, however, Zambian policy meant pursuing two related goals, both of which ultimately proved elusive: an interim government of national unity and an end to foreign military intrusion.

The idea of a government of national unity held a special appeal for Zambians. Not only did it offer the prospect of a happy outcome to the years of effort devoted to pressing for a common front of Angolan nationalist parties, it also had an historical parallel in Zambian colonial experience. In 1962, an uneasy UNIP-ANC coalition had been forged—with the active assistance of other African governments—to guide the country through the tricky period of transition to majority rule; then, once the extent of popular support each of the rival parties commanded had been settled by general elections, the coalition was dissolved.[32] Nevertheless, this predisposition in favor of a national government was not the decisive consideration. More important to Zambian decision makers was their hardheaded assessment of the balance of political forces inside Angola.

All available information cautioned that, not only could no one party hope to command significant national support outside its own region, but no party could effectively govern the country alone with the political and military resources at its disposal. Accordingly, Lusaka felt compelled publicly to point out these harsh political facts to the rival leaders.

As one spokesman explained, unlike some of MPLA's
African supporters who were "far removed from the
Angolan scene" and who "could not care less about
Angola," Zambia, despite her long record of support
for MPLA, was not prepared "to dupe the MPLA into
thinking that the MPLA can run a peaceful Angola at
the complete exclusion of the other parties." On
the contrary, peace and stability could not come to
Angola "until the other movements were accommo-
dated."[33] This was equally true of UNITA and FNLA;
they too were minority parties with regional bases.
No party was strong enough to represent the Angolan
people as a whole but, equally, none was so insignificant that it could be ignored.[34] As President
Kaunda argued at the OAU:

> We cannot pretend that the three political
> parties do not exist in Angola. This would be
> self-deception. The fact that each one is
> ideologically unacceptable to one or other of
> member states of the OAU does not render its
> existence null and void.

Each party had an equally valid claim to a share in
government, pending a definitive verdict by the
Angolan electorate. "Preference for one movement,"
Kaunda added, "does not and should not necessarily
preclude other movements from [participating in]
the gigantic task of national reconstruction."[35]
Thus, for him, the question was not a matter of
ideological bias but of realistic appraisal of the
political realities in a confused and complicated
struggle for power.
     Although the conviction that a government of
national unity was the only way to preserve the
rights of the Angolan people was the overriding
consideration for Zambia, there were also undeniable
national interests involved. An orderly transfer of
power would be an assurance of peace on Zambia's
western borders. This was no inconsequential concern in view of the continued presence in Angola of
a substantial community of Zambian dissidents who
had been armed by the Portuguese. Moreover, in
December 1975, the Northwestern Province had been
invaded by the "Mushala gang."[36] Lusaka also had a
keen interest in an early reopening of the Benguela
Railway, closed since August 1975. In 1974, this
route had carried 55.1% of Zambia's exports and
44.6% of her imports.[37]
     President Kaunda's advocacy of a government of
national unity was pressed with persistence and

eloquence for more than a year. Although it had received OAU endorsement at the Kampala Summit of July 1975—which Kaunda had boycotted—and been re-iterated by the OAU Bureau and its Defence Commission on the eve of Angolan Independence,[38] by the time the emergency session of the OAU Assembly convened the following January, the earlier consensus had begun to crumble. Kaunda's powerful appeal succeeded in stem-ming the erosion temporarily but, within weeks, the military and diplomatic triumph of the MPLA was virtu-ally complete. Nevertheless, Zambia continued, rather optimistically, to urge national reconciliation. In February, her foreign minister was still calling on "the FNLA and UNITA, together with their followers, to forget the past and join hands with the Government of the People's Republic of Angola in the gigantic task of nation building." At the same time, he appealed, "in this same spirit . . . to the MPLA Government, in the interests of peace and national reconstruction, to be more accommodating and extend a brotherly hand of peace to all the people of Angola."[39] As late as the following August at the Non-Aligned Conference in Colombo, Kaunda personally advised Neto to unite with his rivals in a government of national unity, particu-larly with a view to ending the continuing guerrilla warfare in the countryside.[40] His advice was ignored.

Zambia's vigorous espousal of a government of na-tional unity has been condemned on two grounds. To begin with, it was perceived by some critics as a subtle maneuver to subvert the Angolan revolution.[41] Those adopting a world perspective identified the enemy as imperialism, not simply colonialism. Conse-quently, for them, the outcome of the second war of liberation—whether true national liberation or a retreat into neocolonialism—was a matter of profound global significance; in the words of one MPLA parti-san, "Luanda is Madrid."[42] Critics also suggested that Zambia's professed concern for a truly repre-sentative government was less than completely genuine. Rather, the real objective of her campaign was to mask a policy of effectively excluding MPLA from a share of power. Both accusations were hotly and repeatedly repudiated. "Zambia has never been against the MPLA," Foreign Minister Rupiah Banda declared in February 1976. "She is not opposed to the MPLA now and will not be against the MPLA in future. Zambia is ready to work with any established government in Angola." In any case, an analysis of Zambian motives was no answer to the basic Zambian argument that MPLA was a minority party incapable of governing Angola without the presence of a foreign army. "That is all

321

we are saying," President Kaunda contended. The MPLA
"cannot control [Angola] without negotiating with
their colleagues in UNITA and FNLA. . . . It is not
possible to have a military solution to the problems
of Angola."[43]

Four arguments have been advanced to support the
contention that Lusaka harbored hostile feelings towards the MPLA. To begin with, it has been suggested
that President Kaunda's personal relations with
Savimbi were more cordial than those with Neto.
There is some secondary evidence to support this.
Kaunda, along with Nyerere and Machel, regarded
Savimbi as the ablest as well as the most charismatic
of the party leaders. For this reason, he was their
first choice to head a government of national
unity.[44] At the same time, Kaunda appears to have
found that Neto—like de Gaulle—was a difficult
character to deal with; according to one commentator,
"Kaunda probably dislikes Neto as much as he dislikes
Muzorewa."[45] Nevertheless, the suggestion that his
personality preferences affected his political judge-
ments can be discounted. If any bias had existed, it
would have been against Holden Roberto and the FNLA,
with its tribalistic and even racialistic overtones.
In the past, Kaunda had dealt with a fair number of
prickly individuals and, perhaps more than any other
frontline leader, had managed to rise above questions
of personality differences. There is no reason to
believe he reacted any differently to Neto. Certainly, idiosyncratic factors did not prove an obstacle to their subsequent close collaboration.

Secondly, it is argued that Zambia committed a
calculated act of unfriendliness in recognizing
Angolan independence but delaying recognition of the
MPLA regime until 15 April 1976—well after the
effective collapse of organized military resistance,
Angola's admission to the OAU (on 11 February), and
even Zairien recognition (on 28 February). There is
little doubt that initially the government of the
People's Republic of Angola possessed few of the
traditional requisites for international recognition.
In particular, it lacked effective physical control
of the country, despite its claim to have occupied
eleven of sixteen provincial capitals. Yet, this was
not an argument Zambia relied on; her practice has
been to regard official recognition of a government
or a state (such as Biafra in 1968 or Guinea-Bissau
in 1973) as a seal of political approval rather than
the mere acceptance of reality.

During the civil war, the motive for withholding
recognition of either regime was clearly to avoid

prejudicing a political solution. "We are not an electoral college," Kaunda told his fellow heads of state. However, as the war wound down, pressure to fall in line with the OAU majority mounted. Yet, Kaunda still refused to be "stampeded."[46] As far as he was concerned, nothing essential had changed. As one spokesman explained, Zambia was still not entitled

> to usurp the right of the Angolan people of choosing a government for themselves. This is clearly the prerogative of the Angolan people and even if MPLA overruns the whole of Angola . . . that would be no proof of the popularity of the victor or the unpopularity of the vanquished. . . . It is merely proof of the military weakness of the vanquished or the lack of military resources or capacity to mobilize such resources on the part of losers.[47]

Moreover, Lusaka doubted whether an "occupied" country could be regarded as genuinely independent. As Kaunda declared:

> We disagree with the presence of foreign troops in Angola because we don't think it is possible for the MPLA—no matter how progressive—. . . to maintain a line of independence of thought and action with Soviet Union and Cuban troops on their shoulder. It is impossible.[48]

Finally, with Zambia almost the last important holdout, an attempt was made to bargain recognition away in return for political concessions. However, despite the obvious value the Angolans placed on normalizing relations, the strategy failed. None of the assurances Lusaka sought from Luanda was realized: neither the reopening of the Benguela Railway, nor the return of seized Zambian property, nor security of its frontiers, nor amnesty for political opponents—let alone withdrawal of Cuban forces.[49]

The recognition issue gave rise to a third indication of the Zambian government's attitude to the MPLA—and the most difficult to dismiss. Following a peaceful demonstration by pro-MPLA students at the University of Zambia on 15 January 1976, the President reaffirmed the state of emergency in the country and detained a number of expatriates and Zambians, principally University staff and students. Admittedly, there were a number of extenuating circumstances: UNIP's traditional sensitivity to student strictures,[50] the coincidence of an internal crisis within the University, the sustained campaign of criticism to which Zambia had been subjected, disquiet over the domestic political implications of the collapse of the world copper price, and the bitterness felt at the perceived Soviet abuse of Zambian hospitality. Nevertheless, some of the anger and frustration felt in Lusaka undoubtedly spilt over on to the MPLA. Although the MPLA was never officially identified as the source of the reported sabotage and subversion, it was indirectly a target of suspicion, though never the principal target. That distinction was reserved for the Soviet Union, whose alleged infiltration tactics led the President to characterize some student groups as behaving "like an orchestra with an invisible conductor on the payroll of a social imperialist power."[51]

Finally, there was the matter of Zambian assistance to UNITA, the nature, extent and motivation of which are analyzed below.

FOREIGN INTERVENTION

The essential preconditions for a genuine government of national unity were a ceasefire and the withdrawal of all foreign forces. Lusaka's appeals for a ceasefire were as regular and as insistent as its pleading for a government of national unity—and equally unproductive. Part of its concern was humanitarian. The spectacle of "senseless killings of brother by brother" in Angola for the benefit of foreign intruders filled Kaunda with anger and shame.[52] Even more ominous were the political consequences he feared might flow from a prolongation of the conflict: dwindling prospects of a political solution, a further escalation in the level of sophistication of the weaponry deployed, the balkanization of the country,[53] and increasing dependence on external powers. "We must reject the erroneous and dangerous assumption," the President declared, "that a truly independent Angola will only be achieved through intensification of the civil war." In fact, the precise opposite was more probable. The Angolan people, who had "struggled for centuries for freedom and peace against foreign domination and exploitation," had finally won their

legal independence only to be threatened with loss of
their political freedom. As a result of the intransigence of the liberation leaders and the paralysis
of the OAU, the "effective decisions" on Angola were
being "made in Moscow and Washington."[54] The superpower hegemony that Peking had railed against for so
long had become a tragic reality.

For these reasons, Zambia bitterly condemned
foreign military intervention, whether by the
Russians, the Cubans, the South Africans or, with
qualifications, the Americans. (Only the Zairiens—
who fought on both sides—and the French escaped public castigation in Lusaka.) Among major powers,
China alone earned commendation for her restraint in
not exploiting her previous assistance to liberation
movements to impose her hegemony on Africa. "China
helped the struggle in Angola," Kaunda reminded the
OAU. "But she has no imperialist ambitions. She has
therefore refused to be involved in the tragedy of
the Angolan civil war."[55]

Zambia's abhorrence of external, and especially
superpower involvement in the affairs of the continent was a matter of deep conviction, rather than
mere expediency. It was central to the pan-African
principle of "Africa for the Africans," the OAU doc-
trines of nonintervention and nonalignment, and the
concept of the sovereign equality of states. Moreover, keeping the Cold War out of Southern Africa had
been a major objective of Zambian foreign policy
since Independence. One reason Kaunda had pressed
the British so relentlessly to use force in Rhodesia
had been to pre-empt the possibility of superpower
intrusion (see chapter 4). Now, in Angola, it appeared that his worst fears were being realized. The
fact that the US Congress unilaterally limited the
Cold War dimension of the conflict was only partially
reassuring.

The Zambian crusade against foreign military
forces in Angola was not so much one-sided as evenhanded—though, in the eyes of critics, this was
equally reprehensible. While "careful not to lump
[the] interventionists into one camp" morally, Lusaka
denounced foreign involvement from whatever quarter,
and demanded the withdrawal of all alien troops without distinction as to nationality or ideology.[56]
Nevertheless, its condemnation of the behavior of the
socialist states was unaccustomably harsh. "In the
history of independent Africa," Kaunda declared,

> this is the first time that thousands of non-
> African regular troops and heavy sophisticated

military equipment have been brought in to in-
stall one political party into power and in the
service of their hegemonic interests. This is
a most dangerous phenomenon which constitutes a
grave threat to the entire continent and the
unity of Africa.[57]

Or, on another occasion, in a now-famous allusion:

We have witnessed [in Angola] imperialism in all
its manifestations. Africa has fought and driven
out the ravenous wolves of colonialism, racism
and fascism from Angola through the front door.
But a plundering tiger with its deadly cubs is
now coming in through the back door.[58]

Such statements were consistent with Zambia's own
conception of nonalignment, which entitled her to
criticize any superpower whose actions merited it—as
in the case of the United States during the Vietnam
war and of the USSR following her invasion of Czechoslovakia.[59] If the Soviet presence in Angola attracted special attention, it was because of its
novelty, its scale, its spillover effects on domestic
politics, and the doubts it raised concerning its
long-run implications. This Zambian reaction did not
reflect any simple anticommunist fixation; Zambia is
not Zaire or Malawi or the Ivory Coast. Nor was it
merely an echo of the dire warnings emanating from
Peking concerning Moscow's ultimate aims in Africa—
though Kaunda's speeches provide increasing evidence
of Chinese jargon being internalized. Nevertheless,
it clearly revealed a nationalist perception of the
Soviet Union as an imperial power. "Africa must
understand," Kaunda warned,

that imperialism is imperialism. It knows
neither race nor color nor ideology. All nations
which seek to impose their will on others are
imperialists. Africa must not permit these
Trojan imperialist horses, which came under the
guise of furthering the cause of liberation, to
drive us.[60]

The Zambian reaction to Cuba's intervention in
Angola was less reproachful. In part, this reflected
the cordial personal and political relations which had
prevailed between the two countries previously.
President Kaunda had toured the island in April 1975
and had returned enthusiastic about the Cuban experiment, aspects of which he incorporated into the

program outlined in his marathon "watershed speech" in June.[61] Then in December 1975, at the peak of the civil war, a high-powered UNIP delegation attended the First Congress of the Cuban Communist Party. Subsequently, a team of Cuban experts visited Zambia to advise on setting up new sugar estates.[62] A further factor was the tendency to consider the Cubans, somewhat unrealistically, as Soviet "cubs", rather than as autonomous actors. There were even hints that Cuban troops might be welcome in a liberation role elsewhere in Southern Africa. "We can't support the idea of Cubans killing black Africans in Angola in the name of ideology," Foreign Minister Rupiah Banda declared. "But if they go into Namibia to chase out the whites, they will have our blessings."[63] Thus, although Zambia reacted less emotionally to the presence of Cubans in Angola than to Russian involvement, she felt equally strongly that they had no moral right to be there, and firmly and frequently demanded their removal. Lusaka even appears to have attempted (unsuccessfully) to negotiate a Cuban withdrawal as a condition of recognition of the MPLA regime.[64]

It is worth observing that Zambian objections to Cuban and Russian personnel in Angola did not turn on the question whether the MPLA had been entitled to invite in foreign military forces prior to Independence. Lusaka was much too concerned with the broader issues at stake to be greatly agitated by a narrow legal point.

SUPPORT FOR UNITA

The question of Zambia's attitude towards international intervention on behalf of the shaky FNLA-UNITA coalition is considerably more contentious and confused. In particular, much of the evidence concerning Zambian involvement is conflicting, and frequently no more substantial than media speculation, partisan opinion and routine official denials. Nevertheless, an element of ambiguity in Zambia's approach was undoubtedly present. To establish the facts and assess their significance, three areas of inquiry require exploration: assistance to UNITA, American military aid, and the alleged collaboration with South Africa.

The Zambian government believed deeply and sincerely in the doctrine of nonintervention in neighbors' affairs. Why, then, did it depart from its own principles in providing limited assistance to UNITA.

327

A variety of motives have been advanced, most of them wide of the mark. To begin with, it has been suggested that it was the "pro-Western stance" of the anti-MPLA coalition that attracted Zambian support.[65] Apart from the dubious validity of attaching Cold War labels to Angolan parties, this is too simplistic an explanation to carry much conviction; once again, Zambia is not Zaire. A more plausible argument is that Lusaka calculated that the prospects of restoring the Lobito route, on which it had depended so heavily, would be improved if the Benguela Railway were under UNITA rather than MPLA control. For one thing, if the line were in unfriendly hands, Zaire might be unwilling to reopen it to through traffic; this, in fact ɔ what happened.[66]

Pertinent as this consideration was, it is not sufficient on its own to account for Zambia's behavior. The real clue to this was to be found in her desire to establish greater equality in bargaining power among the rival parties. The intention here was to impress OAU members, promote a ceasefire, discourage any further recognitions, and facilitate formation of a government of national unity—not to "exclude MPLA from power." Apart from anything else, this was clearly not feasible, and never suggested. Thus, what appears to have been an inconsistency in Zambia's policy was not perceived as such. Nevertheless, as a contribution to national unity, the assistance rendered UNITA turned out to be inadequate or counterproductive.[67] Accordingly, it was terminated in February 1976—following OAU recognition of the MPLA government but two months prior to Zambia's own decision—though the UNITA office in Lusaka continued to function until its officials were finally expelled the following December.[68]

Savimbi's frequent and well-publicized visits to Lusaka created the impression of a more intimate relationship with Kaunda than was actually the case. Even the most critical accounts agree that direct Zambia aid to UNITA—there was none to FNLA—was modest, though precise details are difficult to come by. Savimbi, as well as his political rivals, maintained a busy office in Lusaka, and on occasion had access to Zambia Radio. He is also said to have used the President's private plane, though there may be confusion here with the Lonrho executive Learjet which certainly was placed at his disposal.[69] More significant but less certain is the extent to which Zambian territory was used to ferry in supplies to UNITA forces in the field; reports that Zambia Air Force planes participated in this

328

airlift, though not improbable, remain unsubstantiated.[70] Finally, there is the delicate question
whether Lusaka used its good offices to enlist
American and possibly even South African military
aid for UNITA.

The United States was not directly involved in
Angola with troops, apart from her contribution to
the rather pathetic band of misguided mercenaries
who quickly discovered—in some cases too late—
that they had bitten off more than they had bar-
gained for. Instead, American military aid took
the form of light arms deliveries and logistical
support. Zambian involvement in this operation was
most apparent at the initial decision-making stage.
President Kaunda first urged the Americans to bolster the military capabilities of MPLA's opponents
in April 1975, in the course of his protocol-
shattering visit to Washington and shortly after
the first major injection of Soviet weaponry into
Angola. While public attention focused on Kaunda's
blunt White House speech expressing "dismay" at US
policy on South Africa, Namibia and Rhodesia, privately he was warning Ford and Kissinger of Soviet
intentions and encouraging them to react effectively.[71]

Initially, this advice was rejected in favor
of the "diplomatic option." As Nathaniel Davis,
US Assistant Secretary of State for African Affairs,
reportedly argued in July in opposition to covert
intervention, "we won't be able to win" and "failure
inevitably would be extremely damaging to the two
leading African moderates who are American supporters": Kaunda and Mobutu.[72] Nevertheless, Kissinger
reportedly overrode the almost unanimous advice of
the State Department, the National Security Council,
the CIA and the Joint Chiefs of Staff and authorized
limited military support.[73] The 17 July 1975 decision of the Forty Committee—a high-powered body
responsible for approving all covert operations
overseas—was subsequently justified, perhaps not
entirely accurately, as a response to appeals from
Angola's neighbors. According to William Schaufele
—who succeeded Davis when the latter resigned in
protest:

> After separate pleas from Zambia and Zaire,
> each of which saw their security threatened by
> the specter of a Soviet supported MPLA, we
> reversed our earlier decision not to provide
> military support to any faction and on June 18
> we authorized the use of covert funds for the
> FNLA and UNITA forces.[74]

He added, in words that might well have been Kaunda's that: "Our goal was to strengthen the two movements sufficiently to preserve a military balance and thereby encourage the establishment of a compromise coalition government."[75] Nevertheless, this parallelism does not indicate that American and Zambian interests and outlook coincided; Washington's perspective was global and strategic, whereas Lusaka's was regional and restricted.

Although the Zambian government never publicly admitted to its part in pressing for American military assistance, and did in fact deny it, President Kaunda continued to defend the right of UNITA and FNLA to receive US arms as long as the Soviet Union was supplying the MPLA. "We are a nonaligned nation," he explained,

> and as such, we spoke out plainly against US policy in Vietnam. We must have political and moral courage, as well as consistency, to tell the Russians that what they are doing in Angola is wrong. . . . It is not the American arms to Angola that caused the crisis. No African leader in his right mind could imagine for a moment that the Soviet Union could have its presence in Angola and expect not to attract the Americans.[76]

Although the fact, if not the extent of Zambian input into the American decision to mount a military assistance program in Angola is well-documented, less certainty surrounds Lusaka's participation in its implementation. Two roles have been suggested. The first was the provision of arms from Zambian stocks. The basis for this claim is that the Forty Committee had authorized

> the replacement of arms that had been previously supplied by Zaire and Zambia, the two neighboring African states that supported the American intervention. It was [also] agreed to permit Zambia and Zaire to provide as much non-American equipment as possible at first in order to minimize the overt link with the United States.[77]

US authorization of a swap arrangement there certainly was. In addition, Zambia appears to have received some American (as well as Soviet) arms during the second half of 1975.[78] Yet whether these represented replacements for Zambian arms transferred

330

to UNITA has not been finally established. In the case of Zaire, the empirical evidence is overwhelming; for Zambia, no firm conclusions are yet possible.

Secondly, there is the question whether any US aid to UNITA was routed through Zambia. The CIA had certainly urged the use of Zambian transit facilities as a means of compromising Kaunda at a time when he was suspected of having dangerous neutralist tendencies. "We wanted no 'soft' allies in our war against the MPLA," John Stockwell asserts and, in this respect, Kaunda presented a "potential problem."

> How could we get him so involved he could never defect? The key seemed to be the transshipment of arms through Zambia. Kaunda had publicly supported the international embargo against the shipment of arms to Angola, and it was felt that if one planeload of arms could be introduced into Zambia, with Kaunda's permission, he would be irreversibly committed to UNITA's support——'pregnant' we said in CIA headquarters.[79]

Stockwell does not reveal if this Machiavellian scheme was ever actualized. Nevertheless, although most American supplies were funnelled through Zaire, at a later stage some undoubtedly reached UNITA through Zambia.

THE SOUTH AFRICAN CONNECTION?

Concerted action with the Americans was one thing; collusion with the South Africans was quite another. Yet this is precisely the accusation levelled at the Kaunda government. It has taken several forms: that Lusaka allowed South African men and supplies destined for Angola to transit Zambian territory; that Kaunda was the intermediary between UNITA and Pretoria in negotiating military support; that he had acquiesced in, tacitly approved or even requested the South African invasion of Angola; and that he was duly rewarded economically for his services. These charges are so grave and so at variance with past Zambian behavior that it would take solid evidence to render them credible. Unfortunately, the information presently available for reaching a judgement is spotty or uncorroborated. Moreover, much of it emanates from sources, notably South Africa and MPLA support groups, which share a vested interest——

331

for opposing reasons—in promoting reports of a
Kaunda-Vorster conspiracy. On the other hand, official disclaimers can be equally suspect.

Towards the end of 1975, vague reports of mys-
terious night flights through remote airports in the
Western Province gave rise to allegations that South
Africa had been accorded transit rights in Zambia to
support UNITA and possibly her own military activities in Angola. The most specific charge was the
claim (in February 1976) that "a Viscount belonging
to the South African company Pearl Air has been flying arms regularly for several weeks to the UNITA
airfield at Silva Porto from Lusaka International
Airport." Some credence was given this report with
the arrest of the aircraft in March, after aid to
UNITA had been suspended.[80] Pearl Air is known to
have been involved in ferrying supplies to UNITA
from Kinshasa via Lusaka. However, there is no
evidence that it was operating from or on behalf of
South Africa. On the contrary, when the Zairien
Foreign Minister arrived in Lusaka at the end of
1975 with an appeal from Mobutu to make Zambian
facilities available to South Africa to supply
UNITA, the request was flatly rejected.[81]

The evidence for Kaunda interceding with
Vorster to procure military hardware and troops to
bolster the ill-equipped and ill-trained opposition
to MPLA is more substantial, but still somewhat
suspect. The major sources are two reports, both
with distinct South African flavors. The first, by
Robert Moss, a rightwing Australian author with
access to South African intelligence sources, appeared in a series of articles in the London Sunday
Telegraph in early 1977.[82] The second, by Bill
Coughlin, an inexperienced staff assistant to US
Senator John V. Tunney (then fighting unsuccessfully for re-election), was an account of his tour
of Southern Africa in January 1976. Significantly,
Coughlin's conclusions were published in Rapport,
a Johannesburg Afrikaans newspaper with close ties
with the Pretoria government, in February 1976 at
a time when South African forces were withdrawing
from Angola and Pretoria was searching desperately
for a scapegoat to blame for the debâcle.[83] The
reports reveal that Savimbi met Vorster in Pretoria
twice, on 10 November and 19 December 1975, and held
a third meeting with South African authorities in
Windhoek at the end of the year.[84] On all three
occasions, he implored Pretoria not to withdraw its
forces prematurely and, indeed, to reinforce them.
South Africa's original intention had been to pull

out immediately after Angolan independence, but (according to these accounts) she was persuaded by Savimbi twice, though not the third time, to postpone her departure.

Only in the case of the second meeting with Vorster is there specific mention of Kaunda using his good offices to facilitate the arrangements, but the implication is that he at least knew about the others. Certainly, other South African-inspired publications, as well as Radio RSA, took up the cudgels eagerly and sought to exploit to the full rumors of Kaunda's role as an intermediary.[85] Despite the gravity of these allegations, Kaunda for many months kept his silence. Finally, in February 1976, in an angry outburst, he challenged his critics to "prove that I sent Savimbi to South Africa," and threatened legal action against his accusers.[86] That challenge still stands. On the basis of present evidence, the most that can be assumed is that Kaunda knew of Savimbi's links with South Africa and chose not to condemn him publicly.

Even more damaging was the charge that Zambia was instrumental in encouraging South African troops to invade Angola in the first place, and had backed UNITA appeals that they stay on. Here the Coughlin report is quite specific. According to Savimbi, Pretoria behaved throughout with "painful correctness"; at no stage did it act militarily without the approval of Kaunda, Mobutu and Houphouët-Boigny. In particular, in early October 1975, all three presidents had, at Savimbi's request, personally appealed to the South African prime minister to provide UNITA with secret assistance. It was in response to this that Vorster launched "Operation Zulu" which took South African forces up the coast almost to Luanda. Again, in December, Pretoria agreed to postpone its withdrawal only after sounding out opinion in Lusaka and Kinshasa.[87]

The Zambian government reacted to the Coughlin report with indignation and exasperation. "I am assured on the highest authority," Colin Legum reported from Lusaka, "that President Kaunda, so far from encouraging South African intervention, did everything possible to discourage Mr. Vorster from the enterprise."[88] Such denials failed to satisfy Kaunda's critics. Nor were they impressed by declarations, such as the President's reiteration at the OAU that, "we have repeatedly condemned South Africa [for intervening in Angola] and do condemn them now. We call for the withdrawal of all South African troops from Angola."[89] Confronted with this

333

irreconcilable conflict of evidence, it is unlikely
that the issue can be finally resolved until all the
diplomatic exchanges are revealed publicly. Pending
that improbable occurrence, certain general considerations may contribute to placing the problem in
perspective.

To begin with, the Zambian president had every
reason to be furious with Vorster. Not only was his
eagerness to appear helpful an acute embarrassment,
but his actions in Angola completely undercut the
moral basis of Kaunda's policies. In particular, it
lost him the support of critical African states,
notably Tanzania and Nigeria, and tipped the balance
of OAU opinion decisively against a government of
national unity and condemnation of Soviet-Cuban (as
well as South African) intervention. There is
little, therefore, which Zambia had reason to feel
grateful to South Africa for.

Secondly, despite the controversy that some of
his détente initiatives had generated, Kaunda's cre-
dentials as a leader of the liberation struggle remained impressive, and his achievements real. Unlike
many more distant countries, Zambia had backed up her
fine words with positive deeds, often at great cost.
This helps explain the depth of resentment felt in
Lusaka at the uninformed criticisms of "microphone
revolutionaries." "We in Zambia," Kaunda remarked
with some asperity at the OAU,

> need no lecturing from anyone about apartheid
> and colonialism. We have fought South African
> apartheid for many years. . . . Some of us will
> forget about the struggle soon after takeoff
> from Addis Ababa, while for Zambia this [fight]
> is part of [our] daily program.[90]

The fact that Zambia has paid such a high price for
her principles, and that Kaunda has been prepared to
gamble on bold initiatives even at great risk to his
own reputation, hardly suggests that Lusaka was abandoning the liberation struggle; on the contrary, it
was a measure of its commitment to the cause. Nor,
on the basis of Kaunda's known character and past
record, does the attempt to cast Kaunda in the role
of a Judas carry conviction. Yet, this is what is
implied in the related charge that he reacted to economic adversity at home by succumbing to the temptation of thirty pieces of South African silver.

334

REGIONAL ECONOMIC DEPENDENCE

There is no disputing that the Angolan conflict coincided with a period of severe economic hardship in Zambia. Just as the country appeared on the point of coping with the economic consequences of the decision to close the Rhodesian border in 1973, but before the Tazara railway had come into operation, it was confronted with a calamitous fall in the world copper price, a fivefold increase in the cost of imported oil, a mammoth balance of payments deficit and the sudden closure of its one remaining rail outlet to the sea (see chapters 1 and 11). What is in dispute is whether these economic constraints compelled Zambia to soften her hostility to South Africa. Had she done so, her reaction might have been understandable. Indeed, the fact that an economic accommodation with Pretoria appeared the most rational policy in terms of the country's immediate national interests has led some observers to suspect that this is what actually happened.

Admittedly, the minority regimes in Southern Africa were quick to appreciate Zambia's plight, and sought to capitalize on it for their own economic and political purposes. They had long cherished a belief with some of their ideological opponents that economic realities must ultimately triumph over political preferences. Accordingly, Salisbury sounded out Lusaka on the prospects of restoring rail service across Victoria Falls. This appeal found some echo within Zambia, particularly in the Southern Province which had suffered most from the border closure. President Kaunda, however, was adamant in spurning the idea as unworthy—until "Zimbabwe is born."[91]

Pretoria was in a stronger position to offer economic inducements and, as a result, mounted a concerted campaign to exploit its opportunities to the full. It also managed to gull the media—in South Africa, and elsewhere in Africa and overseas—into treating its bold initiatives as accomplished facts. This was apparent from the sensational press accounts of massive South African loans to Zambia and the extravagant predictions of expanded exports to Zambia. As noted in chapter 1, the loan story was effectively discredited following a successful Zambian suit in the British courts, and the anticipated trade boom failed to materialize. On the contrary, table 1.2 provides impressive evidence of the success of Zambian efforts to disengage economically from dependence on South Africa.

335

The dependency thesis has also been expressed in more general terms, based on the premise that an emerging Zambian comprador class, with international links that tied it directly or indirectly to South African capital, had taken control of the state. There is little doubt that transnational class linkages had been developing in Zambia, though the bargaining power of the nascent bourgeoisie enabled its members to exercise greater autonomy than their characterization as compradors implied. Certainly, President Kaunda was well aware of the growing danger, judging by the frequency with which he railed against it and the measures he took to contain it, particularly during the period that coincided with the Angolan civil war.[92] The number of politicians and senior officials who were disciplined for breaches of the Leadership Code or prosecuted for corrupt practices is indicative, not so much of the extent of the problem, as of the President's determination not to allow "right wingers" to steer the ship of state.[93] The whole history of Zambia since Independence has been a constant struggle to pursue her political ideals in the face of inherited economic ties. The government's record in this respect offers some assurance that the residual economic dependence on Southern Africa can be largely discounted as a major constraint on Zambian policy on Angola generally and on South African involvement in particular. Nevertheless, as was evidenced in 1978 following a further severe deterioration in the Zambian economy, there are limits, even in the case of Zambia, to the price that the country can be expected to pay for its principles.

CONCLUSIONS

The Angolan civil war was an agonizing experience for Zambia, and especially her President. It opened painful breaches with close colleagues, and led to embarrassing associations with friends who were collaborating with sworn foes. In the process, Zambian motives were misrepresented left and right, north and south, and her leaders abused by traditional allies and praised by longstanding opponents. Moreover, in the end, none of the immediate objectives of Zambian policy was achieved. As an exercise in maintaining control over Zambia's "external environment through the preservation of desired situations and the modification of undesired ones,"[94] Angola was a failure.

Characteristically, Kaunda's policy—to the distress of some of his more pragmatic supporters— was firmly rooted in principles, in particular, pan-Africanism, representative government and nonalignment.[95] Not that national interests, notably access to the Benguela Railway and peaceful borders were entirely absent, but they were never as decisive as was commonly assumed. Zambia, Kaunda declared, "would not be cowed into doing wrong things because of routes."[96] Certainly, any suggestion that, even in the midst of an economic recession, policy on Angola was influenced by tempting offers of South African financial carrots can be dismissed as implausible and unworthy.

One principle was of paramount importance to Zambia. This was the distinction between the obligation of African states to assist in the total liberation of Africa and their obligation to respect the right of liberated people to a government of their own choice.[97] From this basic premise, all else flowed logically: the preoccupation with limiting and, if possible, eliminating foreign military intervention, the insistence on a ceasefire and a political solution, the promotion of a balance of forces and a government of national unity, and the reluctance to accord recognition to only one party to the conflict.

These goals were legitimate, even if unattainable in the short run. The problem arose when it came to implementing them in practice, especially when a variety of other actors with divergent interests joined in the action. As a result, Zambia found herself associated with partners not of her choosing. While the precise nature and extent of the tacit coalitions that emerged still cannot be assessed definitively, it is possible to outline the general parameters of the relationships involved:

1. Zambia supported UNITA morally and, to some slight extent, materially, though Kaunda was never as deeply committed to Savimbi as Mobutu was to Holden Roberto.[98] Moreover, UNITA was always envisaged as only one partner in a government comprising MPLA and possibly FNLA, not as ruling alone or in coalition with FNLA only. Thus, from Lusaka's perspective, there was nothing anti-MPLA in its attitude or actions.

2. American military assistance for the underdogs was welcomed, even solicited, as a means of restoring a military balance and thus encouraging the parties to search for a political rather than a

337

military settlement. There is a close parallel here with Zambian policy on Biafra.

3. Zambia developed a tolerance for UNITA's known South African connection. Whether it went beyond this has never been established. Certainly, there is no evidence of any direct Zambia-South African collusion over Angola. In this respect, as in many others, a clear distinction can be drawn between the policies pursued by Zambia and Zaire. To the extent that Zambian behavior was externally inspired, it was more pro-Peking than pro-Pretoria.

Throughout the Angolan civil war, Lusaka enjoyed firm Chinese support. In Africa, Peking has never had any difficulty in distinguishing between primary and secondary enemies, or qualms about enlisting temporary or indirect allies. Accordingly, although it publicly declared its neutrality shortly before Angola's independence, privately it actively encouraged American involvement, and was not entirely unhappy at South African intervention. In this respect, the Chinese were considerably more hawkish than the Zambians.[99]

Lusaka's increased reliance on Peking was undoubtedly strengthened by its deep suspicion concerning Soviet motives in both Angola and Zambia, especially the failure to respect the right of small, weak states to select their own leaders. Kaunda was particularly critical of the fact that the massive buildup of Soviet arms in Angola came only after the principle of independence had been conceded. That this attitude was not simply blind anticommunism is apparent from the fact that, in April 1977, President Podgorny of the Soviet Union paid a state visit to Zambia, thus formally ending the period of estrangement in bilateral relations as well as a sad chapter in relations among African states.

Repairing the breach with the MPLA government became a protracted exercise. Although transnational relations at the party level were quickly restored—and, in fact, were never severed—Zambia was among the last African states to accord recognition to the Angolan government. Even after the formal announcement on 15 April 1976 and the replacement on 10 May of Rupiah Banda who, as foreign minister, had been closely associated with UNITA,[100] a certain lack of cordiality persisted. A number of intermediaries proffered their good offices, but it was the ZAPU president, Joshua Nkomo who succeeded in effecting a reconciliation; he had, of course, been acutely embarrassed by the open hostility between his two

most important host states. On 25 July 1976, he returned from Luanda with a message that Neto was prepared to meet Kaunda. The next day, Nkomo reported
personally to a meeting of UNIP Central Committee
members, who welcomed the initiative enthusiastically.
Accordingly, the two presidents conferred together at
the summit conference of nonaligned states at Colombo
in mid-August, and Neto stopped off in Lusaka on his
way home.
    Since then, relations have improved dramatically:
UNITA has been expelled from Zambia, the 14,000
Angolan refugees in Mehebe camp have been deported,
trade and cultural agreements have been concluded, a
permanent joint commission established, crossborder
road links are being upgraded, and Zambian goods and
equipment seized in Lobito have been released. In
addition, Kaunda mediated between Neto and Mobutu,
following the incursions into Shaba province in 1977
and 1978, with a view to expediting a reopening of
the Benguela Railway. Moreover, on the issues of
Namibia and Zimbabwe, Kaunda has found more common
ground with Neto than with either Nyerere or Machel.
As in the aftermath of the Nigerian civil war, African
statesmen have again demonstrated a remarkable capacity to overcome the past, face up to the realities of
the present, and build constructive relationships for
the future.

NOTES

    1. The principal accounts of the Angolan civil war
and Zambia's part in it are: John A. Marcum,
The Angolan Revolution (Cambridge, Mass.: MIT Press,
1978), II, 241-75; Colin Legum and Tony Hodges, After
Angola: The War over Southern Africa (New York:
Africana Publishing, 1976); R. W. Johnson, How Long
Will South Africa Survive? (London: Macmillan Press,
1977), pp. 132-63; Alex Callinicos and John Rogers,
Southern Africa after Soweto (London: Pluto Press,
1977), pp. 138-56; Mario J. Azevedo, "Zambia, Zaire,
and the Angolan Crisis Reconsidered: From Alvor to
Shaba," Journal of Southern African Affairs 2, no. 3
(July 1977):275-293; Charles K. Ebinger, "External
Intervention in Internal War: The Politics and
Diplomacy of the Angolan Civil War," Orbis 20, no. 3
(Fall 1976):669-99; Basil Davidson, "Angola: A Success
that Changes History," Race and Class 18, no. 1
(Summer 1976):23-37.

    2. A tacit coalition is a form of ad hoc variable

sum mixed motive cooperative "interaction" involving
two or more actors pursuing independent but parallel
paths with respect to a common conflict object but
for different and often irreconcilable reasons; no
element of coordination, collusion or communication
need be present. It falls short of the degree of
purposeful collaboration implied by such expressions
as "marriage of convenience" and "supping with the
devil"—familiar diplomatic devices to which actors,
such as Biafra, have been driven in extremities.

3. Africa Contemporary Record (ACR), 1974-75,
pp. C221-26; 1975-76, pp. B423-25. For chronologies
of events, see Johnson, How Long Will South Africa
Survive?, pp. 138-54; Gerald Bender, "Kissinger in
Angola: Anatomy of Failure," in American Policy in
Angola: The Stakes and the Stance, ed. René
Lemarchand (Washington: University Press of America,
1978), pp. 122-28; John Stockwell, In Search of
Enemies: A CIA Story (New York: W. W. Norton, 1978),
pp. 257-60; Nathaniel Davis, "The Angola Decision of
1975: A Personal Memoir," Foreign Affairs 57, no. 1
(Fall 1978):121-22.

4. On Soviet intervention generally, see Christopher
Stevens, "The Soviet Union and Angola," African
Affairs 75, no. 299 (April 1976):137-51; Stephen
Larrabee, "Moscow, Angola and the Dialectics of
Détente," World Today 32, no. 5 (May 1976):173-82;
Peter Vanneman and Martin James, "The Soviet Inter-
vention in Angola: Intentions and Implications,"
Strategic Review 4, no. 3 (Summer 1976):92-103. For
a Soviet view of the conflict, see Oleg Ignatiev,
Secret Weapon in Africa (Moscow: Progress Publishers,
1977).

5. Marcum, Angolan Revolution II, 259; US Senate,
US Involvement in Civil War in Angola. Hearings
before the Subcommittee on African Affairs, 6 February
1976, pp. 174, 184. Thirty planeloads of Soviet arms
reached Brazzaville on 25 March 1975, and were quickly
smuggled to MPLA forces in Angola. The first direct
deliveries began in April when chartered aircraft flew
arms into Southern Angola and three Yugoslav freighters
offloaded heavy equipment in Luanda (ACR, 1975-76,
pp. A13-14, B426; New York Times, 25 September 1975,
p. 22; London Times, 1 January 1976, p. 11).

6. Davis, "The Angola Decision of 1975," pp. 110,
120; ACR, 1975-76, p. A124; US Involvement in Civil
War in Angola, p. 175; Bender, "Kissinger in Angola,"

pp. 75-77.

7.   Stockwell, In Search of Enemies, p. 206; Mohamed
A. El-Khawas and Barry Cohen, The Kissinger Study of
Southern Africa (Westport, Conn.:   Lawrence Hill,
1976), pp. 183-84; New York Times, 14 December 1975,
p. 1 and 19 December 1975, p. 1.   Marcum (Angolan
Revolution II, 263) estimates a realistic valuation
of US assistance at twice the published figure.
Other sources on US intervention include: Ernest
Harsch and Tony Thomas, Angola: The Hidden History of
Washington's War (New York: Pathfinder Press, 1976);
Bender, "Kissinger in Angola," pp. 63-143; Roger
Morris, "The Proxy War in Angola: Pathology of a
Blunder," New Republic 174, no. 5 (31 January 1976):
19-23; "CIA's Secret War in Angola," Intelligence
Report (Washington) 1, no. 1 (1975):1-11.
M. A. Venkataramani, "The Ford-Kissinger Safari in
Angola: Ramifications of American Policy," Foreign
Affairs Reports (New Delhi) 25, nos. 9-10 (September-
October 1976):131-78; John A. Marcum, "Lessons of
Angola," Foreign Affairs 54, no. 3 (April 1976):407-
25; Neil C. Livingstone and Manfred von Nordheim,
"The United States Congress and the Angolan Crisis,"
Strategic Review 5, no. 2 (Spring 1977):34-44; also
US Involvement in Civil War in Angola.

8.   On Cuban intervention, see Gabriel Garcia
Marquez, "Operation Carlota," New Left Review,
nos. 101-102 (February-April 1977):123-37; Abraham F.
Lowenthal, "Cuba's African Adventure," International
Security 2, no. 1 (Summer 1977):3-10; Zdenek Cervenka,
"Cuba and Africa," ACR, 1976-77, pp. A84-90; Gerald
J. Bender, "Angola, the Cubans, and American
Anxieties," Foreign Policy, no. 31 (Summer 1978):3-
33; Gregory F. Treverton, "Cuba after Angola," World
Today 3, no. 1 (January 1977):17-21.

9.   Robin Hallett, "The South African Intervention
in Angola, 1975-76," African Affairs 77, no. 308
(July 1978):347-86; Defence Headquarters, Pretoria,
"Nature and Extent of the SADF's Involvement in the
Angolan Conflict," Press Release, 3 February 1977;
Mohamed A. El-Khawas, "South Africa and the Angolan
Conflict," Africa Today 24, no. 2 (April-June 1977):
35-46.

10. Garcia Marquez, "Operation Carlota," p. 125.
The three troopships, with their ports and dates of
arrival, were El Vietnam Heroico (Porto Amboim,
4 October 1975), El Coral Island (Pointe Noire,

Congo B, 7 October) and La Plata (Pointe Noire, 11 October); Brian Crozier claims that "five Cuban ships loaded with troops and weapons sailed for Africa on 5 September" ("The Surrogate Forces of the Soviet Union," Conflict Studies, no. 92 [February 1978], p. 2).

11. Marcum, Angolan Revolution II, 269, 273; US Involvement in Civil War in Angola, pp. 83, 165, 175; Times, 8 January 1976, p. 6; Globe and Mail (Toronto), 31 January 1977, p. 3 and 14 February 1977, p. 3.

12. International Herald Tribune, 31 December 1975, p. 4.

13. Daily Times (Lagos), 10 November 1975, p. 32; James H. Polhemus, "Nigeria and Southern Africa: Interest, Policy and Means," Canadian Journal of African Studies 9, no. 1 (1977):60; J. Isawa Elaigwu, "The Nigerian Civil War and the Angolan Civil War," Journal of Asian and African Studies 12, nos. 1-4 (January and October 1977):233-34; ACR, 1975-76, pp. A23, B798-99. Even after recognition, Nigeria (like Tanzania) continued to urge a government of national unity, and invited the three party leaders to Lagos for discussions on it.

14. Dunstan Kamana, "Our Stand is Based on Firm Principles," Z Magazine (Lusaka), no. 81 (February 1976):4-7. A condensed version appeared in the New York Times, 25 February 1976, p. 37. Kamana argued that the "desperate attempts to equate the position that Zambia has held on Angola with positions and policies of certain African and non-African States," [especially Zaire] represented a "complete misunderstanding, distortion and maligning of her position on Angola."

15. Basil Davidson, "Angola in the Tenth Year," African Affairs 70 (278) (January 1971):43. A week before UDI, the Zambian government reminded the liberation movements that it would "not agree to the Territory of Zambia being used as a military base for operations" (Marcum, Angolan Revolution II, 308). UDI led to the progressive relaxation of the strict enforcement of this regulation.

16. Douglas G. Anglin, "Confrontation in Southern Africa: Zambia and Portugal," International Journal 25, no. 3 (Summer 1970):507-13; Zambia Information

Service (ZIS), Background, no. 1/76, p. 3, 12 January 1976; no. 18/76, pp. 15-16, 20 February 1976.

17. ACR, 1973-74, pp. B277, 519. Colin Legum claims that Kaunda was a party to the decision to invite Chinese support for the FNLA ("A Letter on Angola to American Liberals," New Republic 174, no. 5 [31 January 1976], p. 17).

18. Marcum, Angolan Revolution II, 201-203.

19. Legum claims that, when Moscow tipped off Neto concerning an alleged Chipenda plot to assassinate him, his troops "pre-empted the assassination by launching an attack on Chipenda and his supporters in Zambia, which was put down only with difficulty by the Zambian security forces" ("Letter on Angola," p. 17; see also, ACR, 1973-74, p. B19).

20. Marcum, Angolan Revolution II, 249-50, 431n81. Congo B, Somalia, Tanzania, Zaire, FRELIMO, the PAIGC and the OAU were also represented at the Congress.

21. ZIS Background, no. 18/76, pp. 13-15, 20 February 1976. On the other hand, Marcum claims that Kaunda refused to allow Neto to return to Lusaka on his plane (Angolan Revolution II, 252).

22. Ruth Weiss, "Factionalism Delays Angolan Independence," Montreal Gazette, 14 September 1974, p. 8.

23. Marcum, Angolan Revolution II, 201-202, 214.

24. US Involvement in Civil War in Angola, p. 184; ACR, 1975-76, p. A5; Johnson, How Long Will South Africa Survive?, pp. 134-35; Legum, "Letter on Angola," p. 17, which alludes to Moscow's "extraordinary and unsavory role" in this affaire.

25. Ibid.; Marcum, Angolan Revolution II, 228, 230, 245-46.

26. Ibid., pp. 257, 435n128; US Involvement in Civil War in Angola, pp. 128, 182-86, 191. Garcia Marquez justified Cuban aid by claiming that, in May 1975, MPLA "found itself in a less favorable military position than the others" ("Operation Carlota," p. 124).

27. Neto refused to meet Kaunda, Nyerere, Mobutu and Congo B's Ngouabi in Lusaka in May 1974 to discuss nationalist unity. Instead, Chipenda represented MPLA.

28. _Supra_, pp. 252-53, 255.

29. "Art. 40: The Transitional Government will organize general elections to a Constituent Assembly within the space of nine months from 31 January 1975, the date when it takes office" (_ACR_, 1974-75, p. C234).

30. Broadcasting began in late 1970, and was extended, following the commissioning of the more powerful Chinese transmitters, in May 1973. Broadcasts ceased in late 1974, though a new program "Kwacha-Angola" was aired from August 1975 to April 1976 (Zambia Broadcasting Service, _Television and Radio Programmes_ [Lusaka: ZBS, monthly]).

31. ZIS _Background_, no. 1/76, 12 January 1976, p. 6.

32. The analogy with Zambian nationalism was not entirely appropriate, as Zambia had never been faced with a "war of liberation." Nor was the history and intensity of interparty conflict in any way comparable; revolution, not consensus, was the name of the game. In the January 1964 elections in Zambia, the OAU Liberation Committee had supported UNIP, but not the ANC, financially.

33. _New York Times_, 25 February 1976, p. 37.

34. Colin Legum argued that: "The central reality about the Angolan situation is that none of the [three rival movements] individually commands the majority of all Angolans. . . . for all its strong points, the MPLA is a minority party, confined largely to the elites and to tribal support in the central area. Its only hope of gaining power is through military supremacy. . . . [UNITA], too, is a radical nationalist movement which, if elections had been possible after independence, would undoubtedly have emerged as the largest party" ("Letter on Angola," pp. 16-17). This assessment of relative electoral strengths is consistent with other estimates (Marcum, _Angolan Revolution_ II, 260, 437n164; _Africa_ [London], no. 43 [March 1975]:40), including that of the OAU Committee of Enquiry and Conciliation (_ACR_, 1975-76, p. A23). Kaunda believed that UNITA had "massive support in the southern half of Angola" (_Observer_, 30 May 1976, p. 1).

35. ZIS _Background_, no. 1/76, pp. 2-5, 12 January 1976.

36. UN Security Council, Verbatim Record (S/PV.1944), 27 July 1976, pp. 16, 26-28 (provisional); Africa, no. 69 (May 1977):41-42; Observer, 6 June 1976, p. 9; Times, 27 July 1976, p. 6; ZIS Background, no. 7/76, p. 3, 28 January 1976; ACR 1975-76, pp. C82-83.

37. N.A. Deb., no. 41, 30 January 1976, c.673.

38. ACR, 1975-76, pp. A22-23, 71-72, C16-17.

39. N.A. Deb., no. 41, 18 February 1976, c.1572.

40. Times of Zambia, 20 August 1976, p. 1; Citizen (Ottawa), 24 August 1976, p. 47.

41. E.g., Review of African Political Economy, no. 5 (1976):8, 80.

42. Immanuel Wallerstein, "Luanda is Madrid," Nation 222, no. 1 (10 January 1976):12-17.

43. N.A. Deb., no. 41, 18 February 1976, c.1572; ZIS Background, no. 1/76, p. 3, 12 January 1976 and no. 18/76, pp. 15-16, 20 February 1976. During the Nigerian civil war, Zambia had also argued that there could be "no military solution" (Douglas G. Anglin, "Zambia and the Recognition of Biafra," African Review 1, no. 2 [September 1971], p. 109).

44. Legum, "Letter on Angola," p. 17; ACR, 1975-76, pp. A28, B388.

45. Roy Lewis, "Kenneth Kaunda in 1976," Round Table, no. 263 (July 1976):286.

46. ZIS Background, no. 1/76, p. 9, 12 January 1976; Times, 19 February 1976, p. 8.

47. Dunstan Kamana, Z Magazine, no. 81 (February 1976):6.

48. ZIS Background, no. 25/76, p. 11, 30 March 1976. "You cannot achieve nonalignment with big brother overbearing on you. He will be too heavy for you and you cannot walk straight. . . . What assurance have we that the Soviet Union will act differently in Angola" than in Eastern Europe? (Zambia Daily Mail, 30 March 1976, p. 8).

49. Times, 19 February 1976, p. 15 and 27 May 1976, p. 17. France, Portugal and Yugoslavia had all urged

Zambia to accept the MPLA regime (Times of Zambia, 15 March 1976, p. 1).

50. The strident tone of the lengthy "Statement on Angola" issued by the University of Zambia Students Union on 15 January 1976 was bound—on the basis of past experience—to provoke a strong reaction. It denounced Zambian government policy as "extremely reactionary and retrogressive . . . opportunist, hypocritical, imperialist and impossible," and concluded by charging "the Zambia ruling clique headed by Dr. Kaunda 'our beloved President' with CRIMINAL TREACHERY." See N. J. Small, "Zambia—Trouble on Campus," Index on Censorship 6, no. 6 (November-December 1977):8-14; Michael Burawoy, "Consciousness and Contradictions: A Study of Student Protest in Zambia," British Journal of Sociology 27, no. 1 (March 1976):78-98; Donald Rothchild, "The Beginning of Student Unrest in Zambia: A Study of Political Order and University Power," Transition 8, no. 40 (December 1971):65-74.

51. ZIS Background, no. 7/76, p. 4, 29 January 1976; no. 18/76, p. 17, 20 February 1976; no. 25/76, pp. 9-10, 30 March 1976.

52. According to Kaunda, "The Zambian government see Angola in its starkest dimensions—white South Africans and white Russians are either killing blacks or encouraging blacks to kill other blacks" (Citizen, 3 December 1975, p. 7).

53. ZIS Background, no. 67/75, pp. 10, 12, 2 December 1975; no. 1/76, pp. 7, 8, 12 January 1976. Kaunda's fears for the territorial integrity of Angola were reinforced by reports that the US briefly flirted with the idea of partition.

54. Ibid., no. 1/76, pp. 2, 7-10; no. 67/75, pp. 9-13.

55. Ibid., no. 1/76, pp. 6-7, 12 January 1976.

56. New York Times, 25 February 1976, p. 37.

57. ZIS Background, no. 18/76, p. 4, 20 February 1976.

58. Ibid., no. 7/76, p. 3, 28 January 1976; see also Zambia Daily Mail, 30 March 1976, pp. 1, 8 and Youth (Lusaka, UNIP) 2, no. 3 (31 January 1976):2. For a particularly shrill attack on Soviet lobbying at the OAU summit in January 1976, see Frank Chingwalu,

"Angola: Future Still Unsettled," Z Magazine, no. 80
(January 1976), pp. 5-7.

59. Times, 21 February 1976, p. 6; New York Times
Magazine, 28 March 1978, p. 54; ACR, 1975-76, p. B389.
Kaunda's reference to the Soviet occupation of Czechoslovakia at his press conference on 20 February 1976
led to the Czech ambassador angrily walking out.

60. ZIS Background, no. 1/76, p. 6, 12 January 1976.

61. UNIP National Council, 30 June 1975; see also,
Education for Development: Draft Statement on Educational Reform (Lusaka: Ministry of Education, 1976),
p. 79.

62. Times of Zambia, 13 December 1975, p. 1 and
10 March 1976, p. 7.

63. Globe and Mail, 24 February 1976, p. 10; Zambia
Daily Mail, 19 March 1976, p. 4 and 22 March 1976,
p. 4. But cf. ibid., 30 March 1976, p. 1, Observer,
22 February 1976, p. 13 and Times, 31 May 1976, p. 5
for the view that extra-African aid to liberation
movements should exclude operational forces.

64. Times, 27 May 1976, p. 17. Kaunda told a visiting Cuban delegation bluntly that they were in Angola
on behalf of the Soviet Union (Observer, 30 May 1976,
p. 1).

65. Mohamed A. El-Khawas, "Power Struggle in Angola:
Whose Struggle? Whose Power?," Journal of Southern
African Affairs I (October 1976):60-61.

66. Ibid.; Manchester Guardian Weekly, 16 January
1977, p. 22; New York Times, 25 February 1976, p. 37;
Economist, 27 December 1975, p. 8.

67. El-Khawas, "Power Struggle in Angola," p. 61.

68. ZIS Background, no. 18/76, p. 17, 20 February
1976; Sunday Times of Zambia, 7 March 1976, p. 1;
For Savimbi's letter to Kaunda in early February 1976
acknowledging defeat, see Stockwell, In Search of
Enemies, pp. 235-36.

69. Globe and Mail, 14 February 1977, p. 3.

70. Fifty UNITA vehicles used to transport supplies
into Angola from Kalabo camp in western Zambia were

eventually turned over to the MPLA government (<u>Zambia Daily Mail</u>, 15 July 1977, p. 1).

71. William E. Schaufele, personal interview, 2 May 1977; <u>Washington Post</u>, 6 January 1976. The <u>Times</u> (7 January 1976, p. 12) refers to Kaunda's April 1975 appeal to Ford "to reverse what he considered to be a tide sweeping the MPLA to victory." This was, of course, four months before South Africa intervened to transform the political complexion of the conflict.

72. Memorandum of 12 July 1975 (<u>New York Times</u>, 14 December 1975, p. 2). In "The Angolan Decision of 1975," Davis omits this reference to Kaunda.

73. <u>Journal of Modern African Studies</u> 15, no. 1 (March 1977):146.

74. 6 February 1976, <u>US Involvement in Civil War in Angola</u>, p. 175; also pp. 9, 17. Zambia complained to the State Department at having her Angolan policy equated with Zaire's. To clarify the distinction, her UN representative published an article in the <u>New York Times</u> (25 February 1976, p. 37). René Lemarchand concludes that, "considering the relative depth of past US commitment to Zaire, and published remarks by Kissinger aides, it is reasonable to suppose that Zambia was of secondary importance" in influencing the US decision (<u>American Policy in Southern Africa</u>, p. 405).

75. Kissinger informed the Subcommittee earlier that "Zambia along with other states, told us it supported our efforts to achieve a compromise solution in Angola and that Zambia, along with Zaire, asked the US to provide assistance to UNITA and FNLA" (<u>US Involvement in Civil War in Angola</u>, p. 54). Stockwell reports that Kaunda was briefed on the decision and his "co-operation assured" (<u>In Search of Enemies</u>, p. 86).

76. <u>New York Times Magazine</u>, 28 March 1976, p. 54; <u>ACR</u>, 1975-76, p. A28. Kissinger consulted personally with the Zambian foreign minister in Paris on 17 December 1975 and with Kaunda's special assistant on foreign affairs, Mark Chona, in Washington on 6 February 1976.

77. <u>New York Times</u>, 19 December 1975, p. 14.

78. Though neither the <u>World Armament and Disarmament SIPRI Yearbooks</u> (Stockholm) nor the <u>World</u>

Military Expenditures and Arms Transfers (Washington)
record any US military transfers to Zambia during
1975 or 1976. One Lisbon newspaper claims that UNITA
received 600 Zambian rifles (Expresso, 11 October
1975, cited in John A. Marcum, "The Anguish of
Angola," Issue 5, no. 4 [Winter 1975]:8).

79. In Search of Enemies, p. 193.

80. Tony Hodges, "Zambia–South Africa: A New
Connection?", African Development 10, no. 2 (February
1976):139. The Viscount was reported to have New
Zealand registration and to have made a forced landing in Lusaka (Zambia Daily Mail, 18 March 1976,
p. 7; Sunday Times [London], 21 March 1976, p. 1).
Pearl Air International was a one-plane airline with
headquarters in Grenada (Interavia ABC, 1977, p. 708).

81. Times of Zambia, 30 December 1975, p. 1.

82. 23 January–20 February 1977; also carried in Globe
and Mail, 21 January, 1, 7, 14, and 21 February 1977.

83. Rapport, 15 February 1976; Guardian, 17 February
1976, p. 2; Times, 17 February 1976, p. 6; US Involvement in Civil War in Angola, pp. 163-66, 170. The
full report the authors promised appears never to have
been written.

84. Moss mentions only the first meeting and
Coughlin only the other two. Moss also reports meetings between Savimbi and South African intelligence
officers in Europe in March and in Lusaka on 14 April
1975. Johnson also mentions meetings in Kinshasa in
July and in Namibia in August (How Long Will South
Africa Survive?, pp. 144, 146).

85. E.g., RSA World (Pretoria), 12, no. 2 (April
1976):23 and no. 7 (November-December 1976):13; see
also, Southern Africa 10, no. 2 (March 1977):30.

86. ZIS Background, no. 18/76, p. 10, 20 February
1976. Coughlin in conversation (on 5 October 1977)
denied that he had any evidence that Kaunda served as
an intermediary between Savimbi and Vorster.

87. Times, 17 February 1976, p. 6; Guardian
17 February 1976, p. 2. Moss is less specific but
implies that there was Zambian pressure. Again,
Coughlin has since denied that Kaunda encouraged South
Africa to invade Angola (conversation, 5 October

1977). An unnamed South African officer is reported
as having asserted (somewhat unconvincingly) that
"Zambia, Zaire and many other African states requested
us to intervene. But our government held back until
the United States contacted us, and guaranteed that
. . . they would . . . send their troops if necessary"
(Spotlight [Washington], 12 July 1976, p. 13).

88. Observer, 22 February 1976, p. 1. Asked about
press reports that Zambia had urged Pretoria to send
troops into Angola, Kaunda replied that, if Zambia
could "force" South Africa to do this, "we must be very
powerful" (Zambia Daily Mail, 21 February 1976, p. 8).

89. ZIS Background, no. 1/76, p. 5, 12 January 1976.
Earlier, Kaunda had claimed that the South African
presence in Angola was "an effect of the problem, not
a cause" (International Herald Tribune, 31 December
1975, p. 4).

90. ZIS Background, no. 1/76, p. 5, 12 January 1976.

91. Ibid., no. 25/76, p. 6, 30 March 1976; Hodges,
"Zambia-South Africa," p. 137.

92. E.g., the "Watershed speech," 30 June 1975.

93. ZIS Background, no. 25/76, p. 6, 30 March 1976.

94. James N. Rosenau, The Scientific Study of
Foreign Policy (New York: Free Press, 1971), p. 39.

95. ACR, 1975-76, pp. A27-28; New York Times
Magazine, 28 March 1976, p. 54.

96. Zambia Daily Mail, 26 January 1976, p. 1.

97. ACR, 1975-76, p. A28; New York Times,
25 February 1976, p. 37.

98. Stockwell reports that, on 10 September 1975,
Kaunda "gave Savimbi sixty days, until Angolan independence, to get the Benguela railroad open. Otherwise he could not guarantee continued support" (In
Search of Enemies, p. 193).

99. George T. Yu, "The USSR and Africa: China's
Impact," Problems of Communism 27, no. 1 (January-
February 1978):47-49; Legum, "Letter on Angola," p. 18.

100. Stockwell, In Search of Enemies, pp. 235-36.

Part III
Zambia and the International System: Dependence and Interdependence

9
External Behavior:
An Events Data Analysis

The collection and analysis of events data has
been advocated as one way of gaining new insights into the foreign policy of any state. This essay uses
events data in an attempt to describe, explain, understand and perhaps predict foreign policy. Such an
approach to analysis may also help studies of new
states' foreign policies become more rigorous, sophisticated, and comparative. Further, it may generate
novel perspectives on the nature of Zambia's external
behavior. In particular, it may be usefully contrasted with the organizational and decision-making analysis presented earlier in Chapter 3.
    This collection and analysis of Zambian events
data, then, has three main objectives. First, such
data provide a quantitative overview of Zambia's foreign relations; they indicate what Zambia was doing
with whom over what issues. Second, these events
data can be used to either support or challenge orthodox assumptions and generalizations, based on the more
traditional modes of analysis employed elsewhere in
this volume, about the nature of Zambia's foreign
relations. And finally, Zambian events data may contribute to the generation of both global and local
events data sources and so advance the debate over
the validity, reliability, and drawbacks of this
method of inquiry.[1] Therefore, this chapter is primarily a descriptive case study of the foreign relations of one new African state; but such a study invariably raises, and relates to, other empirical,
theoretical, methodological, and even political
questions.
    We are particularly concerned here, then, with
discovering the content of Zambia's external relations, comparing our findings with the established
wisdom about Zambia's foreign policy, and also with
reinforcing the trend within the events data "movement" toward the use of local rather than "universal"

data sources. We agree with Maurice East that the former are rich and "that significant advances could be made in both our knowledge of Africa and our theories of foreign policy analysis by undertaking further events data research on African and other small, less modern states."[2] Indeed, as he points out,relatively simple descriptive and analytic work on African international relations using events data on particular African states may be more appropriate and useful at the present time than the more sophisticated manipulation of other varieties of empirical data. Certainly, the limited data presented here and their modest statistical manipulation indicate that our findings are only preliminary. Nevertheless, this chapter may point up the utility of events data for the study of new state foreign policies in general and for the study of Zambia's external behavior in particular.

ZAMBIAN EVENTS DATA

The data presented in this essay are based on clippings taken from two daily newspapers published in Zambia during the period 1 October 1973 to 31 July 1974. One of the two, the Zambia Daily Mail, is owned by the government, while the Times of Zambia was then owned by the Lonrho corporation and other private interests though its editor was a presidential appointee; in 1975, it was nationalized and ownership transferred to UNIP. Both papers are of a distinctly high quality compared to most African dailies, in terms of reporting and production. Although both, of course, operate under constraints, they were (and are) more free and critical than most papers on the continent. They provide an unusually comprehensive source for events data as most papers elsewhere in Africa are less reliable in terms of coverage and appearance. The two Zambian dailies are certainly treated as authoritative by both bureaucrats and attentive publics within and concerned with Zambia; and compared with other national, regional or global sources they seem to capture most Zambian events. They both appeared six times each week, with the Times being published as the only Sunday paper, The Sunday Times of Zambia.

These newspaper reports yielded 1,383 events for the ten-month period, almost four events per day. The Zambian Events Data (ZED) file was created by coding events following the rules of our "Zambia Events Data Coding Manual" which was largely based on the established World Events Interaction Survey procedures;

354

some 18 items of information were coded for each event.[3] Although the period covered is quite short, it yielded a rich collection of events data, especially when compared to the fewer Zambian events captured by other files. Over three years (1964-1966), the AFRICA project found 969 Zambian events, but CREON yielded only 173 events over 120 months while WEIS records just 99 events for Zambia over 42 months.[4] Moreover, although the period was characterized by an absence of crises in the region (unlike the November 1965 and January 1973 crises over Rhodesia), the distribution of targets, behavior, issue areas and actors is quite characteristic of Zambia's foreign policy since her independence in October 1964.

Zambia has been a remarkably stable polity and society in its first decade, despite the problems of Southern Africa, her dependence on copper and internal inequalities. We can therefore take this period to be reasonably representative of Zambia's foreign relations over time; the relative shortness of the period covered is compensated for by the richness of the local data. Given the persistence of dependence and underdevelopment, most external interactions of new states are quite stable, despite apparent shifts in rhetoric.

ZED data have been manipulated using cross tabulations both to describe and to analyze the foreign policy of Zambia. This research has, in particular, been stimulated by the innovative work of East[5] on both small countries and the foreign policies of the East African states, and also by Patrick J. McGowan[6] on the foreign relations of African states.

THE FOREIGN POLICY OF ZAMBIA: DEPENDENCE OR INTERDEPENDENCE

In general, the study of foreign policy in Africa is underdeveloped: most analyses have concentrated either on the values of the characteristically charismatic leader or on the formal structures of foreign policy making.[7] However, the elusiveness of development and the availability of new techniques of analysis have led to two novel and apparently divergent approaches: explanations based on theories of dependence and imperialism on the one hand, and quantitative analyses of events, transactions and national attributes on the other. This essay suggests that these two contemporary concerns may be more compatible than they appear at first: events data can be used to examine, among other propositions, hypotheses about dependence and the impact of international in-

355

equality, while a political economy perspective can, in turn, inform events data and transaction surveys.[8]

The foreign policy behavior of Zambia has already received significant attention because of its salience in African, particularly Southern African, affairs and because of the relative openness of her polity to enquiry.[9] The diversity of approaches used to examine and explain her external policy and behavior include historical description, dyadic studies,[10] transaction analysis,[11] decision making,[12] geopolitics,[13] the ideology of foreign policy,[14] economic constraints and imperatives[15] and dependence.[16] In this chapter, we focus on many of the same phenomena considered through these other methods, especially on those factors most amenable to events data research — internal actors, types and patterns of international behavior, issue areas and channels of diplomacy. AFRICA data indicates that between 1964 and 1966 Zambia was among the most participatory states in Africa;[17] this activeness continues and is captured by ZED.

Zambia's foreign policy activeness constitutes one of several simultaneous strategies followed by the regime in an attempt to reduce the impact of its inheritance of dependence and underdevelopment. Her national goals of independence, development and regional liberation have been elusive because of the paucity of power attributes she possesses. Nevertheless, Zambia's essentially promotive foreign policy style portrayed by these events data can be seen as a continuing struggle to overcome the constraints and dilemmas of her relative smallness, poverty and weakness and to establish her autonomy and identity in international politics. Certainly her foreign policy is neither completely passive nor overly cautious; like many new states, she is prepared to be conflictual in deeds and is particularly concerned with economic issues.

In this empirical and quantitative analysis of Zambia's foreign policy, we present findings based on several of the indicators abstracted, identified and coded for the ZED file, and compare these results to the literature on both Zambia's external relations and new states in world politics. We turn initially to the activities of the president and other internal actors in Zambia's foreign relations; we then examine Zambia's role in the region and her nonalignment in world politics; and we conclude with an analysis of her use of diplomacy and her ability to take the initiative over both her national development and the continuing confrontation in Southern Africa.

CHARISMA AND CONTROL: THE ROLE OF PRESIDENT KAUNDA

In many new states, the successful nationalist
leader is also the primary symbol of the nation. In
Zambia, Dr. Kenneth D. Kaunda emerged as the leader
of the dominant nationalist party, UNIP, during the
struggle for freedom from both the British Empire
and the settler-dominated Central African Federation;
he is the first and only president of the new state
and led it into a one-party Second Republic in 1973.
He is also President of UNIP and Commander-in-Chief
of the armed forces; clearly he takes many initiatives
on his own[18] and few decisions in Zambia are made
without his approval. His roles as mediator among
sectional factions and as the most visible representative of his country have led to the common assumption that he dominates the making of Zambia's foreign
policy.[19]
The characteristic approach to presidential dominance over the foreign policy of new states is reflected in two generalizations by Marion Bone: that
"Kaunda is the dominant figure" and that "foreign
policy is almost entirely identified with him."[20]
These assumptions are also reflected by East and Hermann who assert that over significant issues a less
developed country "may resort to head of state involvement more often" than a rich, industrialized state.[21]
In table 9.1, we present our data on the frequency

TABLE 9.1
Ranking of Internal Actors in Zambia's Foreign Policy

Actor Specified	Number of Times Responsible for Event	%	Rank
President Kaunda	231	38	1
Minister of Foreign Affaris	117	19	2
Parastatal organiza-tions	87	14	3
President's office/ State House	70	12	4
United National In-dependence Party	57	9	5
Ministry of Foreign Affairs	26	4	6
Economic Ministry	13	2	7
Security Ministry	1	0	8

with which internal actors participate in Zambia's
foreign policy. They serve to support the proposition of Bone and others that the president dominates
the making of foreign policy in Zambia, with the
Minister of Foreign Affairs, the parastatals, and
the party also playing active roles. On the other
hand, the primacy of the president is increasingly
limited, pointing to the growing complexities of foreign policy making in general and Zambia in particu-
lar.22

FOREIGN POLICY MAKING IN ZAMBIA: COORDINATION AND PENETRATION

The ranking of internal actors may differ according to issue area. Students of foreign policy generally suggest that national leaders are most involved
with "high politics," whereas routine interactions
are processed by government ministries and other less
central actors. James Rosenau suggests that the
ranking of actors differs somewhat for a "small country, underdeveloped economy, open polity, penetrated"
according to issue area; in general, after systemic
variables, the ordering of potency among factors is
individual, role, societal and governmental, with the
individual factor being consistently second in potency
and the other three variables differing according to
issue area.23 Using the ZED categorization of internal actors, a distinction is made between individual and role variables: that is, between the president and his office. However, we are more interested
here in the roles of the Ministry of Foreign Affairs
and other ministries, UNIP and the burgeoning parastatal sector. In general, analyses of African foreign policies suggest that the president is most
dominant in security and regional issues and that
other government agencies handle "low politics"; such
assumptions are reflected for the Zambian case in
chapter 3 of this volume.
Table 9.2 presents data on the relative involvement of domestic actors in Zambia in different external issue areas; it indicates the need for refine-
ment in treating the dominance of the president, especially in economic issues. In the increasingly
complex Zambian foreign policy system, a division of
labor between institutions appears to have been established based on their respective interests. The
president is most dominant in security (conventional
and guerrilla), diplomatic (including international
organization), and sociocultural issue areas.

TABLE 9.2
The Involvement of Zambian Actors in International Issue Areas (Row Percentages)

Issue Area	President	Foreign Affairs	Economic Ministry	Para-statal	UNIP	Totals
Conventional military	60 (N=26)	37 (N=16)	—	—	2 (N=1)	99 (N=43)
Guerrilla	57 (N=54)	30 (N=28)	—	—	13 (N=12)	100 (N=94)
Trade and investment	27 (N=11)	22 (N=9)	7 (N=3)	34 (N=14)	10 (N=4)	100 (N=41)
Economic assistance	32 (N=17)	13 (N=7)	19 (N=10)	36 (N=19)	—	100 (N=53)
Technical and scientific	32 (N=15)	13 (N=6)	—	45 (N=21)	11 (N=5)	101 (N=47)
Socioeconomic	56 (N=34)	20 (N=12)	—	7 (N=4)	18 (N=11)	101 (N=61)
Regional cooperation	43 (N=16)	35 (N=13)	—	22 (N=8)	—	100 (N=37)
International organization	56 (N=9)	31 (N=5)	—	3 (N=2)	—	100 (N=16)
Diplomatic	65 (N=88)	25 (N=33)	—	2 (N=3)	9 (N=12)	100 (N=136)

However, in the three economic issue areas, the parastatals are dominant and economic ministries most active. The Ministry for Foreign Affairs seems to be most concerned with military questions and regional and universal organizations while the party concentrates on sociocultural, guerrilla and diplomatic issues. This growing complexity highlights the problems of coordination of a new state's foreign policy; incompatible statements and actions serve to undermine its credibility.

New states often have different priorities from those of older, richer countries. Their major concerns are reflected not only in the activities of particular domestic institutions, but also in the overall direction of ˙ avior. Further, they lack the experience and capabilities of established states and so tend to concentrate their activities in particular issue areas: "those international issues which are directly related to their economic growth and development will be most salient for small states."[24] Because of the scarcity of resources, new states cannot either monitor or respond to all global issues like major world actors, so "certain functional and geographic areas must be emphasized while others are ignored."[25] Table 9.3 presents data on the concentration of Zambia's behavior in particular issue areas, and table 9.4 looks at the concentration of Zambia's foreign policy targets according to region. These two tables provide support for those propositions which suggest that new state concerns will be limited to questions of diplomacy, development and independence, and that the objects of their actions will be primarily at the regional level or centers of economic exchange: most of Zambia's foreign policy is directed at Africa and Europe. These data help to further substantiate the assumptions made by students of subordinate state systems, as well as those held by proponents of the economic imperatives of statecraft.[26] There is inevitably a tension between the possibilities of regional integration and the necessities of continued exchange with industrialized countries; this dilemma is reflected in the concentration of Zambia's foreign policy according to both issue and region.

Table 9.3 provides partial support for East's proposition about the economic imperatives of new states, but tends to disconfirm his suggestion that small states "have a higher proportion of events involving economic bureaucracies than do large states."[27] In Zambia, economic ministries and parastatals account for a relatively small proportion of her external

TABLE 9.3
The Concentration of Zambia's Foreign Relations in
Issue Areas

Issue Area	Number of Events	%	Ranking
Diplomatic	217	17	1
Technical and Scientific	209	16	2
Guerrilla warfare	183	14	3
Socio-cultural	172	13	4
Economic assistance	142	11	5
Trade and investment	133	11	6
Regional cooperation	130	10	7
Conventional military	62	5	8
International organization	52	4	9

TABLE 9.4
The Concentration of Zambia's Foreign Relations in
International Regions

Targets by Region	Number of Events	%	Ranking
Africa	956	45	1
Europe	452	21	2
Non-regional groups	278	13	3
Asia	169	8	4
Western Hemisphere	154	7	5
Middle East	117	6	6

behavior, although their concerns are concentrated in economic issue areas. Table 9.4 serves to reinforce the ambiguous results obtained by East and Hermann[28] on the propensity of small states to engage in collective, cooperative behavior through international coalitions and organizations. Nevertheless, despite the lag in implementation, Zambia has used her international associations in an attempt to diversify her relations and so reduce the impact of her legacy of dependence.

NONALIGNMENT AND DEPENDENCE: ZAMBIA IN WORLD POLITICS

Zambia, in common with most new states, claims to be nonaligned; however, she inherited an economy and society which were dependent both on the former metropole, Britain, and on the Western economic system. She has attempted to diversify her pattern of external linkages, if not her commodity exports which remain dominated by copper. In particular, Zambia has eliminated trade and other relations with Rhodesia since UDI.[29] However, there has been conflict, at least in the medium term, between her policies towards Southern Africa and her general concern for nonalignment: "Disengagement is beginning to conflict with the aims of diversification."[30] To maintain the profitability of her crucial copper industry, Zambia has at times been forced to increase her dependence on South Africa and Europe. Moreover, she has only marginally increased her trade and other relations with the socialist states, other than China, since independence. Most analyses of Zambia's international relations suggest that her extracontinental linkages have grown since independence with a select group of states including Italy, Yugoslavia, Scandinavia, Canada and China. Using events data, we can discover whether her behavior has been directed more at this group of states than other non-African countries and whether she has achieved a position of nonalignment, or of impartiality or balance, between the two dominant international coalitions centered on the United States and the Soviet Union.

Data presented in tables 9.5 and 9.6 indicate that most of Zambia's international relations continue to be with Western rather than Eastern states, and her "nonalignment" at least in aggregate, empirical terms, is limited to contacts with China rather than with the Soviet Union or other Warsaw Pact countries. In part, this reflects China's benificence, especially in building the Tanzania-Zambia "Uhuru" railway; but it is also indicative of Zambia's own

TABLE 9.5
The Ideology of States with which Zambia Interacts in Different Issue Areas (Row Percentages)

Issue Area	Ideology of Target			
	Western	Eastern	Nonaligned	Totals
Conventional military	29 (N=29)	4 (N=4)	67 (N=66)	100 (N=99)
Guerrilla warfare	20 (N=69)	2 (N=7)	78 (N=271)	100 (N=347)
Trade and investment	41 (N=72)	4 (N=19)	55 (N=95)	100 (N=174)
Economic assistance	40 (N=66)	7 (N=19)	48 (N=77)	100 (N=162)
Technical and scientific	50 (N=122)	14 (N=35)	36 (N=88)	100 (N=245)
Socioeconomic	35 (N=77)	11 (N=24)	54 (N=117)	100 (N=218)
Regional cooperation	3 (N=6)	2 (N=3)	95 (N=175)	100 (N=184)
International organization	24 (N=17)	4 (N=3)	71 (N=50)	99 (N=70)
Diplomatic	29 (N=87)	15 (N=46)	56 (n=167)	100 (N=300)

363

TABLE 9.6
Numbers of Actions by Zambia Directed at Selected
Target States and Organizations

United Kingdom	128	Soviet Union	24
United States	81	China	56
South Africa	63	Portugal	67
Italy	16	Canada	34
Yugoslavia	28	Sweden	34
Tanzania	104	Zaire	72
Botswana	31	Malawi	46
United Nations	13	Commonwealth	20
Organization of African Unity	52	World Bank	13
MPLA	30	FRELIMO	40
UNITA	17		

perceptions of China as a relevant and non-imperialis-
tic Third World model, whereas the Soviet Union is
seen as another industrialized state in the northern
hemisphere. As indicated in table 9.6, the ex-metro-
pole, Britain, continues to be the target of most
Zambian behavior, with Tanzania being of increasing
importance along with the neighboring white states,
although, of course, the qualities of the latter two
types of relationship differ dramatically. Table
9.5 reveals the unimportance of the Eastern bloc in
most issue areas, except the economic and diplomatic,
whereas relations with the West are spread throughout all issue areas other than regional cooperation.
The importance of links with the group of nonaligned
states varies between issue areas, but they are concentrated over select issues such as regional cooperation, security (guerrilla and conventional), and collective activity in international organizations. As
shown in table 9.6, Zambia does have considerable
ties with a small group of relatively disinterested
middle powers in the international system: with Sweden, Canada, and Yugoslavia, as well as with China.[31]
Zambia is also more active in the continental institution — the Organization of African Unity (OAU) —

364

than in other international organizations.

Nonaligned states, despite their characteristic dependence on a few dominant actors in the international system, may be less constrained by specific external relationships than states which belong to blocs such as NATO or the Warsaw Pact. East suggests that the foreign relations of small states usually include "avoidance of behavior and policies which tend to alienate the more powerful states in the system."[32] The case of Zambia, amongst others, suggests two modifications to this generalization. First, the "nonalignment" of new states contains different emphases or "tilts": the balance of conflictual and cooperative words and deeds directed at the superpowers varies depending on the general foreign policy direction of any new state. And second, although such states are concerned not to alienate the powerful, they are nevertheless able to express criticisms at times, especially when particular Third World interests are threatened. So, for instance, they may be highly critical of a particular superpower intervention while in general maintaining a cooperative stance. Such outbursts do not appear to disturb the overall dyadic relationship; perhaps the great powers have become able to shrug off the complaints of the weak.[33]

Zambia's occasional criticisms of the superpowers do not appear to disrupt her characteristically cooperative relationship with both of them. However, as indicated in table 9.7, she does exhibit more frequent and more conflictual interaction with the Western states than with the Eastern group. Further, most of her foreign relations seem to consist of verbal statements rather than actual deeds, although she did carry out almost as many conflictual as cooperative deeds. Zambia interacts most frequently with other Third World states, although the degree of conflict, both words and deeds, within the nonalignment movement is surprisingly high. This finding serves to reinforce our skepticism about the nature and salience of the contemporary nonaligned grouping except as an expression of general Third World frustrations and poverty.

As indicated in chapter 3, we expect the degree of dependence or nonalignment of Zambia in international politics to vary according to issue area. Zambia depends on the Western states, especially the EEC, for markets, imports, technology and investment; she has received some aid and investment from the socialist states, especially from China; and she exchanges political support within the nonaligned states' caucus. She has advocated the development of international organization and has concentrated her diplo-

TABLE 9.7
Ideology of Target according to type of WEIS Action
(Row Percentages)

Type of WEIS Action	Ideology of Target			
	Western	Eastern	Nonaligned	Totals
Verbal conflict	36 (N=148)	2 (N=9)	62 (N=255)	100 (N=412)
Conflictual deeds	50 (N=15)	3 (N=1)	47 (N=14)	100 (N=30)
Verbal cooperation	28 (N=383)	10 (N=146)	62 (N=863)	100 (N=1392)
Cooperative deeds	27 (N=14)	14 (N=7)	59 (N=30)	100 (N=51)

matic resources in Africa and centers of diplomacy, aid and trade. She continues to be dependent on the economies of the Western capitalist system, a factor which may affect her nonalignment policies.

In table 9.8, we present ZED data on the distribution of her targets in different issue areas. It suggests a mixed result: over trade and technological issues Zambia is oriented towards the West; over economic assistance issues, she is more impartial to maximize her resources; her concerns for international organization are divided between the global and continental levels; and her diplomatic behavior, mainly focused on Southern Africa, again reveals her interest in the maximization of support for the region's liberation by adopting a nonaligned, equidistant stance. Zambia is particularly active in Africa over guerrilla conflict, regional cooperation and diplomacy, especially in Black Africa rather than among the Arab states of the Middle East; and she seeks economic assistance from international organizations as well as from Europe. She is infrequently concerned with targets in either Asia, the Middle East or the Western hemisphere; her major focus remains Africa and Europe.

ZAMBIA AS A "MIDDLE POWER" IN CENTRAL AFRICA

The trends toward inequalities and regionalization in world politics mean that most states are

TABLE 9.8
Targets of Zambia's Foreign Policy according to Issue Area (Row Percentages)

Issue Area	Western Hemisphere	Europe	Africa	Middle East	Asia	Non-regional Groupings	Totals
Conventional military	4 (N=4)	17 (N=18)	50 (N=53)	15 (N=16)	3 (N=3)	12 (N=13)	101 (N=107)
Guerrilla warfare	1 (N=3)	18 (N=70)	70 (N=266)	2 (N=8)	1 (N=2)	8 (N=32)	100 (N=381)
Trade and investment	12 (N=25)	17 (N=34)	35 (N=71)	12 (N=25)	10 (N=20)	14 (N=29)	100 (N=204)
Economic assistance	12 (N=25)	33 (N=66)	21 (N=42)	5 (N=11)	6 (N=12)	22 (N=45)	99 (N=201)
Technical and scientific	17 (N=48)	33 (N=92)	17 (N=48)	1 (N=4)	15 (N=41)	17 (N=47)	100 (N=280)
Socioeconomic	8 (N=19)	28 (N=64)	34 (N=78)	8 (N=19)	12 (N=27)	10 (N=23)	101 (N=230)
Regional cooperation	1 (N=1)	2 (N=4)	81 (N=174)	3 (N=6)	2 (N=4)	12 (N=25)	101 (N=214)
International organization	3 (N=3)	11 (N=10)	37 (N=35)	4 (N=4)	10 (N=9)	35 (N=33)	100 (N=94)
Diplomatic	7 (N=22)	24 (N=74)	42 (N=131)	7 (N=21)	13 (N=39)	7 (N=22)	100 (N=309)

regional rather than global actors; that is, much of
their external interaction is concentrated in a subordinate state system which includes their neighbors.
Zambia has been particularly involved in providing
support for the liberation movements of Southern
Africa and in disengagement from Southern Africa and
integration with Eastern Africa.[34] She thus played
two important roles—that of "host" state, providing
facilities for nationalists from minority-ruled
states, and that of "core" for advancing infrastructural and industrial integration in Central Africa.
Zambia is one of several "middle" (or "minor")
powers,

> which play leading roles in the international
> relations of their own subordinate systems,
> either through regional activities or inde-
> pendent policies. . . . [they] attempt to
> alter, in their own favor, the direction of
> domestic and foreign policies in some coun-
> tries within their region.[35]

Whilst we can accept Bone's proposition that
"geography is perhaps the most crucial determinant
of Zambia's foreign policies," we question whether
Zambia is at the same time "strategically insignificant."[36] She has been an important base territory
for the freedom fighters and she was the center for
negotiations to end conflict and advance "détente"
over Rhodesia. In the future, she may become the
industrial and communications core for independent
countries in Central Africa. In table 9.9, we present our findings on the importance of regional
interaction for Zambia and on the distribution of
regional events in each issue area. ZED data indicates that she is concerned mainly with guerrilla
warfare issues in her relations with the white
regimes and the liberation movements. She also acts
in the diplomatic and conventional military issue
areas against Rhodesia and South Africa. By contrast, Zambia concentrates on regional cooperation
and economic issues in her relations with neighboring independent black states, especially with Tanzania, Zaire and Malawi (and increasingly, in recent
years, with Mozambique and Botswana).
These data indicate that Zambia displays a high
level of both economic cooperation and political
conflict in the region because of the distinctive
characteristics of the Southern and Central African
subsystems respectively. Relations with Tanzania
have developed rapidly and now cover several issues

TABLE 9.9
Targets of Zambia's Actions in Africa in Different
Issue Areas: A Partial Listing

Target states and Organizations	Conventional Military	Guerrilla Warfare	Trade and Investment	Economic Assistance	Technical and Scientific	Socioeconomic	Regional Cooperation	Diplomatic	Total for Targets
Ivory Coast	–	–	–	–	1	–	–	3	4
Liberia	–	2	–	2	–	1	1	6	12
Nigeria	–	–	1	2	1	1	3	4	12
Congo (B)	–	4	–	–	–	1	–	–	7
Zaire	1	9	7	4	3	12	21	11	58
Uganda	6	1	–	–	–	1	6	5	19
Kenya	2	2	9	1	5	3	11	7	40
Tanzania	4	9	15	5	8	8	32	12	93
Malawi	–	2	7	2	4	1	12	12	40
Botswana	–	–	9	4	–	1	9	4	27
Angola	2	12	–	–	1	–	3	4	22
Mozambique	1	15	1	–	3	3	3	3	29
Rhodesia	17	19	3	3	2	12	4	15	75
South Africa	9	20	5	2	2	12	3	10	61
Namibia	2	2	–	1	1	2	2	2	12
OAU	5	13	4	1	1	2	9	15	50
EAC	–	1	4	1	2	–	6	–	14
ZAPU	1	7	–	–	–	–	–	1	9
ZANU	–	11	–	–	–	1	–	1	13
MPLA	1	27	–	–	–	–	1	–	28
UNITA	–	14	–	–	–	–	1	2	17
FRELIMO	–	32	–	–	–	–	–	6	38
Totals for African issue areas	50	192	67	28	34	61	149	98	679

TABLE 9.10
The Pattern of Zambia's Relations with Africa, according to WEIS Categories of Action: A Partial Listing (Column Percentages)

WEIS Action Category	Zaire	Tanzania	Rhodesia	South Africa
Verbal Conflict				
Negative comment	13	10	23	24
	(N=9)	(N=10)	(N=17)	(N=15)
Accuse/deny	3	2	15	11
	(N=2)	(N=2)	(N=11)	(N=7)
Protest	-	-	8	13
			(N=6)	(N=8)
Reject	2	1	4	6
	(N=1)	(N=1)	(N=3)	(N=4)
Warn	-	-	9	8
			(N=7)	(N=5)
Conflictual deeds	2	1	7	3
	(N=1)	(N=1)	(N=5)	(N=2)
Verbal cooperation				
Positive comment	34	42	22	22
	(N=23)	(N=43)	(N=16)	(N=14)
Consult	21	31	1	-
	(N=14)	(N=32)	(N=1)	
Approve	3	2	1	-
	(N=2)	(N=2)	(N=1)	
Positive request/ proposal	13	5	11	8
	(N=9)	(N=5)	(N=8)	(N=5)
Promise/agree	7	1	-	2
	(N=5)	(N=1)		(N=1)
Cooperative Acts	2	5	-	3
	(N=1)	(N=5)		(N=2)
Country Totals	100	100	101	100
	(N=67)	(N=102)	(N=74)	(N=63)

and institutions; ZED and other data[37] provide support for the proposition that "relations with Tanzania have been the most specific, wide-ranging and friendly of all Zambia's contacts"[38] and that "Zambia's strongest fraternal ties are with the United Republic of Tanzania."[39] As indicated in table 9.6, Tanzania is second only to the United Kingdom as the most frequent target of Zambia's foreign policy; table 9.9 suggests that this dyadic relationship indeed covers all issue areas.

However, because of her opposition to racism and to express her own policy of Humanism, Zambia has also been very conflictual in her immediate region. ZED data for this period do not provide support for the proposition that "small developing states have the lowest percentage of conflict behavior."[40] As indicated in table 9.10, most conflict is directed by Zambia at the white regimes, whereas most cooperation is with neighboring black states, although, significantly, there is also some cooperation with the white states and some conflict with black regimes. Thus, ZED data provide support for Sklar's assertion that Zambia is concerned with national interests as well as with regional liberation in determining the "mixture of liberationist principle and realpolitik" in her foreign relations.[41]

The pattern of actor involvement also tends to be divided along this cleavage between white- and black-ruled Africa. State House and Foreign Affairs are most concerned with the confrontation in the South, while UNIP, Foreign Affairs and the parastatals concentrate on regional cooperation with independent African states; these assertions are confirmed by data presented in table 9.11. Further, ZED data support the conclusion reached in chapter 6 that, "although Southern Africa has constituted the central focus of Zambian foreign policy, direct support for liberation movements has formed only one element in a broader strategy." This strategy includes active multilateral diplomacy as well as the cajoling of those industrialized states with significant interests in the white South (see tables 9.5-9.8). ZED data capture all of Zambia's actions whether they express a particular "national" or a general "African" interest.

ZAMBIA AS A NEW STATE: MULTILATERAL DIPLOMACY

Rather than entering an alliance as protection against the white regimes, Zambia has actively sought

TABLE 9.11
Pattern of Zambian Actor Involvement in African
Relations

Target States and Organizations	Actor in Zambia							
	President Kaunda	President's Office	Minister of Foreign Affairs	Ministry of Foreign Affairs	Economic Ministry	Parastatal Organization	United National Independence Party	Totals for Targets
Ivory Coast	2	–	–	–	–	–	–	2
Liberia	9	1	–	–	1	–	1	12
Nigeria	1	–	–	–	–	1	1	3
Congo (B)	4	–	5	1	–	1	–	11
Zaire	13	1	6	4	1	3	1	29
Uganda	3	–	4	2	–	2	–	11
Kenya	1	1	2	–	1	4	1	10
Tanzania	20	7	14	3	–	2	2	48
Malawi	4	1	5	2	–	6	1	19
Botswana	2	1	1	1	1	5	3	14
Angola	5	–	2	1	–	–	1	9
Mozambique	13	1	5	2	–	–	4	25
Rhodesia	5	9	11	3	–	3	2	33
South Africa	16	5	3	–	–	5	6	35
Namibia	3	1	2	–	–	–	3	9
OAU	15	3	9	3	–	2	3	35
EAC	2	3	–	–	–	2	–	7
ZAPU	–	–	2	–	–	–	3	5
ZANU	–	–	3	–	–	–	5	8
MPLA	9	–	4	–	–	–	2	15
UNITA	6	–	2	–	–	–	2	10
FRELIMO	15	1	7	1	–	–	5	29

TABLE 9.12
Channels Used by Zambia according to WEIS Action Categories (Row Percentages)

Channel	Verbal Conflict	Conflictual Deeds	Verbal Cooperation	Cooperative Deeds	Totals
Speech to international organization	17 (N=6)	–	80 (N=28)	3 (N=1)	100 (N=35)
'Open' address in Zambia	45 (N=81)	–	55 (N=22)	–	100 (N=40)
'Closed' address in Zambia	18 (N=31)	2 (N=3)	78 (N=138)	2 (N=4)	100 (N=176)
Press Conference	25 (N=104)	2 (N=9)	71 (N=298)	2 (N=7)	100 (N=418)
Written domestic message	24 (N=29)	1 (N=1)	73 (N=89)	2 (N=3)	100 (N=122)
Statement in National Assembly	33 (N=9)	–	67 (N=18)	–	100 (N=27)

support from several international organizations.
Her active participation in many multilateral institutions, both global and continental, is due to diplomatic and financial imperatives: "Because of the
relative lack of resources available for foreign
affairs, the small state must seek methods of interaction that are less costly and more economical."
East also postulates that "small states tend to
minimize the costs of conducting foreign policy by
initiating more joint actions and by directing influence attempts at joint- or multiple-actor targets."[42] In table 9.12, we analyze the proportion
of Zambia's external events in different WEIS action
categories. The data undermine East's generalization that small states usually generate "less verbal
behavior and more non-verbal behavior" than other
types of state.[43] In this and other periods, Zambia
has engaged in conflictual as well as cooperative
acts. Table 9.12 also indicates that most of Zambia's actions are initiated in "closed" or exclusive
domestic forums, such as the UNIP National Council
or in local press conferences, rather than in international arenas or in "open" meetings in Zambia.
New states' foreign policies, including Zambia's,
are often as elitist as those of older nations, if
not more so.

Finally, one indicator of a state's dependence
or subordination in world politics is the proportion
of events it initiates rather than receives, that is,
to what extent its behavior is a response to external
or systemic demands. Table 9.13 lends support to
the proposition that "a small state with low economic development initiates fewer events than does
a small state with high economic development."[44]
However, the degree of adaptation varies in the case
of Zambia according to internal actor and issue.
The President and the Minister of Foreign Affairs
initiate more events than all other actors; further,
ZED data show that Zambia initiates a higher proportion of political and security events than economic
events, again reflecting her economic dependence and
greater degree of political independence or interdependence.

Most of Zambia's actions are responses; her
initiatives are confined to four issues—sociocultural, trade and investment, diplomatic and regional and global organizations. Most of her immediate concerns—the liberation of Southern Africa,
national development, nonalignment and regional integration—are concentrated in these issue areas. Her
responses, however, are mainly expressed in the more

374

TABLE 9.13
Nature of Zambia's Response according to Issue Area
and Actor

Response Related to:	Not a Response	Response
Issue Area		
Conventional military	4	58
Guerrilla warfare	4	179
Trade and investment	8	125
Economic assistance	3	139
Technical and scientific	9	200
Socioeconomic	13	159
Regional cooperation	6	124
International organization	5	47
Diplomatic	7	210
Internal Actor		
President Kaunda	39	192
President's Office/ State House	2	68
Minister of Foreign Affairs	14	103
Ministry of Foreign Affairs	2	24
Security Ministry	–	1
Economic Ministry	–	13
Parastatal organization	2	85
United National Independence Party	7	50

general or less salient diplomatic, warfare and economic issue areas. The President and Minister of
Foreign Affairs usually take initiatives in those
areas of greatest urgency for Zambia; they are less
dominant in other areas of more routine interaction
which are characterized by a greater devolution of
responsibility. So Zambia is capable of taking the
initiative in crises or in "high politics," especially within Southern Africa;[45] in regularized
"low politics," she is more dependent and subject to
systemic constraints, especially to those emanating
from the rich, dominant, industrialized states.

NEW STATES AND EVENTS ANALYSIS

This essay on the case of Zambia suggests that
established propositions about new state behavior
can usefully be evaluated through events data. Local

sources of such data are particularly rich and provide substantial, reliable, and valid evidence by which to support or reject generalizations. Our ZED file may also be used to compare coverage in the two Zambian newspapers, to contrast local sources with continental (AFRICA) or global (WEIS and CREON) data sets,[46] to prepare graphic illustrations of Zambia's "world map," and to assess changes in Zambian behavior over time. Hopefully, events data will both complement and challenge traditional approaches to the study of African international politics and so enhance our understanding of the foreign policies of new states.

This mode of quantitative empirical analysis probably can be profitably employed both to supplement and to examine generalizations on African foreign policy behavior derived from more orthodox modes of inquiry. It has yielded some new insights and understanding about Zambia's external behavior. In particular, ZED data indicate that the foreign policy of a new state such as Zambia has more complexity and subtlety than many analysts would allow; that the targets, actions and channels of her external relations are multiple; and that her world role has reached a definition and maturity to merit serious and continuing academic and political attention.

NOTES

1. See, for example, Timothy M. Shaw and Douglas G. Anglin, "Global, Regional and National Sources of Zambian Foreign Policy Events Data," in Measuring International Behavior: Public Sources, Events, and Validity, Don Munton, ed. (Halifax: Centre for Foreign Policy Studies, Dalhousie University, 1978).

2. Maurice A. East, "Events Data and the Study of Foreign Policy in East Africa," International Studies Association Conference, St. Louis, March 1974, p. 22.

3. See Timothy M. Shaw and Paul Burdett, "Zambia Events Data (ZED) Coding Manual," mimeographed (Centre for Foreign Policy Studies, Dalhousie University, 1975).

4. For a comparative analysis of the Zambian data generated by three events data sets, see Shaw and Anglin, "Global, Regional and National Sources of Zambian Foreign Policy Events Data."

5. See Maurice A. East, "Size and Foreign Policy Behavior: A Test of Two Models," World Politics 25, no. 4 (July 1973):556-76 and "Events Data and the Study of Foreign Policy in East Africa."

6. See Patrick J. McGowan, "The Pattern of African Diplomacy: a Quantitative Comparison," Journal of Asian and African Studies 4 (July 1969):202-21, and with Dale L. Smith, "Economic Dependency in Black Africa: An Analysis of Competing Theories," International Organization 32, no. 1 (Winter 1978): 179-235.

7. See, for instance, I. William Zartman, International Relations in the New Africa (Englewood Cliffs: Prentice-Hall, 1966), pp. 47-85 and chapter 3 in this volume.

8. Contrast for example, Patrick J. McGowan, "Economic Dependence and Economic Performance in Black Africa," Journal of Modern African Studies 14, no. 1 (March 1976):25-40 with Timothy M. Shaw, "The Political Economy of African International Relations," Issue 5, no. 4 (Winter 1975):29-38.

9. For a review of some of these, see chapter 12.

10. See Douglas G. Anglin, "Confrontation in Southern Africa: Zambia and Portugal," International Journal 25, no. 3 (Summer 1970):497-517 and "Zambia and the Recognition of Biafra," African Review 1, no. 2 (September 1971):102-36 and chapter 4 in this volume.

11. See chapter 5.

12. See chapter 3.

13. See chapters 6 through 9.

14. See chapter 2.

15. See Timothy M. Shaw and Agrippah T. Mugomba, "The Political Economy of Regional Détente: Zambia and Southern Africa," Journal of African Studies 4, no. 4 (Winter 1977/78):392-413 and "Zambia: Dependence and Détente," Southern Africa since the Portuguese Coup, ed. John Seiler, forthcoming.

16. See chapter 11.

17. See Patrick J. McGowan and K. P. Gottwald, "Small State Foreign Policies: A Comparative Study of Participation, Conflict and Political and Economic Dependence in Black Africa," International Studies Quarterly 19, no. 4 (December 1975):485.

18. See, for example, Anthony Martin, Minding Their Own Business: Zambia's Struggle against Western Control (Harmondsworth: Penguin, 1975), p. 156.

19. See Irving Kaplan et al., Area Handbook for Zambia, 2nd edition (Washington: Government Printing Office for American University, 1974), p. 237; and Jan Pettman, Zambia: Security and Conflict (New York: St. Martins, 1974), pp. 37-44.

20. Marion Bone, "The Foreign Policy of Zambia," in The Other Powers: Studies in the Foreign Policies of Small States, ed. Ronald P. Barston (London: George Allen and Unwin, 1973), pp. 148 and 131.

21. See Maurice A. East and Charles F. Hermann, "Do Nation Types Account for Foreign Policy Behavior?" in Comparing Foreign Policies: Theories, Findings and Methods, ed. James N. Rosenau (Beverly Hills: Sage, 1974), p. 278.

22. See chapter 3.

23. See James N. Rosenau, "Pre-theories and Theories of Foreign Policy," in Approaches to Comparative and International Politics, ed. R. G. Farrell (Evanston: Northwestern University Press, 1966), p. 149.

24. East, "Size and Foreign Policy Behavior," p. 560.

25. Ibid., p. 559.

26. See, for example, I. William Zartman, "Africa," in World Politics: An Introduction, eds. James N. Rosenau, Kenneth W. Thompson and Gavin Boyd (New York: Free Press, 1976), pp. 569-94; and Shaw and Mugomba, "The Political Economy of Regional Détente."

27. East, "Size and Foreign Policy Behavior," p. 574.

28. See East and Hermann, "Do Nation Types Account for Foreign Policy Behavior?," pp. 279 and 297.

29. See chapter 5.

30. See Douglas G. Anglin, "The Politics of Transit Routes in Land-locked Southern Africa," in Land-locked Countries of Africa, ed. Zdenek Cervenka (Uppsala: Scandinavian Institute of African Studies, 1973), p. 102.

31. See Dunstan Kamana, "Zambia," in Conflict and Change in Southern Africa: Papers from a Canadian-Scandinavian Conference, eds. Douglas G. Anglin, Timothy M. Shaw and Carl G. Widstrand (Washington: University Press of America, 1978), pp. 33-68; and Timothy M. Shaw, "Canada in Zambian Perspective," in How Others See Us: Canada in World Perspective, eds. Denis Stairs and Don Munton, forthcoming.

32. East, "Size and Foreign Policy Behavior," p. 557.

33. See, for instance, the resistance of Britain and the Soviet Union to Zambian entreaties and pressures as described in chapters 4 and 9.

34. See chapters 8 and 9, and 5 respectively.

35. Steven L. Spiegel, Dominance and Diversity: The International Heirarchy (Boston: Little Brown, 1972), p. 105.

36. Bone, "The Foreign Policy of Zambia," p. 141.

37. See chapters 3 and 5.

38. Bone, "The Foreign Policy of Zambia," p. 141.

39. Kaplan et al., Area Handbook for Zambia, p. 241.

40. East, "Size and Foreign Policy Behavior," p. 571.

41. Richard L. Sklar, "Zambia's Response to the Rhodesian UDI," in Politics in Zambia, ed. William Tordoff (Berkeley: University of California Press, 1974), p. 362.

42. East, "Size and Foreign Policy Behavior," pp. 560 and 576. See also, Benedict V. Mtshali, "The Zambian Foreign Service, 1964-1972," African Review 5, no. 3 (1975):303-16 and chapter 3 above.

43.   East, "Size and Foreign Policy Behavior,"
p. 567.

44.   Ibid., p. 564.

45.   See, for instance, chapters 6 and 7.

46.   See Shaw and Anglin, "Global, Regional and
National Sources of Zambian Foreign Policy Event
Data."

10
Zambia: Dependence and Underdevelopment

The political economy of Zambia in many ways
constitutes a classic case of dependence and underdevelopment. Yet analysis of the Zambian state has
largely failed to concentrate on the fundamental
structures of its political economy.[1] The thrust of
the present chapter is that the development as well
as the foreign policy of Zambia during her first
decade of independence cannot be explained without
reference to her inheritance of and response to
dependence. This inquiry is based on the premise
that internal and international inequalities are
interrelated and that domestic "class" formation is
one result of Zambia's status as a peripheral part
of the world capitalist economy. The ideology and
practice of Humanism and planning within Zambia's
one-party state failed during the initial period
after Independence to overcome the essential structures of underdevelopment: dependence on the export
of copper, neglect of agriculture, and the rise of a
dominant class with significant external associations.
Rather, incremental politics and a continuing permissiveness towards embourgeoisement led to the advocacy,
particularly from factions not in power, of coexistence with the prevailing balance of power in Southern
Africa. The occasional ambivalence of the Zambian
state itself towards the liberation movements may be
seen, then, to reflect a disinclination to overcome
the problems of dependence. Until the new class is
challenged by domestic demands, it is likely to maintain its comfortable collaboration with global economic interests and reveal continuing ambiguity about
fundamental regional change.

THE DOMINANT CLASS AND THE ZAMBIAN STATE

Internal inequalities are inseparable from international stratification. In Zambia, as in many

381

African states, the dominant "class" has been able to maintain its domestic control and to increase its affluence through association with external interests. The ability of this small elite to maximize its status and its inability to deal effectively with domestic inequalities can be seen as a function of its cooperation with foreign entrepreneurs and corporations. The pervasive materialist ethic[2] in Zambia is one result of the participation of the national elite in a transnational relationship[3] with external economies, institutions, and values.

The focus of this chapter is on the interrelation of the international hierarchy and the evolution of privilege in a new state such as Zambia. To the extent that the new dominant class has become incorporated into international linkages,[4] it ceases to retain an interest in confronting this central structure of dependence. The underdevelopment of Zambia will likely continue, therefore, until domestic inequalities compel some sort of "revolution" in both Zambia's internal and international relationships, as we suggest in chapter 11. Because the class structure of Zambia is largely a function of her subordinate role in the global economy, any progress towards socialism and self-reliance would necessitate confronting both internal and external inequalities: "In peripheral areas of the world economy . . . the primary contradiction is between the interests organized and located in the core countries and their local allies on the one hand, and the majority of the population on the other."[5]

Although the relationship between a few rich states and many poor states promotes the underdevelopment of the latter, a few within the periphery may benefit from such an unequal relationship. Given the dominance of rich actors globally, the new rulers of the Third World have faced a crucial policy choice of collaboration or confrontation; the response of most leaders in Africa over time has typically been to accept cooperation.[6] The continent's elites have generally welcomed political and economic support, technical and educational services from outside. Their permissiveness has allowed locally produced surplus to be extracted in exchange for foreign capital, skills, techniques and markets, so postponing internal accumulation and national self-reliance. Acceptance of the inherited international division of labor tends to reinforce the concentration of industrial growth in the rich states and condemn Africa to a continuation of dependence and underdevelopment.[7] The characteristic ambivalence of the

382

new states of Africa in their response to the politics of dependence is related, then, to the benefits
which the emerging classes obtain through such
relationships. The "dependence" of countries may be
perpetuated by the "interdependence" of ruling
elites.

However, the relationship between any new ruling class and the global economy is not entirely
predetermined. The dominant class in Zambia, for
example, has been able to bargain for greater control over and returns from foreign investment.[8]
Nevertheless, this new class has remained essentially
a dependent "pseudo-bourgeoisie,"[9] or a "managerial
bourgeoisie."[10] It secured and perpetuated its
power by control, not so much over the means of production but rather over the state and its external
associations. This class is not an orthodox social
class, defined in terms of its relationship to the
means of production and reproduction, as it lacks
autonomy from both the national state sector and
international exchange and values; it is unable to
accumulate and innovate on its own. In this sense,
it is not a national bourgeoisie but has certain
parasitic characteristics; it is in a new form of
"partnership," the local branch of a "transnational
class."[11] It is generally less responsive to its
internal constituency than to the pressures of
foreign entrepreneurs. The ruling class is dependent on the continued supply of foreign capital and
technology and is probably incapable of transforming
itself into a national bourgeoisie unless it separates itself somewhat from its intimate relationship
with established state structures.[12]

The interaction between an African ruling class
and the multinational corporation often occurs
within parastatal institutions,[13] and is legitimized
by reference to "African socialism." There are, of
course, several varieties of state capitalism;[14] in
Zambia, for example, the ideology of Humanism examined in chapter 2 has facilitated the development of
a dominant sector which largely consists of cooperative agreements between the interests of the
state and of foreign capital. The ruling class in
Africa may have formal charge over the national
economy, but it lacks effective control to the
extent that there is joint ownership of the major
means of production. The absence of a contemporary
mercantilist or industrial revolution on the continent has largely prevented the emergence of an
autonomous bourgeoisie thus far. Rather, the rich
in Africa still rely on external linkages to per

petuate their status and power. Although some
Africans benefit from such relationships, their
essential external asymmetry leads to dependence on
foreign trade and technology, the outflow of funds
and to domestic inequalities.

Whilst the "managerial bourgeoisie" is the
major beneficiary of the external estate, one further social group has been able to take advantage of
national dependence—the labor aristocracy.[15] An
elite of workers in the "modern" sector has been
able to demand and receive higher incomes because of
its skills and roles in crucial sectors. In Zambia,
senior African miners, factory workers and artisans
have been able to improve their standard of living
rapidly because of their leverage within strategic
industries; these industries are either located
within, or are crucial to, the parastatal corporations. So, it is the urban poor and the rural
peasantry who are further excluded and impoverished
by dependence. On the other hand, they have yet to
mobilize the political power potentially available
to them and form an alliance to challenge the
collaborative relationship between external interests, the ruling class and the labor aristocracy,
particularly as the latter coalition is of recent
vintage but of considerable importance.[16] Class
conflict in African states such as Zambia is likely
to develop around the maldistribution of control and
affluence.

CLASS FORMATION AND INTER-
NATIONAL DEPENDENCE

The ability of the dominant class to maintain
political order in Zambia has been related to the
production, distribution and price of copper.
Zambia is one of the most dependent economies when
measured in terms of the contribution of a single
dominant industry to exports and government revenue.[17]
As late as 1974, copper contributed 93% of export
earnings, 54% of government revenue, 44% of gross
domestic product, and 15% of direct employment.
Income from copper exports has determined Zambia's
capacity to import both capital and consumer goods;
the affluence of the ruling class and its ability to
perpetuate its control have been directly related to
copper.

Yet copper is a mixed blessing. Zambia has been
able to expand her manufacturing capability and to
reorient her transport routes,[19] but she has tended

to neglect agricultural and rural development and has been permissive of embourgeoisement.[20] Moreover, Zambia reduced her dependence on Southern Africa (especially on Rhodesia) by becoming more dependent on other capitalist economies, such as West Germany and Japan, as well as on China. Humanism is intolerant of racial discrimination,[21] but it has been more permissive towards other social inequalities and the multinational corporation. Further, Zambia's vulnerability in the confrontation over Southern Africa has led it to seek support throughout the rest of the international system, including the noncapitalist economies. For reasons of both domestic order and foreign policy, Zambia has been unwilling to challenge the interdependence of the white economies and the capitalist system too far lest such a challenge rebound on her own prospects.[22] Amongst the economic imperatives of détente in Southern Africa were, therefore, both the need for cheap and reliable transit routes as well as a concern to reinforce cooperation between the ruling class and its external associates. However, countervailing pressures from the front line states prevented any easy or consistent retreat from liberation support.[23]

To enhance her role as a reliable regional core in Central Africa, Zambia has preferred moderate African regimes on her borders. Her advocacy of regional coexistence may be seen to have been an expression of the interests of the ruling class of the Zambian state. The Zambian leadership had hoped that its dependence and copper would lead to upward mobility in the international hierarchy in which the Zambian state became "semiperipheral" rather than "peripheral"; it sought to share the affluence and influence of rich states by playing a subimperial role in one particular region of the international system.[24] Zambia's readiness to act as mediator in Southern Africa, as examined in chapter 7, may have been related to the interests of her ruling class in seeking enhanced influence, status and affluence by being prepared at times to advance moderate solutions to the region's problems.

The transition from a peripheral to a semiperipheral role in Central Africa would not by itself have changed Zambia's relationship of dependence within the global economy. It would, however, indicate the emergence of Zambia from her inheritance of dependence on the White South and the impact of the uneven rate of development in the region. Yet the affluence of the ruling class and the labor aristocracy has made Zambia a high-cost economy;

some consumption may have to be limited if Zambia's regional hegemony is to be assured. Moreover, if Zambia were to become a leading actor in the region in addition to South Africa, her enhanced role might lead to competition between the two dominant regional states, even after majority rule in South Africa.

The underdevelopment of Zambia has its origins in the precolonial, colonial and settler periods of Central African history. Its inheritance in 1964 included investment from and infrastructural links with the White South, dependence on copper exports, and reliance on agricultural output dominated by white commercial farmers. Zambia has begun to confront some of these structures, but in so doing has become increasingly dependent on the global economy and on new large-scale African farmers.

In terms of most of the criteria of under-development and dependence proposed by Glyn Hughes and Tamas Szentes, Zambia rated high scores during her first decade : (1) she exhibited high levels of consumption, particularly of imports for the ruling class and the labor aristocracy; (2) her economy was "foreign" in orientation, origin and ownership; (3) export trade was concentrated in one product and with a few markets; (4) Zambia depended on foreign credit and exchange, if not on orthodox assistance; (5) the "national" economy was not autonomous or internally integrated and relied on foreign technology and skills; and (6) there was a high outflow of "invisibles" in the form of profits, expatriate remittances, costs of transport and insurance, and for debt servicing.

Zambia has been able to support a comparatively indulgent life style for the few because of a highly unequal distribution of copper revenues. During the first decade of independence, her balance of trade was usually sufficient to cover a high level of imports and invisibles. However, since 1974-75, a combination of global inflation and recession has led to a decline in both the demand and price for copper; the cost of Zambia's oil, capital and food imports has escalated; and conflicts in Angola and Zimbabwe as well as congestion in East Africa have hurt her externally oriented economy.

Zambia's diplomatic initiatives in Southern Africa have been in part a response to her economic dilemmas. To maintain its affluent life style and even the basic needs of the peasants and urban poor, the ruling class has had to compromise its ideals at times over the liberation of Southern Africa. Cheap and reliable routes and import sources continue to

be imperatives. Zambia had always combined "liberationist principle and realpolitik";[26] détente was a
reflection of the urgency of the interests of the
state as defined by the dominant class.

The first decade of independence did not alter
the basic structures of Zambia's dependence. It did,
however, enable the local ruling class to extract
more privileges for itself from its transnational
associations in the global economy, particularly
from its participation in the burgeoning parastatal
sector. Enhanced national power over the state produced Africanization of management but not of effective control. Any redistribution of resources
through state capitalism was to the advantage of the
ruling class and the labor aristocracy. Economic
growth has not yet led to a significant reduction in
domestic inequality; rather, the continuing economic
crisis has led to further relative impoverishment
away from the line of rail.

The ability of the new leadership to extract
privilege by adopting a cooperative stance within
the global economy has been a disincentive to a
radical foreign policy. To be sure, Zambia has made
isolated rhetorical gestures such as recognizing
exile governments in South Vietnam, Cambodia and
Guinea-Bissau; it also broke diplomatic relations
with postcoup Chile and with postwar Israel. However, Zambia has not sought to disengage from the
global economy, as noted in chapter 5, and in Southern Africa, she has successfully severed ties with
Rhodesia but not yet with South Africa. Any moves
towards a reduced level of external exchange have
been caused more by foreign currency reserve problems than by a decision either to adopt a greater
degree of self-reliance or to put the interests of
the national economy above those of the international
market. Disengagement from Rhodesia enhanced Zambia's
local manufacturing and distributing capability and
extended the control of the dominant class. The
perpetuation of collaboration with the industrial
economies has been essentially compatible with the
emergence of state capitalism as the dominant ethos
in Zambia.

The preeminence of the parastatal sector thus
far has tended to retard the development of a petit-
bourgeoisie in Zambia.[27] Although the Africanization
of the retail trade, transportation and services has
been advanced through legal instruments and party
actions, these sectors are dominated by parastatal
supermarkets, transport companies and service
industries. Moreover, most successful private

Zambian companies are either foreign, white, or highly dependent on contracts with parastatals. To date, state capitalism in Zambia has, therefore, largely prevented the rise of Zambian entrepreneurs outside the burgeoning parastatal sector. It has, however, reinforced the trend towards concentration and monopoly of decision making in the regime.

The dominant class created the one-party state to maximize order and to eliminate challenges to its definition of development and exclusive control over relations with external interests.[28] Thus far, presidential rhetoric and ethnic balancing have contained opposition to the monopoly of power in Zambia without any significant redistribution of income. However, unless inequalities are reduced, embryonic class formation may be accelerated and class conflict be intensified. The President is necessarily ambivalent towards the new ruling class on the one hand and to a socialist definition of Humanism on the other. However, the perpetuation of inequalities and the development of state capitalism may yet lead to vocal, if not widespread, radical opposition to the growing monopoly possessed by the dominant class in Zambia over the state apparatus.[29]

THE GROWTH OF INHERITED INEQUALITIES

Northern Rhodesia was dependent on two centers— the imperial metropole in Britain and the subimperial cores of South Africa and Southern Rhodesia; copper profits went to Johannesburg and Salisbury as well as to London. Under colonialism, these external interests were largely compatible but, with the rise of African nationalism, many of the white settlers and miners found the neocolonial solution, which the imperial administration and multinational corporations favored, unattractive.[30] Yet race was not the only inequality the new state inherited at Independence. Society was also characterized at the time by ethnic, regional and class differences. The tastes and values of the metropole were adopted by affluent residents, both black and white, and association with the transnational corporations served to perpetuate the acceptability of these life styles. Such an inheritance provided the basis for intensified sectional and class conflict in Zambia over the distribution of new resources, patronage and privilege in the first decade and since.

If Zambia had few choices at Independence over her development, she has in practice even fewer now,

fifteen years later. The Africanization of the
state has introduced a new and indigenous elite committed to the maintenance of the established political order. The inherited problems of dependence on
copper and foreigners, urbanization and rural underdevelopment remain. The post-UDI crisis provided
the resources and urgency for expanded control by
the national elite, and reinforced the uneven structure of the Zambian economy. Indeed, Charles Harvey
pointed out in 1974 that the only major new factor
since 1964 in addition to established inequalities
was the emergence of wage inflation; the major beneficiaries of the postindependence boom in Zambia
were African bureaucrats and workers.[31] Salaries
for the new "bureaucratic bourgeoisie" and for the
"labor aristocracy," notably in the parastatals,
especially in the mining, energy and communication
sectors, multiplied after Independence, far out-
stripping, yet also accelerating, the rate of inflation, at least for the first decade.

The mineworkers in Zambia have always been
relatively affluent and were, perhaps, the first
genuine proletariat in Africa.[32] However, their
status in the labor aristocracy has since been
matched by workers in the new manufacturing and
distribution industries, especially by those in the
strategic transport and energy sectors. Pay awards
to the bureaucracy and wage-earners in Zambia continue to advance the rate of inflation, much of
which was imported initially with the high price of
foreign oil and manufactures. Meanwhile, the real
income of the peasant farmers may have declined, and
certainly has not improved, since Independence.[33]
Moreover, the labor aristocracy is a declining proportion of the population as the number of new jobs
in characteristically capital-intensive industries
fails to keep pace with population growth.

The relative affluence of the labor aristocracy
and the impoverishment of the peasantry, under- and
un-employed in an era of inflation and shortages,
tended to reinforce the collaboration between the
ruling class and labor aristocracy. Their symbiotic
relationship and relative embourgeoisement have been
reflected in the high pay awards of the first decade
and power sharing within the state apparatus, especially senior appointments in parastatals, representation in the Central Committee, Cabinet and
Parliament, as well as a growing awareness of the
need both to placate and to regulate the rest of
society. The rhetoric of one-party and industrial
participatory democracies is largely restricted to

debate within this group; the poor are increasingly excluded from both influence and affluence in contemporary Zambia.

This analysis of class formation in Zambia is intended in part as a corrective to an overemphasis in the past on other social cleavages. "Sectionalism" in Zambia is the politics of linguistic, regional and ethnic divisions; it has been defined to exclude religious or class distinctions.[34] Clearly leaders in Zambia have used a variety of variables to attract support. However, given the increase in social inequalities and the growth of class formation, it has become inappropriate to exclude class identities and relations as a salient sectional phenomenon. The underdevelopment of Zambia has accelerated since Independence with economic growth being concentrated along the line-of-rail and especially in a few urban centers.[35] Agriculture and the rural areas have continued to be overlooked except when the rise of food imports and a weak balance-of-payments situation have coincided, nowadays a rather frequent occurrence. Nevertheless, in addition to ethnic, regional and spatial distinctions, class divisions are now an integral part of Zambian society and politics.

The urban-rural gap and non-class inequalities in Zambia have been studied by Donald Rothchild who argued that regime rhetoric about agricultural development and the need for self-reliance has not halted the underdevelopment of the rural areas.[36] Rather, the imperatives of Africanization and industrialization have increased the dominance both of the cities and of the ruling class. By contrast, Ann Seidman has criticized the preoccupation with this gap and has drawn attention to the inequalities within the cities rather than between them and the countryside.[37] Her analysis of the urban poor is compatible with more orthodox Marxist analysis of the role of the proletariat and tends to contradict the labor aristocracy approach. However, the case of Zambia suggests that the labor aristocracy will continue to identify with the ruling class until its relative affluence is threatened, or until it can assume the leadership of the urban and rural poor. At present, the privileged employed workers of Lusaka, Livingstone and the Copperbelt are more concerned with security than with revolution. Until recently, the managers and workers of Zambia have been able to overcome the high rate of inflation by successfully demanding large pay increases, whereas the peasants' predicament is hardly heard. Moreover,

390

the interaction between ethnicity and class on the Copperbelt makes the regime anxious to secure even minimal support from largely Bemba miners. Any sustained moves against such relative economic privilege would threaten the political base of the ruling class.[38] The trend towards a political economy dominated by the new elite has been hastened by the difficulties confronting an increasingly centralized state capitalist system: concentration of power and popular de-participation have reinforced each other and generated a new agenda for action. As Ian Scott suggests:

> The comparative ease with which the political leadership made the transition from party-based support to class-based support disguised many of the real costs involved. As power and decision making became more centralized, the implementation of policy became more difficult. . . . factionalism and the inability of the government to maintain an extensive patronage system brought about an alliance between the political leadership and what was its natural and only alternative base of support, the middle class. The alliance has, however, created major problems for the political leadership. The middle class is tiny and, while it can provide some of the skills the regime needs, it cannot solve the problem of the communications gap between the center and the countryside. And failure to implement policy and meet real needs is perhaps the critical issue facing the Zambian government today.[39]

And any move to transcend the regime's class base and external associations is likely to be difficult and problematic.

Despite good intentions, postindependence investment in manufacturing and communications have seemed only to accentuate regional inequalities. In the period of the first national development plan, capital expenditure reached or exceeded targets only in the line-of-rail urbanized provinces. The poor rural provinces have continued to suffer from both a lack of capital and attention, and their low incomes contribute to the continual flow of people to the cities. However, output of basic staples, such as maize and cotton, has increased since Independence, particularly on large-scale farms, and agricultural production for the rich in the cities has grown; more eggs, chicken, sugar, pigs and vegetables were produced for the urban areas, again, largely on quite capital-intensive farms.[40] The only major investments outside the established industrial and mineral areas have been parastatal plants in Livingstone, Kafue and Kasama and the construction of pipeline, road and rail links with Tanzania through the Northern Province. Nevertheless, new communications and industrial infrastructures do not of themselves end dependence or produce a more autonomous national economy unless carefully related to a national strategy.

INTERNATIONAL TRADE AND UNDERDEVELOPM:

During the first decade of Independence, the pattern of Zambia's continuing dependence on international exchange was characterized by increased imports of food and raw materials as well as of capital, increased invisible imports and outflows, and diversification among, but not away from, capitalist economies. Zambia's "outward-directed" growth, based on the export of copper and import of most economic necessities, was not really dissimilar from that of other, poorer African states.[41] External trade increased in proportion to GDP; economic growth since Independence has not produced a substantially more integrated, balanced and autonomous economy. Indeed, the Zambian economy remains highly vulnerable to international economic cycles; with the demand for and price of copper reflecting global trends; continuous growth and planning in Zambia remain elusive. The dramatic drop in the price of copper in 1974 has led to predictable problems ever since as noted in chapters 1 and 11. Moreover, over time the price of copper has failed in any case to keep pace with global inflation. Even when the price of copper was high, Zambia could less easily afford new imports; when the price falls, funds available for foreign exchange are very limited, the external payments "pipeline" lengthens and the domestic output of goods declines, thus exacerbating the problem.

This pattern of "dependent development" or "outward-directed growth" in Zambia has intensified the dependence of the new state. The high price of oil has seriously affected Zambia as it has all oil-importing Third World countries. However, Zambia's reliance on foreign materials, food, technology and services for postindependence growth had already

392

reinforced her inheritance. Local manufacturing may
enhance regime control and patronage, and provide
consumer goods for the new dominant class. But it
is not a very viable long-term development strategy,
and it advances both external dependence and internal underdevelopment. So the interests of the elite
largely determine the future of the state in the
direction of continued dependence. By themselves,
import substitution policies tend to perpetuate the
status quo, satisfy the needs only of the rich, and
maintain relations of dependence.[42] The ruling
class as a whole can hardly be expected to advocate
a policy of self-reliant development which would
interfere with its foreign associations and tastes.[43]

The absence of an industrial development strategy in Zambia has made it both permissive and vulnerable to market forces. During the first ten
years of independence, imports of raw materials and
chemicals doubled and imports of machinery and transport equipment quadrupled; food imports reached
record heights in the early 1970s. Although this
situation may be detrimental for the Zambian nation,
it has been acceptable for the present state which
increased its control and affluence through the
parastatal sector and collaboration with the multinational corporation. The interrelated forces of a
high cost of oil imports, a decline in the value of
copper exports, and increased external borrowing
throughout the mid-1970s are only the latest in a
series of economic cycles and crises that have
characterized Zambia as a very open and dependent
economy. And yet a strategy of self-reliance and
labor intensivity has been avoided because of the
entrenchment of a dependent bureaucratic bourgeoisie.

The international dependence of Zambia is
revealed in the increase of her invisible payments,
which erode her balance of trade whatever the price
of copper. The outflow doubled after Independence
and averaged $300 million a year in the early 1970s,
though it has since declined substantially as a
result of the recession. As noted in chapter 5,
Rhodesia's UDI and border closure increased the
costs of transportation, but other major factors
have been expatriate earnings and the transfer of
profits. The expense of an increased use of air-
freight and a variety of routes has also raised the
cost of an externally oriented economy; continued
dependence on foreign investment and skills is reflected in the perpetuation of a considerable invisible outflow. Moreover, Ann Seidman has suggested
that the real outflow of funds is greater than

appears in official statistics; she estimates that the investable surplus produced in Zambia and so potentially available for accumulation is double the reported outflow. She indicated that in the early 1970s K620 million could be saved annually in Zambia if mining profits, transfer payments, and excessive consumption by the few above real necessities were all curtailed.[44]

As noted in chapter 5, Zambia has had to diversify her use of transit routes for her external trade away from reliance on Southern Africa and towards the use of routes through independent Africa.[45] In 1977, over 80% of Zambia's trade passed through Dar es Salaam. Since then, the capacity of this route has dropped and the Lobito route (which accounted for almost 50% of the traffic in 1974) remains closed. As a result, in October 1978 Zambia was forced into the difficult and humiliating position of reopening the southern route through Rhodesia for the importation of key commodities, notably fertilizer. Because Zambia remains dependent on the export of one commodity, she has been unable to diversify her markets very widely. She has been somewhat more successful in seeking new sources of imports. The proportion of trade has declined with Southern Africa and increased with the European Economic Community, China, Japan and East Africa. The elusiveness of significant market diversification away from capitalist economies is related to the entrenchment of a mono-crop, non-socialist political economy in Zambia.

The inability of Zambia to widen her trade links is partly a function of the interests of the ruling class and its definition of development. Zambia will continue to be vulnerable to external exchange and cycles until she becomes more self-reliant in agriculture and manufacturing.[46] She is likely to begin to confront her dependence and to construct a national economy only when the ruling elite places the interests of a broader internal constituency above those of its own class and external associations.[47] The debate over the future direction of the political economy of Zambia is centered on the definition of the national ideology of Humanism.

HUMANISM AND STATE CAPITALISM

The nation of Zambia remains dependent on international trade, external capital and foreign technology. The state of Zambia, symbolized by the new dominant class, has become established through cooperation with the capitalist world economy. State capitalism and collaboration with external interests have advanced both the control and affluence of the new elite. Partial and benign state ownership captures some resources for the ruling class, but does not threaten the basic pattern of unequal relations between Zambia and her main trading partners. Seminationalization may not really disturb the interests and dominance of the multinational corporation; rather, collaboration in the parastatal sector has given both partners security, profitability and patronage.[48] However, transnational relations between the Zambian elite and its foreign associates, no matter how favorable the bargain is to the former, perpetuate dependence between countries and limit the independence of Zambia. The interests of the ruling class are secured at the cost to the Zambian nation of its longer-term autonomy and self-reliant development. Despite presidential rhetoric, there is little reason why the new rulers of Zambia should confront international capitalism or their inheritance of dependence;[49] they can turn it to the advantage of their class despite the implications for the underdevelopment of the rest of the nation.

Zambia has rarely resorted to the politics of confrontation with either foreign, regional or local corporations. Rather, through the 1968 Mulungushi, 1969 Matero, and 1970 and 1973 Lusaka reforms, she has extended state participation and formal control through the mining, industrial, commercial and financial institutions.[50] The parastatal sector is still subject to organizational change and to renegotiation, but the essential structures of cooperation between foreign capital and the Zambian state are likely to be perpetuated.[51] Despite rhetoric about "self-management" and "workers' participatory industrial democracy," through management contracts, the provision of services, and control over technology, the multinationals have continued to determine product "development," methods of production and industrial strategy. Moreover, parastatals still apply orthodox profitability criteria to their performance; at best they have some welfare concerns, but they are in no sense operated along socialist or cooperative lines.[52]

The issue of the control and direction of the parastatals is central to the wider debate over the definition of Humanism in Zambia. Although the President has moved some way himself from a con-

sensual to an advocative interpretation of Humanism,[53] the leading apologists for the ideology have
continued to articulate a traditionalist and synthetic variety of the philosophy. Against this
dominant interpretation, Robert Molteno, Sefelino
Mulenga, Timothy Kandeke and others have advocated a
socialist definition of Humanism (see chapter 2).[54]
Any "radical" orientation for the national ideology
is also opposed by Zambian leaders in the parastatal
sector, the "technocratic" faction most likely to
be adversely affected by any disengagement from the
world economy. Indeed, as in Tanzania,[55] state
functionaries have been constrained in their embourgeoisement only by presidential appeals. President
Kaunda has tended to evolve from a supporter of a
traditionalist, consensual Humanism[56] to an advocate
of a more radical variety. He has abandoned pluralism, at least in proclamations and rhetoric, in his
quest for social order, development and justice in
Zambia, so pitting himself against the emerging
managerial bourgeoisie on which the state as a whole
has come to rely.

In response to this debate over Humanism and to
the interrelated problems of class formation and
external dependence, which had become increasingly
apparent in the first decade, Dr. Kaunda introduced
a redefinition of the national ideology on the
state's tenth anniversary of formal independence.[57]
In this review, he called for further incremental
changes in Zambia's political economy towards redistribution and decentralization, seeing the contemporary mixed economy merely as an intermediate
stage. He advocated a society without divisions and
demanded a reduction of inequalities between regions
and classes; he lamented the "false start" and undesirable byproducts of state participation, and
demanded further political and industrial democracy.
Dr. Kaunda criticized "the rapid emergence of a
powerful Zambian elite whose thoughts and actions
are couched in terms of the very rapine system which
Humanism in Zambia was meant to combat."[58] "We need
to brace ourselves for a fight against those who
have placed themselves in upper and middle classes."[59]
So the President of the state and of the Party seems
recently to have adopted a more critical form of
class-type analysis, and to have followed the advice
of "radical" intellectuals, at least at the level of
rhetoric. He would now appear to recognize that
"the 'revolution from above' in state enterprise,
with its elitist connotations, is directly relevant
to the growth of the managerial bourgeoisie."[60]

However, the entrenchment of the technocratic Zambian elite, with its transnational class associations, limits the President's ability to act without an alternative power base other than the very beneficiaries of the established pattern of dependent growth.[61]

Nevertheless, President Kaunda continues to display a remarkable capacity to take initiatives and a great tenacity to remain in office despite the continuing range of subnational, regional and international challenges identified in chapter 1. He possesses an independent spirit which at times expresses opinions more radical than the "authorized version" of Humanism. For instance, in July 1974 on a state visit to Tanzania, he identified multinational corporations as structures of exploitation with a potential to control African states and charged that they were "invisible opposition parties."[62] In June 1975, in response to global inflation, recession in the copper market and critical reports on the economy, mismanagement and crime, Kaunda advocated frugality, an end to state subsidies and greater discipline and self-reliance. He appealed for popular support for his attack on the nouveau riche:

> The cause of the revolutionary masses, workers and peasants is the cause of the Party. . . . luxuriousness, lavishness and all forms of behavior are found in today's Zambia. . . . Society is sick and the Zambian economy cannot be more sick than the people who run it. We cannot turn Zambia into a socialist state we want it to be, let alone into a Humanist one, in a short time. . . . We are not against foreign capital per se. Therefore, to those who may wish to invest in Zambia again they are welcome. . . . We are building socialism here as an instrument of establishing a Humanist state.[63]

This latest Mulungushi declaration, while it contains "socialist" rhetoric, nevertheless still reveals a certain ambivalence over the direction of Humanism and the Zambian state; at best, it is a more radical expression of reformism. Because of the prevalence of the capitalist and consumer ethic in Zambia, it is unlikely that the institutionalization of a socialist Humanism can be achieved single-handed by the President; a greater degree of political education, participation or coercion may

397

be necessary, as noted in chapter 11.[64]

CONCLUSION: STATE AND
CLASS IN ZAMBIA

The Zambian state has now taken partial control over most economic institutions, except for the foreign banks, but it has resisted moving rapidly or unambiguously towards a socialist economy. Despite the rhetoric about the supremacy of the UNIP, the leadership code, one-party participatory and industrial democracy, and rural development, Zambia remains a stratified society in which access to affluence remains the dominant goal. The President may appeal for popular support outside the ruling class in his attempt to make an opening to the left, but thus far the new "bureaucratic bourgeoisie" remains entrenched and defiant in its new position and opulence.

So whilst the President may have diagnosed correctly the political, economic and social problems of Zambia, it is doubtful whether he can confront the new national elite in the ministries, parastatals and barracks of Lusaka by himself. It is particularly difficult for Dr. Kaunda to confront those groups on which he has depended for support and towards whom he has of necessity been permissive; but the alternative would seem to be intensified inequalities and conflict:

> Bureaucratic and technocratic elitism, nurtured by the state, has arisen to challenge the democratic ideals of the nationalist party in power. Either the party will restrain the pretensions of technocratic elitism, or technocratic elitism, sheltered by the influence of multinational corporations, will transform the populist party into a willing instrument for capitalist development. The struggle between elitist and popular power looms as the central issue of Zambian political development.[65]

This chapter has suggested that we cannot understand the development and foreign policies of an African state such as Zambia without reference to its political economy. Moreover, its political economy is largely determined by the interests of the ruling class; this class will continue to define the state until challenged by internal and/or international opposition. At present, Zambia's political economy is perpetuated by the mutual interests of the dominant indigenous class and those of its external associates. Their collaboration is concentrated in the large parastatal system. So long as their interdependent transnational interests are advanced, Zambia herself will continue to be dependent on the capitalist world economy.

The underdevelopment of certain groups and regions in Zambia has been exacerbated as a result of the process of class formation in a new state. External collaboration intensifies internal inequalities. This potential contradiction may yet threaten the established pattern of linkages between the ruling class in Zambia and the multinational corporation. It may also tend to separate the interests of the bureaucratic bourgeoisie from those of the labor aristocracy, although they have both identified to date with the parastatal strategy. Thus far, the interests of both the dominant class and of the labor aristocracy have been advanced by collaboration with external capital and the political impact of uneven national development has yet to be really felt. As suggested in chapter 1, the continuing crisis may hasten such a day of reckoning. Because "classes obviously do exist in Zambia,"[66] they cannot continue to be overlooked. Presidential rhetoric about Humanism cannot repress or resolve class differences alone: basic changes in the political economy cannot be postponed indefinitely.

NOTES

1. For succinct, sympathetic and informed reviews of recent Zambiana, see Douglas G. Anglin, "Political Scene in Zambia," Canadian Journal of African Studies 9, no. 2 (1975):337-40; William Tordoff, "Zambia: the politics of disengagement," African Affairs 76, no. 302 (January 1977):60-69; and Sholto Cross, "Politics and criticism in Zambia: a review article," Journal of Southern African Studies 1, no. 1 (October 1974):109-15. Cross perceptively points to the need for "a theory of oligarchic statism" (p. 115) to analyze the contradictory roles of the President and the ruling class and to begin to answer the crucial question: are they "the entrepreneurial national bourgeoisie . . . who play-- despite themselves--a progressive role in the uplift of their society, or are they a passive and parasitic elite, masking their pursuit of power and greedy consumerism under a rhetoric of modernization

and development?" (p. 110).

2. Robert Molteno and William Tordoff, "Conclusion—independent Zambia: achievements and prospects," in Politics in Zambia, ed. William Tordoff (Berkeley: University of California Press, 1974), p. 395.

3. For a suggestive review of transnational politics from a 'radical' perspective, see Martin Godfrey and Steven Langdon, "Partners in underdevelopment: The transnationalisation thesis in a Kenyan context," Journal of Commonwealth and Comparative Politics 14, no. 1 (March 1976):42-63. For orthodox introductions to this new approach to the study of world politics, see Robert O. Keohane and Joseph S. Nye, "Transnational relations and world politics: an introduction" in their Transnational Relations and World Politics (Cambridge: Harvard University Press, 1972), pp. ix-xxix and "Transgovernmental relations and international organizations," World Politics 27, no. 1 (October 1974):39-62.

4. For a plea for a more critical analysis of linkage politics, see Timothy M. Shaw, "The political economy of African international relations," Issue 5, no. 4 (Winter 1975):29-38.

5. Immanuel Wallerstein, "Class and class conflict in contemporary Africa," Canadian Journal of African Studies 7, no. 3 (1973):380. See also T. dos Santos, "The crisis of development theory and the problem of dependence in Latin America," in Underdevelopment and Development: The Third World Today ed. Henry Bernstein (Harmondsworth: Penguin, 1973), p. 79.

6. See Timothy M. Shaw, "The actors in African international politics" in Politics of Africa: Development and Dependence eds. Timothy M. Shaw and Kenneth A. Heard (New York: Africana; and London: Longmans and Dalhousie University Press, 1978), pp. 357-396.

7. See Immanuel Wallerstein, "Africa in a capitalist world," Issue 3, no. 3 (Fall 1973):1-11; and "Class and class conflict in Africa," Monthly Review 26, no. 9 (February 1975):34-42.

8. See Anthony Martin, Minding Their Own Business: Zambia's Struggle Against Western Control (Harmondsworth: Penguin, 1975); and Marcia M. Burdette, "Nationalization in Zambia: A Critique of Bargaining

Theory," Canadian Journal of African Studies 11, no. 3 (1977):471-96.

9. Samir Amin, Neocolonialism in West Africa (Harmondsworth: Penguin, 1973), p. 63.

10. See the useful debate over designations and definitions in Sklar, Corporate Power in an African State (Berkeley: University of California Press, 1975), pp. 198-99 and 206.

11. Ibid., pp. 200-201.

12. On the prospects for national accumulation and class differentiation and on the impact of the new class on Zambian politics, see Karen Eriksen, "Zambia: Class Formation and Détente," Review of African Political Economy 9 (May-August 1978):4-26; and Ian Scott, "Middle class politics in Zambia," African Affairs 77, no. 308 (July 1978):321-34.

13. We are here concerned with the "commercial" type of state corporation, rather than the "semi-commercial" or "noncommercial" institutions identi-fied by Sheridan Johns in his paper "State capital-ism in Zambia: the evolution of the parastatal sector," African Studies Association, San Francisco, October 1975.

14. See, for instance, Colin Leys, Underdevelopment in Kenya: The Political Economy of Neo-Colonialism (Berkeley: University of California Press, 1975); Issa Shivji, Class Struggles in Tanzania (London: Heinemann, 1976); and Miles D. Wolpin, "Dependency and conservative militarism in Mali," Journal of Modern African Studies 13, no. 4 (December 1975): 590-620, especially pp. 598-612.

15. See Giovanni Arrighi, "International corpora-tions, labor aristocracies and economic development in tropical Africa" in Essays on the Political Economy of Africa eds. Giovanni Arrighi and John S. Saul, (New York: Monthly Review, 1973), especially pp. 141-42. For a critique of this approach, see Issa Shivji, "Peasants and class alliances," Review of African Political Economy 3 (May-October 1975): 10-18. For an earlier refutation of Shivji's analy-sis, see John S. Saul, "The state in post colonial societies: Tanzania" in Miliband and Saville, eds., The Socialist Register, 1974, pp. 349-72, especially pp. 359-67.

16. Ian Scott argues in his article on "Middle
class politics in Zambia" that UNIP has largely
abandoned its earlier populist political base as
state capitalism and inflation forced a reevaluation
of its development strategy and patronage resources.
The economic reforms, paradoxically, "not only
created conditions conducive to the growth of a
middle class; the political leadership itself gradually became more dependent on the middle class for
support and less dependent on the mass support of
the party" (p. 327).

17. See Charles Elliott, "Introduction" in his
collection Constraints on the Economic Development
of Zambia (Nairobi: Oxford University Press, 1971),
especially pp. 3-6. On the problems of measuring
dependence, see Jan J. Jorgensen and Timothy M. Shaw,
"International dependence and foreign policy choices:
the political economy of Uganda," Canadian Association of African Studies Ottawa, February 1973;
Richard Vengroff, "Neocolonialism and policy outputs
in Africa," Comparative Political Studies 8, no. 2
(July 1975):234-50; and Patrick J. McGowan, "Economic
dependence and economic performance in Black Africa,"
Journal of Modern African Studies 14, no. 1 (March
1976):25-40.

18. See Alistair Young, Industrial Diversification
in Zambia (New York: Praeger, 1973).

19. See chapter 5 and Douglas G. Anglin, "The
Politics of Transit Routes in Land-Locked Southern
Africa" in Land-locked Countries of Africa ed. Zdenek
Cervenka (Uppsala: Scandinavian Institute of
African Studies, 1973), pp. 98-133.

20. See Charles Elliott, "Growth, Development . . .
or Independence?" in Socio-economic Development in
Dual Economies: The Example of Zambia eds., Heide
and Udo Ernst Simonis (Munich: Weltform Verlag for
African Studies Institute, 1971), pp. 61-94; and
King Copper: The Extraction of Copper and Its Impact
on Zambian Society (London: Europe/Africa Research
Report, 1971).

21. See chapter 2 and Richard Hall, The High Price
of Principles: Kaunda and the White South (Harmondsworth: Penguin, 1973).

22. On Zambia's ambivalence towards multinational
corporations with investments in both Black- and

402

White-ruled Africa, see Sklar, Corporate Power in an African State, pp. 164-78. The collaboration between Zambia's ruling class and corporations with established, and sometimes growing, interests in Southern Africa has been facilitated by "the doctrine of domicile" (p. 184).

23. See Eriksen, "Zambia: Class Formation and Détente," p. 18.

24. On the emergence of a few "semiperipheral" states or "regional middle powers" by either invitation or accident, see Immanuel Wallerstein, "Dependence in an interdependent world: the limited possibilities of transformation within the capitalist world economy," African Studies Review 17, no. 1 (April 1974):1-26; and Norman Girvan, "Economic nationalists v. multinational corporations: revolutionary or evolutionary change?" in Multinational Firms in Africa ed. Carl Widstrand (Uppsala: Scandinavian Institute of African Studies, 1975), pp. 26-56.

25. See Glyn Hughes, "Preconditions of socialist development in Africa," Monthly Review 23, no. 1 (May 1970):11-30; and Tamas Szentes, The Political Economy of Underdevelopment (Budapest: Akademiai Kiado, 1971), pp. 166-89.

26. Richard L. Sklar, "Zambia's Response to the Rhodesian Unilateral Declaration of Independence" in Tordoff, ed., Politics in Zambia, p. 362. Cf. chapter 7, Eriksen, "Zambia: Class Formation and Détente" and Timothy M. Shaw and Agrippah T. Mugomba, "The Political Economy of Regional Détente: Zambia and Southern Africa," Journal of African Studies 4, no. 4 (Winter 1977/78):392-413.

27. See Andrew A. Beveridge, "Economic independence, indigenization, and the African businessman: some effects of Zambia's economic reforms," African Studies Review 17, no. 3 (December 1974):477-90; A. Oberschall, "African traders and small businessmen in Lusaka, Zambia," African Social Research 16 (December 1973):474-502; and Carolyn Baylies, "Class formation and the role of the state in the Zambian economy," University of Zambia Political Studies Seminar, Lusaka, January 1974.

28. Ian Scott comments in his "Middle class politics in Zambia" that "the role of the party was

403

essentially devalued in favor of a tacit alliance
with the middle class" (p. 331). Cf. Jan Pettman,
"Zambia's Second Republic: the creation of a one-
party state," Journal of Modern African Studies 12,
no. 2 (June 1974):231-44 and Tordoff, "Zambia: the
politics of disengagement."

29. See Molteno and Tordoff, "Conclusion" in
Tordoff, ed., Politics in Zambia, especially pp. 385-
401. Ian Scott suggests that "within the middle
class, senior civil servants in particular assumed
greater prominence after the creation of the one-
party state. Indeed, the political leadership and
the senior civil servants, who had previously been
suspicious of each other, drew together to the point
where a number of positions became interchangeable"
("Middle class politics in Zambia," p. 331).

30. See Arghiri Emmanuel, "White settler colonialism
and the myth of investment imperialism," New Left
Review 73 (May-June 1972):35-57; Kenneth Good,
"Settler colonialism in Rhodesia," African Affairs
73, no. 290 (January 1974):10-36; and Sklar, Corporate Power in an African State, pp. 179-88.

31. See Charles Harvey, "The Structure of Zambian
Development," University of Zambia Economics Seminar,
Lusaka, January 1974; and Charles Elliott, Patterns
of Poverty in the Third World (New York: Praeger for
World Council of Churches, 1975), passim.

32. See Michael Burawoy, The Colour of Class on the
Copper Mines: From African Advancement to Zambian-
isation, Zambian Papers Number 7 (Lusaka: Institute
for African Studies, University of Zambia, 1972);
King Copper, p. 2; Martin, Minding Their Own Business, p. 22; and Cherry Gertzel, "Labour and the
State: The Case of Zambia's Mineworkers Union—A
Review Article," Journal of Commonwealth and Comparative Politics 13, no. 3 (November 1975):290-304.

33. For data on income distribution between sectors
of the Zambian economy, see ILO Report to the Gov-
ernment of Zambia on Incomes, Wages and Prices in
Zambia: Policy and Machinery (Lusaka: Government
Printer, 1969), p. 9, cited in Frank C. Ballance,
Zambia and the East African Community, Eastern Afri-
can Studies I (Syracuse: Syracuse University Pro-
gram of Eastern African Studies, 1971), p. 84;
Republic of Zambia, Second National Development Plan
(Lusaka: Government Printer, 1971), p. 11; and

404

Timothy M. Shaw, Dependence and Underdevelopment: The Development and Foreign Policies of Zambia, Papers in International Studies, Africa Series No. 28 (Athens, Ohio: University Center for International Studies, 1976).

34. See Robert Molteno, "Cleavage and conflict in Zambian politics: a study in sectionalism," in Politics in Zambia, ed., Tordoff, pp. 62-106, especially p. 100.

35. See Robert H. Bates, Patterns of Uneven Development: Causes and Consequences in Zambia, Monograph Series in World Affairs, 11, no. 3 (Denver: University of Denver, 1974).

36. See Donald Rothchild, "Rural-Urban Inequities and Resource Allocation in Zambia," Journal of Commonwealth Political Studies 10, no. 3 (November 1972):222-42.

37. See Ann Seidman, "Varsity corner: the haves and have-nots," Times of Zambia, 30 March 1974, p. 4; reprinted in Africa Institute Bulletin 12, no. 4 (1974):168-70.

38. For the dilemmas posed by political and economic indulgence since independence, see John Markakis and Robert L. Curry, "The Global Economy's Impact on Recent Budgetary Politics in Zambia," Journal of African Studies 3, no. 4 (Winter 1976/77):403-27.

39. Scott, "Middle class politics in Zambia," pp. 332, 333-34.

40. See Republic of Zambia, Economic Report, 1973 and Annual Review: performance of the Zambian economy (Lusaka: Government Printer, 1974). For more details of rural and agricultural underdevelopment, see Shaw, Dependence and Underdevelopment.

41. See Amin, Neocolonialism in West Africa, especially p. xiv; and Ann Seidman, Comparative Development Strategies in East Africa (Nairobi: East African Publishing House, 1972), especially pp. 1-59.

42. See Ann Seidman, "The Distorted Growth of Import Substitution Industry: The Zambian Case," Journal of Modern African Studies 12, no. 4 (December 1974):601-31.

43. See Ann Seidman, "Multinational corporations and economic dependence in Africa," African Social Research 19 (June 1975):739-50.

44. Seidman, "The haves and have-nots." For further details on the invisible outflow, see Shaw, Dependence and Underdevelopment, pp. 32-35.

45. Cf. R. M. Bostock, "The transport sector" in Constraints on the economic development of Zambia ed. Elliott, pp. 323-76; Anglin, "The Politics of Transit Routes in Land-Locked Southern Africa"; and Sklar, Corporate Power in an African State, pp. 156-64.

46. See D. C. Mulaisho, "When the copper mines fall silent," Enterprise (March 1974):27-30.

47. For a review of alternative development strategies open to African states, from self-reliance and the noncapitalist path to external integration and counterpenetration, see Timothy M. Shaw and Malcolm J. Grieve, "Dependence or development: a review article on international and internal inequalities in Africa," Development and Change 8, no. 3 (July 1977):377-408; "Inequalities and the State in Africa," Review of Black Political Economy 8, no. 1 (Fall 1977):27-42; and "Dependence as an approach to understanding continuing inequalities in Africa," Journal of Developing Areas 13, no. 3 (April 1979).

48. See Sklar, Corporate Power in an African State, especially pp. 192-216; and Eriksen, "Zambia: Class Formation and Détente," pp. 19-22.

49. See Rothchild, "Rural-Urban Inequities and Resource Allocation in Zambia," p. 232.

50. For analyses of this series of reforms, see Bastiaan de Gaay Fortman, ed., After Mulungushi: The Economics of Zambian Humanism (Nairobi: East African Publishing House, 1969); M. L. O. Faber and J. G. Potter, Towards Economic Independence: Papers on the Nationalization of the Copper Industry in Zambia (Cambridge: Cambridge University Press, 1971); Mark Bostock and Charles Harvey, eds., Economic Independence and Zambian Copper: A Case Study of Foreign Investment (New York: Praeger, 1972); and Martin, Minding Their Own Business.

51. For suggestive but preliminary analyses of

parastatals in Zambia, see Sheridan Johns, "Para-
statal bodies in Zambia: problems and prospects,"
in Socio-economic Development in Dual Economies
eds. Simonis, pp. 217-51 and "State capitalism in
Zambia: the evolution of the parastatal sector";
Paul Semonin, "Nationalisation and management in
Zambia," Maji Maji 1 (January 1971); George K.
Simwinga, "The Copper-Mining Industry of Zambia:
A Case Study of Nationalization for Control," in
What Government Does, Sage Yearbooks in Politics
and Public Policy 1 (1975):84-93; and Michael
Williams, "State participation in the Zambian
economy," World Development 1, no. 10 (1974):43-54.

52. See James Fry, "Varsity corner: socialism and
state capitalism," Times of Zambia, 30 July 1971,
p. 4; and "Management question: profits or employment?", Enterprise 1 (1975):37-39.

53. For the major presidential declarations on
Humanism, see Kenneth D. Kaunda, Humanism in Zambia
and a Guide to Its Implementation (Lusaka: Govern-
ment Printer, 1968), Take up the Challenge (Lusaka:
Government Printer, 1970), and The Challenge of the
Future (Lusaka: Government Printer, 1973).

54. See Robert Molteno, "Zambian Humanism: The Way
Ahead," The African Review 3, no. 4 (1973):541-57;
N. Sefelino Mulenga, "Humanism and the Logic of
Self-Sufficiency," Lusaka, September 1973, reprinted
in Zambia Daily Mail, 30 and 31 January 1974; and
Timothy K. Kandeke, Fundamentals of Zambian Humanism
(Lusaka: Neczam, 1977).

55. See Saul, "Socialism in one country: Tanzania,"
in Essays on the Political Economy of Africa eds.,
Arrighi and Saul, pp. 237-335 and "The state in
post-colonial societies: Tanzania."

56. See Kenneth D. Kaunda, A Humanist in Africa:
Letters to Colin M. Morris (London: Longmans, 1966),
and Letter to My Children (London: Longmans, 1973).

57. See Kenneth D. Kaunda, Humanism in Zambia and a
Guide to Its Implementation, Part II (Lusaka:
Government Printer, 1974).

58. Ibid., p. 110.

59. Ibid., p. 98.

60. Sklar, <u>Corporate Power in an African State</u>, p. 207.

61. See Scott, "Middle Class Politics in Zambia."

62. <u>Zambia Daily Mail</u>, 4 July 1974, p. 1.

63. <u>Zambia Daily Mail</u>, 1 July 1975, pp. 8-10.

64. See Molteno and Tordoff, "Conclusion," pp. 385-399.

65. Sklar, <u>Corporate Power in an African State</u>, p. 8.

66. Molteno and Tordoff, "Conclusion," p. 394.

11
Conclusion: Zambia as a Middle Power

Although Zambia was not among the first group of African states to achieve independence, nevertheless she rapidly achieved a considerable stature in continental affairs in general and regional affairs in particular because of her position and role in the front line of the liberation struggle against white minority rule. Furthermore, her considerable economic resources and potential have given her both status and visibility, enabling her to command some attention in world politics as a whole. These two factors, along with the presence and preferences of the President and his advisers, reinforce each other in practice: global resources, regional activism, and national leadership are a compelling combination. After a decade and a half as an independent actor in international relations, Zambia has emerged as an aspiring middle power at both the regional and Third World levels. Although at the global level somewhat dependent, she is increasingly influential in Southern African and continental affairs—an essential qualification for a new middle power in contemporary world politics.

Zambia is a middle power in several senses of the term. At the global level, she is in the middle rank of states on the criteria of national resources and capabilities; these attributes, in turn, find reflection in her ability to exert influence over others as well as in the perceptions held by other actors of her as an influential state. At the level of the Third World and the continent, Zambia is a middle power in terms of both her recognized ability to forge and reflect a consensus and her willingness and capacity to mediate between contending countries and factions in the nonaligned and Pan-African movements. In regional affairs, as a Front Line State she is literally in the middle of the continuing Southern African crisis. In addition to being geographically central, Zambia has also evolved a national political economy that is, in many ways, in the middle in terms of ideology and ethics: it is neither capitalist nor socialist, Western democratic nor authoritarian. Rather, it is a careful amalgam of ideas and institutions combined in a unique manner which reinforces Zambia's claim to a nonaligned middle power status externally.

In this concluding chapter, we attempt to provide an analytic overview of Zambia's emerging role in regional, continental and global relations. In particular, we seek, first, to relate her choice of development strategy to constraints on her foreign policy, pointing to a growing domestic debate over both questions, secondly, to examine alternative explanations of Zambia's external diplomacy and relationships and, thirdly, to compare the Zambian case with other studies of African foreign policy. This final essay is, then, both more analytic and more conceptual than earlier chapters; it is presented in conclusion in an attempt to stimulate further research and debate given the particular problems, opportunities and dilemmas presently confronting the Zambian nation and state.

REORGANIZATIONALIST STRATEGY AND REGIONAL COMMITMENT

Zambia's position as an emergent middle power has not been achieved without skill and effort. Indeed, she might have more readily slipped into a less controversial, less committed, less visible and less costly role by adopting a "Malawi"-type response to entrenched white power in Southern Africa. Despite this, she has at times in the past been accused by some, mainly external, critics of being cautious in her support for the liberation movements, especially when significant national interests have come into conflict with the mounting demands of regional confrontation. Moreover, the "honeymoon" period of the late 1960s, which was characterized by confidence in orthodox development strategies nationally, steady disengagement from dependence regionally, and buoyant copper prices internationally, had by the middle and late 1970s given way to a series of interconnected crises. These revolved around a new scepticism about the prospects for the national political economy, mounting concern over the ineluctable escalation of the conflict in Southern Africa, and the multiple impacts of a continuing low price for copper globally leading to rapidly rising indebtedness and negative

410

growth. As noted in chapter 1, these interrelated
and continuing crises constitute a major challenge,
with both immediate and longer-term implications for
the overall direction of the foreign policy and development strategies Zambia has pursued since
Independence. Together, they pose fundamental questions about the future of Zambia's political economy
and international relations.

Zambia's struggle to overcome her inheritance
of dependence on a network of formative factors—
copper, the White South, and the advanced industrialized economies, particularly Britain—led to the
adoption during the first decade of an essentially
"promotive" style of external behavior at the global
level and of an "intransigent" style at the regional
level, in part as a response to two major crises
with Rhodesia. At the global level, Lusaka has
tried since 1964 to "shape the demands of its present structures and its present environment to each
other" through a series of negotiations, while, at
the regional level, given the pervasiveness of white
minority rule, it has sought "to render its environment consistent with its present structures, thus
engaging in the politics of intransigent adaptation."[1] On the one hand, then, Zambia has eschewed
the more permissive possibilities of either "acquiescent" or "preservative" adaptation;[2] yet, on the
other hand, she has not been able to achieve as
great a measure of self-reliance or disengagement
as she would have liked. Nevertheless, once liberation has been realized throughout the subcontinent,
it is conceivable that the Zambian government will
attempt to advance regional integration through the
articulation of a preservative stance, that is "to
live within the limitations that its present structures and its present environment impose on each
other."[3]

The "middle road" that Zambia has followed in
responding and adapting to her inherited global
links, has been characterized by Donald Rothchild
and Robert Curry as following a strategy of "reorganization" rather than one of either "accommodation" or "transformation."[4] In other words, she
has been neither permissive nor resistant in an
unequivocal way, but rather has adopted a pragmatic
bargaining position through which to achieve a
cluster of goals—national development, regional
liberation and global redistribution.

Zambia has maintained and modified, rather
than simply accepting or rejecting links with Western capitalist economies, and has attempted to make

use of these continuing connections to bring pressure
on the white regimes. Instead of adopting a more
radical posture against the West, such as Tanzania
and Algeria have done on occasion, she has chosen to
pursue a less doctrinaire approach. This is typical
of reorganizationalist states generally which, "as
a consequence of their relative success in gaining
their immediate economic growth objectives, are
highly pragmatic in their approach to economic development questions generally."[5] This strategy may have
significant implications for Zambia's political economy and future international orientation.

In some ways, because of the nature of her transition to independence and because of the character
of her inherited political economy, Zambia had little
choice but to move quite cautiously in revising her
links with the West. Nevertheless, in the 1960s and
since, Zambia did act decisively, though less exten-
sively than Tanzania, to redefine the terms of her
participation in the world economy. In some respects,
Tanzania could afford to pursue a more radical "trans-
formationalist strategy" because she did not share
Zambia's strategic resources, geographical constric-
tions, historical links with the South, or exposure
to retaliation. As Rothchild and Curry explain,
"because Zambians consider their country to be more
dependent and intertwined with the world economy than
its more rural and agriculturally based neighbor, they
are more cautious in redefining their relationship to
the multinational corporations in their midst. . . .
Zambia's inevitable reliance on the production of
copper for export rather than agriculture as the main-
stay of national revenues tends to make the system
reformist rather than revolutionary."[6]

As the price of copper has fallen in the mid-1970s
and Zambia's indebtedness to international banking and
financial institutions for the flow of foreign exchange
has increased, her definition of a "reorganizational"
strategy has in practice tended to moderate. Moreover,
the pressures to accommodate to external demands and
conditions, such as devaluation, austerity budgeting
and investment guarantees, have been reinforced by internal inequalities. Yet, even before the twin constraints of external debt and internal change impinged
so markedly, Zambia's mercantilist objectives were
quite limited. As Rothchild and Curry comment:

Rather than precluding foreign investment, nationalization, pragmatically applied, may facilitate
external participation by removing many of the
uncertainties associated with investment in Third

412

World countries. Surely all of the states adopting a reorganization strategy have gone far, some contend too far, in reaching accommodations with international capitalism. A dramatic case in point is the [initial] agreement on the nationalization of the Zambian mining industry.[7]

The series of negotiations between the Zambian state and multinational corporations in the mining and other sectors have led not only to the state's continued integration into the world economy but also to the incorporation of many of its elite—both private and parastatal—into a transnational network. Thus, the position of the state and of its entrepreneurs and "managers" are mutually reinforcing, and further inform and constrain Zambia's choice of a moderate reorganizational strategy.

During the nation's second decade of independence, the growth in strength and scope of activity, and in competence and confidence of the nascent Zambian middle class has attracted close attention and generated a lively debate over its character, composition and influence, domestically and externally. Nevertheless, no adequate class analysis of Zambian society has yet been attempted; nor is there agreement even on the appropriate terminology to employ. On the other hand, a consensus has emerged among commentators on two points. The first is the existence of identifiable and sometimes competing fractions within the "bourgeoisie", reflecting their differing degrees of dependence on the state, the party, and transnational associations for employment, contracts, licences and loans; these distinctions account for much of the variation observable in the political and social outlooks of the somewhat disparate elements comprising the bourgeoisie. But, secondly, despite its diversity, the Zambian bourgeoisie—whether designated as "bureaucratic," "national," or by some other label—shares a considerable commonality of interest, particularly with respect to rival classes, the acquisition of land and property, national development and external linkages. This convergence of views is reinforced by the prevalence of crosscutting ties characteristic of a small, close-knit community drawn together by common educational experiences, distinctive life styles, and often kinship ties. Moreover, mobility in and out of the public and private sectors remains easy and frequent. The more elusive development goals and regional liberation have become, the more outspoken have certain members of the middle class been in reiterating demands for a more flexible approach to world politics (less "nonalignment"), to

413

regional commitments (less "liberation support"), and
to national economics (less "intervention"). Accordingly, they have sought not only effectively to redefine the reorganizationalist strategy to provide
for less state involvement but also to press for conflict resolution and an economic modus vivendi in
Southern Africa.

Eriksen takes the argument one step further by
asserting that the fractions within the bourgeoisie
have succeeded in imposing their interests on the
state. "The process of internal class formation
since independence," she suggests, ". . . although
less immediate in its effects on state policy" than
the impact of the current economic crisis, is "fundamental to the direction in which Zambia is moving,"
since it involves "the growth of an indigenous property owning group closely tied to the state which is
in turn increasingly prone to articulate its interests."[8] This is the point at which a consensus on
class analysis in Zambia breaks down; there is still
insufficient empirical evidence to establish a clear,
causal connection between the expression of elite
demands and foreign policy behavior, especially with
respect to Southern Africa.

The task of assessing official regime respon-
siveness to class concerns is complicated by the
fact that, not only do some of the demands arise from
within the government itself, but also bourgeois
spokesmen, in arguing that Zambia's Southern African
stance is the major cause of domestic shortages, inflation, negative growth, unemployment, inefficiencies
and other grievances, are merely articulating and
amplifying upon widely shared popular perceptions. As
suggested in chapter 1, even in the case of tactical
retreats such as the partial reopening of the Rhodesian
border in 1978, it is not possible automatically to
assume that this decision is solely or even mainly a
response to bourgeois economic interests. Eriksen
concedes that the costs of confrontation, if perhaps
not the policy itself, have become "a point of contention not only among Zambia's businessmen, large and
small, foreign and national, but also among the mass
of its urban and rural populations." At the same time,
she is skeptical that the masses are capable of seeing
"their problems as deriving from support of the liberation struggle"; on the contrary, "the couching of demands for policy change in populist terms" is explained
away as middle class "manipulation of mass discontent
to promote changes ultimately in accord with the long
run interests of the emergent bourgeoisie."[9] That may
very well be the eventual outcome; it is less certain
that it is the cause.

414

The ability of the Zambian bourgeoisie to affect foreign policy, particularly at the regional level, is limited by the force of nationalism on the one hand and by the dominance of the President in such matters on the other hand. Moreover, classes are still in formation in Zambia, and so rather inchoate in ideology and action. Finally, domestic pressures for moderation are counterbalanced by the relative militancy of the liberation movements and other influential African states with whom Zambia seeks to collaborate closely—especially Tanzania and Mozambique on whom she is heavily dependent for transit rights. Consequently, as Rothchild and Curry observe, "on questions of colonialism or white racism, there is little to differentiate [reorganizationalist] policies from those put forth by the states adopting a transformationist strategy."[10] Even Eriksen concedes that,

> it could be argued that, in the light of Zambia's historically defined orientation towards the West and envelopment within the Southern African regional economy, its foreign policy would automatically have meshed with that of the Western powers. Such a simplistic argument, however, overlooks the very real attempts made by the government to weaken such constraints and to stake out an independent position for the country.[11]

Nevertheless, it is necessary to recognize that the intrusion of class-type politics into Zambia's political economy has potentially important implications for her foreign policy at all levels of interaction, including the regional. If the first decade of independence was characterized by a consensus on external affairs, then the second, more difficult decade may provoke a new debate over objectives and options in foreign policy in its several forms.

IMPLICATIONS OF DEVELOPMENT STRATEGY FOR EXTERNAL RELATIONS

Although empirical data on class formation and effectiveness in Zambia is limited and controversial, there is mounting evidence of growing dissension within the country over both external and internal policies, despite the constraints of national ideology, unity and security. The intensification of this "grand debate" has coincided with and been fueled by the low price of copper and consequent economic

415

difficulties nationally, the escalation of military, political and racial conflict regionally, and the elusiveness of economic and strategic support globally.

A major forum for the articulation of alternative directions in development strategies and external economic relations, especially overseas linkages, was the high-powered Special Parliamentary Select Committee, appointed in October 1977 under the chairmanship of Finance Minister John Mwanakatwe to "consider and endorse" the President's emergency program of action for economic development.[12] The Committee reflected a wide spectrum of ideological perspectives and interests, both public and private.[13] Although its recommendations represented a consensus or at least a composite of the views of its members, it is possible to reconstruct in rough outline the lines of division between what may be loosely characterized as the "progressive" and the "conservative" interpretations of Zambian Humanism and nationalism. While economic orthodoxy by no means went unchallenged, it received greater prominence, more explicit expression, and greater legitimacy than on any previous occasion since Independence. In fact, in many respects, the Committee's Report may be considered a conservative manifesto.

Evidence of a "progressive" input into the Mwanakatwe Report can be found in the proposal for an Emergency Development Plan which would be "primarily rural oriented" with a view, among other things, to promoting self-reliance in food production. This Plan was also intended to accord priority to "employment generation through labor intensive techniques" and "small-scale industries." Other recommended reforms included action to narrow the urban-rural gap in terms of incomes and services, urgent measures to "diversify the economy away from copper" and into other minerals, manufacturing and markets, and a reduction in the "real burden" of external debt. In addition, there were sweeping proposals for a reorganization of UNIP along more democratic lines.[14]

The "conservative" prescription for Zambia's ills was outlined in greater detail. The Report noted the "alarming increase" in government expenditure over the past decade and urged an immediate, drastic reduction by reallocating resources from defense to development,[15] ending free social services, phasing out consumer subsidies, and reducing "overemployment" in the public and parastatal sectors. Moreover, in order to ensure that the "redeployment" of redundant workers and others into "productive

416

farming" become a "reality", the Report considered
it essential to have careful and proper planning,
including "attractive incentives," and some revision of the Leadership Code; moreover, in the case
of the urban unemployed, "some form of coercive redeployment compatible with our humanistic requirements" was necessary. More directly relevant to
Zambia's external relations was the strong recommen-
dation that further steps be taken to "encourage
private investment from within and without the country," along with a plea that "inflammatory statements by leaders which have the effect of scaring
away potential investors should be discouraged."
Coupled with this was strong support for the institutionalization of "a major and meaningful advisory
role" for the private sector in the formulation of
economic policy, including direct representation on
a revitalized National Commission for Development
Planning and close involvement in the government's
"export promotion efforts."
    The Mwanakatwe Report may usefully be con-
trasted with recent, if somewhat earlier, writings
of a rather more "radical" persuasion, notably
Timothy Kandeke's socialist interpretation and defense of the ideology of Humanism. As noted in
chapter 2, he sees many of the very solutions proposed by the Select Committee—insistence on strict
economic criteria, cutbacks in social services, and
increased private investment—as obstacles to the
achievement of a socialist, and therefore a Humanist, political economy.[16]
    The report of the 1975 International Labour
Office (ILO) employment advisory mission, by focusing attention on a "basic needs" approach to development, also raised issues with important implications
for Zambia's external economic linkages. The start-
ing point of its inquiry was the assertion that development strategies since Independence had reinforced rather than reduced class disparities. On the
basis of limited data for 1972-73, the report estimated that "the richest 2 per cent of all households
account for roughly 20 per cent of the entire national
household income which is about the same as the share
of the poorest 50 per cent." Not only do "few countries elsewhere in the world display a comparable
degree of income inequality," but "the inequality seems
to have widened over time";[17] since 1973, with the
dramatic decline in real terms of the national product, the gap has undoubtedly increased further. The
Mission readily acknowledged that the country had
achieved "remarkable progress" since Independence and

that its failures were often for reasons beyond the government's control. Time and again, external developments had

> obstructed Zambia's attempts to pursue a steady path of sustained development. Beginning with UDI in late 1965, Zambia has been forced on several occasions to undertake major, rapid and extremely costly measures to restructure its trade links, its transportation routes, its fuel supplies and sources, the types and specifications of imported equipment—in short, to replace the whole set of inherited links with the South [with] new alignments consistent with priorities of Independence.

Nevertheless, despite heroic efforts to break with the patterns of the past, the "old dualities" had unfortunately reappeared over and over again: "the rural-urban gap has widened; the dominance of large-scale, formal sector, capital-intensive production persists; and the inequalities in the structure of incomes has increased." In spite of the "enormous expenditures" on development during the first decade, the report concluded, "the majority of Zambians have so far gained little from them and most of the rural population have not benefited very much."[18]
 A major policy prescription arising from this ILO assessment was the need for a radical restructuring of the pattern of Zambia's foreign trade. This required not only the energetic promotion and diversification of exports but, even more important, the gearing of imports to "the basic needs of all the population, rather than the luxury consumption of a few." Although some changes have since been effected to limit "non-essential" foreign expenditure, in the early seventies Zambia's list of imports was "that of an affluent society" and bore "little relation to the needs of the vast majority of the country's population."[19]

> Despite numerous Party and government pronouncements to the contrary, much manufacturing development in Zambia has been largely capital-intensive, urban-located, and oriented towards the production of luxury goods . . . . Even in consumer goods production, many of the new consumer goods factories catered more for the luxury market than for the provision of necessities. Thus we find that Zambia assembles Fiat . . . and Land Rover motor vehicles, but has no plant to manufacture bicycles or hoes.

418

Hence the report recommends a "major shift" in the allocation of investment resources in favor of rural areas.

> The way to a self-reliant economy in Zambia is clearly to build up the productive potential in the rural sector. Increased production of food grains will help to meet the country's basic needs for food, while reducing Zambia's dependence on imports. It will help produce the raw materials which can feed indigenous industries . . . . Over the longer run it must contribute also to the diversification of Zambia's exports.[20]

The ILO report recognizes that Zambia is "at present committed to an acceptance of foreign and private domestic investment in certain sectors," and outlines the basis of "a mutually beneficial trade-off" which would enable the country to attract investment "at least possible cost to the Zambian economy." Accordingly, it urges the government to adopt an Investment Code providing specific "guarantees against sudden arbitrary changes in the conditions affecting private enterprise," but in return to introduce an excess profits tax and make full use of other instruments of governmental control. In particular, it should employ discriminatory investment allowances, employment subsidies, tariff protection and other fiscal techniques to encourage the use of more labor-intensive technology, the location of factories away from the line of rail, greater use of local inputs, and more rapid Zambianization.[21]

The Mission's greatest concern was not that the government would reject its recommendations but fear that it would accept them but fail to implement them. As it reiterated repeatedly, "the problem is not that past policies are wrong, but that many have not been implemented. . . . One of the striking features about Zambian development planning is the gap between policies, plans and actions," between Humanist rhetoric and reality. Although the authors are cautious in attributing blame for the poor performance in the past, they do suggest that "one of the major bottlenecks" is "the lack of will and commitment" on the part of the government. This raises the question whether the decision makers—who also constitute the principal beneficiaries of the present inequities—can reasonably be expected to press ahead with changes in domestic and foreign policies designed to effect "a sustained and concerted shift of priorities" in favor of the majority who still lack the basic necessities of life.[22]   As Dresang explains with reference to the Zambian bureaucracy,

> the wealth and status of civil servants in a generally poor country set them apart and gave them a vested interest in a specific kind of political order. The absence of egalitarianism is underlined by the limited capacity of the administrative system to engineer rapid and widespread economic development.[23]

This is a dilemma of development in a reorganizationalist mode: the inability of the Zambian bureaucratic bourgeoisie to effect fundamental change because its own values and interests stand in contrast to the intent and goals of Humanist principles. Paradoxically, the very class that Humanism seeks to constrain is also the central instrument of state policy and action. Recognition of this contradiction helps account for the ambivalence underlying much of the Report of the Special Parliamentary Select Committee and the factional politics it reflects. A further obstacle to a Humanistic development strategy stems from the ever-increasing claims of Southern African liberation on Zambia's dwindling resources; for proponents of social justice, domestic development and regional confrontation represent competing goals in terms of salience and sequence.

Zambia's foreign and development policies, like those of many African and Third World countries, contain a series of apparent inconsistencies or contradictions, in part because of continuing yet changing sets of internal and external demands. Nevertheless, as Tordoff and Molteno assert,

> despite the powerful presence of foreign capital and a large domestic capitalist system, the UNIP government has carried through radical measures which have placed the control of the economy in Zambian hands . . . . Finally, despite a colonial legacy of extreme dependence on the South and vulnerability to its pressures, Zambia has been consistently in the forefront of the struggle to liberate Southern Africa.[24]

On the other hand, they recognize that such policies are fragile, in particular because of the small base of support available to the President in his attempts to confront privilege and radicalize the country:

420

The problem of institutionalizing Humanism is
compounded by the fact that its values run
counter to the dominant values in Zambian
society. Among all classes materialism is
more firmly entrenched than ever before as the
supreme ethic.[25]

ALTERNATIVE EXPLANATIONS
FOR FOREIGN POLICY

The identification of interrelated internal and
external factors and complexities in the making of
Zambia's foreign and development policy points not
only to certain difficulties in policy formulation
for Zambia herself, but also to the need for more
sophisticated analysis as well. In chapters 3 and
10, we pointed to some structures and processes involved in Zambia's foreign policy system. But, to
advance our understanding of Zambia's decision making
and external behavior further, we need to recognize
a series of alternative factors and explanations. We
begin this task by reviewing several approaches to
the study of foreign policy in Africa in general before turning back, in conclusion, to the case of
Zambia in particular.

Remarkably few attempts have been made thus far
to develop either an approach to or a theory of foreign policy making in Africa, despite the growth of
studies in comparative foreign policy in recent
years, stimulated initially by James N. Rosenau's
work on "pre-theory".[26] W. A. E. Skurnik has used
Rosenau's typology in an effort to organize and
explain Senegal's foreign policy in different issue
areas. Skurnik concluded, unlike Rosenau himself,
that for Senegal, systemic factors were most salient,
followed by domestic variables (governmental, societal and role), with individual and idiosyncratic
being the least salient variables.[27] He suggested
that, while President Senghor tends to set the tone
for his country in terms of orientation and philosophy, in practice "both adaptation and change . . .
appear largely as responses to threats emanating
from, and as a search for opportunities inherent in,
the international environment."[28]

Okwudiba Nnoli, in an analysis of Tanzania's
foreign policy, also uses a linkage approach, but
combines it with a rather orthodox concern for national power and interest.[29] He too emphasizes the
predominant role of the president and examines the
evolution of Tanzanian socialism towards self-

reliance. However, he goes beyond previous modes of analysis of African foreign policy by dealing with the roles of the state and parastatals and by treating the internal debate over development strategy and foreign policy. Indeed, his own concluding chapter on the future of Tanzania's self-reliance shares many concerns with the present conclusion—continuity and change, choice and constraints, class conflict and the country's position in the world system[30]—issues over which more traditional inquiries like that of Skurnik have paid insufficient attention.

A contemporary and general framework through which to examine the foreign policies of African states, comparable to that of Nnoli, has also been presented by Olajide Aluko. He categorizes variables according to the orthodox internal-external dichotomy but incorporates some novel and characteristically "African" factors within them as well, in an attempt to render his framework more applicable to OAU members. Within the "domestic setting", Aluko includes the economy, internal political pressures, colonial heritage, and the nature and ideology of the governing elites, while within the "external environment" he treats geographical location, the proximity of colonial territories and white supremacist regimes, and the cold war environment.[31] Whilst Aluko has not ranked these factors in order of potency for African states in his volume of case studies, he has evaluated their relative strengths in a comparative historical analysis of Nigerian-Ghanaian interactions and policy making.[32]

Aluko's collection of essays on African foreign policies includes one of our own on Zambia in which we attempt to identify alternative factors and explanations for Zambia's policy and behavior. These range from the "idiosyncratic" or individual—Kaunda's character and style, especially his "mission" in Southern Africa—through geopolitics and the political economy of regionalism to global dependency. Other factors mentioned, as in the present chapter, include the new class structure of Zambia, strategic questions—notably the regional and global balances of power and the strategic importance of Southern Africa—Zambia's interest in popular, united and viable regimes in neighboring states, and national economic imperatives, such as transit routes, the price of copper and security of supply.[33]

This set of possible explanations ranges, then, from state-as-actor assumptions (for instance, stable neighbors and national mercantilism) through internal institutions (e.g., class formation and Kaunda's

422

personality) to external factors (regional pressures and global dependency). Clearly, as Skurnik recognizes in his own study of Senegal and we suggest in chapter 3, the ranking of factors for any country varies according to time period, issue area and degree of crisis.

Whilst the development of even a pre-theory of either Zambian or African foreign policy is still for the future, nevertheless, the recognition of a range of actors, issue areas and rankings is an essential beginning. Given the wide variety of policies and behaviors to be analyzed, some combination of variables and approaches seems essential for comprehensive and confident explanation. However, a greater degree of self-consciousness about different levels of analysis and interaction and alternative approaches and explanations is likely to advance understanding. Accordingly, we attempt to identify three possible explanatory approaches to the study of the foreign policy of Zambia and other African states, based on the level of actor involvement.

As earlier intimated, domestic and external pressures are inextricably linked in determining the foreign policy of any state. This is especially so for relatively open, poor and dependent political economies such as Zambia's. This approach means discounting two increasingly inappropriate distinctions—firstly, between domestic and international forces and, secondly, between governmental and non-governmental institutions—and accepting instead that all kinds of influences affect policy making and outputs to a greater or lesser extent. At the same time, for purposes of analysis of foreign policy formulation and execution, it is useful to distinguish between internal and external organizations as authoritative and regular actors, and also, within the state, between central decision makers and other institutions.

We have already identified several types of actors in Zambia's foreign policy system in chapter 3, and several varieties of explanation in chapters 1 and 9. Here, we try to situate such typologies and the debates about them in the context of more general questions of foreign policy in Africa. Table 11.1 represents an attempt to summarize some of the basic distinctions that can be usefully made amongst levels of analysis and types of approach in the case of Zambia. As this table indicates, most of our own work, and indeed most of the work in the fields of both Zambian and African

423

TABLE 11.1
Types of Actors, Goals and Analysis in Zambia's Foreign Policy

	Actor Type		
	State	Internal Institutions	External Institutions
Examples of actors	Zambia State House UNIP	Ministries Parastatals Factions & classes	International organizations Multinational corporations Liberation movements
Goals	Development Unity/social harmony Security Freedom Liberation	Growth/resources Status/recognition Accumulation	Access Support Association

Modes of analysis	National interest/
	  ideology/power
	Transactions
	Rational actor
	  model
		Decision making
		Bureaucratic politics
		Transnationalism
		Pluralism
			Geopolitics
			Dependence
			Diplomacy
			Bargaining

Relevant chapters	all	2, 3, 7, 9, 10, 11	3, 4, 6, 8, 10, 11

foreign policy, is based on the premise that the
state is the dominant actor. There is still only
limited recognition or analysis of the growing range
of other internal and external institutions involved
in influencing foreign policy outcomes in an African
state like Zambia.

Obviously the centrality of the state cannot be
ignored, particularly at times of crisis. However,
during noncrises, and over issue areas involving
"low" politics, such as routine economic and social
questions, a much broader range of actors are involved and influential. As previously noted, both
Zambia's development strategy of "reorganization"
and her regional policy of "disengagement" are under
attack from internal and external interests.
Clearly we cannot expect fully to explain either the
continuities or the discontinuities, the consisten-
cies and the contradictions in Zambia's foreign
policy without reference to nonstate, nonofficial
actors as well as to official national institutions.

The ultimate test of the validity and utility
of any particular approach or theory is whether it
can predict the future and not merely explain the
past and present. Given the volatility of African
politics, especially in Southern Africa, we hesitate
to hazard projections on the future of Zambia in
world politics. However, we hope that this set of
essays, particularly those which identify salient
forces and factors, will aid understanding and
analysis. Clearly Zambia's foreign policy will
continue to reflect the interests of the state as
well as other internal and external institutions,
but the balance between President and Party, classes
and copper, regional and global interactions remains
problematic.

Nevertheless, the developing national political
economy, the changing regional situation, and shifts
in the global order will all impact, in varying
degrees, on the foreign policy orientation and actions of Zambia. These three levels of interaction
are, of course, interrelated and are inseparable
from the growing debate inside Zambia herself about
foreign and development policies. While Zambia is
unlikely to abandon a reorganizational stance, the
definition, interpretation and implementation of
Humanism and liberation will continue to evolve in
the future as they have since Independence. Moreover, given her considerable resources, established
role and distinctive position, Zambia will continue
to merit recognition as an important middle power
in world affairs.[34]

425

NOTES

1.   James N. Rosenau, The Adaptation of National
Societies: A Theory of Political System Behavior and
Transformation (New York: McCaleb-Seiler, 1970),
p. 4.

2.   James N. Rosenau, "Foreign Policy as Adaptive
Behavior: Some Preliminary Notes for a Theoretical
Model," Comparative Politics 2, no. 3 (April 1970):
365-387.

3.   Rosenau, The Adaptation of National Societies,
p. 4.

4.   Donald Rothchild and Robert L. Curry, Scarcity,
Choice, and Public Policy in Middle Africa (Berkeley:
University of California Press, 1978), pp. 114, 147.

5.   Ibid., pp. 119-120.   For a discussion of alternative development strategies in Africa, see Timothy
M. Shaw and Malcolm J. Grieve, "Dependence or Development: A Review Article on International and Internal Inequalities in Africa," Development and Change
8, no. 3 (July 1977):377-408, and "Inequalities and
the State in Africa," Review of Black Political
Economy 8 (Fall 1977):27-42.

6.   Rothchild and Curry, Scarcity, Choice and Public Policy in Middle Africa, pp. 136-137.

7.   Ibid., p. 132.

8.   Karen Eriksen, "Zambia: Class Formation and
Detente," Review of African Political Economy 9
(May-August 1978):5.

9.   Ibid., pp. 14, 15.

10.   Rothchild and Curry, Scarcity, Choice and Public Policy in Middle Africa, p. 133.

11.   Eriksen, "Zambia: Class Formation and Detente,"
p. 18.

12.   National Assembly, The Report of the Special
Parliamentary Select Committee appointed on Friday,
14th October, 1977 (Lusaka: Government Printer,
1977).   Appendix I contains the President's address
of 11 October 1977 to the first emergency session of
the National Assembly.   The themes of this address

426

were repeated in Kaunda's speech to the UNIP National
Council, 12 June 1978.

13. Half of the 10-member Committee were ministers,
including the Finance Minister (as well as two former
Finance Ministers and a future one). Four members
retired as MPs at the time of the 1978 general elections, including the two most outspoken "conservative" critics of the government as a result of being
"vetted" as candidates by the UNIP Central Committee.
Five of the continuing MPs currently hold senior ministerial posts—Prime Minister, Finance, Agriculture,
Industry, and Education—and the sixth is a minister
of state.

14. These were largely rejected by the President
though, in a major reorganization of the government
following the 1978 general elections, he placed each
ministry under the supervision of the chairman of the
corresponding Central Committee subcommittee. Thus,
Foreign Minister Wilson Chakulya operates under
Political and Legal Affairs Committee Chairman Reuben
Kamanga. Nevertheless, the latter does not report to
Parliament on foreign affairs as, unlike 5 other
chairmen including the Secretary of State for Defence
and Security, he was not nominated an MP (Zambia
Daily Mail, 3 January 1979, p. 1).

15. The Rhodesian raids in late 1978 forced the government to divert even more funds from social services to arms purchases (ibid., 21 November 1978,
p. 1). It is a measure of the inappropriateness of
imported political labels, and of the nature of the
regional conflict, that a preference for butter over
guns must be characterized as "conservative" rather
than "progressive". The withdrawal of consumer subsidies can also be regarded as a progressive move
designed to narrow the urban-rural gap; for this
reason, it was advocated in the ILO Report discussed
below.

16. Fundamentals of Zambian Humanism (Lusaka: Neczam,
1977), especially pp. 17-30 and 63-142.

17. International Labour Office, Narrowing the Gaps:
Planning for Basic Needs and Productive Employment in
Zambia (Addis Ababa: ILO Jobs and Skills Programme
for Africa, 1977), pp. 26, 213, 292-293.

18. Ibid., pp. 2, 6-8, 53.

19. Ibid., pp. 195-197, 201.

20. Ibid., pp. 14, 25, 114-115, 203.

21. Ibid., pp. 26-27, 199-200, 216-218.

22. Ibid., pp. 2, 34-37, 200, 265-266, 270.

23. Denis L. Dresang, The Zambia Civil Service
(Nairobi: East African Publishing House, 1975),
p. 164.

24. William Tordoff and Robert Molteno, "Introduction," in Politics in Zambia, ed. William Tordoff
(Berkeley: University of California Press, 1974),
p. 38.

25. Robert Molteno and William Tordoff, "Conclusion. Independent Zambia: Achievements and
Prospects," in ibid., p. 395.

26. See James N. Rosenau, "Pre-theories and
Theories of Foreign Policy," in Approaches to Comparative and International Politics, ed. R. Barry
Farrell (Evanston: Northwestern University Press,
1966), pp. 27-92.

27. See W. A. E. Skurnik, The Foreign Policy of
Senegal (Evanston: Northwestern University Press,
1972), pp. 250-284.

28. Ibid., p. 275.

29. Okwudiba Nnoli, Self-Reliance and Foreign Policy
in Tanzania: The Dynamics of the Diplomacy of a New
State, 1961 to 1971 (New York: NOK, 1978).

30. Ibid., pp. 297-325.

31. Olajide Aluko, "The Determinants of the Foreign
Policies of African States," in The Foreign Policies
of African States, ed. Olajide Aluko (Atlantic High-
lands: Humanities Press, 1977), pp. 1-23.

32. See Olajide Aluko, Ghana and Nigeria, 1957-70:
A Study in Inter-African Discord (New York: Barnes
& Noble, 1976).

33. See Timothy M. Shaw, "Zambia's Foreign Policy,"
in Aluko, ed., Foreign Policies of African States,
pp. 220-234.

34. One indication that Zambia's middle power status
has received international recognition is the fact
that she is the only African state, other than Egypt
and Nigeria, to have been elected to the UN Security
Council a second time; a majority of African members
have never served on the Council.

Bibliography

Anglin, Douglas G. "Confrontation in Southern
    Africa: Zambia and Portugal." International Jour-
    nal 25, no. 3 (Summer 1970):497-513. Reprinted in
    Zambia and the World, pp. 10-22. Lusaka: Univer-
    sity of Zambia, 1970.

————. "Zambia and the Recognition of Biafra."
    African Review 1, no. 2 (September 1971):102-136.

————. "The Politics of Transit Routes in Land-
    Locked Southern Africa." In Land-Locked Countries
    of Africa. Edited by Zdenek Cervenka, pp. 98-133.
    Uppsala: Scandinavian Institute of African
    Studies, 1973.

————. "Britain and the Use of Force in Rhodesia."
    In Freedom and Change: Essays in Honour of Lester
    Pearson. Edited by Michael G. Fry, pp. 43-75.
    Toronto: McClelland and Stewart, 1975.

————. "Political Scene in Zambia." Canadian
    Journal of African Studies 9, no. 2 (1975):337-340.

————. "Zambia and Southern African Détente."
    International Journal 30, no. 3 (Summer 1975):471-
    503.

————. "Zambian versus Malawian Approaches to
    Political Change in Southern Africa." In Profiles
    in Self-Determination: African Responses to Euro-
    pean Colonialism in Southern Africa 1652-present.
    Edited by David Chanaiwa, pp. 371-414. Northridge:
    California State University Foundation, 1976.

————. "Zambian Disengagement from Southern Africa
    and Integration with East Africa, 1964-1972: A
    Transaction Analysis." In Cooperation and Con-
    flict in Southern Africa: Papers on a Regional

Subsystem. Edited by Timothy M. Shaw and Kenneth A. Heard, pp. 228-289. Washington: University Press of America, 1976.

———. "Zambia and the Southern African Liberation Movements." In *Politics of Africa: Development and Dependence*. Edited by Timothy M. Shaw and Kenneth A. Heard. London: Longmans; New York: Africana and Dalhousie University Press, 1978.

Arnold, Guy and Weiss, Ruth. "Zambia." In *Strategic Highways of Africa*, pp. 67-86. London: Julian Friedmann, 1977.

Azevedo, Mario J. "Zambia, Zaire and the Angolan Crisis Reconsidered: From Alvor to Shaba." *Journal of Southern African Affairs* 2, no. 3 (July 1977):275-293.

Bailey, Martin. *Freedom Railway: China and the Tanzania-Zambia Link*. London: Rex Collings, 1976.

Ballance, Frank C. *Zambia and the East African Community*. Eastern African Studies, no. I. Syracuse University Program of Eastern African Studies, 1971.

Bone, Marion. "An Investigation of the Relations between Zambia and East Africa with Particular Reference to the Potential for Future Political and Economic Integration." M.A. thesis, University of Sussex, 1968.

———. "Foreign Policy in the Republic of Zambia, 1964-1971." Ph.D. thesis, University of Sussex, 1973.

———. "The Foreign Policy of Zambia." In *The Other Powers: Studies in the Foreign Policies of Small States*. Edited by Ronald P. Barston, pp. 121-153. London: George Allen and Unwin, 1973.

Bostock, Mark and Harvey, Charles, eds. *Economic Independence and Zambian Copper: A Case Study of Foreign Investment*. New York: Praeger, 1972.

Burawoy, Michael. *The Colour of Class on the Copper Mines: From African Advancement to Zambianization*. Zambian Papers no. 7. Lusaka: Institute of African Studies, University of Zambia, 1972.

431

Burdette, Marcia M. "Nationalization in Zambia: A Critique of Bargaining Theory." Canadian Journal of African Studies 11, no. 3 (1977):471-496.

Burgess, Julian. "Zambia." In his Interdependence in Southern Africa: Trade and Transport Links in South, Central and East Africa. Special Report No. 32, pp. 39-55. London: Economist Intelligence Unit, July 1976.

Canter, Richard S. National and International Events and Ethnic Conflict: Lenje/Black Rhodesia Relations in Zambia. Working Papers in African Studies no. 3 (1976). Boston: Boston University African Studies Center, 1976.

Cervenka, Zdenek and Weiss, Ruth. Zambia: The First Ten Years, 1964-1974. Stockholm: Swedish Zambian Association, 1974.

Cliffe, Lionel and Lawrence, Peter. "The Zambian State and Détente." Review of African Political Economy 5 (1976):8-11.

Craig, James. "Zambia-Botswana Road Link." In Zambia and the World, pp. 25-29. Lusaka: University of Zambia, 1970.

Curry, Robert L. "Global Market Forces and the Nationalization of Foreign-Based Export Companies." Journal of Modern African Studies 14, no. 1 (March 1976):137-141.

Doganis, R. S. "Zambia's Outlets to the Sea." Journal of Transport Economics and Policy 1, no. 1 (January 1967):46-51.

Dresang, Dennis. "The Political Economy of Zambia." In The Political Economy of Africa. Edited by Richard Harris, pp. 187-226. Cambridge, Mass.: Schenkman, 1975.

Dumont, René. "Kenneth Kaunda's Humanist Socialism in Zambia." In Socialisms and Development, pp. 123-142. London: Deutsch, 1973.

Elliott, Charles, ed. Constraints on the Economic Development of Zambia. Nairobi: Oxford University Press, 1971.

Elliott, Charles. "Growth, Development . . . or

Independence?" In Socioeconomic Development in Dual Economies. Edited by Heide and Udo Ernst Simonis, pp. 61-95. Munich: Weltform Verlag for African Studies Institute, 1971.

Eriksen, Karen. "Zambia: Class Formation and Détente." Review of African Political Economy 9 (May-August 1978):4-26.

Faber, Michael L. O. and Potter, J. G. Towards Economic Independence: Papers on the Nationalization of the Copper Industry in Zambia. Department of Applied Economics Occasional Paper, no. 23. Cambridge: Cambridge University Press, 1971.

Fortman, Bastiaan de Gaay, ed. After Mulungushi: The Economics of Zambian Humanism. Nairobi: East African Publishing House, 1969.

Fortman, Bastiaan de Gaay. "Zambia's Economic Reforms." Kroniek van Afrika 1 (1972):20-29.

Gertzel, Cherry. "Labour and the State: The Case of Zambia's Mineworkers Union—A Review Article." Journal of Commonwealth and Comparative Politics 13, no. 3 (November 1975):290-304.

Good, Robert C. UDI: The International Politics of the Rhodesian Rebellion. Princeton: Princeton University Press, 1973.

Gordenker, Leon. International Aid and National Decisions: Development Programs in Malawi, Tanzania, and Zambia. Princeton: Princeton University Press, 1976.

Griffiths, I. L. "Zambian Links with East Africa." East African Geographical Review no. 6 (April 1968):87-89.

Grundy, Kenneth W. "The 'Southern Border' of Africa." In African Boundary Problems. Edited by Carl Gosta Widstrand, pp. 119-160. Uppsala: Scandinavian Institute of African Studies, 1969.

Hall, Richard. Zambia. New York: Praeger; and London: Longman, 1965, 1976.

————. "Zambia and Rhodesia: Links and Fetters." Africa Report 11, no. 1 (January 1966):8-12.

————. "Zambia's Search for Political Stability."
The World Today 25, no. 11 (November 1969):488-495.

————. *The High Price of Principles: Kaunda and the
White South.* London: Hodder and Stoughton, 1969.
Rev., Harmondsworth: Penguin, 1973.

———— and Peyman, Richard. *The Great Uhuru Railway: China's Showpiece in Africa.* London:
Gollancz, 1976.

Harkema, Roelof C. "The Ports and Access Routes of
Landlocked Zambia." *Geografisch Tijdschrift* 6,
no. 3 (May 1972):223-31.

————. "Zambia's Changing Pattern of External
Trade." *Journal of Geography* 71, no. 1 (January
1972):19-27.

Harvey, Charles. "The Control of Inflation in a
Very Open Economy: Zambia, 1964-1969." *Eastern
African Economic Review* 3, no. 1 (June 1971):41-61.

————. "State Participation and the Zambian Banks."
Discussion Paper no. 28 (1972). Nairobi: University of Nairobi. Institute of Development Studies,
1972.

————. "International Corporations and Economic
Independence: A View from Zambia." In *Economic
Independence in Africa.* Edited by D. P. Ghai,
pp. 176-189. Nairobi: East African Literature
Bureau, 1973.

————. "The Structure of Zambian Development." In
Development Paths in Africa and China. Edited by
Ukandi Damachi, pp. 136-151. Boulder: Westview,
1975.

———— and Fry, James. "Copper and Zambia." In
Commodity Exports and African Economic Development.
Edited by Scott R. Pearson and John Cownie.
Lexington: Heath, 1974.

Hatch, John. "Zambia—A Case Study." In his *Africa
Emergent,* pp. 154-183. London: Secker & Warburg,
1974.

————. *Two African Statesmen: Kaunda of Zambia and
Nyerere of Tanzania.* London: Secker and Warburg,
1976.

434

Hill, Christopher R. "The Botswana-Zambia Boundary
Question: A Note of Warning." Round Table no. 252
(October 1973):535-541.

International Defence and Aid Fund. The Rhodesia-
Zambia Border Closure: January-February, 1973.
London: International Defence and Aid Fund, 1973.

International Labour Organisation, Jobs and Skills
Programme for Africa. Narrowing the Gaps: Plan-
ning for Basic Needs and Productive Employment in
Zambia. Report to the Government of Zambia by a
JASPA Employment Advisory Mission, Addis Ababa,
January 1977.

International Monetary Fund. "Zambia." In Surveys
of African Economies 4, pp. 370-444. Washington:
International Monetary Fund, 1971.

Jardim, Jorge. Moçambique: Terra Queimada. Lisbon:
Editorial Intervençao, 1976.

————. Sanctions Double-Cross: Oil to Rhodesia.
Lisbon: Editorial Intervençao, 1978.

Kaemba, L. F. "Building the Image of a New Nation."
In The Diplomatic Persuaders. Edited by John Lee,
pp. 37-44. New York: Wiley, 1968.

Kamana, Dunstan. "Zambia." In Conflict and Change
in Southern Africa: Papers from a Scandinavian-
Canadian Conference. Edited by Douglas G. Anglin,
Timothy M. Shaw and Carl G. Widstrand. Washington:
University Press of America, 1978, pp. 33-68.

Kandeke, Timothy K. Fundamentals of Zambian
Humanism. Lusaka: Neczam, 1977.

Kaplan, Irving et al. Area Handbook for Zambia.
2nd ed. Washington: Government Printing Office
for American University, 1974.

Kaunda, Kenneth D. Zambia Shall Be Free. London:
Heinemann, 1962.

————. A Humanist in Africa: Letters to Colin M.
Morris. London: Longmans, 1966.

————. "Crisis in Southern Africa." African Forum
2, no. 3 (Winter 1967):11-16.

435

————. Letter to My Children. London: Longmans, 1973.

Leech, John. "Zambia Seeks a Route to a Fuller Independence." Issue 2, no. 4 (Winter 1972):6-11.

Legum, Colin. ed. Zambia: Independence and Beyond: The Speeches of Kenneth Kaunda. London: Nelson, 1966.

Lewis, Roy. "Kenneth Kaunda in 1976: A Leader in the Front Line." Round Table no. 263 (July 1976): 283-288.

Lubetsky, Robert. "The Foreign Policy of Zambia since Independence, With Special Reference to the Rhodesian Crisis." M.A. thesis, Manchester University, 1967.

MacPherson, Fergus. Kenneth Kaunda of Zambia: The Times and the Man. Lusaka: Oxford University Press, 1974.

Madu, Oliver V. Models of Class Domination in Plural Societies of Central Africa. Washington: University Press of America, 1978.

Makoni, T. "The Economic Appraisal of the Tanzania-Zambia Railway." African Review 2, no. 4 (1972): 599-616.

Markakis, John and Curry, Robert L. "The Global Economy's Impact on Recent Budgetary Politics in Zambia." Journal of African Studies 3, no. 4 (Winter 1976-1977):403-427.

Martin, Anthony. Minding Their Own Business: Zambia's Struggle Against Western Control. London: Hutchinson, 1973. Rev., Harmondsworth: Penguin, 1975.

Mazrui, Ali A. "Kenneth Kaunda: from Satyagraha to Détente: A Review Article." African Social Research no. 22 (December 1976):155-159.

McKay, Vernon. "The Propaganda Battle for Zambia." Africa Today 17, no. 2 (April 1971):18-26.

Meebelo, Henry S. "The Concept of Man-Centredness in Zambian Humanism." African Review 3, no. 4 (1973):559-575.

436

————. Main Currents of Zambian Humanist Thought. Lusaka: Oxford University Press, 1973.

Melady, Thomas Patrick. ed. Kenneth Kaunda of Zambia: Selections from His Writings. New York: Praeger, 1964.

Mingst, Karen A. "Cooperation or Illusion: An Examination of the Intergovernmental Council of Copper Exporting Countries." International Organization 30, no. 2 (Spring 1976):263-288.

Molteno, Robert. "Zambian Humanism: The Way Ahead." African Review 3, no. 4 (1973):541-557.

Morris, Michael. "Zambia." In Armed Conflict in Southern Africa, pp. 241-264. Cape Town: Jeremy Spence, 1974.

Mtshali, Benedict V. "Zambia's Foreign Policy." Current History 58, no. 343 (March 1970):148-153. Reprinted in Zambia and the World, pp. 1-9. Lusaka: University of Zambia, 1970.

————. "South Africa and Zambia's 1968 Election." Kroniek van Afrika 2 (1970):125-135.

————. "Zambia's Foreign Policy Problems." African Social Research 11 (June 1971):50-54.

————. "Zambia's Foreign Policy: The Dilemmas of a New State." Ph.D. thesis, New York University, 1972.

————. "Zambia and the White South." In Land-Locked Countries of Africa. Edited by Zdenek Cervenka, pp. 188-193. Uppsala: Scandinavian Institute of African Studies, 1973.

————. "The Zambian Foreign Service 1964-1972." African Review 5, no. 3 (1975):303-316.

Mubako, Simbi V. "The Rhodesian Border Blockade of 1973 and the African Liberation Struggle." Journal of Commonwealth and Comparative Politics 12, no. 3 (November 1974):297-312.

Mudenda, Gilbert M. "Class, Politics and Development in Zambia." MSS thesis, Institute of Social Studies, The Hague, 1977.

Mujaya, Murungo S. Zambia's Foreign Policy: A Study. Political Science Paper no. 7. Dar es Salaam: University of Dar es Salaam, 1970.

Mulenga, N. S. "Humanism and Logic of Self-Sufficiency." Lusaka, 1973, mimeo. Reprinted in the Zambia Daily Mail, 30 and 31 January 1974.

Murapa, Rukudzo. "Nationalization of the Zambian Mining Industry." Review of African Political Economy 7, no. 1 (Fall 1976):40-52.

Mutukwa, Kasuka S. "The International Implications of the Tanzania-Zambia Railway Project." M.A. thesis, George Washington University, 1971.

————. "Imperial Dream Becomes Pan-African Reality." Africa Report 17, no. 1 (January 1972):10-15.

————. "Political Control of Parastatal Organizations in Zambia." Zango 1 (September 1976):39-59.

————. Politics of the Tanzania-Zambia Rail Project: a study of Tanzania-China-Zambia relations. Washington: University Press of America, 1977.

Mwaanga, Vernon J. "Zambia's Policy Toward Southern Africa." In Southern Africa in Perspective: Essays in Regional Politics. Edited by Christian P. Potholm and Richard Dale, pp. 234-241. New York: Free Press, 1972.

————. "Zambia's Foreign Policy: To Play a Full Part in the Affairs of the Human Family." Enterprise no. 3 (1974):25-27.

————. "US-Africa Relations: The View from Zambia." Africa Report 19, no. 5 (September-October 1974): 37-39.

Ngwenya, Martyn. "The Role of Foreign Aid in Development: A Case Study of Zambia." Ph.D. thesis, University of Ottawa, 1974.

Nolutshungu, Sam C. "Zambia." In South Africa in Africa: A Study of Ideology and Foreign Policy, pp. 218-258. Manchester: Manchester University Press, and New York: Africana, 1975.

Nyerere, Julius. "Zambian-Tanzanian Relations."

Pan-African Journal 4, no. 3 (Summer 1971):272-278.

Ohadike, Patrick. "Immigrants and Development in Zambia." *International Migration Review* 8, no. 3 (Fall 1974):395-412.

Ostrander, Taylor F. "Zambia in the Aftermath of Rhodesian UDI: Logistical and Economic Problems." *African Forum* 2, no. 3 (Winter 1967):50-65.

Oudes, Bruce. "US-Africa Relations: Kaunda's Diplomatic Offensive." *Africa Report* 20, no. 3 (May-June 1975):41-45.

Parsons, Q. M. "A New Link Between Two Nations: Economics of the Zambia-Botswana Highway." *Enterprise* no. 3 (1974):56-59.

Pettman, Jan. *Zambia: The Search for Security*. New York: St. Martin's, 1974.

Pettman, Rosalyn J. "The Tanzania Rail Link: China's Loss-Leader in Africa." *World Affairs* 136, no. 3 (Winter 1973-1974):232-258.

Radmann, Wolf. "Intergovernmental Cooperation: The Case of Foreign Investment in Zambia and Chile." *Pan-African Journal* 5, no. 2 (Summer 1972):201-221.

Payne, William. "The USSR and Zambia." *Mizan* 11, no. 5 (September 1969):265-270.

"Report of the Zambian Trade Mission to the People's Republic of China, 14th-23rd October 1969." In *China's African Policy*, by George T. Yu, pp. 173-183. New York: Praeger, 1975.

de Rham, Gérard. *La politique étrangère de la République de Zambie*. Bern: Peter Lang, 1977.

Roberts, Andrew. *A History of Zambia*. London: Heinemann, and New York: Africana, 1977.

Rothchild, Donald. "Rural-Urban Inequities and Resource Allocation in Zambia." *Journal of Commonwealth Political Studies* 10, no. 3 (November 1972): 222-242.

Scarritt, James R. "Elite Values, Ideology and Power in Post-Independence Zambia." *African*

Studies Review 14, no. 1 (April 1971):31-54.

―――――. "European Adjustment to Economic Reforms and Political Consolidation in Zambia." _Issue_ 2, no. 2 (Summer 1973):18-22.

―――――― and Hatter, John L. _Racial and Ethnic Conflict in Zambia_. Studies in Race and Nations 2, no. 2 (1970-71). Denver: University of Denver Center on International Race Relations, 1970.

Scott, Ian. "Middle Class Politics in Zambia." _African Affairs_ 77, no. 308 (July 1978):2-14.

Seidman, Ann. "An Alternative Development Strategy in Zambia." Mimeographed. Occasional Paper LTC no. 89. Madison: University of Wisconsin Land Tenure Center, 1973.

―――――. "The Distorted Growth of Import-Substitution Industry: The Zambian Case." _Journal of Modern African Studies_ 12, no. 4 (December 1974): 601-631.

Shaw, Timothy M. "The Foreign Policy of Zambia: Interests and Ideology." _Journal of Modern African Studies_ 14, no. 1 (March 1976):79-105.

―――――. "The Foreign Policy System of Zambia." _African Studies Review_ 19, no. 1 (April 1976):31-66.

―――――. _Dependence and Underdevelopment: The Development and Foreign Policies of Zambia_. Papers in International Studies Africa Series, no. 28 (1976). Athens, Ohio: Ohio University Center for International Studies, 1976.

―――――. "Zambia and Malawi—The Politics of Dependence and Development." _ASA Review of Books_ 2 (1976):180-183.

―――――. "Zambia: Dependence and Underdevelopment." _Canadian Journal of African Studies_ 10, no. 1 (1976):3-22.

―――――. "Zambia's Foreign Policy." In _The Foreign Policies of African States_. Edited by Olajide Aluko, pp. 220-234. London: Hodder and Stoughton, and New Jersey: Humanities, 1977.

————. "The Foreign Policy of Zambia: An Events Analysis of a New State." Comparative Political Studies 11, no. 2 (July 1978):181-209.

————. "Canada in Zambian Perspective." In How Others See Us: Canada in World Perspective. Edited by Denis Stairs and Don Munton. Halifax: Dalhousie University Centre for Foreign Policy Studies, forthcoming.

————. "Zambia: Dependence and Détente." In Southern Africa Since the Portuguese Coup. Edited by John Seiler, forthcoming.

Shaw, Timothy M. and Mugomba, Agrippah T. "The Political Economy of Regional Détente: Zambia and Southern Africa." Journal of African Studies 4, no. 4 (Winter 1977-1978):392-413.

Shaw, Timothy M. and Anglin, Douglas G. "Global, Regional and National Sources of Zambian Foreign Policy Events Data." In Measuring International Behavior: Public Sources, Events and Validity. Edited by Don Munton. Halifax: Dalhousie University Centre for Foreign Policy Studies, 1979.

Shaw, Timothy M. and Anglin, Douglas G. "Zambia: The Crises of Liberation." In Southern Africa: The Continuing Crisis. Edited by Patrick O'Meara and Gwendolen M. Carter. Bloomington: Indiana University Press, 1979.

Simwinga, George K. "The Copper-Mining Industry of Zambia: A Case Study of Nationalization and Control." In What Government Does. Edited by Matthew Holden and Dennis L. Dresang. Sage Yearbook in Politics and Public Policy 1 (1975):84-93. Beverly Hills: Sage, 1975.

Sklar, Richard L. "Zambia's Response to UDI." Mawazo 1, no. 3 (June 1968):11-32.

————. "Zambia's Response to the Rhodesian Unilateral Declaration of Independence." In Politics in Zambia. Edited by William Tordoff, pp. 320-363. Berkeley: University of California Press, 1974.

————. Corporate Power in an African State: The Political Impact of Multinational Mining Companies in Zambia. Berkeley: University of California Press, 1975.

441

Small, N. J. "Zambia—Trouble on Campus." Index on Censorship 6, no. 6 (November-December 1977):8-14.

Sutcliffe, R. B. "Zambia and the Strains of UDI." World Today 23, no. 12 (December 1967):506-511.

Tordoff, William, ed. Politics in Zambia. Berkeley: • University of California Press, and Manchester: Manchester University Press, 1974.

————. "Zambia: The Politics of Disengagement." African Affairs 76, no. 302 (January 1977):60-69.

Young, Alistair. "Patterns of Development in Zambian Manufacturing Industry Since Independence." Eastern African Economic Review 1, no. 2 (December 1969):29-38.

————. Industrial Diversification in Zambia. New York: Praeger, 1973.

Yu, George T. "Chinese Aid to Africa: The Tanzania-Zambia Railway." In Chinese and Soviet Aid to Africa. Edited by Warren Weinstein, pp. 29-55. New York: Praeger, 1975.

Index

320, 328, 350n98
Berkeley, Humphry,
118, 158n41
Biafra, 6, 25, 91, 99,
281, 288
Bone, Marion, 357, 368
Botswana, 9, 26, 74, 193,
206, 207, 290, 296
Bottomley, Arthur, 117,
138, 164n101
bourgeoisie, 15, 20-21,
35n14, 37n36, 52, 59,
63, 383, 389, 396,
398, 402n16, 403n28,
404n29, 413, 420; and
foreign policy, 20,
29, 30-31, 54, 414-15;
embourgeoisement, 381,
385, 389; see also
classes, comprador
Britain, 5, 10, 33n2,
48, 88-89, 148, 170,
292, 364; and Rhodesia,
10, 237, 263, 284,
290; arms for South
Africa, 46, 126, 289;
force in Rhodesia,
113-23, 116, 129,
133-34, 136-37, 143-
44, 146-54, 156n12,
158n41, 159n43, 167n
127; military support,
138-42; see also
Kaunda
British South Africa
Company, 6, 10
broadcasting, 8, 208-9,
242-43, 318, 344n30
Broederbond, 232n81
Burundi, 26

cabinet, see Zambia
Canada, 88, 90, 92, 134,
145, 166n66, 362, 364
capitalism, 52-54, 59-65,
387-88
Central Africa, 47, 49,
136, 150
Central African Airways,
177-79, 181-82, 200

Central African Empire,
26, 128
Central African Power
Corporation, 177-79,
182, 226n32, 227n43
Chad, 26
Chikerema, James, 254-55
Chile, 49-75
China, 6, 24, 25, 28, 37n
40, 46, 59, 90, 91,
107, 135, 208, 308n62,
310, 311, 315, 325,
362, 364
Chipenda, Daniel, 255,
270n69, 315-17, 343n19,
n27
Chitepo, Herbert, 8, 92,
274
Chivuno, Leonard, 69n57
Chona, Mainza, 82, 98
Chona, Mark, 73, 83, 188,
275, 293, 302n3, 348n
76
CIPEC, 6, 29
classes, 15, 23, 30, 40,
54, 59, 62, 381-85,
387-91, 393, 395, 398-
99, 413, 415; see also
bourgeoisie, labor
aristocracy, political
economy
coal and coke, 30, 165n
101, 197-200, 231n70
colonialism, 10, 42, 45,
235
Common Fund, 29
common services, with
Rhodesia, 176-83, 185;
with Tanzania, 183-85
Commonwealth, 6, 24, 29,
43, 48, 95, 194; and
Rhodesia, 116, 119,
123-26, 137, 145-46;
and South Africa, 45,
288-89; conferences,
116, 123-26, 144, 157n
28, 288; Declaration
of Principles, 7, 43,
45
communism, 56, 138
comprador, 15, 30-31, 83,

336
Congo (Brazzaville), 26,
158n42
Congo (Kinshasa), see
Zaire
copper, 17, 24, 31, 37n
37, 41, 60, 136, 169,
171, 172, 205, 234,
355; prices, 4, 5, 8,
17, 20, 52, 171, 301,
324, 335, 384, 392,
412
COREMO, 239, 240, 248,
252
Coughlin, Bill, 332, 333,
349n83-n87
Credit Guarantee Insurance
Corporation of Africa,
36n31
Cuba, 312, 313, 327, 341
n10, 343n26, 347n64
Cyprus, 148
Czechoslovakia, 28, 347
n59

Dag Hammarskjold Founda-
tion, 97
Dar es Salaam, 194, 198,
199, 206; Declaration,
43, 44, 105, 294; port,
20, 193, 203
Davis, Nathaniel, 329
decision-making, see
Kaunda
Defence, Ministry of, 76,
106-7, 155n6
dependence, 5, 16, 23-24,
39-40, 52, 55-56, 58,
75, 83, 90, 92, 95,
169, 171, 173-74, 190,
198, 201, 203, 206,
335, 355-56, 362, 366,
374, 381, 384, 385-
86, 392, 394; see also
underdevelopment
"détente", 19, 21, 42,
43, 44, 95, 235, 273,
275, 290-302, 304n19,
308n65-n66, 385
dialogue, 42, 44, 273,

284, 286-90, 305n34,
309n71
diplomatic relations, 37n
40, 49, 83, 84-87, 91,
98-100, 102-4, 187-89,
303n14, 305n28
disengagement, see South-
ern Africa

East Africa, integration
with, 26, 90, 170-74,
183-89, 193-98, 201-7,
209, 214, 216-18, 220-
23, 230n64
East African Community
(EAC), 25, 49, 59, 91,
95, 96, 99, 171, 172,
196
East and Central African
States Conference, 26,
43, 44, 285; see also
Front Line States
Eastern Africa National
Shipping Line, 184
East Germany, 27, 83
East, Maurice, 95, 354,
355, 357, 360, 362,
365, 374
East-West conflict, 28
Economic Commission for
Africa (ECA), 26, 170
economic reforms, 52, 54,
64, 397
economy, Zambian, see
Zambia
Egypt, 48, 127, 130, 158
n42
Equatorial Guinea, 26
embourgeoisement, see
bourgeoisie
Eriksen, Karen, 414, 415
Ethiopia, 26, 128, 130,
132
Europe, 90, 198
European Economic Commun-
ity (EEC), 29, 38n43,
48, 86, 394

Fearless, 125, 284, 285

445

Federation of Rhodesia
and Nyasaland, 10,
41, 49, 115, 155n6-
n7, 174, 176-79, 183
Finland, 89
FNLA, 239, 240-41, 248-
49, 252, 271n84; see
also Roberto
Foley, Maurice, 151
Fourie, Brand, 274, 293
Foreign Affairs, Minister
of, 74, 77, 81-82, 95,
101, 427n14
Foreign Affairs, Ministry
of, 57, 72-78, 86, 91,
94-108, 110n28
Foreign Affairs Committee,
of Cabinet, 76, 83;
of Central Committee,
73, 76, 80-81, 427n14
foreign aid, 17, 21-22,
24, 27-28, 30, 60,
92, 185, 230n68
foreign investment, 22,
39, 58, 88-89
foreign policy, ix, 11,
50, 368, 381, 410,
421, 424; actors, 24,
37n38, 72, 73-77, 96,
357-59, 371-72, 374-
75, 424
France, 28, 206, 290,
312, 345n49
FRELIMO, 8, 44, 66n7, 95,
229n55, 239, 240, 243,
248, 252, 264, 271n
78, 290, 296
FROLIZI, 238, 240, 249,
251, 255, 306n47
Front Line States (FLS),
8, 18, 26, 44, 47,
49, 74, 80, 92, 133,
189, 246, 251, 273,
274, 292, 294, 296,
300-2, 303n4, 409

Gabon, 26
Gandhi, M., 51, 237
General Assembly, see
United Nations

Ghana, 25, 99, 128, 129,
130-32, 158n42, 160n
54, 161n61, 276
Good, Robert, 150, 162n79
Goodman, Lord, 284
good neighborliness, 49,
57, 74, 94
Guardian, 21, 151, 152
Guerrilla warfare, 127,
129
Guinea, 128, 130, 158n42

Hart, Judith, 151
Healey, Dennis, 147, 166
n121
Houphouet-Boigny, F.,
288-90, 333
Humanism, ix, 6, 8, 14,
27, 28, 39-42, 51-55,
57-59, 61, 62-65, 93,
371, 381, 394

ILO report, 417, 418-19
imperialism, 42, 94, 235
INDECO, 57, 60, 61, 87-90
India, 46, 134
inequalities, see Zambia
integration, see Southern
Africa, East Africa
Intergovernmental Council
of Copper Exporting
Countries, see CIPEC
International Monetary
Fund (IMF), 7, 9
International Red Locust
Control Service, 186
Israel, 90
Italy, 88-90, 206, 362
Ivory Coast, 99, 101, 275

Jamaica, 162n71
Japan, 6, 30, 88-90, 385,
394
Jardim, Jorge, 229n55
Joanna V, 134
Jordan, 161n65, 245, 256

446

297, 305n32

MacDonald, Malcolm, 137,
  163n86
Machel, Samora, 44, 274,
  291, 322
Madagascar, 26, 128
Mafeje, Archie, 15
maize, 17, 171, 192
Malawi, 13, 16, 26, 37n32,
  47, 117, 125, 128, 177,
  193, 280, 305n31;
  routes, 203, 206, 207
Malaysia, 134, 148, 166n
  121
Mali, 158n42
Mandela, Nelson, 279
Marais, Jan, 36n30
Mauritania, 128, 158n42
Mauritius, 26
Mbeya agreement, 251
McGowan, Patrick, 355
Meebelo, Henry, 62, 63,
  70n69
MEMACO, 30, 38n45
middle class, see bourg-
  eoisie, classes
Middle East, 46, 91, 130,
  366
middle power, 49, 368,
  385, 403n24, 409, 429n
  34
migration, 209, 211-18
military coups, 25, 48,
  49, 75
Mobutu, Sese Seko, 25, 48,
  311, 313, 317, 332,
  333
Mogadishu Declaration,
  251
Molteno, Robert, 13, 64,
  70n71, 396, 420
Morocco, 245
Mountbatten, Lord, 163n
  87
Mozambique, 26, 45, 75;
  liberation, 8, 16,
  43, 44, 56, 251, 272,
  291, 292; routes, 14,
  45, 92, 170, 201,

205, 415; see also
  FRELIMO
Mozambique-Rhodesia Pipe-
  line Company, 134
MPLA, 239, 240-41, 243,
  248-49, 252-53, 255,
  311, 314-18, 321-22,
  323, 344n34; see also
  Angola
Mtshali, Benedict, 108
Mudenda, Elijah, 81, 82,
  109n20, 251
Mugabe, Robert, 293
Mulenga, Sefelino, 64,
  71n74, 396
Muller, Hilgard, 275, 286
multinational corporations,
  29-30, 37n35, 55-56,
  63, 73, 75, 76, 83,
  190, 385, 395, 397,
  402n22
Mulungushi Club, 26, 80,
  249, 252, 317
Mulungushi reforms, see
  economic reforms
Mushala gang, 12, 320
Muzorewa, Bishop A., 36n
  26, 251, 274, 306n47,
  322
Mwaanga, Vernon, 42, 82,
  96, 97, 101, 298, 299,
  306n44, 309n71
Mwale, Sitake, 82, 101
Mwanakatwe, John, 82,
  416; Report, 416-17
Mwinilungu, 13, 14

Nakuru accord, 319
Namibia, 12, 26, 44, 45,
  272, 292, 299, 301
National Development
  Plans, 6, 27
National Institute of
  Public Administration,
  97
nationalism, 56
nationalization, 29, 51,
  53
National Progress Party
  (NPP), 13, 14

448

NATO, 37n40, 42
neocolonialism, 50, 52,
  55-57, 94
Netherlands, 92
Neto, Agostinho, 255, 315,
  316, 317, 322, 339,
  343n19, 343n21, n27;
  see also MPLA
New International Economic
  Order, 29, 47
new states, 73, 94
New Zealand, 134, 165n114
NIBMAR, 120, 125
Nigeria, 25, 48, 101, 127,
  130, 133, 313, 343n13,
  345n43
Nkomo, Joshua, 8, 247,
  251, 274, 293, 306n47,
  307n51, 338-39
Nkoloso, Mukuka, 256
Nkrumah, Kwame, 25, 48,
  125, 128-32, 136, 140,
  159n47, 160n54, 235,
  276, 278
Nnoli, Okwudiba, 421, 422
Nonaligned conferences,
  7, 28, 47, 101, 339
nonalignment, 24, 27,
  37n40, 40, 41, 46-47,
  56, 62, 80, 90, 92,
  93, 94, 194, 345n48,
  362-65
Northern Ireland, 150,
  167n127
North-South, 28, 29
Nye, Joseph, 175, 176
Nyerere, J.K., 24-25
  44, 115, 123, 126,
  140, 174, 274, 293,
  299, 308n66, 322; see
  also Tanzania

Obote, Milton, 25, 48
Observer, 117, 151
oil sanctions, 9, 35n20,
  134, 162n74, 198-99,
  230n66
one-party participatory
  democracy, see Zambia
"Operation Carlota", 313

"Operation Tembo", 132
"Operation Zulu", 313, 333
Organization of African
  Unity (OAU), 7, 24,
  25, 28, 43, 44, 45, 47,
  49, 57, 74, 75, 92,
  93, 119, 126, 129, 138,
  145, 158n42, 159n43,
  235, 247, 248-49, 286,
  300, 364; and Angola,
  252, 328, 344n34; army,
  127-33, 150, 159n47,
  160n58; Council of
  Ministers, 8, 44, 122,
  128, 139, 159n50, 297;
  Liberation Committee,
  19, 47, 74, 92, 240,
  241, 251, 256, 299;
  Heads of State con-
  ferences, 48, 127, 245,
  247, 250; see also
  pan-Africanism
Owen, David, 168n136

PAFMECSA, 26, 170
Pakistan, 134
Palestine Liberation
  Organization, 161n65,
  245, 256
pan-Africanism, 24-25, 40,
  41, 47, 56, 80, 93,
  193, 319
Pan-Africanist Congress
  (PAC), 238, 240-41,
  254, 279
parastatals, 30, 57-63,
  73, 75, 78-79, 87-90,
  388, 395; external
  links, 60, 90, 358,
  371
Parliament, 73, 416, 427n
  13-n14; Special Parli-
  amentary Select Commi-
  ttee, 413-17, 420,
  427n13
Peace Corps, 27
Pearl Air, 332, 349n80
Pearson, Lester B., 116,
  146
peasants, 64, 384, 389

449

327-31, 344n34,
347n70, 349n78
United National Inde-
pendence Party (UNIP),
23, 28, 52, 57, 64,
74, 80, 81, 90, 92,
93-94, 170, 241, 246,
402n16, 403n28; and
press, 52, 354; Cen-
tral Committee, 77,
80, 81, 98, 108n6;
external relations,
80, 102, 240, 257,
266n18, 327; see also
Foreign Affairs Commi-
ttee
United Nations, 17, 51,
75, 86, 90, 92, 95,
127, 138, 145, 170,
235, 237; General
Assembly, 38n40, 46,
126, 162n72, 285;
Rhodesia, 17, 119,
133, 134, 156n16,
158n37, 170; Security
Council, 7-9, 47, 126,
134, 162n72, 429n34;
South Africa, 51, 272
United Party, 13
United Progressive Party
(UPP), 7
United States, 24, 28, 88,
90, 101, 135, 148,
156n12, 158n39, 325,
329-30, 346n53, 348n71,
348n74-n75
Unity Movement of South
Africa, 238, 240
University of Zambia, 7,
8, 323, 346n50

Verwoerd, H., 277, 280,
304n16
Victoria Falls, 8, 115,
206, 218, 274, 293-94
Vietnam, 28, 113, 134,
135, 312
violence, 44, 50, 236,
237, 261-62, 282-83
Vorster, B.J., 7, 8, 44,

188, 273-75, 279-85,
288-90, 293, 296, 297,
299-302, 304n18, 305n
31, 307n58; see also
South Africa

Walston, Lord, 151
Welensky, Sir Roy, 38n43,
165n111, 278
WENELA, 12, 213
West Germany, 88-89, 91,
199, 385
Willoughby, J.E.F., 142
Wilson, Sir Harold, 113-
14, 117-25, 127, 133-
36, 138-39, 142-46,
151-54, 161n70, 163n
85, 164n101, 167n123,
168n135, 237, 284
Wina, Arthur, 23, 32n1,
37n33, 82
workers, 63, 64; see
labor aristocracy
World Bank, 9, 145-46,
177

Yarborough, William, 291
Yemen, 130
Yugoslavia, 8, 24, 28,
107, 340n5, 345n49,
362, 364

Zaire, 13, 25, 26, 33n5,
48, 130, 132, 136,
174, 198, 203, 312,
331, 342n14, 348n74;
see also Mobutu,
Tshombe
Zambia Airways, 90, 177,
206, 207
Zambia, 3, 11, 24, 47,
170, 183, 198, 234,
388; inequalities, 5,
15, 52, 53, 58, 59,
355, 381, 384, 385,
388, 412, 417-18,
419; regionalism, 3,
12-13

452